T0368375

Communications
in Computer and Information Science 2447

Rationale

The CCIS series is devoted to the publication of proceedings of computer science conferences. Its aim is to efficiently disseminate original research results in informatics in printed and electronic form. While the focus is on publication of peer-reviewed full papers presenting mature work, inclusion of reviewed short papers reporting on work in progress is welcome, too. Besides globally relevant meetings with internationally representative program committees guaranteeing a strict peer-reviewing and paper selection process, conferences run by societies or of high regional or national relevance are also considered for publication.

Topics

The topical scope of CCIS spans the entire spectrum of informatics ranging from foundational topics in the theory of computing to information and communications science and technology and a broad variety of interdisciplinary application fields.

Information for Volume Editors and Authors

Publication in CCIS is free of charge. No royalties are paid, however, we offer registered conference participants temporary free access to the online version of the conference proceedings on SpringerLink (http://link.springer.com) by means of an http referrer from the conference website and/or a number of complimentary printed copies, as specified in the official acceptance email of the event.

CCIS proceedings can be published in time for distribution at conferences or as post-proceedings, and delivered in the form of printed books and/or electronically as USBs and/or e-content licenses for accessing proceedings at SpringerLink. Furthermore, CCIS proceedings are included in the CCIS electronic book series hosted in the SpringerLink digital library at http://link.springer.com/bookseries/7899. Conferences publishing in CCIS are allowed to use Online Conference Service (OCS) for managing the whole proceedings lifecycle (from submission and reviewing to preparing for publication) free of charge.

Publication process

The language of publication is exclusively English. Authors publishing in CCIS have to sign the Springer CCIS copyright transfer form, however, they are free to use their material published in CCIS for substantially changed, more elaborate subsequent publications elsewhere. For the preparation of the camera-ready papers/files, authors have to strictly adhere to the Springer CCIS Authors' Instructions and are strongly encouraged to use the CCIS LaTeX style files or templates.

Abstracting/Indexing

CCIS is abstracted/indexed in DBLP, Google Scholar, EI-Compendex, Mathematical Reviews, SCImago, Scopus. CCIS volumes are also submitted for the inclusion in ISI Proceedings.

How to start

To start the evaluation of your proposal for inclusion in the CCIS series, please send an e-mail to ccis@springer.com.

Kun Zhang · Xianhua Song ·
Mohammad S. Obaidat · Anas Bilal · Jun Hu ·
Zeguang Lu
Editors

Computer Science and Educational Informatization

6th International Conference, CSEI 2024
Haikou, China, November 1–3, 2024
Revised Selected Papers, Part I

 Springer

Editors

Kun Zhang 🆔
Hainan Normal University
Haikou, China

Mohammad S. Obaidat 🆔
University of Jordan
Amman, Jordan

Jun Hu 🆔
Harbin University of Science and Technology
Harbin, China

Xianhua Song 🆔
Harbin University of Science and Technology
Harbin, China

Anas Bilal 🆔
Hainan Normal University
Haikou, China

Zeguang Lu 🆔
National Academy of Guo Ding Institute
of Data Science
Beijing, China

ISSN 1865-0929   ISSN 1865-0937 (electronic)
Communications in Computer and Information Science
ISBN 978-981-96-3734-8   ISBN 978-981-96-3735-5 (eBook)
https://doi.org/10.1007/978-981-96-3735-5

This Springer imprint is published by the registered company Springer Nature Singapore Pte Ltd.
The registered company address is: 152 Beach Road, #21-01/04 Gateway East, Singapore 189721, Singapore

If disposing of this product, please recycle the paper.

Preface

The 6th International Conference on Computer Science and Educational Informatization (CSEI 2024) was held in Haikou, China, on November 1–2, 2024, hosted by Hainan Normal University, CCF Computer Applications Technical Committee, and co-organized by CCF Haikou Member Activity Center, Hainan University, Hainan Tropical Ocean University, Hainan College of Economics and Business, the First-level discipline Master's Program in Cyberspace Security of the School of Information Science and Technology at Hainan Normal University, and the Master's Program in Computer Technology of the School of Information Science and Technology at Hainan Normal University. The goal of this conference was to provide a forum for computer scientists, engineers, and educators.

This conference attracted 171 paper submissions. After the hard work of the Program Committee, 51 papers of CSEI 2024 were accepted to be presented in the conference, with an acceptance rate of 29.82%. There were at least 3 reviewers for each article, and each reviewer reviewed no more than 4 articles. The major topics of this conference were Computer Science, Education Informatization, and Engineering Education. The accepted papers cover a wide range of areas related to educational information science and technology, educational informatization and big data for education, innovative applications for the deeper integration of education practice and information technology, and university engineering education.

We would like to thank all the Program Committee members for their hard work in completing the review tasks. Their collective efforts made it possible to attain quality reviews for all the submissions within a few weeks. Their diverse expertise in each research area helped us to create an exciting program for the conference. Their comments and advice helped the authors to improve the quality of their papers and gain deeper insights.

We thank the team at Springer, whose professional assistance was invaluable in the production of the proceedings. A big thanks also to the authors and participants for their tremendous support in making the conference a success.

Besides the technical program, this year CSEI offered different experiences to the participants. We hope you enjoyed the conference.

January 2025

Xianhua Song
Yu Zhou
Anas Bilal

Organization

Honorary Chair

Rajkumar Buyya   University of Melbourne, Australia

General Chairs

Mohammad S. Obaidat   University of Jordan, Jordan
Kun Zhang   Hainan Normal University, China
Bin Wen   Hainan Normal University, China

Program Chairs

Xianhua Song   Harbin University of Science and Technology, China
Yu Zhou   Hainan Normal University, China
Anas Bilal   Hainan Normal University, China

Program Co-chairs

Xiaowen Liu   Hainan Normal University, China
Haixia Long   Hainan Normal University, China
Zhengjie Deng   Hainan Normal University, China
Ali Haider Khan   Lahore Garrison University, Pakistan
Mostafa Ghobaei-Arani   Islamic Azad University, Iran
Sibghat Ullah Bazai   Balochistan University of Information Technology, Engineering, and Management Sciences, Pakistan

Organising Chairs

Qingchen Zhang   Hainan University, China
Haifeng Wang   Hainan Tropical Ocean University, China
Heping Gou   Qiongtai Normal University, China

Yuxi Liu	Harbin Normal University, China
Hongzhi Wang	Harbin Institute of Technology, China
Mir Muhammad Nizamani	Hainan University, China
Amin Qourbani	Amirkabir University of Technology, Iran

Publication Chairs

Jun Hu	Harbin University of Science and Technology, China
Emad Mahrous Awwad	King Saud University, Saudi Arabia
Uzair Aslam Bhatti	Hainan University, China

Registration/Financial Chair

| Fa Yue | National Academy of Guo Ding Institute of Data Science, China |

Academic Committee Chairman

| Hongzhi Wang | Harbin Institute of Technology, China |

Academic Committee Vice Presidents

Jianhou Gan	Yunnan Normal University, China
Dong Liu	Henan Normal University, China
Guanglu Sun	Harbin University of Science and Technology, China

Academic Committee Secretary General

| Zeguang Lu | National Academy of Guo Ding Institute of Data Science, China |

Academic Committee Executive Members

Xiaoju Dong	Shanghai Jiao Tong University, China
Qilong Han	Harbin Engineering University, China
Lan Huang	Jilin University, China
Ying Jiang	Kunming University of Science and Technology, China
Junna Zhang	Henan Normal University, China
Junxiang Zhou	Yunnan Normal University, China

Program Committee Members (In Alphabetical Order)

Jinliang An	Henan Institute of Science and Technology, China
Hongtao Bai	Jilin University, China
Chunguang Bi	Jilin Agriculture University, China
Xiaochun Cao	Sun Yat-sen University, China
Yuefeng Cen	Zhejiang University of Science And Technology, China
Wanxiang Che	Harbin Institute of Technology, China
Juntao Chen	Hainan College of Economics and Business, China
Lei Chen	Sanya Aviation and Tourism College, China
Yarui Chen	Tianjin University of Science and Technology, China
Haoran Chen	Zhengzhou University of Light Industry, China
Fei Dai	Southwest Forestry University, China
Shoujian Duan	Baoshan University, China
Congyu Duan	Shenzhen University, China
Yuxuan Feng	Jilin Agricultural University, China
Ping Feng	Changchun University, China
Jianhou Gan	Yunnan Normal University, China
Qiuei Han	Changchun University, China
Jia Hao	Yunnan Normal University, China
Yaqiong He	Zhengzhou University of Light Industry, China
Xinhong Hei	Xi'an University of Technology, China
Wenjuan Jia	Dalian University of Finance and Economics, China
Ying Jiang	Kunming University of Science and Technology, China
Jiaqiong Jiang	Hunan University, China
Zhejun Kuang	Changchun University, China

Guohou Li	Henan Institute of Science and Technology, China
Yuanhui Li	Sanya Aviation and Tourism College, China
Shanshan Li	Sanya Aviation and Tourism College, China
Hua Li	Changchun University of Science and Technology, China
Yanting Li	Zhengzhou University of Light Industry, China
Zedong Li	Dalian Nationalities University, China
Zijie Li	Yunnan Normal University, China
Chengrong Lin	Hainan University, China
Zongli Lin	University of Virginia, USA
Kaibiao Lin	Xiamen University of Technology, China
Chunhong Liu	Henan Normal University, China
Dong Liu	Henan Normal University, China
Xia Liu	Sanya Aviation and Tourism College, China
Kang Liu	Sanya Aviation and Tourism College, China
Ying Liu	Tianjin University of Science and Technology, China
Wanquan Liu	Sun Yat-sen University, China
Sanya Liu	Central China Normal University, China
ChinaDong Liu	Henan Normal University, China
Shijian Luo	Zhejiang University, China
Juan Luo	Hunan University, China
Wei Meng	Guangdong University of Technology, China
Yashuang Mu	Henan University of Technology, China
Cong Qu	Hainan University, China
Jiannji Ren	Henan Polytechnic University, China
Jinmei Shi	Hainan Vocational University of Science and Technology, China
Xiaobo Shi	Henan Normal University, China
Yancui Shi	Tianjin University of Science and Technology, China
Wenjun Shi	Zhengzhou University of Light Industry, China
Jing Su	Tianjin University of Science and Technology, China
Peng Sun	University of Electronic Science and Technology of China, China
Weizhi Sun	Sanya Aviation and Tourism College, China
Guanglu Sun	Harbin University of Science and Technology, China
Lin Tang	Yunnan Normal University, China
Mingjing Tang	Yunnan Normal University, China
Hongwei Tao	Zhengzhou University of Light Industry, China
Yiyuan Wang	Northeast Normal University, USA

Junchao Wang	North Dakota State College of Science, China
Xiaoyu Wang	Jilin Normal University, China
Cong Wang	Tianjin University of Science and Technology, China
Yuan Wang	Tianjin University of Science and Technology, China
Jun Wang	Yunnan Normal University, China
Min Wang	Yunnan Normal University, China
Haiyan Wang	Changchun University, China
Xiao Wang	Zhengzhou University of Light Industry, China
Cunru Wang	Dalian Nationalities University, China
Xinkai Wang	Ningbo Technology University, China
Yongheng Wang	Hunan University, China
Zumin Wang	Dalian University, China
Wei Wei	Xi'an University of Technology, China
Changji Wen	Jilin Agriculture University, China
Bin Wen	Yunnan Normal University, China
Yang Weng	Sichuan University, China
Huaiguang Wu	Zhengzhou University of Light Industry, China
Di Wu	Yunnan Normal University, China
Yonghui Wu	Fudan University, China
Bin Xi	Xiamen University, China
Yuelong Xia	Yunnan Normal University, China
Xiaoxu Xiao	Shaanxi Normal University, China
Meihua Xiao	East China Jiaotong University, China
Min Xie	Yunnan Normal University, China
Jian Xu	Qujing Normal University, China
Mingliang Xue	Dalian Nationalities University, China
Yajun Yang	Tianjin University, China
Fan Yang	Xiamen University, China
Kehua Yang	Hunan University, China
Chen Yao	Zhejiang University, China
Zhenyan Ye	Sanya Aviation and Tourism College, China
Shouyi Yin	Tsinghua University, China
Xiaohui Yu	Shandong University, China
Yue Yu	Beijing Institute of Technology, China
Lingyun Yuan	Yunnan Normal University, China
Ye Yuan	Northeastern University, China
Congpin Zhang	Henan Normal University, China
Junna Zhang	Henan Normal University, China
Chuanlei Zhang	Tianjin University of Science and Technology, China

Yanan Zhang	Tianjin University of Science and Technology, China
Yaming Zhang	Yunnan Normal University, China
Weiwei Zhang	Zhengzhou University of Light Industry, China
Hua Zhang	University of Chinese Academy of Sciences, China
Tingting Zhao	Tianjin University of Science and Technology, China
Bo Zhao	Yunnan Normal University, China
Jian Zhao	Changchun University, China
Zhongtang Zhao	Zhengzhou University of Aeronautics, China
Huan Zhao	Hunan University, China
Tongtao Zheng	Xiamen University, China
Wei Zhong	Yunnan Normal University, China
Juxiang Zhou	Yunnan Normal University, China
Qifeng Zhou	Xiamen University, China
Jun Zhu	Northwestern Polytechnical University, China

Contents – Part I

Contents – Part II

**Innovative Application for the Deeper Integration of Education
Practice and Information Technology**

Educational Information Science and Technology

Digital Transformation of Higher Education: Research Status, Conceptual Connotation, and Analytical Framework

Shoujian Duan[1,2], Yanli Yang[2(✉)], and Dongxiang Song[3]

[1] Key Laboratory of Education Informatization for Nationalities, Ministry of Education, Yunnan Normal University, Kunming, China
[2] School of Big Data, Baoshan University, Baoshan, China
35701741@qq.com
[3] School of Information, Dehong Teacher's College, Dehong, China

Abstract. In the face of the new requirements for talent cultivation in higher education in the digital age, the integration of digital transformation and governance capabilities in higher education is an inevitable trend. Clarifying the conceptual connotation and analytical framework of digital transformation in higher education is an important part of promoting the practice of digital transformation in higher education. On this basis, this article summarizes the current situation of digital transformation in higher education, analyzes its conceptual connotation, and uses TOE theory to design an analysis framework for digital transformation in higher education from the dimensions of technology, organization, and environment. It explains the promotion scenarios of digital teaching, digital learning, digital governance, and digital evaluation to explore the digital analysis framework of higher education from a theoretical perspective and promote the modernization of higher education governance.

Keywords: Digital Transformation of Education · TOE Theory · Analytical Framework

1 Introduction

In the digital age, digital education transformation has become an inevitable requirement for education to respond to changes in time and the need for realistic development. The construction of an efficient and high-quality education system is a policy orientation and a key requirement for the development of higher education in China in the new era, which urgently requires the innovative empowerment of digital transformation in higher education. The digitization of higher education is not only a new track of education development but also an important way to shape new advantages of education. Owing to the complexity and special nature of education digitization, he has not achieved satisfactory results, as many other fields have achieved [1]. The digital transformation of education is the innovation and transformation of all the elements, processes, and fields of education. The digital transformation of higher education in China is currently in its early stages

K. Zhang et al. (Eds.): CSEI 2024, CCIS 2447, pp. 3–13, 2025.
https://doi.org/10.1007/978-981-96-3735-5_1

of development [2]. Although some progress has been made in promoting the digital transformation of education, there are significant differences in the understanding of conceptual connotations, model frameworks, and practical paths. The main issues are as follows: First, the academic research community has not yet formed a unified consensus on the digital transformation of education. Second, there is a shortcoming of top-level design at the national level, and there is a lack of a digital maturity model framework and a clear practical path for education digital transformation in practice [3]. Third, there are significant differences in environmental conditions, organizational culture, and practical abilities among schools of different levels and types in different regions. Currently, a hierarchical and classified framework for guiding and analyzing digital transformation is lacking. Concerning digital transformation in higher education, scholars, decision-makers, and the public commonly face confusion in terms of why, what, and how to transform. Therefore, it is particularly urgent and necessary to understand the current situation of digital transformation in higher education and analyze its conceptual connotations and theoretical analysis framework to guide universities in promoting digital transformation in education.

2   Research Status of Digital Transformation in Higher Education

2.1   Research Status on Digital Transformation

Digital transformation begins with the practice of the enterprise. For enterprises, the purpose of transformation is to improve efficiency, innovation capabilities, and market adaptability through technology-driven change, thereby achieving long-term growth and success. According to Matt C. [4], a digital transformation tactic, is a blueprint that allows a company to manage changes due to the synthesis of digital technologies and to support smooth operation after the transformation. Tobias K. [5] suggested that digital transformation is a transformation based on digital technologies, resulting in distinctive alterations to corporate functioning, workflow procedures, and the generation of value. X. [6] suggested that the essence of digital transformation is to resolve the uncertainty of complex systems through the automatic flow of data, optimize resource allocation efficiency, and build a new competitive advantage for enterprises.

As digital technology becomes increasingly prevalent across different sectors, the notion of digital transformation has experienced broader conceptual evolution. Scholars such as Agarwal R. [7] and Majchrzak A. [8] believe that digital transformation denotes the application of digital technology to effect significant shifts in societal and industrial landscapes. According to Chanias S. [9], the objective of digital transformation is to pursue elemental alterations in an organization's infrastructure, offerings, business processes, models, and strategies, as well as in the relationships and networks between organizations. Zhai Y. [10] and other academics contend that digital transformation constitutes a process of transforming and reconfiguring the economic, social, and governmental spheres, driven by the combined influence of ongoing innovation in information technology applications and the steady expansion of data resources. It has high efficiency, added value, a global scope, and openness and can effectively empower the modernization of national governance.

2.2 Research Status of Digital Transformation in Higher Education

Recently, the issue of digital transformation in higher education has received increasing attention from countries and scholars around the world. For example, the United States emphasized the significant support and promotion role of information technology in digitizing higher education [11]. France is committed to implementing the "digital campus" and "digital university" strategies [12]. Germany has focused on implementing the digital transformation of higher education and technical education [13]. Russia has proposed a series of digital transformation development strategies to improve the quality of higher education and international competitiveness and to adapt to the development trend of the cyber age [14]. European countries emphasize the empowering role of data in educational transformation and actively construct digital education systems from a systemic perspective to promote the digital education ecosystem [15]. In 2018, the Education Informatization 2.0 Action Plan issued by the Ministry of Education of China emphasized that education informatization is the basic connotation and significant feature of education modernization. In 2021, the Guidance on Promoting the Construction of New Infrastructure for Education and Building a High-quality Education System issued by the Ministry of Education and six other departments noted that it is necessary to "promote the digital transformation, intelligent upgrading, integration and innovation of education, and support the high-quality development of education". China has made historic progress and breakthroughs in the digital transformation of education, and a new ecosystem of digital education is emerging [16]. However, the basic situation and trend of China's current and future digital education is that the results have been remarkable in some aspects, but the overall situation is worrying[17]. Some schools in developed regions have achieved significant results in the digital transformation of education, but in more regions, especially in relatively backward border ethnic areas, digital education transformation is still in a passive state.

3 The Concept and Connotations of Digital Transformation in Higher Education

3.1 Definition of Digital Transformation in Higher Education

The advancement and transformation of society in the digital realm necessitate that education progresses in tandem and often assumes a pioneering role. When a strong country is built through education, the institution of higher learning is the leader. Transformation is a type of reform, and the key to digitizing education lies in "transformation", which means systematically transforming education in the digital age and building a new educational ecosystem. By revolutionizing teaching approaches, learning paradigms, administrative frameworks, and assurance strategies, we will gradually achieve process reengineering, structural restructuring, and cultural reconstruction. Yu S. [18] noted that digital education transformation includes three levels: technology, business, and people-oriented. Zhu Z. [19] suggested that digital education transformation involves the incorporation of digital technology into various levels of the education field, promoting comprehensive innovation and changes in educational methodologies, organizational structures, instructional procedures, assessment techniques, and other aspects of educational organizations. Its value orientation is based on digital transformation and upgrading, and by fully utilizing the advantages of digital technology in the education ecosystem, it promotes structural, functional, and cultural changes in the educational structure, making the educational structure more dynamic and service-oriented.

Therefore, based on the above analysis, we define the "digital transformation of higher education" under the guidance of the Party and the state's education policy, driven by digital technology, supported by the organizational structure, and guaranteed by the external environment, promoting deep-level digital transformation of universities; optimizing the allocation of institutions of greater learning resources; individualizing educational services; and comprehensively improving educational quality through digital teaching, digital learning, digital governance, and digital evaluation, thus nurturing socialist contributors and successors who are well rounded in character, mind, body, aesthetics, and work skills.

3.2 The Value Connotation of Digital Transformation in Higher Education

High quality, fairness, and efficiency are known as the "impossible triangle" or "difficult triangle" of education. Traditional educational methods find it difficult to balance them, whereas digital education has the potential to break through the "difficult triangle". What remains unchanged in the realm of education is the essence of education services based on human development, as well as the quest for high-quality, fair, and efficient education. Digital transformation is the merging of digital technology into all areas of activity, fundamentally altering the way humans engage in these activities and bringing value to humanity and society as a whole. From this perspective, digital transformation involves the profound impact of digital change on human behavior, habits, and various sociocultural phenomena at a deeper level. The digital transformation in higher education's greater importance involves promoting personalized learning, lifelong education, and competency-based educational concepts, which aim to enhance educational quality through technological empowerment, promote educational equity, and cultivate talent with an innovative spirit, critical thinking, and an international perspective.

Digital transformation originates from the human pursuit of increasing certainty and the active development of productivity. Shannon [20] posits that "information serves to diminish uncertainty, and its worth is measured by the enhancement of certainty it brings". The digital transformation of universities is a deep exploration and reshaping of the connotation of educational value, which stems from the continuous pursuit of educational efficiency and quality, as well as the improvement of knowledge dissemination and innovation capabilities. The digital transformation of universities means integrating digital technology into diverse facets of educational processes and instruction, significantly improving the certainty of education through precise data analysis and intelligent teaching management. The value connotation of digitalization in universities lies in optimizing resource allocation, enhancing teaching interactivity and personalized learning experience, increasing the predictability and controllability of educational outcomes, and providing strong support for cultivating innovative talent that adapts to future social development.

4 Analysis Framework for the Digital Transformation of Higher Education

4.1 TOE Analysis Framework

The technology-organization-environment (TOE) framework is a conceptual model introduced by Tornatzky L. et al. [21] in 1990 and is based on the classical technology acceptance model and innovation diffusion theory. The proposed framework originated from enterprise technological innovation and has strong adaptability, flexibility, and scalability. Currently, it has been extensively applied across multiple domains, including the fields of education, government data open-sharing, and enterprises. The digital transformation of institutions of greater learning is constrained in its development path because of its unclear and complex structure during its dynamic changes [22]. The TOE framework, as a theoretical model based on the application context of emerging technologies, includes three dimensions, i.e., technology (T), organization (O), and environment (E), which are highly compatible with the dynamic interaction factors between digital education transformation and the superior advancement of education. The driving forces of digital transformation in higher education can be classified into three categories: digital technology-driven, school organization-driven, and educational environment-supported.

4.2 Analysis Framework for the Digital Transformation of Higher Education Based on TOE Theory

Based on the literature and practical work in universities, we design an analytical framework for the digital transformation of higher education based on TOE theory, as shown in Fig. 1. This analytical framework demonstrates the transformation of scenarios such as digital teaching, digital learning, digital governance, and digital evaluation in universities through the collaborative linkage of technology, organization, and environment. The ultimate objective is to cultivate socialist builders and successors with comprehensive development in morality, intelligence, physical fitness, aesthetics, and labor skills.

Technical Dimension Analysis. The dependence on technology in the digital transformation of higher education means that technological innovation has become the motivation for advancement. In terms of technology, key technologies such as big data, artificial intelligence, the Internet of Things, and metaverse methods play a vital role in the digital transformation of higher education. The application of big data technology in the field of education provides abundant data resources for universities. Big data platforms can also help universities identify problems in teaching and management processes, providing data support for teaching reform. Through big data learning analysis, universities can gain a clearer perception of students' learning behaviors and needs, thereby achieving personalized teaching. Artificial intelligence provides vigorous support for the digital transformation of higher education, offering personalized learning advice and guidance to students to help them better grasp knowledge. Moreover, intelligent teaching assistants can reduce the workload of teachers and increase teaching output. The Internet of Things provides a more convenient and efficient teaching environment, which can achieve intelligent management and efficient utilization of teaching resources and improve teaching

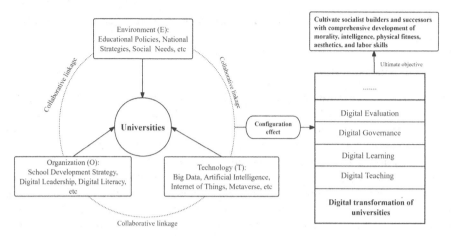

Fig. 1. Analysis Framework for the Digital Transformation of Universities Based on TOE Theory

quality and efficiency. Metaverse technology can create a virtual teaching environment, allowing students to learn and communicate in the virtual world. Metaverse technology can also achieve cross-regional and cross-cultural teaching exchanges, promoting international educational cooperation and communication.

Organizational Dimension Analysis. At the organizational level, the development strategy of universities, the digital leadership of cadres, and the digital literacy of teachers are the three key factors driving the digital transformation of higher education. First, the development strategy of universities plays a leading role. Schools must develop clear strategic plans, specifying the goals, directions, and paths of digital transformation. This includes identifying priority areas for digital transformation, such as online teaching, digital resource development, and intelligent education platforms, as well as developing corresponding implementation plans and timelines. The formulation of development strategies for universities needs to consider the actual situation of the school, such as its resources, capabilities, and culture, to ensure the feasibility and effectiveness of the strategy. Second, the digital leadership of cadres is essential in the digital transformation of education. Cadres are the leaders of schools, and their decisions and behaviors have a profound effect on the digital transformation of schools. Therefore, enhancing the digital leadership of cadres, including strengthening their understanding and comprehension of digital transformation, improving their decision-making and leadership abilities, and promoting innovation and change within the organization, is necessary. Third, teachers' digital literacy plays a fundamental role. Teachers are the direct executors of teaching activities, and their digital literacy is directly related to the quality of teaching and the learning experience of students. Therefore, enhancing teachers' digital literacy, which includes strengthening their understanding and mastery of digital teaching tools and methods, improving their teaching and innovation abilities, and cultivating their knowledge and skills related to digitalization, is necessary.

Environmental Dimension Analysis. As a subsystem of the social system, education lays the human and cultural foundation for the operation of society through talent output and cultural dissemination. Education demonstrates its value by meeting the needs of society, the state, and individuals for education. The environmental dimensions of digital transformation in universities include educational policies, national policies, and social needs.

The Party's educational policy is the fundamental guideline. In April 2021, the Education Law of the People's Republic of China defined "what kind of people to cultivate" as "socialist builders and successors with comprehensive development in morality, intelligence, physical fitness, aesthetics, and labor" and "how to cultivate people" as "combining production labor and social practice" and "for whom to cultivate people" as "serving socialist modernization construction and the people" [23]. The Party's educational policy provides guidance and theoretical support for the digital transformation of higher education, and digital transformation is a specific practical means to achieve educational policy. The Party's educational guidelines highlight the nurturing of socialist constructors and heirs who are holistically developed in ethics, intellect, physical health, artistic appreciation, and work skills. Therefore, the digital transformation of universities serves this overall goal by improving excellence and productivity in educational processes.

National policies are a solid guarantee. In recent years, China has introduced multiple policies and measures in the digital transformation of higher education. The Ministry of Education issued the "Education Informatization 2.0 Action Plan" in 2018, which aimed to promote the updating of educational concepts, the transformation of models, and the reconstruction of the education system. In 2021, the Ministry of Education issued the "Norms for the Construction of Digital Campuses in Higher Education Institutions (Trial)" to foster the comprehensive merging of information technology with educational instruction and improve the level of information construction and application in higher education institutions. The work points released by the institution of the higher learning department of the Ministry of Education in 2023 focus on deepening the execution of digital strategic actions and shaping new advantages for the transformation and advancement of higher education. In 2024, the Ministry of Education held the World Digital Education Conference to explore the practice and innovation of digital education with nations across the globe, aiming to promote inclusive and equitable quality education through educational digitization. These policies and actions reflect the country's emphasis on the transformation of higher education, providing a solid guarantee for promoting the transformation of higher education.

Social demand is the intrinsic driving force. First, in the age of the information economy, innovation ability, critical thinking, and digital skills have become important indicators of talent. This demand prompts universities to innovate in curricular content, pedagogical approaches, and assessment strategies. To adapt to the rapidly changing social environment. Second, the realignment of the societal industrial framework and the shift in economic growth paradigms necessitate universities to produce graduates equipped with cross-disciplinary expertise, creative capabilities, and hands-on competencies. Digital transformation can help universities demolish conventional disciplinary boundaries, encourage multidisciplinary synergy, nurture individuals with intricate knowledge frameworks, and meet the demand for diversified talent in society. Furthermore, lifelong learning has become an inevitable trend in social development, and the demand for continuing education and lifelong learning among members of society continues to increase. The transformation of universities meets the educational requirements of various cohorts at diverse times and locations by providing flexible and convenient learning methods, thereby promoting the fair distribution of educational resources and the realization of social education equity.

4.3 Scenario Analysis of Digital Transformation in Universities

The scenario design should be guided by educational needs and aimed at solving practical problems in higher education. Therefore, "teaching-learning-management-evaluation" is taken as the key area of digital transformation, and the use cases of "digital teaching, digital learning, digital governance, and digital evaluation" are designed to form a mutually supportive and promoting digital education ecosystem.

Digital Teaching. Classroom teaching is the pivotal arena of teaching, and its digitalization process not only relies on technological support but also cannot be separated from human participation. Human-machine interaction and collaboration are the keys to achieving the synergistic effect of "one plus one is greater than two" in digital classroom teaching. Currently, large-scale language models such as ChatGPT, ChatGLM, and iFlytek are increasingly widely used in university teaching. They can provide personalized tutoring, intelligent Q&A, automatic homework correction, and other functions. The classroom of human-machine collaboration, especially the collaborative teaching of local teachers, remote teachers, and robot teachers, will become a routine classroom form in the age of AI [24]. In digital teaching scenarios, teachers utilize technological tools such as intelligent teaching platforms and virtual reality simulators to innovate teaching content and optimize teaching methods. These tools not only enhance the interactivity and personalization of teaching but also enable teachers to monitor student's learning progress and performance in real time through learning analytics technology, thereby achieving precise teaching. Although human-machine interaction has partially replaced the functions of teachers, this does not mean that teachers are no longer important but rather that teachers must play a more important role. In the digital teaching environment, the functions and methods of teachers' roles have changed. At this time, teachers are leaders who understand the essence of digital education, have digital literacy, and are constantly learning and improving themselves [25].

Digital Learning. Tailored, customized, and student-centered education represents an ideal and terminal objective of human schooling, and educational digitization makes it possible to provide suitable education for everyone. The construction of a personalized adaptive learning environment is an important component. In this environment, learners are proactive, content is personalized and pushed for learners, and rules and processes are reorganized and reconstructed around learners' needs, providing learners with a more autonomous and personalized learning environment. The learning form of "everyone can learn, everywhere can learn and anytime can learn" is beginning to emerge. In the digital age of education, students' learning focus has shifted from knowledge and skills to adaptive learning, with a greater emphasis on cultivating critical and higher-order thinking, including the ability to analyze and address issues through data utilization.

Digital Governance. How to transform the potential of digitalization, leading to enormous changes in the education field, into practical results and how to facilitate the transition to and elevation of educational digitization constitute not only a technical challenge but also a major issue in testing governance capabilities and levels. Carrying out digital governance is not only an inherent requirement for the reform of universities but also an essential route to advance the modernization of higher education institutional governance [26]. From the perspective of application scenarios, teachers and students are the main participants in the digital governance of universities. The main purpose of carrying out digital governance in universities is to provide high-quality services for teachers and students. With the advancement of data-driven teaching management processes and the diversification of data collection methods, education management is gradually moving toward a more efficient and accurate regulatory stage, thus continuously optimizing management processes and mechanisms. By real-time collection of comprehensive data related to students' learning status, teachers' teaching activities, resource utilization efficiency, platform operation, and usage, a big data governance platform for schools can be constructed. On this basis, an education governance mechanism centered on data-driven and efficient decision-making has been established, achieving intelligent management and dynamic governance of the platform.

Digital Evaluation. Comprehensive development is the fundamental purpose of education, and comprehensive cultivation is the basic process and means to achieve comprehensive development. A comprehensive evaluation is an important means and guarantee to grasp and supervise the basic process of comprehensive cultivation and to measure whether the fundamental purpose of comprehensive development has been achieved[27]. The main functions of traditional education evaluation are identification, selection, and digital evaluation. The digital evaluation of universities will achieve a deep-level transformation in education evaluation, primarily by leveraging digital advancements such as large data analytics, AI, distributed ledger technology, digital twins, and the virtual universe, to form an interconnected and common education evaluation big data system that connects multiple organizational levels, communicates multiple educational subjects, and integrates multidimensional spaces. It fully integrates and mobilizes multiple resources and forces, gradually realizing the all-around, full process, full time and space, and full elements of education evaluation [28]. A comprehensive evaluation is committed to a comprehensive examination of student cultivation and development, covering the balanced development of the "five educations" of morality, intelligence, physical fitness, aesthetics, and labor. The whole process evaluation focuses on the dynamic monitoring of students' cultivation and growth trajectories, recording their development and changes in real-time. Expanding the evaluation of the whole time and space to the multidimensional dimensions of student cultivation fully considers the differences in growth under different time and spatial backgrounds. The total factor evaluation comprehensively considers the key elements of student cultivation and development, including diverse educational subjects, guaranteed conditions, the educational environment, and other comprehensive influencing factors.

5 Conclusion

In most industries or fields, the success of digitalization is usually inversely proportional to the level of human participation. In other words, the greater the degree of digitalization is, the less human involvement is needed, leading to more efficient operations and a more effective transformation. If people are completely replaced, it is the complete success of digitalization. However, education is not like that. Education cannot exclude people from digitization and intelligence. If students and teachers are replaced, then education ceases to exist. The core of education lies in the interaction and communication between people. In the process of digital transformation, only through the profound fusion of humans and machines, attaining the sphere of human-machine interaction and synergy, can the full potential of digital education be realized and unleashed. Therefore, in the process of promoting digital transformation, universities not only simply emphasize the utilization of digital technology but also need to examine it with a systematic analysis framework to ensure that digital education conforms to the laws of education, revolves around the fundamental goal of promoting comprehensive, free, and personalized development of people, fully utilizes the unique value of digital means, and truly allows digital technology to serve education.

Acknowledgments. The following projects funded this research effort: Joint Special Project for Basic Research of Local Undergraduate Universities in Yunnan Province (202301BA070001–051), Key Laboratory of Education Informatization for Nationalities, Ministry of Education, Yunnan Normal University (EIN202114), Yunnan Key Laboratory of Smart Education and Yunnan International Joint R&D Center of China-Laos-Thailand Educational Digitalization (202203AP140006).

References

1. Yuan, Z.: Digital Transformation in Education: What to Turn and How? Journal of East China Normal University (Educational Sciences) **41**(03), 1–11 (2023)
2. Zhu, Z., Hu, J.: The Logic of Practice and Opportunities for Digital Transformation in Education. E-Education Research. **43**(01), 5–15 (2022)
3. Lan, G., Wei, J., Huang, C., Li, P., Cui, Y., Guo, Q.: Digital Transformation of International Higher Education and Implementation Path in China. Open Education Research. **28**(03), 25–38 (2022)
4. Matt, C., Hess, T., Benlian, A.: Digital transformation strategies. Bus. Inf. Syst. Eng. **57**(5), 339–343 (2015)
5. Tobias, K., Pooyan, K.: Digital Transformation and Organization Design: An Integrated Approach. Calif. Manage. Rev. **62**(4), 86–104 (2020)
6. An, X.: Keywords for digital transformation. Informatization Construction. **06**, 50–53 (2019)
7. Agarwal, R., Gao, G., DesRoches, C.: The digital transformation of healthcare: Current status and the road ahead. Inf. Syst. Res. **21**(4), 796–809 (2010)
8. Majchrzak, A., Markus, M., Wareham, J.: Designing for digital transformation: Lessons for information systems research from the study of ICT and societal challenge. MIS Q. **40**(2), 267–277 (2016)

9. Chanias, S., Myers, M., Hess, T.: Digital transformation strategy making in predigital - organization: The case of a financial services provider. J. Strateg. Inf. Syst. **28**(1), 17–33 (2019)

10. Zhai, Y., Jiang, W., Wang, W.: Theoretical Explanation and Operational Mechanism of China's Digital Transformation. E-Government. **06**, 67–84 (2021)

11. Du, L.: The Reform and Innovation of Higher Education Driven by Technologies——Interpretation and Implication of U.S. National Education Technology Plan: 2017 Higher Education Edition. Digital Education, **4**(03), 87-92 (2018)

12. Ren, Y.: Educational Informatization Strategy Planning and Its Enlightenment in France. Journal of World Education. **31**(18), 14–17 (2018)

13. Xu, X., Zhang, C.: The Essentials and Approaches of Higher Education Digitalization Reformation in China. China Higher Education Research. **07**, 31–35 (2022)

14. Wang, X., Li, Y.: Research and Implications on The Digital Transformation of Russian Higher Education. Chinese Journal of ICT in Education. **28**(01), 78–88 (2022)

15. Shi, J., Kong, H., Wu, J., Wang, Y.: Data Enabled Engineering Education Transformation: Analysis of European Digital Strategy Report. Research in Higher Education of Engineering. **01**, 17–23 (2021)

16. Cheng, L.: Connotative Characteristics, Basic Principles and Policy Elements of Digital Transformation of Education. E-Education Research. **44**(4), 53–56 (2023). 71

17. Tian, A., Gao, W., Xiao, M., Hou, C., Wang, Y.: A Study of Model Construction and Development of Principal's Digital Leadership. J. Chin. Soc. Educ. **05**, 89–95 (2024)

18. Yu, S.: Levels of Digital Transformation in Education. China Educational Technology. **2**, 55–59 (2023). 66

19. Zhu, Z., Hu, J.: A Theoretical Framework of Digital Transformation in Education. J. Chin. Soc. Educ. **04**, 41–49 (2022)

20. Shannon, C.: A mathematical theory of communication. The Bell System Technical Journal **27**(3), 379–423 (1948)

21. Tornatzky, L., Fleischer, M., Chakrabarti, A.: The Process of Technological Innovation, pp. 12–15. Lexington Books, Massachusetts (1990)

22. Zhang, M., Jiang, Q., Zhao, W.: Digital Transformation Enabling High-quality Development in Higher Education–An Analysis of Configuration Path Based on TOE Framework. e-Education Research. **45**(03), 54–61 (2024)

23. Qu, T., Yu, P.: Educational Policy of the Communist Party of China: Evolution Achievement and Prospect. Education Sciences in China (In Chinese and English) **6**(04), 3–12 (2023)

24. Jiao, J.: ChatGPT Boosting Education Digital Transformation in Schooling: What to Learn and How to Teach in the Era of Artificial Intelligence. Chinese Journal of Distance Education. **43**(04), 16–23 (2023)

25. Yuan, Z.: Educational Governance from the Perspective of Digital Transformation. Journal of the Chinese Society of Education. **2022**(08), 1–6 (2022). 18

26. Feng, X.: Research on the Constituent Elements of Digital Governance in Higher Education. Mod. Educ. Technol. **32**(02), 44–53 (2022)

27. Tan, H., Wang, Y.: A Study on the Key Elements and Institutional System of Monitoring and Evaluation of Moral Education. Curriculum, Teaching Material, and Method. **41**(12), 115–121 (2021)

28. Tan, H., Wang, Y.: The Digital Transformation of Educational Evaluation: Endogenous Motivation and Core Issues. Educational Research. **44**(12), 143–151 (2023)

Exploration of the Ecological Popular Science Education Model in the Context of Neuroscience and Big Data

Ling Quan[1]([✉]), Cheng Luo[1], Ruoting Yao[1], and Yangsong Zhang[2]

[1] University of Electronic Science and Technology of China, No.2006, Xiyuan Ave, West Hi-Tech Zone, Chengdu 611731, Sichuan, China
quanling@uestc.edu.cn
[2] Southwest University of Science and Technology, No.59, Qinglong Road, Mianyang 621010, Sichuan, China

Abstract. Within a university's practice-oriented education system, the incorporation of practical scientific applications into students' areas of study can effectively cultivate a wide range of skills necessary for success in the modern era. Nevertheless, current research fails to conduct a methodical investigation into the fundamental aspects, models, and assessment criteria of popular scientific education. The capacity to analyze large datasets precisely offers opportunities for the development of an ecologically popular science education system. This study utilizes neuroscience and big data to develop a comprehensive popular science education model. The model consists of four dimensions: cultivating ecology based on data profiling, collaborative education ecology within and outside of schools, carrier ecology for three-dimensional development, and evaluation ecology from the perspective of data resource integration. This study may be tailored to the specific traits of students at various levels, harnessing their intrinsic drive for personal growth and advancement. As a result, it enhances the caliber and effectiveness of nurturing talent in higher education institutions, thereby boosting national innovation and development.

Keywords: Neuroscience · Big data · Higher education institutions · Popular science education

1 Introduction

The brain is the most important organ of the human body, and understanding the structure and function of the brain is the most challenging scientific issue in the 21st century. The global prevalence of brain diseases is increasing annually, causing a disease burden that accounts for nearly 30% of the total disease burden of humanity, seriously endangering human health. In September 2021, after years of planning, the 'China Brain Project' was officially launched, and the exploration of cognitive impairment-related brain diseases became an important part of the China Brain Project [1]. The importance of popular science and technological innovation is equally important in addressing the practical requirements of serving people's health. At the scientific and technological innovation level, significant scientific and technological innovations have the crucial tasks of analyzing the causes of major brain diseases associated with cognitive impairment and developing novel technologies that can set international standards for the early diagnosis and optimal treatment of brain diseases. Conversely, the general public's understanding of cognitive disorders remains inadequate, leading to the potential for cognitive biases and misunderstandings. Scientific popularization plays a crucial role in the dissemination of scientific knowledge to the public. Its main objective is to increase public awareness of cognitive disorders; promote early prevention, detection, and treatment; and foster understanding and support for families of patients with cognitive disorders. Additionally, it aims to create a caring and respectful environment for patients and their families.

As the innovation highlands of the country, colleges and universities shoulder the important mission of cultivating high-level talent with both morality and ability and carrying out innovation and creation. How to constantly guide college students to find and solve problems such as "promoting science and technology development and science and technology promoting development", encourage them to continue exploring their own professional knowledge and closely integrate their own knowledge with the needs of the country and society, is a topic that needs to be constantly explored in the process of higher education [2]. As a special way of educating students, science popularization has built two bridges for college students. A bridge connects the ivory tower with society. It helps college students fully grasp scientific knowledge, scientific spirit, scientific thought and scientific methods in the ivory tower and then transforms what they have learned into the scientific cognition and behavioral guidelines needed by society through popular science practices. The other bridge connects the present and the future. College students need a long growth time to become leaders in the field of scientific and technological innovation in the future. Focusing on their study stage in school, the practice of popular science can help college students fully understand the value of serving social development and human health with professional services at this stage and can effectively increase their professional pride. According to statistics, 129 institutions of higher learning in China offer brain science-related majors, and all of them have professional activities such as brain science lectures and popular science support education. However, the current model of popular science education still has several problems, such as a lack of systematization, a lack of cross-regional linkages, a lack of matching degree between students' characteristics and content forms, an insufficient impetus of popular science activities to local brain health-related economic development, and a lack of evaluation indicators of popular science.

In the era of big data, "data" has spread to all areas of social life, greatly affecting and changing people's lives, and the field of education is no exception. The influence and change of big data on higher education is grand and profound. The continuous progress of data science and technology has injected new momentum into science popularization and education in colleges and universities. The growth needs of college students in the practice of popular science and the cognitive needs of the public for brain health can be described more comprehensively, and the direction of popular science education is clearer. Popular science content based on big data can provide more professional information and make popular science more convincing. Data visualization works have the characteristics of authority and visualization, which is conducive to the dissemination of brain health science in the new media environment and the subsequent radiation of more people. The use of the internet to build a comprehensive diagnosis and treatment platform for cognitive disorders, improve the ability to diagnose and treat grassroots mental diseases through remote science popularization, and promote the formation of hierarchical diagnosis and treatment modes are also important means of big data that enable the popularization of science [3]. In summary, strengthening the whole process analysis and personalized optimization of mental health knowledge popularization through big data and forming an ecological model of popular science education significantly affects the effectiveness of popular science education in colleges and universities and improves the brain health literacy of the whole population.

2 Analysis of the Current Situation and Problems of Popular Science Education in Colleges and Universities

2.1 Characteristics of Students at Different Stages are not Connected in Series

Undergraduates, masters and doctoral students in universities are in different training stages of higher education. From the perspective of training methods, undergraduates pay more attention to general education, doctoral students pay more attention to academic cultivation, and the training of master's students is relatively diverse. From the perspective of the training mode, academic postgraduates emphasize theory and academic research, whereas professional postgraduates aim to cultivate application-oriented high-level talent. From the perspective of personnel composition, compared with those of undergraduates, the social roles of postgraduates are more complex, their social contacts are more positive, and their contact groups are more diverse and complex. From the perspective of innovation ability and specialization, undergraduates are in the stage of understanding their major, postgraduate students are in the stage of being able to carry out professional operations and practices with existing methods, and doctoral students are more focused on using innovative thinking to overcome difficulties and solve unsolved problems in the field of scientific research. From the perspective of participating in popular science practice activities, undergraduates have high activity and lack professional knowledge, master's degree students have moderate activity and strong professionalism, and doctoral students have low enthusiasm for participation but a strong knowledge frontier.

In the traditional process of popular science education, students at different stages are usually trained separately, which has the advantage of designing educational practices on the basis of group characteristics. However, popular science education needs to be closely aligned with the way society operates, where students' professionalism, enthusiasm, and innovation are all indispensable. Therefore, it is necessary to fully clarify the characteristics and growth needs of students at different stages in popular science education, allowing different features to flow among students at different stages, thus achieving better educational effectiveness.

2.2 Different Educational Links Are not Connected

Popular science education plays a strategic supporting role in the self-reliance of science and technology and the modernization of national governance, making it a systematic project. The practice process of science popularization involves demand analysis, content positioning, carrier design, display output, effect evaluation and other aspects, and it is necessary to integrate experts at the university level and the social level to provide systematic guidance in each link [4]. However, in the traditional link between science popularization and education in colleges and universities, the instructor of a student organization is often responsible for the construction subject, the construction goal, the construction focus, the service object, the effect evaluation and many other aspects. At present, the construction of think tanks with popular science as the core business field is still in the exploratory stage at home and abroad, and there are few studies on expert tanks of popular science think tanks. In the individual studies involved in this area, the expert resources of each link are only briefly mentioned in the analysis of the macrogroup functional characteristics of popular science education. Therefore, there is still a wide range of research space on how to use big data technology to integrate resources, develop the construction of science popularization expert think tanks for changes in the new social environment, and explore the expert intervention mode for the characteristics of different links of science popularization and education in universities.

2.3 Lack of Connection Between Popular Science Content and Media and the Real Needs of Society

The essence of popular science work is to convey scientific theories, scientific spirit, and scientific methods to the public in a simple and easy-to-understand manner. However, the popular science content presented by college students is usually highly specialized. Owing to the lack of interactivity, fun, and diversity in popular science work, popular science work often remains superficial, making it difficult for the public to accept and internalize it as their own knowledge reserve. In terms of popular science content, the interests, content needs, and topic preferences of the public in different regions, ages, and genders vary [5]. Traditional university student science popularization practices tend to focus on what can be said and what can be done while ignoring extensive research on the real needs of the public. They have not accurately grasped public opinion, thus failing to meet the increasing demand for scientific knowledge from the public in the development of society. In terms of science popularization forms, traditional science popularization education carriers are mainly lectures, with a single form that cannot effectively convey scientific content. Therefore, improving the personalized and intelligent level of science popularization education and science popularization communication based on big data technology is urgently needed.

2.4 Less Attention Has Been Given to the Evaluation of the Effects of Science Popularization and the Sense of Achievement of Science Popularization

The evaluation of science popularization effects is an important means to promote and lead the healthy development of science popularization undertakings. The quality assessment of popular science education includes the core links of tracking the development trend of education, measuring the development level, evaluating development problems, and developing development strategies. Its accuracy, validity and reliability have all become core indicators affecting the level of education quality management. There are many scientific education and practical activities in colleges and universities. The existing evaluation indicators focus mainly on the number of participants and the influence of media reports, and evaluations of their scientific, comprehensive and pioneering effects are rarely carried out. How well the function of science popularization and education is played, whether it can meet the needs of the public, whether it can be combined with formal education in schools, etc., needs to be evaluated by scientific methods to understand the situation and find problems in a targeted way to continuously improve it and promote the improvement of education effects. Therefore, theoretical research on science popularization evaluation should be consistent with the development of science popularization practice, conform to the development trend of information technology, and develop scientific methods of science popularization evaluation.

In addition, as the subject and object of popular science education, college students' sense of gain in the process of preparing, carrying out and summarizing popular science practice is mostly presented in a few words, and there are almost no quantitative indicators to measure it. To determine how to provide guidance value for future popular science education, the sense of acquisition of popular science subjects should be taken as an important reference dimension.

In general, how to rely on big data to form an integrated innovative work system that guides teachers in multiple dimensions, diverse practical scenarios, diverse practical content, and diverse student growth and ultimately form high-quality popular science works and projects is a question that needs to be considered in the education process.

3   Construction of an Ecologically Popular Science Education Model Supported by Big Data

3.1   Cultivation Ecology Based on Digital Portraits

In the era of big data, the traditional student work mode can no longer accurately identify students, personalize services for students, comprehensively evaluate students, and actively predict students, whereas the rational characteristics of big data, massive data analysis, and information sharing are conducive to comprehensive and accurate feature analysis of students at the initial stage of education [6]. In view of the scenario of science popularization and education, big data technology is used to carry out data collection, data processing, label extraction and label system establishment for the characteristics of students in the three stages of undergraduate, master's and doctoral studies of brain science-related majors to form a comprehensive portrait of students' growth.

On the basis of the use of big data to picture students, this paper proposes a path for personalized science popularization and education, including the accurate supply of personalized education resources, the reform of personalized teaching methods and the evaluation of personalized training effects. On the one hand, with the gradual deepening of students' exploration of subject knowledge at different stages of undergraduate and doctoral studies, the content design of popular science practice should also be gradually deepened, forming a hierarchical development trend to ensure that students can make contributions and grow in each stage of academic development. Specifically, the characteristics of undergraduates, master's students and doctoral students in their respective development stages can be evaluated from the dimensions of innovation ability, specialization, and participation in student activities, the strengths of each stage can be selected to compensate for the shortcomings of each stage, and the science popularization practice of "efficiency maximization" can be designed comprehensively so that students can gain cognition beyond a single group. On the other hand, in the process of preparing for and implementing "input–output-enabling" science popularization practices, college students are both knowledge acquisition and knowledge dissemination parties. College education should analyze the needs of students at various stages from the perspectives of teachers, society and students; design the form and content of popular science practices that can fully connect professional literacy and comprehensive literacy; and fully connect the ivory tower and society. Students can help in the process of science popularization, not only to meet the comprehensive needs of understanding the profession, understanding the industry, and enriching their own ability reserves but also to improve their understanding of the discipline, the cognitive power of industry development, and the thinking power of personal planning. This method can better adapt to the characteristics of students at different stages, mobilize the internal power of students' growth and talent, and then realize the personalized, accurate, sensitive and intelligent training ecology of college science popularization and education.

3.2 Coordinated Education Ecology Inside and Outside the School

The combination of professional characteristics can effectively mobilize multiple resources and become closer to the essence of education. The practice of popular science provides a new way of thinking for educating people through practice—a new integration mechanism of practice and business. When science popularization is the core of practice, first, the stability of the discipline direction of colleges and universities can greatly promote the development of practice education toward a more systematic, in-depth and inheritable direction, avoid the "fast food" of practice activities, and better conform to the law of education. Second, it can effectively combine one classroom, two classrooms and three classrooms, and high-level teachers can be integrated into them. High-level research platforms and professional practice platforms can provide support. High-level scientific research and discipline competitions can provide content assurance. Third, this education mechanism is not an overnight type but can continue to transform the cutting-edge science and technology and knowledge mastered by students into a strong guarantee for serving social hot spots and national development with the continuous help of multiple education resources.

To this end, using big data technology to promote the open sharing of resources; mobilize the flow, transmission and sharing of education resources across groups, time and space; and accelerate the construction of a collaborative ecology of science popularization and education can fully enhance the appeal of education and education. First, there is cross-group and cross-regional sharing of resources. To realize collaborative education, the barriers between universities and other subjects and between other regions must be overcome [7]. The establishment of communication channels and open big data exchange platforms relying on the network can promote different subjects to form mutual relationships under the connection of the data carrier and accelerate information exchange, data sharing and cross-border cooperation between teachers and students, colleges and departments, colleges and parents, social organizations, government departments and enterprises. An open, interconnected and common cyberspace environment can encourage education subjects to build and share data and information networks, give full play to the multiple benefits and values of big data information resources, integrate a variety of educational forces, and improve collaborative education models. Second, there is a collaborative model of different dimensions of education subjects. Science popularization and education are facilitated by a diverse range of professionals, including counsellors, high-level teachers, industry experts, and platform specialists. This collaborative effort creates an effective teaching matrix. Counsellors play a crucial role in guiding students' development. They should take the lead in promoting and spreading scientific knowledge and education. Their aim is to help college students develop a strong sense of responsibility and purpose in contributing to a "healthy China" and serving the country through science and technology. This can be achieved through engaging students in science popularization activities. The school's teaching staff at a senior level should incorporate the essence of the scientific spirit and the latest advancements in brain health science and technology into the development of science popularization practices and educational outcomes. This collaborative effort aims to increase the influence of education. Contemporary college students are eager to learn and grasp the essential aspects of the industry frontier in China's brain plan, including the craftsman spirit of industry specialists and the technical requirements of the future market, as they progress in their personal growth. To successfully incorporate themselves into the practice of popularizing science and education, they must receive direction from industry specialists. To improve the impact of scientific and technological innovation on society, it is important to involve experts who understand the audience and the goals of science popularization. This can be achieved by integrating these experts into the collaborative education system, aligning the levels of science popularization and education, and ensuring that the scientific communication efforts are effective.

3.3   Carrier Ecology of Diversified Development

The current model of brain health popularization has the problems of a single form, too much specialized content and insufficient interest, often too much scientific language, and less integration with social life, and the public cannot understand it well. In the era of rapid development of information technology, big data has deeply affected all walks of life, and the means and content of brain health popularization should also conform to the trend of big data, integrate the visualization of health big data into popular science design, and create a popular science carrier that is three-dimensional, visible and highly adaptable to the audience [8]. In the process of the development of the Global Brain Project, a large amount of cross-age, cross-gender, cross-industry and cross-regional brain health data has been accumulated. However, in the process of science popularization, these data are often highly professional and difficult to understand, which increases the difficulty of integrating them into science popularization. How to output brain health big data into the content that the public can understand is a major challenge for the innovation of brain health science content.

Popular science content suitable for different audiences. The demand for brain health science is increasingly cutting-edge, refined, and diversified. In the face of the changes in the times and needs of the people, the design of science popularization and education in the new era needs to be fully integrated into various fields and linked to economic and social development with a higher position, updated concept and wider vision. Therefore, the design of popular science content should fully stimulate students' innovative thinking, comprehensively improve the systematization of popular science content, and comprehensively improve the sense of "propriety" in the depth of content for different popular science objects to serve the general public, professional groups, and industry development. Specifically, to integrate big data into popular science works on brain health, innovation and creation must be carried out in aspects of life and popularization. Mining, analyzing and extracting relevant information from massive amounts of brain health data, using visual methods to express information, and producing in depth, valuable and low-threshold brain science popularization topics are the only way and effective means to meet the public's demand for brain-related professional information and improve the level of science popularization.

Popular science forms adapted to different platforms. The parallel practice platform offers customized practice scenarios for both universal popular science popularization sites and specialized institutions such as clinical hospitals and nursing homes. Adapting popular science content to various platforms can enable students to directly engage with the practical aspects of popular science, experience real-time audience reactions, and consequently address genuine societal needs. This allows the kids to experience the transition from their individual identity to a larger, collective identity. The creation of practical mediums such as "popular science stage plays" and "popular science teaching aids" that effectively combine education with entertainment requires a high level of creativity from the student team, as well as rigorous content and extensive knowledge expansion. Although the creation process is time-consuming, these media increase the effectiveness and longevity of knowledge transmission and are well received by the public. Simultaneously, it has a notable effect on enhancing the overall quality and capability of the student team. By utilizing platforms such as partner hospitals, enterprises, governments, and communities and collaborating on scientific research projects focused on depression diagnosis and treatment as well as sleep disorder treatment, we aim to create popular science resources that facilitate practical application scenarios. With the involvement of master's and doctoral groups, we collectively develop educational materials that serve as a bridge for students to transition from academia to society.

3.4 Evaluation Ecology from the Perspective of Data Resource Integration

Against the background of digital transformation, the construction of digital portraits focuses on the process of diagnosing and improving the quality of science popularization and education. From the three dimensions of education carrier, education subject and education object, the quality evaluation platform is constructed to carry out data collection analysis and index system description: the construction of a soft work integrated display platform—the design of a work evaluation index system; the construction of a popular science sharing and communication platform—the description of dimensions of students' sense of gain; and the construction of a professional development platform—the characterization of dimensions of teachers' sense of gain. From the perspective of data resource integration, an effect label is established so that the effects of science popularization and education can be presented comprehensively, three-dimensionally and objectively. Considering the difficulty and technical requirements of collecting data of different dimensions in the index system, a data model containing mandatory data items, optional data items and extended data items is proposed, and the evaluation index of the effectiveness of science popularization and education is further mapped and transformed with the three types of data items [9].

At the specific operational level, the first is to build a soft, popular science display platform. The existing brain health science popularization materials from universities should be compiled and categorized, outstanding science popularization works that can be disseminated should be identified, a platform for showcasing these works (such as case studies, portfolios, and exhibitions) should be established, the elements and design concepts of exceptional science popularization works should be analyzed, and the educational mechanisms employed in these works should be examined and evaluated. Metrics, including measures of communication efficacy, influence, and social engagement, should be developed to assess the societal impact of science popularization efforts. Signs indicate the conversion and transmission of practical accomplishments in popular science, such as the capacity to convert popular science works into marketable popular science products and the standardized system of popular science instruction that can be disseminated across schools. The second is to build a platform for sharing and exchanging science popularization. Excavating vividly popular science characters and popular science stories, building a popular science sharing and exchange platform, "My popular science story", telling students' sense of gain as the subject of popular science in various stages of popular science practice, and inheriting the spirit of popular science education. The evaluation index of sense of gain is established to quantify the actual gains of college students, who are both the subject of implementation and the object of education in different stages of popular science practice, to provide possibilities for continuously optimizing the effectiveness of popular science practice and education from the root. Third, the professional development path should be explored. On the one hand, science popularization tasks are encouraged to be included in the budget and evaluation indicators of scientific research projects, and science popularization achievements are included in the performance assessment and professional title promotion conditions of scientific researchers to stimulate the initiative of scientific researchers to participate in science popularization work [10], promote the transfer and transformation of scientific and technological resources to science education resources, and promote the deep integration of scientific and technological innovation and the science education system. On the other hand, the 'recognition' track of achievements in educating students through collaborative science popularization practices by counselors and full-time teachers in universities, such as awards, projects, and expert databases, should be explored to provide a clear development path for teachers in science popularization education and form a virtuous cycle of education (Fig. 1).

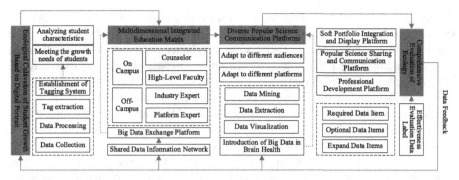

Fig. 1. Construction of an ecological science popularization education model supported by big data

4   Overview of Implementation Strategies for the Ecological Science Popularization and Education Model

Taking the training of undergraduate students in the field of neuroscience at a key Chinese '985' university as an example, in the ecological science popularization and education model designed in the previous text, the first step is to fully utilize the school's existing intelligent educational administration system and intelligent student work system, mine the growth data of students during their school years, and form personalized student growth records. On this basis, we assess the characteristics of students and their growth needs via three layers of data labels, namely, 'professional exploration group', 'innovation design group', and 'professional development group'. Step two: Integrate existing expert databases and platform databases; build a data exchange platform at the expert and platform levels; use big data technology, artificial intelligence and other technologies to explore the educational expertise of different experts and the educational attributes and resources of different platforms; form a 2x2 integrated education matrix; and assign corresponding data labels. Matching student groups with experts and platform matrices on the basis of data labels enables the design of popular science content in neuroscience. For example, when students from the 'Professional Development Group' are paired with mental health doctors as 'industry experts', they focus on combining practical clinical problems with on-campus research exploration to design a mild cognitive impairment detection system with high public acceptance. In the third step, by clarifying the popular science topic and seed keywords and using search engines as the data platform, relevant data are crawled, analyzed, and visualized to form a knowledge graph. This helps to obtain the popular science topics needed by different audiences, determine the best timing for popular science dissemination, and design appropriate popular science content and formats. For example, when a comprehensive search across the entire web is conducted via keywords such as "elderly people", "brain aging", and "needs", the topic of greatest concern for the elderly population is identified as "internet adaptation for the elderly", and a corresponding knowledge graph is constructed. To this end, the school organized students to visit nursing homes during the summer social practice, bringing the cutting-edge technological achievements of the China Brain Project to elderly individuals, offering lectures on the theme of "aging the brain slowly and gracefully," helping the elderly to fully understand the brain and scientifically protect it; creating a popular science stage play called the "brain family" to help the elderly vividly understand the functions and division of different brain areas, thus better understanding how to train the brain; and establishing a closed-loop regulation system based on VR games to help the elderly engage in long-term brain training in the most attractive way. During this process, students' understanding of the profession is greatly enhanced, effectively shaping their sense of mission to serve society professionally. Step four: Build a comprehensive evaluation platform from the dimensions of public evaluation of popular science activities, the quality of popular science works, and the sense of achievement of popular science participants. The evaluation data are linked to students' honor recognition system, university teachers' promotion indicators, and external experts' performance appraisals. The relevant data analysis feeds back into the first three stages of the model, forming a cycle of iteration.

The ecologically popular science education model constructed in this article relies heavily on data exchange at various stages, so comprehensive data mining, good data communication, and timely data feedback are key to the success and challenges of this model. In the process of development, the focus will be on breaking down the barriers between various datasets related to students' growth profiles and integrating expert resources, platform resources, public demand, award channels, etc., to build a specialized database for science popularization education.

5 Discussion and Conclusion

Science popularization and technical innovation are considered essential components of innovative growth and have become indispensable tools for enhancing a country's soft power in the modern era. The Brain Project in China aims to popularize brain health science by addressing critical societal concerns such as the prevention and management of mental diseases and the challenges posed by an aging population, with the goal of serving the general public.

This study incorporates popular science education into the practical education system of universities by utilizing the accurate profiling capability of big data. It establishes an ecologically popular science education model, which serves as a significant method for fostering innovative talent in the modern era. In this article, as the project is still in progress, there are no comprehensive data analysis results after the implementation of the overall solution. In future research, we will conduct corresponding comprehensive analysis and argumentation to further improve the proposed solution.

In the future, it is imperative to prioritize the ongoing dissemination of scientific and technological resources in institutions. On the one hand, it helps college students use their professional talent, enhances the dissemination and exchange of knowledge on a broader scale, and contributes to enhancing the innovation efficiency of the overall national innovation system. Furthermore, it empowers college students with a wide range of practical skills to contribute to the development of an innovative culture in society. It also fosters a passion for science and a scientific mindset through popular science services and encourages a societal inclination toward embracing and promoting science.

Acknowledgments. This research was funded by the boutique project of ideological and political work at the University of Electronic Science and Technology of China (UESTC), titled "Three Initiations and Three Stages: Innovative Education Model Based on Life Popular Science Practice", and supported by the counselor workshop of UESTC, as well as the Special Funding Project for Quality Education Reform (Youth Development Research) at Southwest University of Science and Technology (No. 23 szjg06).

References

1. Pan, F.W.: China Brain Project" Helps More People Overcome Mental "Barriers"—An Interview with Academician of the Chinese Academy of Sciences and Director of Peking University Sixth Hospital. Professor Lu Lin. China Medical Herald. **19**(11), 1–3 (2022)
2. Yang, Y.L.: Reflections on Popular Science and the Future Development of China. Bulletin of Chinese Academy of Sciences. **38**(5), 719–725 (2023)
3. Li, H., Li, X.: Research progress on intelligent cognitive screening tools for cognitive impairment in elderly individuals. Acta Academiae Medicinae Sinicae. **46**(1), 104–110 (2024)
4. Hu, H., Ao, N.H., Cui, L.W.: Research on the practice model of scientists participating in popular science[J]. Studies on Science Popularization. **112**(5), 22–30 (2023)
5. Pang, X.D., Qi, X., Zhang, L.: Research on the current situation and countermeasures of collaborative scientific education in primary and secondary schools in China. Studies on Science Popularization. **110**(4), 72–78 (2023)
6. Zhang, Z., Liu. X.L., Xu, B.B.: Comprehensive quality evaluation based on digital images: framework, indicators, models, and applications. China Educational Technology. (8), 10 (2021)
7. Hao, S.: Research on the development mechanism of sharing scientific popularization resources in the Beijing-Tianjin-Hebei region from the perspective of big data. Journal of North China Institute of Aerospace Engineering. **4**, 24–26 (2023)
8. Zhou, S., Tang, X.W.: Research on Ecological Popular Science Gamification from the Perspective of Participatory Culture: An Analysis Based on the UN's "Play Games, Save the Earth" Project. Studies on Science Popularization. **109**(4), 56–64 (2023)
9. Wang, G., Du, J.B.: Evaluation of the Effect of Innovation Practice Education in Colleges and Universities from the Perspective of Cultivating Students' Research Ability: An Empirical Analysis of N Universities Using Propensity Score Matching Method. China University Teaching. **000**(012), 63–68 (2021)
10. Xie, Q.H., Li, S.R., Han, Y.S.: How to Enhance the Popular Science Willingness of University Teachers: Environment, Resources, Costs, and Satisfaction. Studies on Science Popularization. **108**(1), 60–69 (2023)

Exploring Predictors of Reading Achievement in Macao's Primary Students via Social-Ecological Theory: Machine Learning

Ziqi Chen[1] , Wei Wei[1] , Sheng Chang[2(✉)] , Ting Liu[1] , and Xueyan Cao[1]

[1] Faculty of Applied Sciences, Macao Polytechnic University, Macao, China
[2] Shiqiao Qiaoxing Middle School, Guangzhou, China
18922203823@163.com

Abstract. Recent studies in Macao have focused primarily on the international assessments of higher-grade students, with relatively little attention given to the performance of younger learners in primary school. This research seeks to fill that gap by examining data from 4,059 fourth-grade students who participated in the Progress in International Reading Literacy Study (PIRLS) and identifying the key factors influencing their reading achievements. On the basis of Bronfenbrenner's (1979) social-ecological theory, we explore the roles of individual-, family-, classroom-, and school-level variables in shaping students' reading achievements. Employing the random forest algorithm along with a tenfold cross-validation technique, we assessed the relative importance of 18 distinct predictors. Our findings reveal that family-related factors, particularly parents' attitudes toward reading, are significant predictors of reading performance. Further validation through additional analyses strengthens the robustness of these results and highlights the effectiveness of the machine learning approach used. Building on these insights, this study offers a set of policy recommendations aimed at enhancing the primary school educational environment.

Keywords: Machine Learning · Social-Ecological Theory · Reading Achievement · Macao

1 Introduction

The reading proficiency of students in the early grades plays a crucial role in shaping both their academic success and long-term learning trajectories [1]. A notable example is a comprehensive five-year study [2] examining the effects of policy reforms aimed at closing the reading gap in the U.S. This research revealed that the reforms had a far greater impact on students in the early grades than on those in higher grades. In light of the distinct nature of the reading reforms required in the lower grades and the lack of sufficient research on such reforms in Macao [3], this study aims to identify the key factors that influence reading achievement at this foundational stage. Using machine learning techniques guided by social ecological theory [4], we explore how various factors across multiple dimensions affect early-grade reading outcomes. The

K. Zhang et al. (Eds.): CSEI 2024, CCIS 2447, pp. 26–38, 2025.
https://doi.org/10.1007/978-981-96-3735-5_3

findings from this study are expected to offer valuable, evidence-based insights for districts seeking to improve performance in international reading assessments while also enriching the research on early-grade reading in Macao.

2 Literature Review

2.1 International Assessments Taken in Macao

Before the Sino-Portuguese Declaration of 1987, the government's noninterventionist stance resulted in a fragmented and disjointed educational system, which hindered the development of education, causing it to stagnate [5]. Following reunification, the Macao government faced the challenge of a decentralized and 'nonstandardized' education system [6], alongside efforts to phase out grade repetition, enabling students to progress with their peers [3]. Additionally, there has been a growing emphasis on diverse forms of assessment [7].

In the last two decades, large-scale assessment surveys have become increasingly important in educational research and policy [8]. These assessments, broadly defined, evaluate students' knowledge, skills, or behaviors across specific subjects, often generating extensive datasets that include educational and social factors such as student demographics, teacher characteristics, and school environments [9, 10]. International assessment programs, which collect comparable data from various education systems worldwide, have played a key role in evaluating educational reforms in certain regions [11]. In the case of the Progress in International Reading Literacy Study (PIRLS) in Macao [12], considerable attention has been given to exploring the regional variables that influence reading achievement, as reflected in the assessment results. However, despite these efforts, few studies have provided a comprehensive analysis of the significance of each variable covered by PIRLS and developed a theoretical framework to prioritize these factors.

2.2 Social-Ecological Theory

Recently, social-ecological theory has gained prominence in understanding the factors influencing student achievement. Originally developed by Bronfenbrenner [4], this theory explores the complex relationships within a community and their impact on individual behavior.

As shown in Fig. 1, the key variables related to student reading achievements are framed within the social-ecological perspective [4]. At the core of these variables are individual factors, which encompass student demographics and behaviors. The immediate environments to which students are exposed, such as family, classrooms, and teachers, are categorized as microsystem factors. In addition, mesosystemic factors represent broader social systems, such as schools, which influence student development through interactions with students' microsystems. For example, this study examines the school environment and issues such as school violence. The exosystem and macrosystem layers, situated at the outermost level, include more abstract influences, such as cultural values, societal norms, and laws.

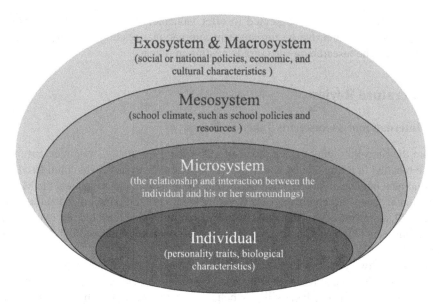

Fig. 1. Elements of social-ecological theory

Building on social-ecological theory, this study hypothesizes that multiple dimensions contribute to student achievement. Similarly, Chen [13] used this theoretical framework to examine the factors at various levels: individual, family, and school. Since the individual, microsystem, and mesosystem represent the levels that most directly influence student learning, this study focused on these socioecological factors. The conceptual model for this study is illustrated in Fig. 2.

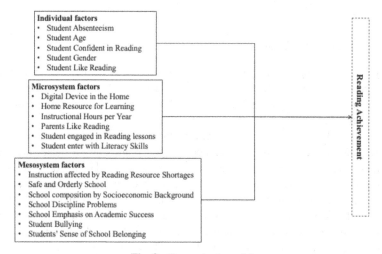

Fig. 2. Conceptual model

2.3 Strengths of Machine Learning Methods

Machine learning, as a technology driven by algorithms, offers a range of capabilities, including prediction, diagnosis, and classification. Artificial intelligence (AI) has become an increasingly influential force in education in recent years, with the promise of revolutionizing learning experiences across various settings [14]. Despite this growing interest, many prior studies investigating the factors that influence student performance have been constrained by conventional statistical approaches. These traditional methods often limit the scope of analysis by focusing on a restricted range of variables, which can hinder a comprehensive understanding of the complex dynamics at play in educational achievement [15]. In contrast, machine learning techniques are well suited for analyzing data involving multiple levels of variables.

With the rapid evolution of machine learning, a growing number of studies have applied these methods to large-scale international assessment data. The advantages of machine learning in educational research are evident in numerous studies. For example, machine learning makes no prior assumption about the relationships between educational factors and student performance, allowing it to model both linear and nonlinear interactions without constraints. This flexibility was highlighted in the work of Wang and colleagues [15], who applied machine learning mapping techniques to analyze data from urban and rural students in China via the PISA 2018 dataset. Furthermore, tree-based machine learning methods have proven particularly effective, as they can account for the hierarchical structure of data [16]. This approach not only reveals the varying contributions of different levels of influence but also allows for clear graphical representations that can aid policymakers in interpreting the results.

Given these strengths, the machine learning approach, particularly random forest regression, is well suited to the research problem for several reasons. First, machine learning enables model evaluation without relying on traditional null hypothesis testing and p values [17], which shifts the focus from binary conclusions (rejection or failure to reject) to providing quantitative evidence in support of the original hypothesis. Second, machine learning models can be assessed through multiple performance metrics, reducing the risk of overfitting [18]. Third, random forest techniques excel in handling high-dimensional data and managing complex interactions and nonlinearities [19].

2.4 Research Questions

Historically, large-scale studies in Macao have focused predominantly on examining the effects of specific factors on students' reading achievements, typically investigating individual-, family-, and school-level influences in isolation [20]. Few studies have adopted a multidimensional approach to explore the complex interactions of various factors affecting reading achievement in Macao. In contrast, previous research has shown that machine learning techniques are highly effective for analyzing multidimensional data, achieving notable success in evaluating large-scale assessment outcomes [15]. Given the ability of machine learning methods to handle complex, multivariable data, they represent an ideal approach for this study. Drawing on social-ecological theory, this research aims to investigate how individual, microsystem, and mesosystem factors collectively contribute to predicting reading achievement among students in Macao. This study is guided by the following primary research question:

1. Which key variables, among individual, microsystemic, and mesosystemic factors, are most significant in predicting the reading achievements of students in Macao?

3   Methodology

3.1   Data Collection

The data used in this study were sourced from the 2016 PIRLS database, which can be accessed freely on the official website (https://timssandpirls.bc.edu/pirls2016/internati onal-database/index.html). The 2016 PIRLS database encompasses information from 50 countries and regions, with data for the Macao region split into seven distinct datasets.

In this study, the main dataset selected was from the Macao region and consisted of a sample of 4,059 fourth-grade students. The mean age of the participants was 9.99 years (SD = 0.53), with a nearly balanced sex distribution. The male student cohort comprised 51% of the sample (N = 2,070), whereas the female student cohort constituted 49% (N = 1,989). In addition to the student data, a range of surveys were conducted to collect information from other key stakeholders. These included surveys targeting parents (n = 4,059) that inquired about their reading habits, as well as surveys administered to 138 teachers (e.g., questions such as "Do you feel safe at your current school?") and 49 school principals (e.g., "How many types of computer software are available at your school?"). The surveys were designed to capture essential data about classroom dynamics and school-level factors, offering a more holistic understanding of the various contextual elements influencing students' reading performance.

The independent variables for this study were selected on the basis of three key criteria. First, they had to be present in the PIRLS 2016 questionnaires completed by students, teachers, and headmasters. Second, the selection needed to align with the framework of Bronfenbrenner's social-ecological theory. Finally, the variables were required to have been recognized in prior research as reliable predictors of student achievement. Using these guidelines, 18 variables were identified and classified into three distinct groups: individual factors, microsystem factors, and mesosystem factors. A comprehensive explanation of each variable and its categorization is illustrated in Fig. 3.

The independent variable for this study was students' reading achievement, which was measured via a set of tasks aimed at assessing both their purposes for reading and their comprehension strategies. This variable functioned as the study's dependent measure, representing an overall indicator of students' reading proficiency. The assessment employed a standardized scale with an average score of 500 and a standard deviation of 100, which is consistent with commonly accepted evaluation frameworks. To ensure clarity and comparability, this measurement approach aligns with established norms in educational research, providing a reliable proxy for general reading ability.

Variable name	Sample item
Individual factors	
Student Absenteeism	About how often are you absent from school?
Student Confident in Reading	I usually do well in reading.
Student Like Reading	I enjoy reading
Microsystem factors	
Digital Device in the Home	How many digital information devices are there in your home?
Home Resource for Learning	In a typical week, how much time do you usually spend reading for yourself at home, including books, magazines, newspapers, and materials for work (in print or digital media)? (week)
Instructional Hours per Year	How many days per year is your school open for instruction?
Parents Like Reading	When you are at home, how often do you read for your own enjoyment?
Student engaged in Reading lessons	My teacher encourages me to say what I think about what I have read.
Student enter with Literacy Skills	Recognize most of the letters of the alphabet
Mesosystem factors	
Instruction affected by Reading Resource Shortages	How much is your school's capacity to provide instruction affected by a shortage or inadequacy of the following? Instructional materials (e.g., textbooks)
Safe and Orderly School	I feel safe at this school.
School Discipline Problems	Intimidation or verbal abuse among students (including texting, emailing, etc.)
School Emphasis on Academic Success	Teachers' understanding of the school's curricular goals
Student Bullying	Said mean things about my physical appearance (e.g., my hair, my size)
Students' Sense of School Belonging	I like being in school.

Fig. 3. Data processing process

3.2 Data Analysis

Data Processing. Following the introduction of the data sample and selection criteria for this study, the overall data processing workflow is presented in Fig. 4.

Fig. 4. Data processing process

Data cleaning revealed that the amount of missing data across all variables was relatively minimal, with missing data ranging from 0% to 12.27%. To address this, the study applied Markov chain Monte Carlo (MCMC) multiple imputation techniques via SPSS 26.0. This method was chosen to accurately estimate the missing values and ensure that the dataset remained complete for subsequent analysis.

In our study, we employed the "randomForest" package in R to build a random forest regression model aimed at predicting reading achievement, utilizing 18 independent variables. To evaluate the model's effectiveness, we implemented cross-validation (CV). Specifically, we conducted k-fold cross-validation, where the dataset was randomly partitioned into k nearly equal-sized subsets. In each round of the process, one subset was designated the test set, while the remaining k-1 subsets formed the training set. The model's performance was then assessed on the test set for each iteration. Upon completion of all k iterations, we calculate the average performance across all folds to obtain a comprehensive evaluation of the model's robustness. This approach allowed for a more reliable estimate of the model's predictive accuracy by reducing the risk of overfitting. To further enhance model reliability, we sequentially reduce the number of predictor variables and compute the mean squared error (MSE) for each reduction. This process aimed to ensure more stable and dependable performance estimates. Specifically, a five-replicate, tenfold cross-validation was conducted to identify the most important predictor variables, which resulted in a notable reduction in the MSE, confirming the robustness of the model. The PIRLS2016 dataset provides five distinct reading score values. To address this issue, we adopted the methodology advocated by earlier educational research [10, 15] and applied individual random forest regressions to each of the five scores. The overall results were then derived by calculating the average across these separate regression outcomes. This approach ensured consistency and reliability in the analysis.

4   Results

4.1   Descriptive Statistics

Descriptive statistics for the 18 independent variables, along with reading achievement, were first calculated and are presented in Table 1. The correlation coefficients between the predictor variables and reading achievement varied, ranging from a low value of -0.145 for the variable "Instruction Affected by Reading Resource Shortages" to a high value of 0.392 for "Student Confidence in Reading." As detailed in Table 1, when considering the factors derived from the social-ecological framework, student confidence in reading demonstrated the strongest positive relationship with reading achievement, yielding a correlation coefficient of 0.392. Among the microsystem and mesosystem variables, family learning resources and school emphasis on academic success had the highest correlation coefficients, with values of 0.230 and 0.166, respectively. These findings highlight the varying degrees of influence that different contextual factors, both individual and environmental, have on reading achievement.

Table 1. Descriptive statistics and bivariate correlations

Name of variables	Mean	SD	r
Students Reading Achievement	545.94	62.07	-
Individual factors			
Student Absenteeism (e.g., frequency of school absences)	3.72	0.68	0.247[**]
Student Age	9.99	0.53	0.020
Student Confident in Reading (e.g., students' self-reports on their perceived ability to succeed in reading)	8.91	1.71	0.392[**]
Student Gender	1.51	0.50	-0.003
Student Like Reading (e.g., students' self-reports on their attitudes toward reading)	9.54	1.70	0.257[**]
Microsystem factors			
Digital Device in the Home (e.g., access to digital tools)	9.93	1.58	0.165[**]
Home Resource for Learning (e.g., availability of educational materials at home)	9.75	1.55	0.230[**]
Instructional Hours per Year	926.33	106.61	-0.013
Parents Like Reading (e.g., parents-self report on frequency of reading for enjoyment at home)	9.11	1.48	0.141[**]
Student engaged in Reading lessons (e.g., (e.g., students' self-reports on their engagement with reading lessons at school)	9.26	1.80	0.110[**]
Student enter with Literacy Skills (e.g., early literacy skills upon entering school)	11.54	1.94	0.002
Mesosystem factors			
Instruction affected by Reading Resource Shortages (e.g., the impact of limited teaching resources on instruction)	8.40	1.11	-0.145[**]
Safe and Orderly School (e.g., a safe, well-organized environment supporting learning)	10.94	1.96	0.110[**]
School Composition by Socioeconomic Background (e.g., socioeconomic diversity)	1.95	0.86	0.044[**]
School Discipline Problems (e.g., frequency of behavioral issues)	11.41	1.36	0.020
School Emphasis on Academic Success (e.g., focus on promoting academic achievement)	9.56	1.18	0.166[**]
Student Bullying (e.g., students' self-reports on the frequency of being bullied by peers)	9.34	1.61	0.120[**]
Students' Sense of School Belonging (e.g., students' self-reports on their feelings about their school)	9.09	1.75	0.146[**]

4.2   Random Forest Regression and Tenfold Cross-Test

A random forest regression model was developed utilizing 18 different variables. As shown in Fig. 5, the variables are ranked by their relative importance in predicting reading achievement, with a clear hierarchy emerging. The analysis reveals that these variables each contribute to the prediction process to varying extents. Notably, the variable "parents like reading" emerged as the most significant predictor of reading performance, whereas "school composition by socioeconomic background" refers to the socioeconomic characteristics of the schools attended by fourth-grade students and was found to have the least impact on the outcome. This finding highlights the varying weight each factor holds in shaping students' reading success, with familial influences proving more influential than school demographics in this context.

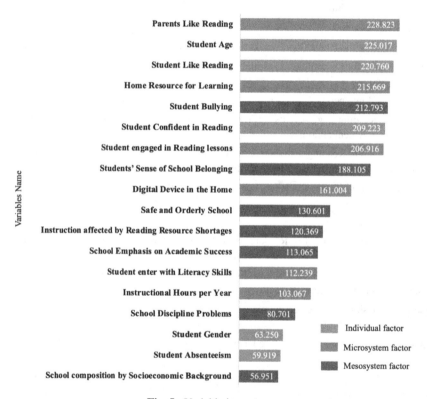

Fig. 5. Variable importance

Next, we performed a tenfold cross-validation with five replications to pinpoint the most significant predictor variables. For the key predictors, we anticipated a marked reduction in the mean squared error (MSE). As indicated in Table 2, the MSE progressively decreases with each additional variable, stabilizing after the inclusion of the eighth variable. This suggests that the first eight predictors are sufficiently robust, offering a strong and reliable foundation for predicting reading achievement. As shown in Table 2, the eight key variables that have been identified are as follows: (1) parent-like reading; (2) student age; (3) student interest in reading; (4) home resources for learning; (5) student bullying; (6) student confidence in reading; (7) student engagement in reading lessons; and (8) student sense of school belonging. The model incorporating these eight variables accounted for 82.6% of the variance in reading achievement, with an error rate of 0.809.

Table 2. Predictive performance identified by tenfold cross-validation

Variable sets	Average MSE reduction
Top 1	0.985
Top 5	0.888
Top 8	0.809
Top 12	0.762
Top 18	0.711

5 Discussion

This study aimed to evaluate the relative importance of 18 socioecological factors concurrently, employing a machine learning methodology based on reading scores from Macao's fourth-grade students in an international assessment. To ensure the robustness of the analysis, tenfold cross-validation was utilized, allowing for the identification of the eight most significant factors influencing reading achievement in Macao. By integrating these advanced analytical techniques, this research contributes to a deeper understanding of the variables affecting reading performance among primary school students in Macao, offering an important extension to the current body of literature on this topic.

This study pinpointed several crucial predictors of reading performance among students in Macao, particularly within the individual, microsystemic, and mesosystemic domains. At the individual level, factors such as students' age, enjoyment of reading, and confidence in reading stand out as significant contributors to reading achievement. These results are consistent with those of McGeown et al. [21], who demonstrated that children's attitudes toward reading, their confidence in reading, and their enjoyment of learning to read were strongly associated with their ability to read words, with reading confidence emerging as a particularly influential predictor of reading success.

Among the microsystemic factors, an interesting observation is that parents' enjoyment of reading emerged as the most critical predictor of students' reading achievement, surpassing even home resources for learning and student engagement in reading lessons. This finding supports the notion that parental involvement plays a crucial role in shaping children's academic performance. Fan and Williams [22] suggested that environmental factors, such as parental engagement, influence children's motivation and behaviors, thereby impacting their self-efficacy and development. In the context of Macao, it is likely that the value parents place on reading significantly affects their children's enjoyment of reading, which in turn influences their academic performance. This highlights the importance of parental behavior and suggests that further research into the cultural influences of Macao parents could provide deeper insights into how these behaviors impact student achievement.

With respect to mesosystemic factors, student bullying and a sense of school belonging were also found to significantly affect reading achievement. This finding is consistent with previous research, such as that of Contreras et al. [23], who reported that bullying negatively impacts students' academic performance and that high rates of bullying can erode students' sense of belonging at school [24], leading to a cycle of increased bullying behavior [25].

Our findings, in line with earlier studies comparing PIRLS data from Macao with those from other high-performing regions, underscore the importance of parental enjoyment of reading as a positive influence on student reading outcomes. The role of policy reformers and educators in fostering this behavior cannot be overstated. To foster increased parental engagement in children's reading, the government could introduce initiatives that provide families with access to affordable or even free e-readers, coupled with comprehensive training programs for maximizing their use. Furthermore, collaborating with online bookstores and digital libraries would offer families a vast selection of reading resources, such as e-books and audiobooks, making literature more accessible to diverse households. In addition, public awareness campaigns that highlight the crucial role of reading and literacy, which are aimed not only at parents but also at the broader community, have been launched. Such multifaceted efforts would contribute to a more literate and engaged society, where reading becomes a shared priority across all levels of the community.

6 Limitations

There are two main limitations in this study. The first relates to the sample used, which is based on the 2016 PIRLS data. Owing to the time lag, we were unable to incorporate the more recent 2021 PIRLS data. The inclusion of these updated data would have provided more timely insights and enhanced the practical relevance of the findings. The second limitation of this study lies in its reliance on secondary data drawn from the 2016 PIRLS. Since the PIRLS framework focuses on assessing student performance within a relatively brief period, we recommend that future investigations adopt longitudinal and experimental approaches to gain deeper insights into the academic trajectories of Macao students. These studies could provide deeper insights into the key factors that influence reading achievement over time.

Additionally, we noted that, according to the PISA results, Grade 8 students in Macao demonstrated better reading performance than their Grade 4 peers did in the PIRLS assessment. However, this study focused only on a comparison of these two groups and did not combine the results or investigate them together in depth. We hope that future research will examine the longitudinal trends and assessment results of PIRLS across different time levels in Macao. Such studies could open new directions for further research on reading achievement in Macao, providing a more comprehensive understanding of the factors at play.

References

1. Chapman, J.W., Tunmer, W.E., Prochnow, J.E.: Early reading-related skills and performance, reading self-concept, and the development of academic self-concept: A longitudinal study. J. Educ. Psychol. **92**, 703–708 (2000)
2. Betts, J.R., Zau, A.C., Koedel, C.: Lessons in reading reform: finding what works. Public Policy Institute of California. (2010)
3. Cheung, K.C., Sit, P., Mak, S., Ieong, M.: Why Macao is commended as a fast-improving economy in PISA 2018 study: An Insider perspective. (2021)
4. Bronfenbrenner, U.: The ecology of human development: experiments by nature and design. (1979)
5. Tang, K., Bray, M.: Colonial models and the evolution of education systems - Centralization and decentralization in Hong Kong and Macao. Journal of Educational Administration. **38**, 468–485 (2000)
6. Morrison, K., Joan, T.F.H.: Testing to Destruction: A problem in a small state. Assessment in Education Principles Policy and Practice. **9**, 289–317 (2002)
7. Xie, H., Ng, W.S., Zou, D., Wang, F.L.: A comparative study on recent educational policy changes of primary and secondary schooling in Hong Kong and Macao. (2018)
8. Kamens, D.H., McNeely, C.L.: Globalization and the growth of international educational testing and national assessment. Comp. Educ. Rev. **54**, 5–25 (2010)
9. Mullis, I.V.S., Martin, M.O.: PIRLS 2016 Assessment Framework. 2nd Edition. International Association for the Evaluation of Educational Achievement. (2015)
10. Organization for Economic Co-operation and Development: PISA 2018 Assessment and Analytical Framework. (2019)
11. Schuelka, M.J.: Excluding students with disabilities from the culture of achievement: the case of the TIMSS, PIRLS, and PISA. J. Educ. Policy **28**, 216–230 (2013)
12. Government Information Bureau of Macao: Macao Yearbook 2016: Macao At a Glance. (2016)
13. Chen, F., Sakyi, A., Cui, Y.: Linking student, home, and school factors to reading achievement: the mediating role of reading self-efficacy. Educ. Psychol. **41**, 1260–1279 (2021)
14. Hwang, G.-J., Xie, H., Wah, B.W., Gašević, D.: Vision, challenges, roles and research issues of Artificial Intelligence in Education. Computers and Education Artificial Intelligence. **1**, 100001 (2020)
15. Wang, F., King, R.B., Leung, S.O.: Why do East Asian students do so well in mathematics? A machine learning study. Int. J. Sci. Math. Educ. **21**, 691–711 (2022)
16. Masci, C., Johnes, G., Agasisti, T.: Student and school performance across countries: A machine learning approach. Eur. J. Oper. Res. **269**, 1072–1085 (2018)
17. Grömping, U.: Variable Importance Assessment in Regression: Linear Regression versus Random Forest. Am. Stat. **63**, 308–319 (2009)
18. Hanafy, M., Ming, R.: Classification of the insureds using Integrated Machine Learning Algorithms: A Comparative study. Applied Artificial Intelligence. 36, (2022)
19. Fawagreh, K., Gaber, M.M., Elyan, E.: Random forests: from early developments to recent advancements. Systems Science & Control Engineering. **2**, 602–609 (2014)
20. Zhou, Y., Wong, Y.-L.: Efficacy of grade retention in Macao. International Journal of Chinese Education. **6**, 57–80 (2017)
21. McGeown, S.P., Johnston, R.S., Walker, J., Howatson, K., Stockburn, A., Dufton, P.: The relationship between young children's enjoyment of learning to read, reading attitudes, confidence and attainment. Educational Research. **57**, 389–402 (2015)
22. Fan, W., Williams, C.M.: The effects of parental involvement on students' academic self-efficacy, engagement and intrinsic motivation. Educ. Psychol. **30**, 53–74 (2009)

23. Contreras, D., Elacqua, G., Martinez, M., Miranda, Á.: Bullying, identity and school performance: Evidence from Chile. Int. J. Educ. Dev. **51**, 147–162 (2016)
24. Davis, J.P., Merrin, G.J., Ingram, K.M., Espelage, D.L., Valido, A., Sheikh, A.J.E.: Examining Pathways between Bully Victimization, Depression, & School Belonging Among Early Adolescents. J. Child Fam. Stud. **28**, 2365–2378 (2019)
25. Bradshaw, C.P., Waasdorp, T.E.: Measuring and changing a "Culture of bullying." Sch. Psychol. Rev. **38**, 356–361 (2009)

FusionASAG: An LLM-Enhanced Automatic Short Answer Grading Model for Subjective Questions in Online Education

He Zheng, Qing Sun[✉], Qiushuo Li, Yunxin Liu, Yuanxin Ouyang, and Qinghua Cao

Beihang University, Beijing 100191, China
sunqing@buaa.edu.cn

Abstract. Subjective questions are crucial to assess students' ability to analyze, synthesize, evaluate and create knowledge. In the massive online education scenarios, the manually scoring of subjective questions is time-consuming. Instead, it could be supported by the task of Short Answer Grading in Natural Language Process. However, it is worth noting that most existing automatic scoring system does not perform well on domain-specific and long questions. In this paper we address the challenges of automated short answer grading (ASAG) by proposing a novel scoring approach that strategically integrates a fine-tuned large language model (LLM), a neural network (NN) for feature extraction, and an answer-question relevance assessment module (RELEVANCE). Our method effectively scores student responses based on a set of predefined rubrics and reference answers. Our experiments on the ASAP-SAS dataset demonstrate that our method achieves an average Quadratic Weighted Kappa (QWK) score of 0.797, surpassing current state-of-the-art AutoSAS model, particularly excelling in longer tasks with a 11.9% improvement. Overall, our proposed method offers a robust solution for subjective question grading, ultimately contributing to more efficient educational assessment in a rapidly evolving learning environment.

Keywords: Automatic Short Answer Grading · Generative Language Model · Model Fine-Tuning · Text Feature Extraction

1 Introduction

Subjective question, as a crucial aspect of the educational field, plays an important role in evaluating students' abilities to understand and apply knowledge. Online education market is growing rapidly year by year, so that manual marking is not realistic. To save teachers' time and educational resources, subjective question automated scoring becomes an essential part of online education. The main solution is *Automated Short Answer Grading* (ASAG).

ASAG is the task to automatically score a given student answer to a prompt based on existing rubrics and reference answers. Similar to other text classification tasks, ASAG takes a piece of discrete text, the answer, as input and requires the output to be a score corresponding to the answer.

© The Author(s), under exclusive license to Springer Nature Singapore Pte Ltd. 2025
K. Zhang et al. (Eds.): CSEI 2024, CCIS 2447, pp. 39–52, 2025.
https://doi.org/10.1007/978-981-96-3735-5_4

Currently, there are three main categories of methods to achieve the goal of ASAG tasks: text similarity-based, corpus-based and machine learning methods. Text similarity-based methods, like ATM [1] and c-rater [2], utilize rules and linguistic approaches to perform grading. These methods require experts to manually break down reference answers into multiple smaller pieces. Corpus-based methods exploit statistical properties or large document corpora [3, 4]. These methods depend on long-term accumulation of vocabulary and can be difficult to practice for emerging subjects. Machine learning methods typically utilize some number of measurements extracted from natural language processing, which are then combined into a single score using a classification or regression model [5–9]. Later it was found through hyperparameter optimization and early stopping that the ensemble of several large networks achieved state-of-the-art performance in paper scoring tasks [10]. Recently, researchers attempted to use GPT-4 for short answer scoring tasks and provided a data augmentation solution for imbalanced training data [11].

However, those current ASAG methods that mainly rely on traditional neural networks or manually constructed features for scoring either have difficulty identifying the complex semantic information contained in the answers or require a large amount of manual work, placing high demands on human resources. Those methods using GPT for the ASAG task have difficulties with factual questions, particularly due to hallucinations [12–14]. Therefore, proposing a precise and efficient method for subjective question grading is of great significance for educational evaluation.

Compared to scoring by manual experts, it is difficult for the generative large language model to automatically construct reasonable scoring metrics for specific subjective automatic scoring tasks, and give explainable scoring details. To leverage the excellent text comprehension ability of generative language models, we fine-tuned the LLM to adapt to the task of ASAG, so that it better simulates the performance of manual experts.

Current models are typically pre-trained using general-purpose text corpora, which results in suboptimal performance in specific domains. To address this issue, we designed a network for extracting answer-related features. This network is trained on a given corpus to extract answers as a set of feature vectors that encode key characteristics of the answers. These vectors can enhance the performance of our approach in the target domain.

For longer tasks, such as reading comprehension, existing models struggle with direct processing. To address this challenge, we propose an evaluation mechanism based on the matching degree between key information from the answer and the question. This mechanism is used to assess whether the response contains essential scoring elements. By employing this approach, the system calculates the coverage rate of key information from the question contained within the answer, thereby quantifying the degree of matching between the two.

We used different training hyperparameters and module combinations and conducted multiple experiments on the English short answer scoring dataset ASAP-SAS [15] to verify the superiority of our method. The experimental results show that on ten subsets of the ASAP-SAS dataset, our proposed method achieved an average Quadratic Weighted Kappa (QWK) score of 0.797, which is the best scoring performance among existing ASAG methods. For certain subsets, the improvements are more than 11%.

2 Methodology

In this section, we present our proposed framework, as shown in Fig. 1. It consists of 3 main parts: LLM fine-tuning for short answer scoring tasks, feature extraction network for construction for short answers, and the assessment on the reference answers to targeted question. Finally, these three parts are integrated based on stacking approach to give a more accurate score.

2.1 LLM Fine-Tuning

The fine-tuning goal of the model is to enable it to understand the evaluation criteria of expert graders after fine-tuning with graded answers, then use its complex model structure to construct corresponding answer features based on these criteria, so that the grading results can reach the grading accuracy of expert graders.

We fine-tune the model with training data provided with ASAP-SAS dataset. We used the P-tuning v2 [16] approach to fine-tune the model, which replaces traditional predefined discrete text prompts with continuous learnable prompts. This method solves the problem where P-tuning [17] could only adjust a limited number of parameters in the first few layers of the model, and the deeper parameters could not be updated. It can achieve similar effects to full parameter fine-tuning in tasks of various scales while significantly reducing the number of parameters that need to be adjusted during training. Our fine-tuning setup and parameter selection are listed in Sect. 4.2.

2.2 Neural Network Construction

Based on the work of Taghipour et al. on paper evaluation [5], we designed a network model that scores based on sentence and word features in short answers. The network structure is shown in Fig. 1. To improve the accuracy of feature extraction, word vector models are trained using domain-related corpora such as reference materials and QA pair. A masked CNN layer was used to extract features of word vectors, and an RNN layer was used to extract sequence features.

Bi-LSTM [18] is used as the RNN layer to extract the sequence features embedded in the answers. It solves the problems of gradient explosion and vanishing gradients in traditional RNNs, and can better focus on the context of the text. To ensure the results comprehensively cover features from all parts of the sentence, we aggregated the network's recurrent layer output using the mean-over-time (MoT) method and introduced an attention mechanism [19]. This mechanism processes the output of the network's recurrent layers, transforming the two-dimensional vector form of word sequences into a one-dimensional vector that can be used for classification. The resulting vector is then combined with features extracted from the answer sentence vector. The combined vector is fed into a fully connected layer to obtain the result.

To improve model performance and accelerate convergence, we initialized the embedding layer parameters using word vectors trained with the Word2Vec [20] and GloVe [21] models. We also used the BERT [22] model to encode the answers as vector representations, using the output of the last hidden layer of the BERT model as the vector representation of the input content.

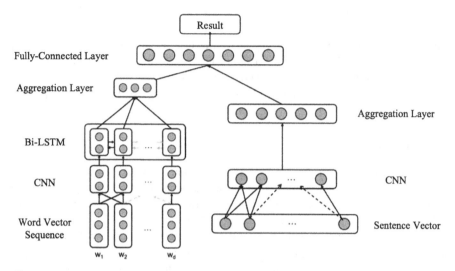

Fig. 1. Network Structure for Short Answer Grading Based on Word and Sentence Features

2.3   Assessment of Answer-Question Relevance

Two evaluation metrics are used to assess the answer-question relevance: keyword over-lap and semantic similarity between given answer and reference text (which includes various sample answers, rubric information and related teaching materials). Adding rubrics and keyword to the training data gives us the ability to judge keyword overlap. For each rubric, if the answer contains one of the candidate keywords, the answer is considered to score on that rubric. The sum of scores for each rubric is the final score for that question. For the second metric, we used the BERT model to compute cosine similarity between the vector representations to determine text similarity. Finally, the results of the two metrics are normalized and classified using an SVM classifier to obtain the scoring result based on the answer-question relevance.

2.4   Model Fusion Strategy

The three parts above corresponds to three modules in our model. In the following sections, we will refer to them as the LLM scoring module, NN scoring module, and RELEVANCE scoring module.

To obtain the final scoring result, focusing only on the modules with better scoring performance would ignore answer features present in the weaker-performing modules. To solve this issue, we used the Stacking approach to integrate the scoring results from the three modules as shown in Fig. 2. Since the answer-question relevance module contains fewer answer features, we use it as a calibration module, introducing its results only when there is a significant discrepancy between the scores of the other two modules.

There are three methods of model fusion. The first one is to calculate weighted summation of the three intermediate results. The second one is Bagging, and the last

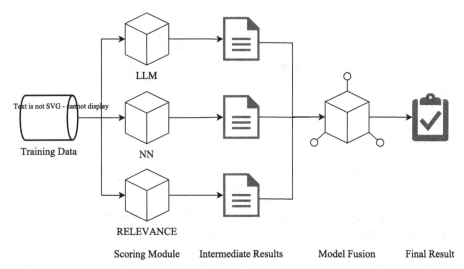

Fig. 2. Fusion of Scoring Modules for Short Answer Grading

one is Boosting. After the experiment, we selected weighted summation as our fusion method, and the comparison between these three methods are conducted in Sect. 4.2.

3 Experiments

3.1 Dataset and Evaluation Metrics

Our experiments are conducted on the ASAP-SAS [15] dataset, which is derived from the Kaggle short answer scoring competition Automated Student Assessment Prize. The ASAP-SAS dataset, provided by ETS, aims to assess high school students' understanding of specific educational topics. It is the largest publicly available dataset, consisting of 10 questions and more than 16000 responses from students.

The 10 questions comprised of varied subject matter at the high school level from arts to science. The description of questions includes prompt and scoring rubric. The responses were given by students and manually graded by ASAP graders, with their length ranging from 1 to 300 words. Expected answers may be derived either from the question itself or from the respondent's own knowledge. It is ideal for evaluating model performance due to its realistic nature and diversity, and is widely used by other researchers as well.

When evaluating the performance of the model we proposed, we mainly used the Quadratic Weighted Kappa (QWK) as the evaluation metric (Eq. 1) to measure the consistency between the scoring results of our proposed method and expert scores. Compared to simply using model accuracy as an evaluation metric, this method can provide greater penalties for parts with large scoring errors, balancing the accuracy and reliability of the scoring results.

$$QWK = 1 - \frac{\sum\limits_{i,j} \omega_{i,j} \times \mathbf{O}_{i,j}}{\sum\limits_{i,j} \omega_{i,j} \times \mathbf{E}_{i,j}} \tag{1}$$

3.2 Experiment Settings

We chose the ChatGLM-6B [23] model with 6.2 billion parameters as the base model. ChatGLM-6B is an open-source, bilingual language model supporting both Chinese and English dialogues. Its moderate parameter size means that it is relatively easy to meet the hardware resources requirements for fine-tuning. Other parameters are set according to the result of experiments on parameters in Sect. 4.2.

3.3 Experiments on Parameters

During the fine-tuning of the LLM module with the P-tuning v2 method, the selection of fine-tuning hyperparameters will affect the performance of the fine-tuned model. The hyperparameters that may significantly impact fine-tuning results include batch size, learning rate, maximum steps, gradient accumulation steps, prompt type, and P-tuning prefix length. During the experiments, the model output will be affected by the randomness of the generative language model.

Different types of word vector models in the embedding layer will affect the performance of NN module. We tried different models and compared their performance with the effect of using sentence vectors directly for classification tasks. In this part of the experiment, the number of training epochs was set to 30, the output feature dimension of the convolutional layer was set to 50, and the output feature dimension of the recurrent layer was set to 300. To prevent overfitting, we set the dropout rate in the Bi-LSTM of the recurrent layer to 0.5, and to prevent excessive dependency between adjacent states in the Bi-LSTM, we set the recurrent dropout rate to 0.1. To accelerate the experiments, we used the MoT method in the aggregation layer, as it does not involve training learnable parameters and can directly complete aggregation through simple calculations. During the experiments, we selected the Adam optimizer with a learning rate of 0.0005.

Through comparison, we decided to use word vectors trained with GloVe to initialize the embedding layer parameters while using sentence vectors generated by BERT. The features extracted by the two models were then combined in the aggregation layer. During the scoring process, we trained the model on the scored data separately using the two embedding forms. To better combine their features, we set a threshold QWK_bottom of 0.500. When both models exceed this threshold, we combine the vector representations of answer features obtained in the two forms in the aggregation layer and complete the classification through the fully connected layer. Otherwise, we selected the better-performing embedding method for network training. We conducted experiments on the combination of embedding layers on the ten subsets of the ASAP-SAS dataset.

RELEVANCE module relies only on a few features in the answers, which are often more significant when the answer needs to include more information from the question. Therefore, we conducted experiments on this module on more typical reading comprehension question subsets 3 and 10.

We also conducted experiments on model fusion methods. A module is integrated only when its QWK reaches 0.60.

4 Results and Discussion

4.1 Comparison with Other Models

We selected three models using different methods for automatic scoring as baseline models to compare with our experimental results. The automatic scoring system AutoSAS [7], which scores based on multiple feature extractions in the answer text, is the current state-of-the-art model. B. Riordan et al.'s scoring work [6], which is relatively lightweight and based on neural networks, also achieved good results. Ramachandran et al.'s work [24] on manually constructed features achieved expert-level scoring results on some subsets of the ASAP-SAS dataset. We compared our model's performance with these models on the ASAP-SAS dataset. The scoring performance is shown in Table 1.

Table 1. Comparison of Our Model with Other Models' Results

Model	1	2	3	4	5	6	7	8	9	10	Mean
FusionASAG	**0.881**	**0.843**	0.740	**0.760**	0.828	0.847	**0.725**	**0.705**	**0.847**	0.793	**0.797**
AutoSAS	0.760	0.828	**0.847**	0.743	**0.845**	0.858	**0.725**	0.624	0.843	**0.832**	0.791
Riordan	0.795	0.718	0.684	0.700	0.830	0.790	0.648	0.544	0.777	0.735	0.723
Ramachandran	0.86	0.78	0.66	0.70	0.84	**0.88**	0.66	0.63	0.84	0.79	0.78

Our method shows excellent performance on most subsets of the ASAP-SAS dataset. FusionASAG outperforms current state-of-the-art model AutoSAS on 6 out of 10 sets. In the remaining 4 of the short answer sets, it performs equally well in one of them, in one of the sets it performs slightly worse and in set 3 and 10 it lags behind AutoSAS.

FusionASAG performs exceptionally well on set 8, performing 11.9% better than the current state-of-the-art model AutoSAS. The question in set 8 is a relatively long reading comprehension task that requires students to read a text excerpt and answer questions based on that text. FusionASAG utilizes the NN module to extract features from lengthy texts, a capability that distinguishes it from other models. While most answers derive from the question itself, their length exceeds the processing capacity of standard models. Therefore, specialized information extraction tailored for long questions is essential to achieve improved performance on such tasks.

4.2   Result of Experiments on Parameters

Result of Experiments on LLM Module
We selected the most representative subsets of each question category (subsets 2, 3, 5, 7, and 10) for this part of the experiment with different hyperparameter combinations. The results are shown in Table 2.

From Table 2, it can be concluded that for various types of questions, fine-tuning with long prompts outperforms or is comparable to fine-tuning with short prompts. Regarding the number of training steps, although fine-tuning with 3000 steps is slightly better than 2000 steps on most question types, the difference is almost negligible. Considering the resource consumption and time cost of fine-tuning, we chose to fine-tune with 2000 steps.

Table 2. Impact of Prompt Type and Training Steps on LLM Performance

Prompt Type	Step	Subset 2	Subset 3	Subset 5	Subset 7	Subset 10
Long Prompt	2000	**0.832**	0.725	0.831	0.703	**0.764**
	3000	0.830	**0.734**	0.832	**0.710**	0.724
Short Prompt	2000	0.779	0.719	**0.838**	0.696	0.731
	3000	0.761	0,716	0.833	0.698	0.716

Table 3. Impact of Prefix Length and Batch Size on LLM Performance

Prefix Length	Batch Size	Subset 2	Subset 3	Subset 5	Subset 7	Subset 10
128	4	0.832	0.725	0.831	**0.703**	0.764
128	8	0.832	0.720	**0.835**	0.702	0.749
256	4	**0.834**	**0.737**	0.831	0.697	**0.784**

There is little difference in model scoring performance when the batch size is set to 4 or 8. However, when the batch size is set to 8, the time and computational resources required for fine-tuning are twice as much as the former. Therefore, we fine-tuned with 4 sets of data in a single batch. From the perspective of the tunable prefix parameter length, a prefix length of 256 achieved better results in most question types during fine-tuning (Table 3).

After determining the fine-tuning hyperparameters, we repeated the experiments three times with the model fine-tuned using the optimal hyperparameters selected in the previous experiment to prove the stability and reliability of the scoring results. The experimental results are shown in Table 4.

From the experimental results shown in Table 4, we can conclude that, except for minor differences in a few subsets, the other results are consistent, which proves that the fine-tuning hyperparameters and model randomness parameters we selected can ensure the reliability of the scoring results.

Table 4. Impact of Different Hyperparameters on LLM Performance

Group	1	2	3	4	5	6	7	8	9	10
1	0.884	0.824	0.737	0.725	0.831	0.834	0.697	0.695	0.848	0.782
2	0.885	0.823	0.737	0.725	0.831	0.834	0.697	0.695	0.848	0.784
3	0.884	0.824	0.737	0.725	0.831	0.834	0.697	0.695	0.848	0.784

Results of Experiments on NN Module

The experimental results on different subsets of the ASAP-SAS dataset for each embedding method are shown in Table 5. "-" indicates the QWK is less than 0.500.

Table 5. Impact of Different Embedding Methods on NN Performance

Embedding Method	1	2	3	4	5	6	7	8	9	10
Word2Vec	0.729	**0.676**	-	0.606	-	-	**0.601**	-	0.756	0.678
GloVe	**0.730**	0.669	-	0.597	-	-	0.590	-	0.759	0.673
BERT	0.690	0.582	-	**0.647**	**0.771**	**0.771**	0.567	**0.599**	**0.772**	**0.728**

Comparing the experimental results of the two different word vector embedding models, we found both perform similarly. To simplify the model, we chose GloVe for word vector training.

Table 6. Impact of Different Aggregation Methods on Network Performance

Subset	1	2	4	7	9	10
MoT	0.730	**0.669**	0.597	**0.590**	**0.759**	**0.673**
Attention	**0.731**	0.677	**0.619**	0.579	0.723	0.656

As shown in Table 6, introducing the attention mechanism did not significantly improve model performance. In contrast, the simple MoT method performed better on more subtasks, which may be because the randomly initialized attention mechanism parameters may require more training data to allocate more reasonable weights to the outputs of each time step in the Bi-LSTM.

The results on the combination of embedding layers on the ten subsets of the ASAP-SAS dataset is shown in Fig. 3.

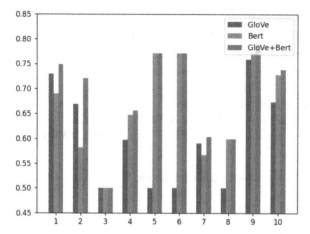

Fig. 3. Results on Different Combination of Embedding Layers

Results of Experiments on the RELEVANCE Module
We compared the performance of the baseline LLM module (blue line in Fig. 4) with the results after introducing RELEVANCE module (green line in Fig. 4).

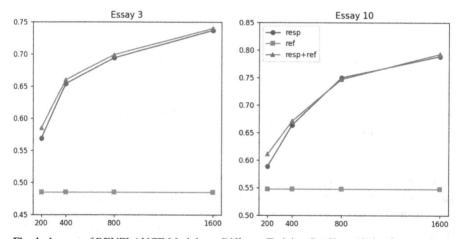

Fig. 4. Impact of REVELANCE Module on Different Training Set Sizes (Color figure online)

When the training data was 200 entries, introducing this module significantly improved the scoring performance, with improvement of about 0.02 in the QWK evaluation metric. As the size of the training data gradually increased, the effect of LLM and NN modules improved correspondingly, and the role of the RELEVANCE module, which did not rely on a large amount of graded data, remained unchanged. When the training data reached 800 entries or more, the role of this module diminished as the amount of data increased. This demonstrates that this module is more important when training data is scarce.

Results of Experiments on Model Fusion Strategy

For bagging and boosting method, we set the number of base classifiers to 100. As shown in Fig. 5, the integration of scoring modules via a simple weighted approach performs slightly worse on certain subsets compared to the other two integration methods; thus, we adopt this method for model fusion.

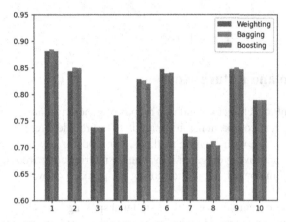

Fig. 5. Impact of Different Model Fusion Strategies

4.3 Ablation Study

Ablation experiments were conducted to demonstrate the impact of the NN module on model performance, with the results illustrated in Fig. 6. The result indicates that the introduction of the NN module based on answer phrase features significantly enhances the model's scoring effectiveness across most subsets of the ASAP-SAS dataset.

Ablation study for this module were conducted on subset 3 and 10, with results indicating that using this module for calibration alongside the first two scoring modules yields a slight improvement in model performance. Specifically, the QWK metric of the model's scoring results improved from 0.737 to 0.740 in subset 3; in subset 10, the metric increased from 0.789 to 0.793.

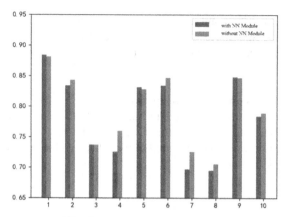

Fig. 6. Importance of NN Module

5   Conclusion and Future Work

We used the complex architecture and rich corpus of generative language models, leveraging their strong text comprehension capabilities to provide a reasonable solution for ASAG tasks. Compared with existing methods, our model is expected to achieve superior performance, improving on general evaluation metrics compared to previous work and enabling machine-based automatic scoring to approach or even reach the accuracy of expert grading.

During the experimental process, we found that spelling errors in the answers, especially those involving important keywords, had a significant impact on the performance of our proposed scoring model. We attempted to use the ChatGLM-6B model to correct and regularize the text, but the results often changed the semantics of the answers, requiring manual review and correction, which is intolerable in automatic scoring. If better open-source models capable of handling this task emerge in the future, the scoring performance of the model could be improved to some extent.

We found that in some subsets of the dataset, the word-sentence features in the answer text did not correspond well to the scoring results, resulting in suboptimal performance of the answer word-sentence feature scoring module for this type of question. For such questions, future work could optimize the model by extracting other types of features from the answers.

The answer-question relevance scoring module only plays a role in specific types of questions, and since reading comprehension questions contain a large amount of information, we tried using models like Key-BERT to extract key information, but the results were not satisfactory, and manual specification of key information may still be necessary.

Acknowledgements. This work is supported by the National Natural Science Foundation of China (No. 62377002).

References

1. Callear, D., Jerrams-Smith, J., Soh, V.: CAA of short non-MCQ answers. In: Danson, M., Eabry, C.: In: Proceedings of the 5th Computer Assisted Assessment Conference, pp. 1–14. Loughborough University, Loughborough (2001)
2. Leacock, C., Chodorow, M.: C-rater: Automated scoring of short-answer questions. Comput. Humanit. **37**, 389–405 (2003)
3. Park, K.: Corpora and language assessment: The state of the art. Lang. Assess. Q. **11**(1), 27–44 (2014)
4. Chang, T.H., Chen, J.L., Chou, H.M., et al.: Automatic scoring method of short-answer questions in the context of low-resource corpora. In: 2021 International Conference on Asian Language Processing (IALP), pp. 25–29. IEEE (2021)
5. Taghipour, K., Ng, H.T.: A neural approach to automated essay scoring. In: Proceedings of the 2016 Conference on Empirical Methods in Natural Language Processing, pp. 1882–1891 (2016)
6. Riordan, B., Horbach, A., Cahill, A., et al.: Investigating neural architectures for short answer scoring. In: Proceedings of the 12th Workshop on Innovative Use of NLP for Building Educational Applications, pp. 159–168 (2017)
7. Kumar, Y., Aggarwal, S., Mahata, D., et al.: Get it scored using AutoSAS—An automated system for scoring short answers. In: Proceedings of the AAAI Conference on Artificial Intelligence, vol. 33, pp. 9662–9669 (2019)
8. Chamieh, I., Zesch, T., Giebermann, K.: LLMs in Short Answer Scoring: Limitations and Promise of Zero-Shot and Few-Shot Approaches. In: Proceedings of the 19th Workshop on Innovative Use of NLP for Building Educational Applications (BEA 2024), pp. 309–315. Association for Computational Linguistics, Mexico City (2024)
9. Sung, C., Dhamecha, T., Saha, S., et al.: Pre-training BERT on domain resources for short answer grading. In: Proceedings of the 2019 Conference on Empirical Methods in Natural Language Processing and the 9th International Joint Conference on Natural Language Processing (EMNLP-IJCNLP), pp. 6071–6075 (2019)
10. Ormerod, C.M., Malhotra, A., Jafari, A.: Automated essay scoring using efficient transformer-based language models. arXiv:2102.13136 (2021)
11. Fang, L., Lee, G.G., Zhai, X.: Using GPT-4 to augment unbalanced data for automatic scoring. arXiv:2310.18365 (2023)
12. Chang, L.-H., Ginter, F.: Automatic Short Answer Grading for Finnish with ChatGPT. In: Proceedings of the AAAI Conference on Artificial Intelligence, vol. 38(21), pp. 23173–23181. (2024)
13. Kortemeyer, G.: Performance of the pre-trained large language model GPT-4 on automated short answer grading. Discov Artif Intell **4**, 47 (2024)
14. Jukiewicz, M.: The future of grading programming assignments in education: The role of ChatGPT in automating the assessment and feedback process. Thinking Skills and Creativity **52**, 101522 (2024)
15. The Hewlett Foundation: Short Answer Scoring, https://www.kaggle.com/competitions/asap-sas/data, last accessed 2012/9/6
16. Liu, X., Ji, K., Fu, Y., et al.: P-tuning v2: Prompt tuning can be comparable to fine-tuning universally across scales and tasks. arXiv:2110.07602 (2021)
17. Li, X.L., Liang, P.: Prefix-tuning: Optimizing continuous prompts for generation. arXiv:2101.00190 (2021)
18. Huang, Z., Xu, W., Yu, K.: Bidirectional LSTM-CRF models for sequence tagging. arXiv:1508.01991 (2015)

19. Bahdanau, D., Cho, K., Bengio, Y.: Neural machine translation by jointly learning to align and translate. arXiv:1409.0473 (2014)
20. Mikolov, T., Chen, K., Corrado, G., et al.: Efficient estimation of word representations in vector space. arXiv:1301.3781 (2013)
21. Pennington, J., Socher, R., Manning, C. D.: GloVe: Global vectors for word representation. In: Proceedings of the 2014 Conference on Empirical Methods in Natural Language Processing (EMNLP), pp. 1532–1543 (2014)
22. Papineni, K., Roukos, S., Ward, T., et al.: BLEU: A method for automatic evaluation of machine translation. In: Proceedings of the 40th Annual Meeting of the Association for Computational Linguistics, pp. 311–318 (2002)
23. Du, Z., Qian, Y., Liu, X., et al.: GLM: General language model pretraining with autoregressive blank infilling. arXiv preprint arXiv:2103.10360 (2021)
24. Ramachandran, L., Cheng, J., Foltz, P.: Identifying patterns for short answer scoring using graph-based lexico-semantic text matching. In: Proceedings of the Tenth Workshop on Innovative Use of NLP for Building Educational Applications, pp. 97–106 (2015)

Virtual Reality Technology in Digital Health Education: Current Research Status and Future Trends

Yuanze Xia[1] (ID), Patrick Cheong-Iao Pang[1]([⊠]) (ID), Zhaoyang Xiong[1] (ID), Xia Liu[2] (ID), and Ting Liu[1] (ID)

[1] Faculty of Applied Sciences, Macao Polytechnic University, Macao, China
mail@patrickpang.net
[2] Sanya Aviation and Tourism College, Sanya, China

Abstract. Virtual reality (VR) technology is revolutionizing the landscape of digital health education by providing learners with increasingly immersive and interactive experiences. This study aims to understand the current usage, main research topics, and future directions of VR in digital health education through a bibliometric analysis. Using data from the Web of Science Core Collection from 2008–2024, alongside CiteSpace software, this study examined trends in publication volume, prevalent keywords, keyword co-occurrence, clustering, keyword bursts, timelines, time-zone distributions, and author networks. Research on VR in digital health education has increased over the years. The main topics are medical simulation training, health education, and rehabilitation therapy. Additionally, the study demonstrated a transition from mere exploration of the technology to its widespread application across diverse fields. Future trends may include creating more immersive and interactive VR education platforms, designing personalized learning experiences, studying how to measure the effects of VR education, and discussing ethical concerns. This research provides a reference for others in the field and provides insights into future VR applications in digital health education.

Keywords: Virtual reality · digital health · education · bibliometric analysis

1 Introduction

In recent years, the proliferation and utilization of digital technology have been steering society toward increased digitalization and intelligence, prompting the education field to adapt to this evolving trend [1]. In the health education field, digital technology is accelerating the transformation of healthcare and facilitating the construction of a digital health ecosystem. Covering a wide range of technologies and applications offers the potential for further enhancing healthcare services and increasing public health standards [2]. The swift emergence of new applications, including mobile health, telemedicine, and AI-assisted diagnosis, has transformed the accessibility of health information and services for individuals. These advancements are also opening new opportunities within the digital health education domain [3, 4].

Virtual reality (VR) [5], a computer technology capable of creating simulated environments, has shown great potential in education in recent years. VR technology can build highly immersive and interactive learning environments for learners, breaking the time and space limits of traditional education and offering more direct and vivid learning experiences [5]. Applying VR technology to digital health education can translate abstract medical knowledge into visual 3D models and convert intricate medical procedures into secure simulation training sessions, offering students a more efficient and safe learning approach [6].

Integrating VR technology with digital health education is a crucial way to drive reform in medical education and enhance the quality of training for healthcare professionals. VR technology can provide strong technical support for digital health education. For example, through the establishment of virtual anatomy labs, students can perform dissections and observe organs in a virtual environment, overcoming the constraints of traditional anatomy teaching, such as limited specimens and high operational risks [7]. Virtual surgery simulation systems can also be developed to allow students to practice surgical procedures repeatedly in a safe and controlled virtual environment, improving their surgical skills and clinical decision-making without the concern of error-related risks [7, 8].

Additionally, the digital health field provides a wealth of data and real cases that can offer rich content for the development of VR educational materials. For example, authentic patient data can be used to generate virtual patients, simulating genuine doctor–patient interaction scenarios to aid students in enhancing their clinical communication and diagnostic skills [9]. VR technology can also build remote medical teaching platforms, allowing students to observe live surgery remotely and participate in case discussions, expanding their learning resources and opportunities [10].

However, the integration of VR technology and digital health education is still in the exploration stage and faces numerous challenges. For example, developing high-quality VR educational resources is costly, making it difficult to share and promote quality resources [11]. The use of VR technology requires specific hardware and software platforms, which poses a challenge in reducing costs and enhancing the accessibility of these devices [11]. Additionally, long-term use of VR devices may cause visual fatigue and motion sickness, raising concerns about the well-being of students [12]. To advance the development of VR technology in digital health education, it is imperative to systematically review the current research, key trends, and future directions in this field.

2   Research Methods

This study used bibliometric analysis methods [13] to systematically review and analyze the relevant literature on digital health, virtual reality, and education from the Web of Science Core Collection database for 2008–2024. The search was conducted in September 2024 via Boolean logic search terms [14]. A total of 537 relevant papers were found. Data analysis was performed via CiteSpace software [15], and eight charts were created:

(1) Annual publication volume trend chart: annual trend of the number of publications in this field. As shown in Fig. 1.

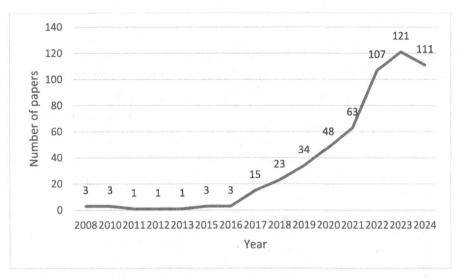

Fig. 1. Annual publication trend

(2) Peak map: This diagram directly displays the keywords that appear frequently in the field. As shown in Fig. 2.
(3) Keyword co-occurrence graph: This graph reveals the correlation between keywords, as shown in Fig. 3.

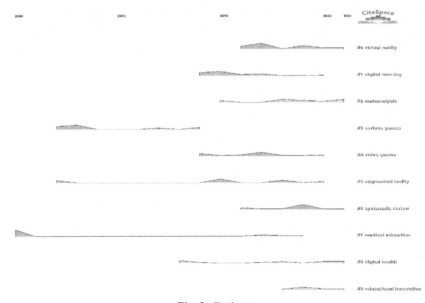

Fig. 2. Peak map

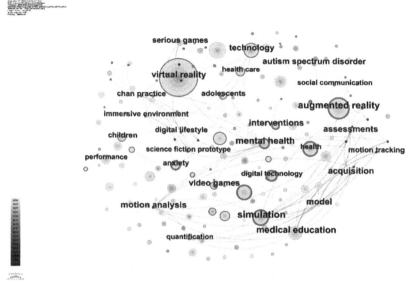

Fig. 3. Keyword co-occurrence graph

(4) Keywords clustering diagram: dividing keywords into different research topics. As shown in Fig. 4.
(5) Keyword emergence map: Identify emerging research hotspots in the field. As shown in Fig. 5.

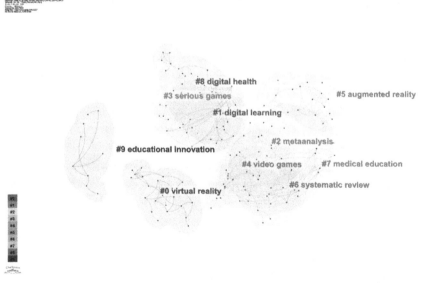

Fig. 4. Keyword clustering diagram

Top 15 Keywords with the Strongest Citation Bursts

Keywords	Year	Strength	Begin	End	2008 - 2024
serious games	2010	2.28	2010	2017	
technology	2017	2.2	2017	2018	
systematic review	2019	4.16	2019	2019	
skills	2019	2.97	2019	2021	
randomized controlled trials	2019	2.56	2019	2019	
medical education	2008	1.89	2019	2019	
tool	2020	2.1	2020	2020	
social media	2020	2.01	2020	2020	
behavior	2020	1.98	2020	2021	
surgical training	2021	2.19	2021	2022	
digital learning	2020	1.89	2022	2022	
online learning	2022	1.87	2022	2022	
internet	2022	1.87	2022	2022	
design	2023	3.36	2023	2024	
people	2016	1.88	2023	2024	

Fig. 5. Keyword emergence graph

(6) Timeline diagram showing the evolution of different research topics. As shown in Fig. 6.

(7) The time zone map shows the research contributions of different regions in this field. As shown in Fig. 7.

(8) Author co-occurrence map: This map shows the cooperation between authors and identifies the main research teams in the field. As shown in Fig. 8.

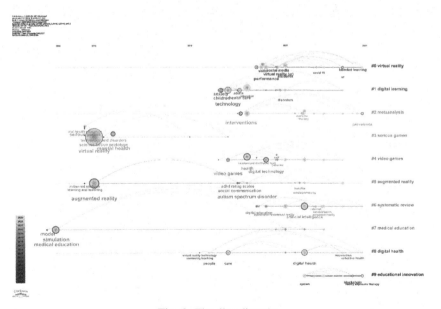

Fig. 6. Timeline diagram

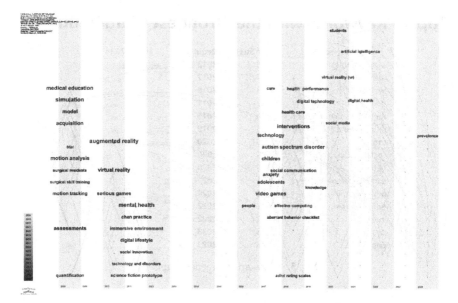

Fig. 7. Time zone diagram

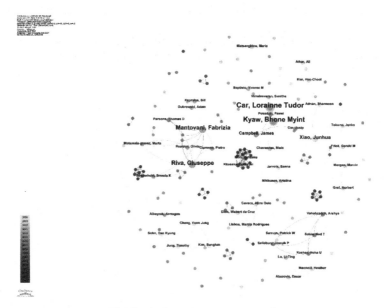

Fig. 8. Author co-occurrence graph

3 Results and Analysis

3.1 Analysis of Publication Trends

The publication trend chart clearly shows the research trend of applying virtual reality technology in the field of digital health education. From 2008–2016, the number of related papers remained low, with no more than three papers published per year, indicating that research in this field was still in its early stages. Starting in 2017, the number of publications began to increase slowly, reaching 48 papers by 2020. After 2021, the number of publications grew rapidly, reaching 107 papers in 2022 and peaking at 121 in 2023. Although 2024 has not yet been published, there are already 111 papers. This showed that since 2017, the application of virtual reality technology in digital health education has gradually attracted academic attention and has experienced explosive growth in recent years. Several factors may drive this growth:

(1) Rapid development and cost reduction of VR technology: In recent years, the performance of VR devices has continuously improved while prices have decreased, making it easier for educational institutions and researchers to adopt them [6].
(2) There is a growing demand for immersive learning experiences: VR technology can offer highly immersive and interactive learning experiences, which aligns with the current education demand for innovative teaching methods and improving learning efficiency [16].
(3) The development of the digital health field: The rapid growth of the digital health field has created a wide range of scenarios and needs the application of VR technology [17].

It is clear from this trend that the application of VR technology in digital health education has enormous potential for growth, and research in this field is expected to continue rising in the coming years.

3.2 Analysis of Publication Trends

High-frequency Keyword Analysis. The peak map visually represents the high-frequency keywords and their trends in research on VR technology in digital health education. As depicted in the map, the top ten most frequently occurring keywords are "virtual reality", "digital learning", "meta-analysis", "serious games", "video games", "augmented reality", "systematic review", "medical education", "digital health", and "educational innovation".

(1) As the most frequent keyword, "virtual reality" spans the entire research timeline and has exhibited an upward trend in recent years. This indicates that VR technology has consistently been a central research theme in this field, and its significance is growing with technological advancements and wider adoption.
(2) The close association of "digital learning" with "virtual reality" highlights the increasing emphasis on utilizing VR technology within digital learning environments.

(3) The frequent occurrence of "meta-analysis" and "systematic review" reflects a growing trend among researchers in this field to synthesize and summarize existing research, aiming to provide clearer directions for future studies.
(4) The high frequency of "serious games" and "video games" suggests that game-based learning represents a significant application of VR technology in digital health education.
(5) The presence of "augmented reality," another technology related to VR, among the high-frequency keywords signifies that combining VR and AR technologies is a crucial trend for the future.
(6) The appearance of "medical education," "digital health," and "educational innovation" indicates that the applications of VR technology in digital health education encompass multiple aspects, including medical education, health education, and educational innovation.

Overall, the analysis of high-frequency keywords reveals the hot topics and development trends in research on VR technology within the field of digital health education, providing a foundation for subsequent keyword co-occurrence and cluster analysis.

Keywords Co-occurrence Analysis. The keyword co-occurrence map illustrates the interrelationships between different research topics concerning VR technology in digital health education. As shown on the map, keywords such as "virtual reality," "serious games," "augmented reality," "medical education," and "mental health" appear as larger nodes with numerous connections to other keywords, indicating their significance within the field's research landscape. A detailed analysis is provided below:

(1) "Virtual reality" is a Central Research Cluster: The close relationship between "virtual reality" and keywords such as "serious games," "immersive environment," "video games," "digital lifestyle," "simulation," and "medical education" suggests the widespread application of VR technology in areas such as medical simulation training, the development of health education games, and the creation of immersive learning environments [18].
(2) "Serious games" and their integration with diverse populations and application scenarios: The co-occurrence of "serious games" with keywords such as "children," "adolescents," "autism spectrum disorder," "social communication," and "anxiety" illustrates the extensive use of VR games in health education and skills training for children, adolescents, and individuals with special needs, such as those with autism [19].
(3) "Augmented reality" complements VR technology: The association of "augmented reality" with keywords such as "assessments," "motion tracking," and "acquisition" implies that the advantages of AR technology in assessment, motion capture, and data acquisition can complement VR technology, providing more comprehensive technical support for digital health education [20, 21].
(4) Applications of VR technology in medical education: The close connection between "medical education" and keywords such as "simulation," "model," and "quantification" indicates that VR technology is utilized primarily in medical education for simulation training, model construction, and quantitative evaluation [22].

(5) Applications of VR technology in mental health: The co-occurrence of "mental health" with keywords such as "interventions," "health," and "digital technology" demonstrates that VR technology is employed for interventions and treatments related to mental health issues, including anxiety and depression [23, 24].

In conclusion, the keyword co-occurrence analysis reveals the interweaving relationships among various research themes related to VR technology in the field of digital health education, highlighting key research directions such as VR games, medical simulation training, and mental health interventions.

3.3 Research Topic Analysis

The keyword cluster map shows the distribution of different research themes pertaining to VR technology in the field of digital health education. On the basis of Figs. 2–4, the research primarily concentrates on the following ten clusters:

(1) #0 VR: As the largest cluster, VR technology itself is the core research focus within this field.

(2) #1 Digital Learning: This cluster's close relationship with the "virtual reality" cluster indicates that VR technology is considered a crucial tool for digital learning.

(3) #2 Meta-analysis: This cluster demonstrates a growing trend of studies conducting meta-analyses on the effectiveness of VR technology in digital health education, aiming to reach more reliable conclusions.

(4) #3 Serious games: This cluster highlights the significant role of VR games in health education.

(5) #4 Video games: The overlap between this cluster and the "serious games" cluster signifies that game-based learning is a crucial direction for VR technology applications.

(6) #5 Augmented reality: This cluster indicates a correlation between AR and VR technologies, suggesting that the integrated development of both technologies deserves attention in the future.

(7) #6 Systematic review: Similar to the "meta-analysis" cluster, it reflects the increasing emphasis on systematic reviews and summaries of existing research within this field.

(8) #7 Medical education: This cluster identifies medical education as one of the essential areas where VR technology is applied.

(9) #8 Digital health: This relatively minor cluster suggests that VR technology represents merely one application within the broader field of digital health, emphasizing the need for further exploration of combining VR technology with other digital health technologies.

(10) #9 Educational Innovation: This cluster positions VR technology as a vital force driving educational innovation.

In summary, the keyword cluster analysis results demonstrate that the application research of VR technology in digital health education encompasses multiple themes. VR games, medical education, digital learning, and the integration of AR/VR technologies stand out as current research hotspots. Future research can delve further into the inter-section and convergence of these themes, as well as explore the combined applications of VR technology with other emerging technologies.

3.4 Research Trend Analysis

Keyword Burst Analysis. The keyword emergence map reveals the trends of different research themes related to VR technology in the field of digital health education. As depicted on the map, certain keywords demonstrated rapid growth during specific periods, indicating that these themes garnered substantial attention from the academic community:

(1) "Serious games" (2010–2017): As the earliest emerging term, this term highlights the early adoption of VR games in digital health education, which has rapidly become a research hotspot.
(2) The
    emergence of "technology" (2017–2018) and "systematic review" (2019) reflects the field's initial focus on exploring the technology itself and conducting summaries and reviews of existing research during its early developmental stages.
(3) The emergence of "skills" (2019–2021) and "randomized controlled trials" (2019) indicated that researchers have shifted their attention toward the impact of VR technology on learners' skills and the adoption of more rigorous experimental methods for evaluation.
(4) "Medical education" (2008–2019), as a long-term emerging keyword, highlights the continuous emphasis on the application of VR technology within the field of medical education.
(5) The emergence of tools (2020), social media (2020), and behavior (2020–2021) suggests that researchers are beginning to explore the use of VR technology as a tool in broader contexts, such as social media and behavioral interventions.
(6) The emergence of "surgical training" (2021–2022), "digital learning" (2020–2022), and "online learning" (2022) reflects the application of VR technology in areas such as surgical simulation training, digital learning, and online learning.
(7) The emergence of "internet" (2022) indicates that with the increasing availability of internet technology, internet-based VR health education platforms are gradually becoming a research focus.
(8) The emergence of "design" (2023–2024) demonstrates that researchers are placing greater emphasis on the design of VR educational content and platforms to enhance user learning experiences and outcomes.

In conclusion, the keyword emergence analysis reveals the evolutionary trajectory of research hotspots concerning VR technology in digital health education. From early technological exploration and application attempts to focus on learning outcomes and evaluation methods and further expand application scenarios and emphasize the user experience, research in this field is progressing in a more in-depth and multifaceted direction.

Analysis of Research Topic Evolution. The timeline illustration illustrates the evolution of different research themes regarding VR technology within the field of digital health education. As depicted in the illustration, certain themes persist throughout the entire research period, whereas others emerge and rapidly develop during specific timeframes:

(1) Persistent research themes: Themes such as "virtual reality," "digital learning," "serious games," "video games," "augmented reality," and "medical education" have persisted throughout the entire research period, indicating their enduring significance as focal points within this field. For example, the term "virtual reality" has maintained a high level of research interest from 2008 to the present, indicating that both VR technology itself and its application in education remain central to scholarly attention. "Serious games" and "video games," as early forms of VR technology applications, have also attracted research attention and are continuously evolving with new applications and scenarios. "Medical education," as a traditional stronghold for VR technology applications, has persistently attracted significant research efforts.
(2) Emerging research themes: Certain themes have emerged and rapidly developed during specific periods, reflecting evolving research hotspots and trends within the field. For example, "mental health" appeared approximately 2010 and has gained increasing traction in recent years, demonstrating the growing emphasis on the use of VR technology for mental health education and interventions. "Social media" emerged approximately 2020, establishing connections with terms such as "virtual reality," "skills," and "performance," implying that researchers are exploring the use of VR technology and social media platforms for health education and skills training. "COVID-19" emerged prominently in 2020 and was associated with terms such as "digital learning" and "online learning," highlighting how the pandemic accelerated the development of online education and telemedicine. VR technology, as a crucial technological tool, has played a vital role in health education during the pandemic.

In conclusion, the application research of VR technology in digital health education has undergone a developmental journey from technological exploration to application expansion and from a single domain to cross-domain integration. In the future, with the continuous advancement of VR technology and the expansion of application scenarios, research in this field will become more in-depth and diverse.

3.5 Research Strength Analysis

Time Zone Distribution Analysis. The time zone map reveals the evolving trends of three key themes—"digital health," "virtual reality," and "education"—within the research landscape. Early studies focused predominantly on the applications of virtual reality (VR) technology in medical education, particularly in surgical skills training, simulation training, and motion analysis, reflecting the significance of VR in enhancing practical skills in medical education.

Over time, research has gradually expanded to encompass mental health and interventions, notably the use of VR and augmented reality (AR) technologies for mental health treatment and rehabilitation. This shift signifies that digital technologies not only increase practical skills in education but also hold vast potential in healthcare.

In recent years, keywords such as "digital health," "artificial intelligence," and "autism spectrum disorder" have reflected further integration and development of digital technologies within health education, especially their applications in mental health interventions and health management for children and adolescents. This highlights the growing diversity of research in this field and the deepening of interdisciplinary collaboration. This trend suggests that future research will continue to focus on effectively integrating VR and other digital technologies to drive innovative convergence in health and education.

Author Co-occurrence Network Analysis. The author co-occurrence map reveals the collaborative relationships among scholars researching VR technology in the field of digital health education. As depicted on the map, the research community exhibits a relatively dispersed pattern, yet several primary research teams or collaborative networks can be observed:

(1) Mantovani, Fabrizia & Riva, Giuseppe: These two scholars and their collaborators constitute the largest cluster within the network, signifying their roles as key researchers in this field with high centrality.
(2) Car, Lorraine Tudor & Kyaw, Bhone Myint: This pair of scholars and their collaborators form another significant research cluster, demonstrating collaborative ties with researchers such as James Campbell and Xiao Junhua.
(3) Other small-scale collaborative networks: In addition to the two major collaborative networks mentioned above, several smaller-scale collaborative networks exist, such as the research team centered around Wiederhold, Brenda K., and the team with Sohn, Dae Kyung; Jung, Timothy; Kim, Sunghak; and Chang, Yoon Jung as its core.

In conclusion, the author co-occurrence analysis suggests that research collaboration in the field of VR technology for digital health education is still in its early stages and that a highly centralized and stable collaborative network has yet to emerge. However, as research in this area continues to deepen and expand, we can anticipate stronger collaboration among diverse research teams, leading to more cohesive and efficient collaborative networks. This enhanced collaboration will be instrumental in driving the rapid advancement of this field.

4 Discussion

The results of this bibliometric analysis indicate that research on virtual reality (VR) technology in digital health education is undergoing rapid growth. Current research hotspots focus primarily on areas such as medical simulation training, health education and training, and rehabilitation therapy. VR technology offers new possibilities for overcoming the limitations of traditional teaching methods by providing immersive, interactive, and personalized learning experiences. However, research in this field is still in its exploratory phase, and future efforts should focus on strengthening the following aspects:

(1) VR Educational Resource Development and Sharing: Develop high-quality VR educational resources that meet pedagogical needs, establish resource-sharing mechanisms, and formulate standards and specifications for resource development to promote standardization and enhance the quality of resources.

(2) VR Education Platform Construction and Application: Develop user-friendly and feature-rich VR education platforms, explore their integration with technologies such as artificial intelligence and big data, and conduct research on application models for VR education platforms to establish replicable and generalizable best practices.

(3) Development of a VR education evaluation system: Establish a multidimensional and multilevel evaluation indicator system for VR education outcomes and develop scientifically sound and standardized evaluation tools for a comprehensive assessment of VR education effectiveness.

(4) Ethical and Safety Issues in VR Education: To formulate ethical guidelines for VR education, strengthen safety education regarding the use of VR equipment, and conduct research on the societal impact of VR education to ensure the safe, ethical, and effective application of VR technology.

(5) Interdisciplinary Collaboration and Integrated Innovation: Enhance collaboration among disciplines such as medicine, education, computer science, and psychology to promote knowledge exchange and integrated innovation, thereby driving significant breakthroughs in the application of VR technology within digital health education.

5 Summary and Prospects

VR technology presents unprecedented opportunities for digital health education. This bibliometric analysis reveals that research on VR technology applications is experiencing rapid growth, encompassing a wide range of fields, including medical simulation training, health education and training, rehabilitation therapy, and mental health interventions. By transcending the limitations of traditional teaching methods, VR technology offers learners immersive, interactive, and personalized learning experiences.

However, this field is still in its exploratory stage. Future research should prioritize the following: developing high-quality, shareable VR educational resources; constructing feature-rich VR education platforms and exploring their integration with technologies such as artificial intelligence and big data; establishing scientifically sound and standardized evaluation systems for VR educational outcomes; formulating ethical guidelines and safety protocols for VR education; and fostering interdisciplinary collaboration to drive the deep integration of VR technology and digital health education. VR technology holds immense promise for cultivating highly qualified medical professionals and improving public health literacy.

References

1. Frolova, E.V., Rogach, O.V., Ryabova, T.M.: Digitalization of education in modern scientific discourse: new trends and risks analysis. Eur. J. Contemp. Educ. **9**(2), 313–336 (2020)
2. Al-Shorbaji, N., Al-Shorbaji, N.: Improving healthcare access through digital health: the use of information and communication technologies. Healthcare Access 10 (2021)

3. Chintala, S.: Improving healthcare accessibility with AI-enabled telemedicine solutions. Int. J. Res. Rev. Tech. **2**(1), 75–81 (2023)
4. Amjad, A., Kordel, P., Fernandes, G.: A review on innovation in healthcare sector (telehealth) through artificial intelligence. Sustainability **15**(8), 6655 (2023)
5. Burdea, G.C., Coiffet, P.: Virtual Reality Technology, 2nd edn. John Wiley & Sons, New York (2024)
6. Kyaw, B.M., Saxena, N., Posadzki, P., et al.: Virtual reality for health professions education: systematic review and meta-analysis by the digital health education collaboration. J. Med. Internet Res. **21**(1), e12959 (2019)
7. Falah, J., Khan, S., Alfalah, T., et al.: Virtual Reality medical training system for anatomy education. In: 2014 Science and Information Conference, pp. 752–758. IEEE, London (2014)
8. Kuppersmith, R.B., Johnston, R., Moreau, D., et al.: Building a virtual reality temporal bone dissection simulator. In: Medicine Meets Virtual Reality, pp. 180–186. IOS Press, Amsterdam (1997)
9. Danforth, D.R., Procter, M., Chen, R., et al.: Development of virtual patient simulations for medical education. J. Virtual Worlds Res. **2**(2) (2009)
10. Almousa, O., Zhang, R., Dimma, M., et al.: Virtual reality technology and remote digital application for tele-simulation and global medical education: an innovative hybrid system for clinical training. Simul. Gaming **52**(5), 614–634 (2021)
11. Smith, M.S., Casserly, C.M.: The promise of open educational resources. Change Mag. High. Learn. **38**(5), 8–17 (2006)
12. Martinez, K., Checa, D.: Are Virtual Reality Serious Games Safe for Children? Design Keys to Avoid Motion Sickness and Visual Fatigue. In: International Conference on Extended Reality, pp. 367–377. Springer, Cham (2023)
13. Alsharif, A.H., Salleh, N., Baharun, R.: Bibliometric analysis. J. Theor. Appl. Inf. Technol. **98**(15), 2948–2962 (2020)
14. Frants, V.I., Shapiro, J., Taksa, I., et al.: Boolean search: Current state and perspectives. J. Am. Soc. Inf. Sci. **50**(1), 86–95 (1999)
15. Chen, C.: The CiteSpace Manual. Coll. Comput. Inf. **1**(1), 1–84 (2014)
16. Dede, C.: Immersive interfaces for engagement and learning. Science **323**(5910), 66–69 (2009)
17. Riva, G.: Virtual reality in psychotherapy. Cyberpsychol. Behav. **8**(3), 220–230 (2005)
18. Bailenson, J., Patel, K., Nielsen, A., et al.: The effect of interactivity on learning physical actions in virtual reality. Media Psychol. **11**(3), 354–376 (2008)
19. Kandalaft, M.R., Didehbani, N., Krawczyk, D.C., et al.: Virtual reality social cognition training for young adults with high-functioning autism. J. Autism Dev. Disord. **43**, 34–44 (2013)
20. Bacca Acosta, J.L., Baldiris Navarro, S.M., Fabregat Gesa, R., et al.: Augmented reality trends in education: a systematic review of research and applications. J. Educ. Technol. Soc. **17**(4), 133–149 (2014)
21. Akçayır, M., Akçayır, G.: Advantages and challenges associated with augmented reality for education: A systematic review of the literature. Educ. Res. Rev. **20**, 1–11 (2017)
22. Jiang, H., Vimalesvaran, S., Wang, J.K., et al.: Virtual reality in medical students' education: scoping review. JMIR Med. Educ. **8**(1), e34860 (2022)
23. Freeman, D., Reeve, S., Robinson, A., et al.: Virtual reality in the assessment, understanding, and treatment of mental health disorders. Psychol. Med. **47**(14), 2393–2400 (2017)
24. Maples-Keller, J.L., Bunnell, B.E., Kim, S.J., et al.: The use of virtual reality technology in the treatment of anxiety and other psychiatric disorders. Harv. Rev. Psychiatry **25**(3), 103–113 (2017)

DKTM-SA: A Deep Knowledge Tracing Model Based on a Sparse Attention Mechanism

Xuzheng Zhang, Zhengzhou Zhu[✉], and Mingyang Jia

Peking University, Beijing 102600, China
zhuzz@pku.edu.cn

Abstract. In modern outcome-based education practices, knowledge tracing technology has emerged as an essential tool for comprehending and optimizing the student learning process. However, existing knowledge tracing models exhibit deficiencies in terms of prediction accuracy and efficiency, as well as limited generalizability and interpretability. This paper introduces a deep knowledge tracing model based on sparse attention (DKTM-SA). Comparative experiments on several public datasets, including Algebra2005, validate that this model enhances prediction accuracy, significantly reduces the computational cost of processing long interaction sequences, and effectively aligns with learners' cognitive development patterns.

Keywords: Knowledge tracing · Deep learning · Sparse attention mechanism · Feature fusion · Item response theory

1 Background

In recent years, the rapid advancement of artificial intelligence and data science has introduced transformative changes to the field of education [1]. From primary schools to universities, an increasing number of educators and students are opting to use intelligent tutoring systems and smart education platforms for teaching, research, and learning activities [2]. These online learning platforms amass substantial amounts of student interaction data. Leveraging technologies such as data mining and machine learning, these platforms can more scientifically decipher students' cognitive patterns, cater to personalized learning needs, and deliver tailored educational content and services [3]. Personalized learning optimizes the student learning experience and enhances learning outcomes. It proves to be more efficient than traditional classroom education and aligns more closely with the contemporary demands of student-centered, outcome-based education [4].

To increase the quality of personalized learning services, the task of knowledge tracing (KT) has been introduced by the academic community. As illustrated in Fig. 1, knowledge tracing predicts the probability of a student correctly answering the next question by establishing a binary classification model that tracks the evolution of a student's knowledge state over time, thereby assessing their grasp of the material [5]. Knowledge tracing estimates a student's knowledge level in a specific domain on the basis of their

K. Zhang et al. (Eds.): CSEI 2024, CCIS 2447, pp. 67–86, 2025.
https://doi.org/10.1007/978-981-96-3735-5_6

observed performance. The goal is to diagnose what the student knows and does not know and to provide them with appropriate questions [6]. Deep learning techniques, known for their significant advantages in handling large-scale data and uncovering complex patterns, have become a focal point of research for modeling knowledge tracing problems over the past few years. Deep knowledge tracing models have been widely applied in the field of personalized education, yielding substantial results [7].

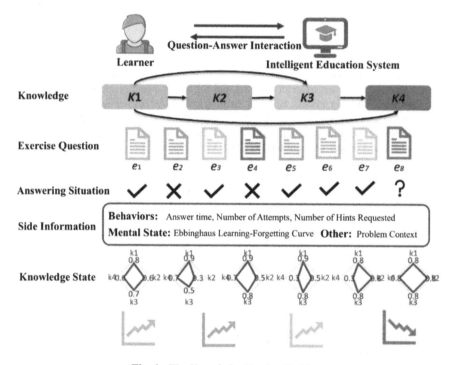

Fig. 1. The Knowledge Tracing Problem

Designing a knowledge tracing model that effectively utilizes diverse types of learning information, improves predictive performance, and accurately reflects cognitive learning processes still has substantial room for exploration [8]. Particularly in the context of learning situation analysis, the development and implementation of a deep knowledge tracing model that precisely depicts students' learning states, offers high interpretability, and optimizes computational efficiency is crucial. Integrating such a model into learning situation analysis systems holds significant theoretical and practical value for advancing personalized education and improving teaching quality.

2   Literature Review

Inspired by deep learning techniques, Piech et al. [7] pioneered the research in deep knowledge tracing by introducing a model known as deep knowledge tracing (DKT). In recent years, both domestic and international studies have expanded the research on deep knowledge tracing models from various perspectives, which can be categorized into the following five categories.

2.1 Models Based on Attention Mechanisms

On the basis of the foundational transformer architecture [9], numerous studies have integrated attention mechanisms into deep knowledge tracing models. Pandey et al. [10]. Were among the first to incorporate attention mechanisms, introducing the self-attentive knowledge tracing (SAKT) model. SAKT employs the scaled dot-product attention mechanism proposed by Vaswani et al. to encode students' response records, capturing dependencies between different time points in students' answer sequences. Ghosh et al. [11]. Proposed the attentive knowledge tracing (AKT) model, whereas Choi et al. [12]. Built upon the self-attention mechanism to enhance and optimize SAKT, introducing the separated self-entive neural knowledge tracing (SAINT) model. Huang et al. [13]. Improved model generalization by proposing the diagnostic transformer (DTransformer), which constructs an architecture from the problem level to the knowledge level and designs a temporal and cumulative attention (TCA) mechanism to diagnose learners' knowledge states at each time step.

2.2 Models Based on Memory Neural Structures

Zhang et al. [14] introduced key-value memory networks into the field of deep knowledge tracing and designed the dynamic key-value memory network (DKVMN). The DKVMN uses two memory matrices, 'keys' and 'values', to store representations of knowledge points and students' mastery levels for each knowledge point, respectively, enhancing the model's ability to dynamically represent students' knowledge states. Abdelrahman et al. [15] built upon DKVMN to address issues related to potentially irrelevant associations between knowledge points. They proposed the sequential key-value memory network (SKVMN), which employs a structure called "Hop-LSTM" for sequence modeling.

2.3 Models Based on Graph Representation Learning

Inspired by the representational power of graph neural networks and other graph learning techniques, several studies have incorporated graph learning methods to leverage the rich structural information within graphs and flexibly model the relationships between problems and knowledge skills. Yan Qiuyan et al. [16] used graph attention networks to learn the structural relationships between students and problems, proposing the SPKT model. Yang et al. [17] introduced a spatiotemporal knowledge tracing method based on heterogeneous graphs (TSKT), which tracks the evolution of students' knowledge states along both temporal and spatial dimensions and obtains a knowledge space with more enriched representations of practice through hierarchical aggregation.

2.4 Models Incorporating Contextual Features of Question Texts

Chen et al. [18] addressed the issue of information sparsity caused by the lack of integration of text-related features by proposing a model called IFKT. IFKT uses embedding propagation to capture various relational structures. Liu et al. [19] introduced an exercise-aware knowledge tracing model that integrates multiple types of knowledge point information during answer prediction. In this model, students' knowledge states are represented by a knowledge state matrix rather than a knowledge state vector.

2.5 Models Incorporating Learning Forgetting Characteristics

Educational psychology research indicates that forgetting is crucial for accurately estimating students' knowledge states. Simulating forgetting effects presents one of the major challenges faced by many studies. Im et al. [20] analyzed the impact of learners' forgetting behavior on existing attention-based knowledge tracing models and proposed the FoLiBi model, which incorporates a forgetting-aware attention mechanism. Xu et al. [21] introduced a Learning Behavior-oriented Knowledge Tracing Model (LBKT), which explicitly explores the impact of learning behaviors, including forgetting, on learners' knowledge states. This model combines forgetting factors with knowledge acquisition to update the evolving knowledge states of learners comprehensively.

Summarizing both domestic and international literature, research in deep knowledge tracing continues to evolve. Scholars are diligently working to increase the accuracy, interpretability, and practical applicability of knowledge tracing by integrating innovative algorithms, advanced model architectures, and contemporary educational theories.

3 Model Design and Implementation

3.1 Definition of the Knowledge Tracing Problem

The knowledge tracing task involves processing and analyzing students' historical problem-solving records through a model to extract latent information for predicting answers at the next time step. Let $Q = \{q_1, \ldots, q_{|N|}\}$ represent the set of all the distinct problem labels in the dataset. Each $q_i \in Q$ may have different difficulty levels, which are usually not explicitly provided. Each exercise x_i is a pair (y_i, b_i), where q_i is a problem label, $y_i \in (0,1)$ is a binary variable indicating the answer—0 for a wrong answer and 1 for a correct answer—and where b_i represents the student's response behavior. When a student interacts with problems in Q, their exercise history $X = \langle x_1, x_2, \ldots, x_t \rangle$ can be observed over t time steps. Furthermore, problems in Q are associated with a set of learning concepts $C = \{c_1, c_2, \ldots, c_N\}$(e.g., skills within a course). Given the answering history X, the goal is to estimate the probability $p(y_t = 1|q_t, X)$ of correctly answering a problem at time step t.

3.2 Model Design

Feature Interaction Analysis
Before the model was designed, a series of interaction feature explorations were conducted on the Junyi Academy dataset. Through visual analysis of the data, this section presents the results of feature interaction exploration via stacked histograms and heatmaps, revealing the relationships between student behavior characteristics and learning outcomes.

The stacked histogram in Fig. 2 illustrates the relationship between 'Hint Usage and Answering Results'. Consistent with previous analyses, students who used hints answered all the questions incorrectly, whereas those who did not use hints achieved a correct answer rate of 88.5%. This finding underscores the value of independent problem solving in the learning process, emphasizing the need for this study to focus on enhancing students' autonomous learning capabilities in both learning situation analysis and knowledge tracing modeling.

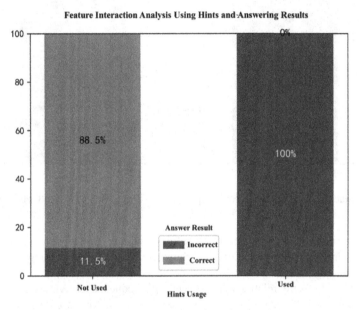

Fig. 2. Stacked histogram of feature proportions for 'Hint Used' and 'Answering Results'

The stacked histogram in Fig. 3 illustrates the relationship between 'Acquired Problem-Solving Proficiency' and 'Hint Usage'. The chart reveals that among students who did not achieve problem-solving proficiency, 6.8% opted to request hints. This finding indicates that some students encountered difficulties during problem solving and required additional guidance to aid their understanding and resolution of the problems.

The results indicate a significant negative correlation between problem-solving proficiency and whether students requested hints. This negative correlation suggests that when models and systems are designed to assess student learning outcomes, accounting for the potential impact of hint usage on students' problem-solving proficiency is crucial.

The heatmap in Fig. 4 illustrates the relationship between 'Hint Usage' and 'Answering Results'. The data show that approximately 37.5% of the students who used hints answered all the questions incorrectly, whereas approximately 37.5% of those who answered incorrectly used hints. This result further underscores the importance of independent problem solving for learning outcomes. This reveals that independent problem solving plays a critical role in the learning process. When students solve problems without external assistance, they are more likely to truly understand and master the

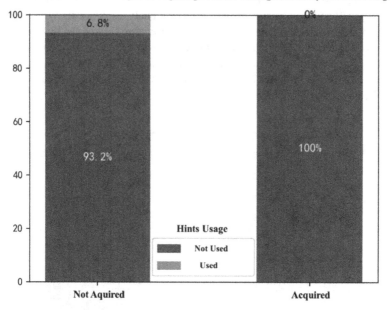

Fig. 3. Stacked histogram of feature proportions for 'Proficiency Gain' and 'Hint Used'

knowledge points. Independent problem solving encourages deeper thinking, fosters problem-solving strategies and skills, and thus helps to reinforce learning outcomes in long-term memory.

Figure 5 explores the relationship between 'hint request and review behavior'. The analysis revealed that none of the students who requested hints engaged in review, whereas 95.3% of the students who did not request hints reviewed their material. This suggests a positive correlation between postclass review behavior and reduced reliance on hints.

Through the analysis of these interaction features, this study provides deep insights into the complex relationships between student learning behaviors and outcomes. By integrating these critical behavioral features, the model can more accurately predict student learning outcomes, thereby offering more robust support for educational interventions.

Model Architecture Overview

This study designs a deep knowledge tracing model based on sparse attention Mechanism (DKTM-SA) to better accommodate knowledge tracing and learning situation analysis tasks. The comprehensive architecture of the DKTM-SA model is as follows: illustrated in Fig. 6, which comprises the following four core components.

Feature Extraction and Fusion Network

To address the issues of insufficient extraction of student behavior features and the relative scarcity of deep interaction analysis in existing knowledge tracing models, this study

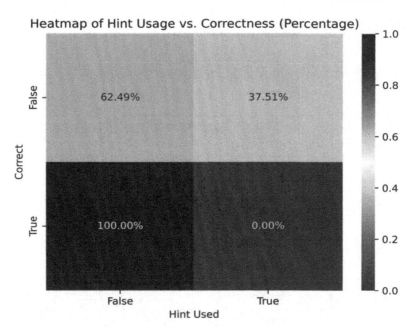

Fig. 4. Heatmap of 'Hint Usage' vs. 'Correctness' (percentage)

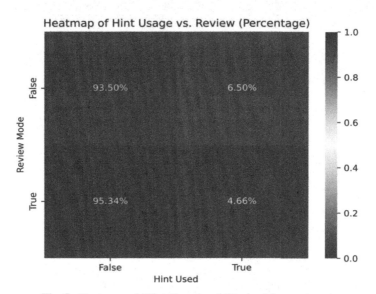

Fig. 5. Heatmaps of 'Hint Usage' and 'Review' (percentages)

designed a feature extraction and fusion network to optimize the interaction modeling process. Initially, the network performs fine-grained extraction of behavior and problem features from the dataset. For example, it incorporates distinguishing factors and problem context information into problem features and introduces behavior characteristics

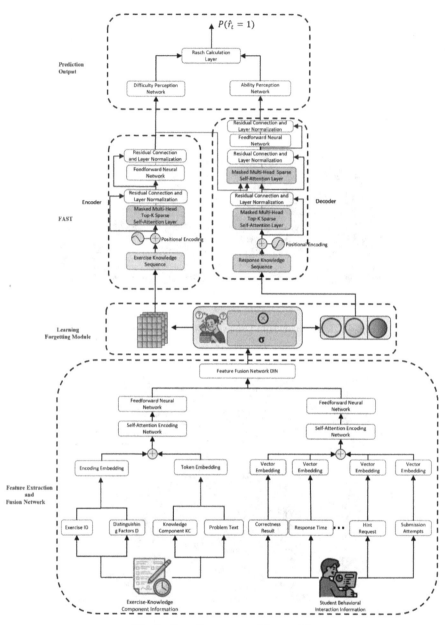

Fig. 6. Overall structure of the model

such as hint usage, review, and problem-solving speed into the interaction sequences. This approach enhances the richness and realism of the depiction of students' knowledge states and learning profiles. These relatively sparse features from different dimensions are then dimensionality-reduced through an embedding layer into dense vectors with a unified dimension.

A deep interaction network (DIN) with a self-attention mechanism is subsequently employed to perform feature interaction fusion on students' learning behavior data and problem text data. This network captures the latent interaction patterns between features, laying the foundation for the model to understand students' knowledge states and learning habits and to perform accurate predictive learning situation analyses.

The integrated feature vectors processed by the feature extraction and fusion network are used as inputs for the subsequent learning forgetting module and sparse attention network. As shown in Eq. (1), the fusion feature vector can be expressed as:

$$F_{st} = \text{ReLU}\big(W_f\big[F_s; F_t; m_q \odot F_t\big] + b_f\big) \tag{1}$$

In this representation, $mq \odot Ft$ represents the elementwise product of problem-specific distinguishing factors and problem text features, thereby directly integrating the distinguishing factors into the problem features. Here, W_f and W_f denote the weights and biases of the fusion network, respectively.

Learning Forgetting Module

The Learning Forgetting Module incorporates a gating mechanism to model the process of student learning and forgetting, which is a critical component of the design, as illustrated in Fig. 7. This module performs learning context-aware processing on the fusion

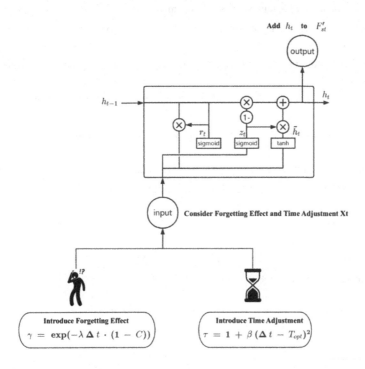

Fig. 7. Detailed structure of the learning and forgetting module

feature vectors from the previous network. It adjusts the student's mastery of knowledge points over time by incorporating time adjustment factors and forgetting factors. The module employs GRU update and reset gates to control the flow of information, determining the extent to which historical answer information is retained. This approach captures the gradual decline in knowledge over time, tracks the learning pace of different students, and enhances the model's adaptability to individual differences, thus improving its interpretability and robustness.

The module takes as input the feature vectors F_{st} from the feature extraction and fusion network and the time intervals Δ_t associated with each problem, representing the elapsed time since the last interaction with that knowledge point. The output is the adjusted feature embedding /F_{st}/, which accounts for the forgetting effect and is updated through the GRU mechanism. The detailed algorithm for this process is provided in Algorithm 1.

Algorithm 1   GRU-Based Algorithm for Simulating the Forgetting Effect

---

Input: Feature vector list F, time intervals Δt associated with each problem, and the student's proficiency level C for each problem.

Output: Feature embeddings adjusted through an enhanced GRU to account for the forgetting effect F'_{st}

1: Initialize the GRU state $h0$ as a zero vector.//GRU state initialization

2: Initialize the list of adjusted feature vectors F' as empty.

3: for each feature vector $feature\_vector$, corresponding time interval Δt, and proficiency level C do:

4:     Compute the forgetting factor $\gamma = \exp(-\lambda \Delta t \cdot (1 - C))$ //Forgetting factor considering proficiency level

5:     Compute the time adjustment factor $\tau = 1 + \beta(\Delta t - Topt)2$ //Time   optimization adjustment

6:     $feature\_vector adjusted \leftarrow feature\_vector \cdot \gamma \cdot \tau$ //Considering both forgetting effect and time adjustment

7:     $GRU\_input \leftarrow$ Integrated ($feature\_vector adjusted$, Δt)

8:     Compute the update gate $zt = \sigma (Wz \cdot [ht-1, GRU\_input] + bz)$ //Update   gate calculation

9:     Compute the reset gate rt and candidate hidden state $\tilde{h}t$ (according to standard GRU operations).

10:     Update the hidden state as $ht = (1 - zt) * ht-1 + zt * \tilde{h}t$

11:     Append ht to F'//Update the feature vector list

12: end for

$$\gamma = \exp(-\lambda \Delta t \cdot (1 - C)) \tag{2}$$

$$\tau = 1 + \beta\left(\Delta t - T_{opt}\right)^2 \qquad (3)$$

$$z_t = \sigma\left(W_z \cdot \left[h_{t-1}, x_t\right] + b_z\right) \qquad (4)$$

$$r_t = \sigma\left(W_r \cdot \left[h_{t-1}, x_t\right] + b_r\right) \qquad (5)$$

$$h_t = (1 - z_t)*h_{t-1} + z_t*\widetilde{h}_t \qquad (6)$$

In the given formulas, σ represents the sigmoid function, and tanh is the hyperbolic tangent activation function. The matrices W_z and W_r are the weight matrices for the update gate and reset gate, respectively, and b_z and b_r are the corresponding bias terms. The hidden state at the previous time step is denoted as h_{t-1}, while $\widetilde{h}_t$ is the candidate hidden state at time t. The current input feature vector x_t consists of the feature vector adjusted for the forgetting effect and Δt. The symbol [,] represents the concatenation operation. The update gate regulates the balance between retaining and forgetting information, thereby modeling the impact of the forgetting effect on the knowledge state.

Encoder-Decoder Based on Sparse Attention
The encoder-decoder, which is based on a sparse attention design, is a core component of our model, as illustrated in Fig. 8. In this work, we introduce a sparse attention mechanism to replace the classical scaled attention mechanism used in transformers for handling time series data. By focusing on key moments, this approach mitigates information overload, reducing the computation of attention scores for unnecessary time steps. Instead, it selects the K time steps with the highest attention weights, which are likely the moments when students exhibit significant progress or difficulties. This enhances the model's understanding of student learning behavior, thereby improving the effectiveness and interpretability of knowledge tracing and learning situation analysis. Sparse attention ensures efficient processing of long sequence data.

The encoder processes the feature representations after being refined by the GRU-based forgetting gate module. The decoder then generates predictions of the student's knowledge state on the basis of the encoder's output and previous states. This structure effectively captures and utilizes student behavior features, reduces computational overhead, and maintains predictive performance.

The core task of the encoder-decoder component is to extract high-level representations from the feature vectors that integrate student learning behavior features and exercise text features, i.e., from the input sequences, to capture key information and its contextual relationships. This is achieved through the introduction of a top-k interaction selection mechanism, where each attention head focuses on only a subset of the sequence rather than the entire sequence. This significantly reduces the computational complexity and enhances the efficiency of processing long sequence data. The computation for the sparse self-attention layer is described by the following equations:

$$\text{SparseCrossAttention(Q, K, V)} = \text{softmax}\left(\frac{M\prime \odot \left(QK^T\right)}{\sqrt{d_{k\prime}}}\right)V \qquad (7)$$

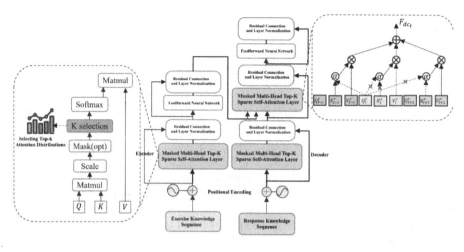

FAST

Fig. 8. The encoder–decoder network structure

Prediction Output Based on the IRT-Rasch Model

Following the processing results from the encoder-decoder, this study designs an IRT-Rasch module to output prediction results. The prediction output component includes the Learning Ability Measurement Layered Perceptron (LAMLP), the Question Difficulty Measurement Layered Perceptron (QDMLP), and the Rasch computation layer. These components collectively estimate the probability $p(rt)$ of a student answering a question correctly at the next time step. This module carefully considers both the student's ability and the question's difficulty, enhancing the accuracy, transparency, and interpretability of the predictions.

The prediction network, which is based on Rasch measurement theory, calculates the probability of a student correctly answering a question via the student's ability parameter θ_i and the question's difficulty parameter β_j. The probability is computed as follows:

$$P\left(y_{ij} = 1 | \theta_i, \beta_j\right) = \frac{1}{1 + e^{-(\theta_i - \beta_j)}} \tag{8}$$

where θ_i represents the ability parameter of student i and where β_j represents the difficulty parameter of question j.

Loss Function Design

To accurately capture a student's performance on various questions over time, this study employs a specifically designed cross-entropy loss function. This loss function focuses on the actual answer results y_{itc} of student i on question k at time t and compares them with the model's predicted answer probabilities $\widehat{y_{itc}}$. The mathematical expression of the loss function is defined as follows:

$$\text{Loss} = -\sum_{i=1}^{N} \sum_{t=1}^{T_i} \sum_{k=1}^{K} \left[y_{itk} \log\left(\widehat{y_{itk}}\right) + (1 - y_{itk}) \log\left(1 - \widehat{y_{itk}}\right) \right] \tag{9}$$

4 Experimental Analysis and Evaluation

This chapter uses five major educational datasets [53–55], ASSIST2009, ASSIST2015, ASSIST2017, Algebra2005, and Junyi Academy 2015, to comprehensively evaluate the performance of the DKTM-SA model in various scenarios. These datasets were chosen for their rich diversity of features and extensive coverage, ensuring that the DKTM-SA model can be effectively trained and evaluated in a variety of learning environments.

4.1 Data Preprocessing

Data File Construction
Taking the Junyi Academy dataset as an example, the dataset contains multiple files. The 'junyi_ProblemLog_original.csv' file records students' answer behaviors, including the user ID, exercise name, correctness of the answer, and time spent answering. The 'junyi_Exercise_table.csv' file contains metadata about the exercises, providing information such as exercise names, availability on the website, and prerequisite exercises.

Data Type Conversion
Upon evaluating the raw data, several key fields that required conversion were identified. For example, the 'time_done' field was originally in Unix timestamp format (integer type), whereas the 'count_attempts' and 'count_hints' fields, which should represent numerical information, were recognized as string types during data loading. On the basis of the actual meanings of these fields, target data types were set, and corresponding conversion strategies were formulated:

Time Type Data Conversion
The 'time_done' field was converted from the Unix timestamp (integer) to Python's datetime format to facilitate subsequent time series analysis. The earliest timestamp in the dataset was selected as a reference point, and all timestamps were converted to time differences relative to this reference point, effectively reducing the range of data representation while maintaining the time order and relative distances.

Discrete Data Conversion
Discrete data in the dataset, such as exercise names, topics, and fields, were originally in text format. Handling large volumes of categorical data in this form can increase storage and computation costs. To address this, appropriate encoding techniques were applied to convert these categorical features into numerical formats suitable for model training.

Outlier Handling
By identifying and handling outliers, we can ensure the accuracy of the input data. Using the Junyi dataset as an example, this study visualizes the distribution of key behavioral features, such as 'count_hints' and 'count_attempts'. Figure 9 presents the distribution histogram of these fields. On the basis of the commonly used Z score method, which considers values exceeding the mean by three standard deviations as outliers, we calculate

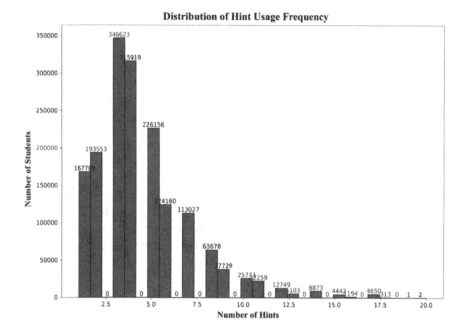

Fig. 9. Distribution of 'count_hints'

the mean and standard deviation for the corresponding fields. These outliers are then replaced with the mean values via data imputation techniques.

Construction of Feature Sequences, Including Student Behaviors
When student behavior sequence data are processed, various anomalies can occur, such as short sequences and exercises with unmarked knowledge points. Considering that learning sequences with fewer than five interactions are insufficient to reflect knowledge acquisition and forgetting patterns, we set a minimum threshold of five interactions. Sequences below this threshold and exercises with unmarked knowledge points are removed to ensure that the data accurately represent students' learning processes.

4.2 Experiment

For the experiments, we utilized the AutoDL platform to create a standardized GPU cloud server environment. To reduce the implementation complexity of the sparse attention mechanism, we employed the PyTorch deep learning framework and conducted parameter analysis experiments on the Weights & Biases platform to increase the training efficiency and performance of the model.

We evaluated the DKTM-SA model on datasets that broadly cover the dimensions of student interaction data and compared it against several benchmark models: DKT, SAKT, SAINT, SKVMN, DTransformer, and FolibiKT. All the models were trained and tested under identical hardware conditions and data preprocessing protocols to ensure experimental consistency. The comparative results are shown in Fig. 10, leading to the following observations:

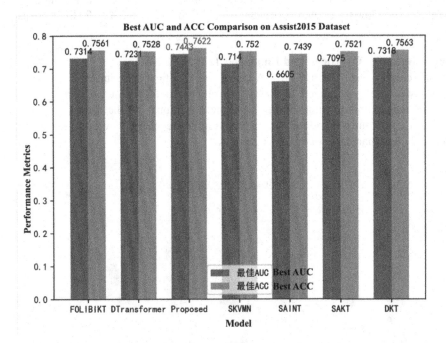

Fig. 10. Model performance comparison on the ASSIST2015 dataset

Superior Performance of DKTM-SA

For the ASSIST2017 dataset, the DKTM-SA model achieved an AUC of 0.7606, an improvement of 2.27% compared with the best-performing benchmark model, FolibiKT.

For the Junyi2015 dataset, DKTM-SA attained an AUC of 0.8095, an improvement of 1.62% over the next best model, FolibiKT. Additionally, the RMSE decreased to 0.3526, a 2.95% reduction compared with FolibiKT, indicating higher prediction accuracy.

For the Algebra2005 dataset, DKTM-SA reached an AUC of 0.9089, surpassing the closest benchmark model, DTransformer, which had an AUC of 0.8794, a 3.35% increase. This was the most significant improvement across all datasets.

Limitations of the DKT Model

Compared with the other encoder-decoder models, the DKT model exhibited lower accuracy and higher RMSE values. This performance gap is due primarily to the structural and processing limitations of the DKT model. As an early model in the knowledge tracing domain, DKT relies on recurrent neural networks (RNNs) to process student answer sequences. RNNs struggle with gradient vanishing or explosion issues when handling long sequences and have difficulty parallelizing data processing, which affects both training efficiency and prediction performance. Therefore, this study adopted an encoder–decoder architecture.

The results of the comparative experiments on memory consumption and training time between DKTM-SA and the other models are shown in Fig. 11. The experiments controlled for other parameters, with all models trained for 10 epochs, adjusting only the sequence window parameter to evaluate resource consumption. The findings are as follows:

Reduced Resource Overhead and Enhanced Training Efficiency
The resource overhead of the DKTM-SA model was significantly reduced, and training efficiency was notably improved. In contrast, the other models presented higher memory usage and longer training times under the same conditions. As the sequence length increased, the GPU memory usage and training time of the DKTM-SA model increased significantly less than those of the other models.

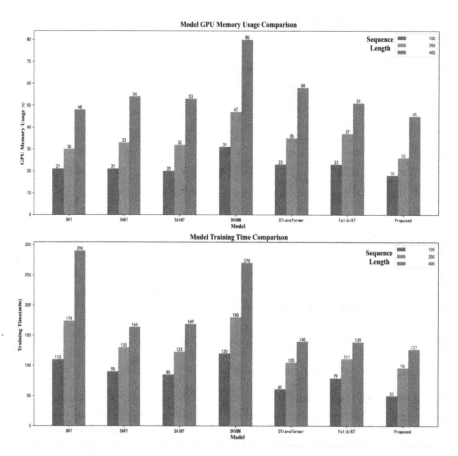

Fig. 11. Resource consumption and training time comparison

Effectiveness of the Sparse Attention Mechanism

The sparse attention mechanism effectively reduces unnecessary computations, thereby decreasing GPU memory usage and training time. This enables the model to maintain low resource consumption even when processing long sequence data.

To align with real cognitive processes and enhance model interpretability, this study designs a GRU-based forgetting module to simulate the natural decline in students' knowledge over time, which is grounded in the Ebbinghaus forgetting curve. To validate the effectiveness of this module, two ablation experiments were set up:

(1) − GRUforget: Directly remove the GRU forgetting gate, feeding the feature-fused vectors directly into the encoder-decoder component.
(2) − GRUalter: This replaces the GRU with a multihead attention layer, adhering to Occam's razor principle to minimize changes to the model's scale.

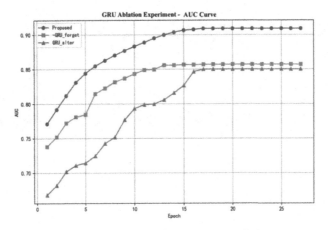

Fig. 12. GRU Ablation Experiment - AUC Curve

To further explore the impact of the forgetting control module on model performance, we conducted ablation experiments using the Algebra2005 dataset. Figures 12–14 illustrate the changes in training metrics before and after the removal of the GRU forgetting gate. The overall trend in the curves indicates a significant performance decline when the GRU forgetting control module is removed or replaced. Additionally, the training convergence process shows noticeable volatility, and the convergence speed is affected to some extent.

The first graph on the top left in Fig. 15, which shows the RMSE versus sequence length, shows that, except for the DKTM-SA model, the RMSE increases with sequence length for all the models. However, the RMSE of the DKTM-SA model continues to decrease as the sequence length increases, particularly at a sequence length of 1000, where it maintains a low error rate, demonstrating its robust ability to handle long sequence data. The subsequent graphs depicting the relationship between sequence length and the ACC/AUC further validate the performance of the DKTM-SA model. Compared with the other models, the DKTM-SA model consistently achieves greater

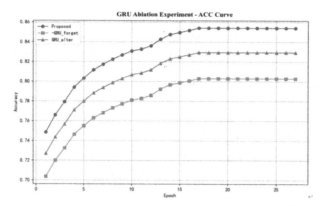

Fig. 13. GRU Ablation Experiment - ACC Curve

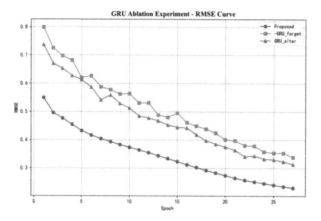

Fig. 14. GRU Ablation Experiment - RMSE Curve

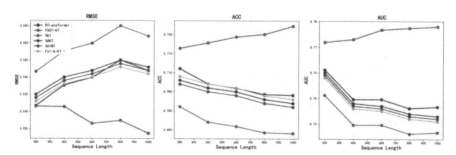

Fig. 15. Comparative Results of Model Sequence Window Hyperparameter Experiments

accuracy across all sequence lengths, especially in long sequence processing, with the former being the only model that shows an increasing trend. This finding indicates that the DKTM-SA model better captures knowledge states in long sequences, enhancing prediction accuracy. This advantage is attributed to its optimized internal structure, such as the incorporation of sparse attention mechanisms, which not only reduce computational complexity but also improve the model's ability to capture long-sequence dependencies. Additionally, the model's deep feature extraction and integration provide richer information for accurate predictions.

5 Summary and Future Work

This study aimed to improve the accuracy and efficiency of knowledge tracing models by deeply exploring student behavior characteristics and refining the granularity of information representations to achieve more precise and efficient learning analytics. Despite advancements in current knowledge tracing algorithm research, shortcomings and areas for improvement remain, particularly in feature extraction, feature fusion methods, model interpretability, and prediction output accuracy. To address these issues, this paper proposes a deep knowledge tracing model named "DKTM-SA," which applies sparse attention to enhance the encoder-decoder structure. While the research achieved significant results, using knowledge tracing for learning outcome prediction is an evolving field. Future research can improve by expanding and enriching datasets, further optimizing the model algorithms and enhancing model interpretability.

Acknowledgments. This paper is supported by the Humanities and Social Sciences Research Planning Fund Project of the Ministry of Education: "Research on Metacognitive Diagnosis Theory and Technology Driven by Multimodal Learning Data" (23YJA880091) and the Fundamental Research Funds for the Central Universities. Additionally, we would like to acknowledge the Undergraduate Teaching Reform Project of Peking University in 2024: "Gamified Interactive Experimental Teaching in Software Engineering" (Project No. 7100903145).

References

1. Bai, Y., Zhao, J., Wei, T., et al.: A Survey of Explainable Knowledge Tracing. arXiv preprint arXiv:2403.07279 (2024)
2. Block, A., Simchowitz, M., Tedrake, R.: Smoothed Online Learning for Prediction in Piecewise Affine Systems. arXiv preprint arXiv:2301.11187 (2024)
3. Goudar, D.M., Goudar, R.H., Kulkarni, A.A., Rathod, V.N., Hukkeri, G.S.: A Digital Recommendation System for Personalized Learning to Enhance Online Education: A Review. IEEE Access **12**, 34019–34041 (2024)
4. Zhu, Z., Zhang, Q., Song, X., et al.: A Classroom Teaching Design of Software Engineering for Cultivating Students' Autonomous Learning Ability. Computer Education (05): 155–159 (2023)
5. Corbett, A.T., Anderson, J.R.: Knowledge tracing: Modeling the acquisition of procedural knowledge. User Model. User-Adap. Inter. **4**, 253–278 (1994)
6. Huang, C., Wei, H., Huang, Q., Jiang, F., Han, Z., Huang, X.: Learning consistent representations with temporal and causal enhancement for knowledge tracing. Expert Syst. Appl. **245**, 123–128 (2024)

7. Piech, C., Spencer, J., Huang, J., Ganguli, S., Sahami, M., Guibas, L., Sohl-Dickstein, J.: Deep Knowledge Tracing. arXiv preprint arXiv:1506.05908 (2015)
8. Wang, Y., Zhu, M.X., Yang, S.H.: Review and Performance Comparison of Deep Knowledge Tracing Models. Journal of Software **34**(3), 1365–1395 (2023)
9. Vaswani, A., Shazeer, N., Parmar, N., Uszkoreit, J., Jones, L., Gomez, A.N., Kaiser, Ł., Polosukhin, I.: Attention Is All You Need. arXiv preprint arXiv:1706.03762 (2023)
10. Pandey, S., Karypis, G.: A Self-Attentive Model for Knowledge Tracing. arXiv preprint arXiv:1907.06837 (2019)
11. Ghosh, A., Heffernan, N., Lan, A.S.: Context-Aware Attentive Knowledge Tracing. arXiv preprint arXiv:2007.12324 (2020)
12. Choi, Y., Lee, Y., Cho, J., Baek, J., Kim, B., Cha, Y., Shin, D., Bae, C., Heo, J.: Toward an Appropriate Query, Key, and Value Computation for Knowledge Tracing. In: Proceedings of the Seventh ACM Conference on Learning @ Scale, pp. 341–344. Association for Computing Machinery, New York, NY, USA (2020)
13. Huang, S., Liu, Z., Zhao, X., Luo, W., Weng, J.: Toward Robust Knowledge Tracing Models via k-Sparse Attention. In: Proceedings of the 46th International ACM SIGIR Conference on Research and Development in Information Retrieval, pp. 2441–2445. Association for Computing Machinery, New York, NY, USA (2023)
14. Zhang, J., Shi, X., King, I., Yeung, D.-Y.: Dynamic Key-Value Memory Networks for Knowledge Tracing. arXiv preprint arXiv:1611.08108 (2017)
15. Abdelrahman, G., Wang, Q.: Knowledge Tracing with Sequential Key-Value Memory Networks. In: Proceedings of the 42nd International ACM SIGIR Conference on Research and Development in Information Retrieval, pp. 1155–1158. ACM, New York, NY, USA (2019)
16. Yan, Q.-Y., Si, Y.-Q., Yuan, G., Wang, Z.-X.: Student-Problem Association Based The heterogeneous graph knowledge tracing model. Acta Electronica Sinica **51**(12), 3549–3556 (2023)
17. Yang, L., Adam, S., Chatelain, C.: Dynamic Graph Representation Learning with Neural Networks: A Survey. arXiv preprint arXiv:2304.05729 (2023).24
18. Chen, Z., Shan, Z., Zeng, Y.: Informative Representations for Forgetting-Robust Knowledge Tracing. User Model User-Adap Inter (2024)
19. Liu, Q., Huang, Z., Yin, Y., Chen, E., Xiong, H., Su, Y., Hu, G.: EKT: Exercise Aware Knowledge Tracing for Student Performance Prediction. arXiv preprint arXiv:1906.05658 (2019)
20. Im, Y., Choi, E., Kook, H., Lee, J.: Forgetting-Aware Linear Bias for Attentive Knowledge Tracing. In: Proceedings of the 32nd ACM International Conference on Information and Knowledge Management, pp. 3958–3962. ACM, New York, NY, USA (2023)
21. Xu, B., Huang, Z., Liu, J., Shen, S., Liu, Q., Chen, E., Wu, J., Wang, S.: Learning Behavior-oriented knowledge tracing. In: Proceedings of the 29th ACM SIGKDD Conference on Knowledge Discovery and Data Mining, pp. 2789–2800. ACM, New York, NY, USA (2023)

A Differentiated Neurocognitive Diagnostic Model Based on Student Level, Exercise Difficulty and Discrimination

Dongkai Qi[1], Xiaoyu Han[1], Zijie Li[1], Jia Hao[1,2], and Jun Wang[1,2(✉)]

[1] Key Laboratory of Education Informatization for Nationalities, Ministry of Education, Yunnan Normal University, Chenggong District, Juxian Street 768, Kunming 650500, China
`wangjun@ynnu.edu.cn`
[2] Yunnan Key Laboratory of Smart Education, Yunnan Normal University, Chenggong District, Juxian Street 768, Kunming 650500, China

Abstract. After years of development, cognitive diagnostic technology has garnered significant attention and has been extensively applied in various areas of contemporary psychological and educational measurement. In the context of smart education, cognitive diagnostic techniques can effectively identify students' mastery of specific knowledge concepts. Although neural network-based cognitive diagnostic methods have achieved excellent results compared with traditional approaches, the relationship between students' levels and exercise diagnostic factors has not yet been comprehensively considered, resulting in less accurate diagnostic results. On this basis, this study presents a differentiated neurocognitive diagnostic model based on students' level, difficulty exercising and differentiation, which effectively solves the above problems; this model is referred to as DCDM. The model is structured around three key modules: the embedding module, the differentiation matching factor calculation module and the prediction module. Through the embedding module, the proficiency vector of the student's knowledge concepts, the knowledge concept association vector of the exercises, the knowledge concept difficulty vector and the differentiation vector are obtained; through the differentiation matching factor module, the relationship between the student's knowledge concept proficiency vector, the knowledge concept difficulty vector of the exercises and the differentiation vector obtained by the embedding module is calculated, and the differentiation matching factor is obtained; finally, in the prediction module, the vectors obtained before are fused with the Distinctiveness Matching Factor are fused, and then the students' responses to the tasks are anticipated. The results of the experiment indicate that the differentiated neurocognitive diagnostic model on two publicly available datasets, ASSISTments2009–2010 and FrcSub, which is based on students' level, difficulty exercising and differentiating improves the diagnostic effect compared with other methods.

Keywords: Smart Education · Neurocognitive Diagnosis · Differentiation Matching Factor

K. Zhang et al. (Eds.): CSEI 2024, CCIS 2447, pp. 87–102, 2025.
https://doi.org/10.1007/978-981-96-3735-5_7

1 Introduction

Cognitive Diagnosis (CD) has been used in the field of educational psychology for decades [1], and the approach more effectively models students' cognitive states at the level of knowledge concepts, thereby representing proficiency in specific knowledge concepts [2], and has been used with good results in applications such as student corrective programs and early warning of academic withdrawal [3]. Figure 1 illustrates a representative example of a cognitive diagnostic model, where typically, students first choose a subset of tasks (e.g., e1,···, e4), give their answers (e.g., right/wrong), and then, our objective is to deduce their true level of comprehension regarding the relevant concept (e.g., three-dimensional geometry). In practical applications, these diagnostic reports are essential because they serve as the foundation for understanding students' abilities and can provide them with targeted training [4, 5].

Fig. 1. An example diagram of cognitive diagnosis.

Within the realm of prevailing cognitive models, they can generally be delineated into two primary classifications: the traditional approach and the neural network-based approach. Among the traditional approaches include Matrix Factorization (MF) [6], Item Response Theory (IRT) [7], Multidimensional Item Response Theory (MIRT) [8, 9] and Deterministic Inputs, Noisy and Gate Model (DINA) [10]. Although traditional cognitive diagnostic models have achieved some results and the predictions of the models are more interpretable, the majority of contemporary cognitive diagnostic models rely on handcrafted functions to replicate the interactions between learners and tasks, and finally, the results are obtained through parameter estimation. Simultaneously, the interactions between students and exercises are often complex, and hand-designed functions usually suffer from oversimplification problems, ultimately resulting in inaccurate diagnostic results.

To surmount the constraints inherent in conventional methodologies, Neural Cognitive Diagnosis (NCD) has been proposed [11], which automatically performs cognitive diagnosis on a large amount of data by incorporating a computational model utilizing artificial neural networks to encapsulate the intricate nonlinear dynamics that occur between learners and their respective exercises, with good results. However, many challenges remain within the domain of cognitive diagnosis.

Research has shown that for a student, exercises of different levels of difficulty and differentiation have a greater impact on whether he or she is able to answer the exercises

[12]. Specifically, the likelihood of correctly answering the same task varies across students with different proficiency levels. In the case of simple and less discriminating exercises, the likelihood of providing an accurate response is greater for both lower and higher level students; in the case of complex and more discriminating exercises, the likelihood of providing an accurate response is lower for lower level students and still higher for higher level students. However, none of the mainstream methods, including IRT and DINA, can accurately obtain the relationship between students' level and the diagnostic factors of the exercises.

To overcome the aforementioned challenges, this study presents a differentiated neurocognitive diagnostic model based on student level, exercise difficulty, and discrimination (DCDM), which captures the relationship between the student factor and the exercise difficulty factor as well as the exercise difficulty factor and the exercise discrimination factor, and obtains the differentiation matching factor, which is input into the interaction function and adjusts the weight of the diagnostic factors of the exercises according to the differences at the student level.

The principal contributions of the present research are delineated as follows:

- A differentiated neurocognitive diagnostic model (DCDM) based on students' level, difficulty of exercising and differentiation is proposed to comprehensively consider the relationship between students' level and the diagnostic factors of exercises and to adjust the weights of the diagnostic factors of exercises according to the students' abilities to achieve more precise diagnostic outcomes and enhance the accuracy of cognitive diagnosis.

- A differentiation matching factor calculation module was designed to derive the differentiation matching factor by calculating the relationship between the difficulty and differentiation of the exercises as well as the students' proficiency and the difficulty of the exercises and to determine whether students can answer the exercises correctly according to their mastery of the knowledge concepts, with the aim of enhancing the veracity of the diagnostic outcomes.

- Extensive experiments were conducted on two publicly available datasets, both of which outperformed the benchmark model, confirming the validity of the model.

2 Related Work

2.1 Traditional Cognitive Diagnosis

Cognitive diagnostic models mainly originate from cognitive psychology and have achieved many results after decades of development, among which the two classic models are IRT [7] and DINA [10]. IRT assumes that the students' answers to the exercises follow an independent homogeneous distribution, articulates the cognitive condition of each student as a singular, continuous competence metric, and then combines with the characteristics of the exercises to model the students' answer situation. DINA, on the other hand, introduces the Q matrix (the association matrix of knowledge concepts of the exercises), which characterizes students' potential knowledge capabilities as a multidimensional vector of mastery over knowledge concepts, thereby ensuring the clarity and interpretability of the diagnostic outcomes.

There are many forms of IRT models, among which the more widely used is the three-parameter logistic regression IRT model, which is formulated as follows:

$$P(X_{ij} = 1|\theta_j, a_j, b_j, c_j) = c_j + \frac{1 - c_j}{1 + exp(-1.7a_j(\theta_j - b_j))} \tag{1}$$

where θ_j denotes the cognitive ability of the students, a_j is the differentiation of the test questions, b_j indicates the complexity of the examination questions, and c_j represents the guessing level of the test questions.

The explicit expression of the DINA model is delineated as follows:

$$P(Y_{ij} = 1|\alpha_i) = (1 - s_j)^{\eta_{ij}} g_j^{1-\eta_{ij}} \tag{2}$$

where η_{ij} indicates whether student i has acquired proficiency in the knowledge constructs assessed by test item j.

$s_j = P(Y_{ij} = 0|\eta_{ij} = 1)$: The probability that a student i erroneously fails to answer test question j correctly despite having assimilated essential knowledge reflects the likelihood of such an occurrence.

$g_j = P(Y_{ij} = 1|\eta_{ij} = 0)$: The probability that a student i fortuitously provides the correct response to test question j notwithstanding an absence of the pertinent conceptual understanding, delineates this particular likelihood.

$\eta_{ij} = \prod_{k=1}^{K} \alpha_{ik} q_{jk} : \alpha_{ik}$ represents the proficiency of student i in relation to the knowledge construct k, and q_{jk} denotes the examination of knowledge concepts k by the exercise j, which is derived from the Q matrix. If $\eta_{ij} = 1$, student i has attained comprehensive mastery over all the knowledge constructs evaluated in test question j. If $\eta_{ij} = 0$, student i has failed to demonstrate proficiency in all the knowledge concepts assessed in at least one instance of test question j.

The IRT model is widely used for its flexibility and accurate estimation of proficiency levels; however, it may require larger amounts of data to estimate parameters accurately and may be overly complex in some cases. The DINA model provides insight into the mastery of individual attributes, which can help educators or test designers understand a test taker's specific weaknesses; however, it is not as applicable as the IRT model to a wide range of test types, and the model may need to be adapted to fit specific test needs in particular situations.

2.2 Neural Network-Based Cognitive Diagnosis

In recent years, artificial neural networks have experienced swift advancements and considerable progress, and many fields have been well developed using neural network techniques, such as speech recognition [13] and facial recognition [14]. In recent years, several methods [6, 15] that incorporate artificial neural networks have achieved good results in educational applications. The capacity of neural networks to effectively model continuous functions has been demonstrated across the aforementioned domains, and Deep Knowledge Tracing (DKT) [16] first used a Recurrent Neural Network [17] to model the learning process of students and achieved good results. However, knowledge tracking dynamically captures the changes in students' knowledge acquisition, which is more applicable to continuous daily practice scenarios, and DKT is unsuitable for cognitive diagnosis because its primary objective is to forecast student performance; however, it does not adequately distinguish between an exercise and the fundamental knowledge concepts it embodies. Moreover, DKT does not solve the problem of poor interpretability of neural networks. For this reason, the teams of Chen, Enhong, Liu, and Qi used a neural network approach to elucidate the intricate synergies between learner attributes and exercise factor vectors and proposed interpretable neurocognitive diagnosis (NCD) [11]. Later, Tsutsumi et al. [18] combined IRT with deep learning to build a student network and an item network for better feature characterization. Tong et al. [19] proposed Incremental Cognitive Diagnosis (ICD), which uses a deep trait network (DTN) to obtain feature parameters in an inductive manner to adapt to the cognitive diagnosis needs of smart education online scenarios. Huang et al. [20] introduced a Multitask-based Group-level Cognitive Diagnosis (MGCD) framework that effectively models the relationship between group competence and individual competence across various learning contexts. Zhou et al. [21] proposed an Educational context-aware Cognitive Diagnosis (ECD) framework through an analysis of the characteristics of the educational context. Recently, Liu et al. [22] analyzed four aspects of cognitive diagnosis based on deep learning technologies: higher-order latent traits, multiple representation responses, multiple representation attributes, and multilevel latent traits. Zeng et al. [23] employed an autogenous oversight methodology to facilitate graph-theoretic cognitive assessment, thus enhancing the efficacy of learners in contexts characterized by data paucity. Wang et al. [24] proposed a model called Boosting Neural Cognitive Diagnosis with Student's Affective State Modeling (ACD), confirming that affective states are indispensable subjective factors in cognitive diagnosis models. Additionally, Zhang et al. [25] introduced a framework named FairCD, aimed at eliminating the impact of sensitive attributes on the assessment of students' mastery levels, thus achieving fairer diagnostic outcomes.

The aforementioned methods integrate cognitive diagnosis with advanced techniques, such as deep learning and multitask learning, to address the complexities of diverse educational environments and requirements. However, they fail to sufficiently account for the relationship between a student's proficiency level and the diagnostic factors of exercise, which may result in reduced accuracy of the final diagnostic outcomes.

3   DCDM Model

3.1   Overview of the Mandate

In the cognitive diagnosis-based task learning analysis task involving N students, M exercises and K knowledge concepts are denoted as $S = \{s_1, s_2, s_3...s_N\}$, $E = \{e_1, e_2, e_3...e_M\}$, and $C = \{c_1, c_2, c_3...c_K\}$, respectively. Each individual learner will autonomously elect specific exercises for engagement, subsequently obtaining an evaluative score r. The student s_i exercises e_j, and the score r can form a log R, denoted as (s_i, e_j, c).. The Q matrix is a manually labelled knowledge correlation matrix, which can be denoted as $Q = \{Q_{ij}\}_{M \times K}$, where $Q_{ij} = 1$ when the exercises contain knowledge concepts and $Q_{ij} = 1$ otherwise.

Problem Definition: Using the input log R and Q matrices, cognitive diagnostics can analyze a student's history of answering questions to predict the student's performance in future exercises. This process not only assesses students' mastery of knowledge concepts but also provides valuable feedback on the teaching and learning process.

3.2 DCDM Framework

The DCDM model framework is shown in Fig. 2, which contains three main components: the embedding module, the discriminant matching factor calculation module, and the prediction module.

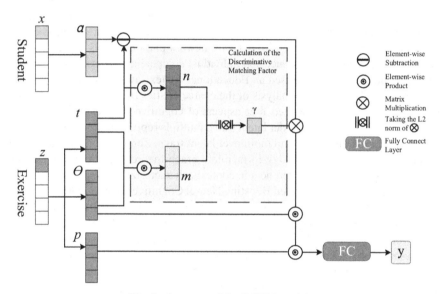

Fig. 2. Structure of the DCDM model.

Embedding Modules
On the student side, the proficiency vector of the student's knowledge concepts α is first obtained via multiplication of the student's one-hot encoding x with the trainable matrix A:

$$\alpha = sigmoid\,(x \times A) \tag{3}$$

where $\alpha \in (0, 1)^{1\times K}$, $x \in (0, 1)^{1\times N}$, and $A \in R^{N\times K}$.

In terms of test problems, the knowledge concept association vector p is obtained directly from the given Q-matrix:

$$p = z \times Q \tag{4}$$

where $p \in (0, 1)^{1\times K}$, $z \in (0, 1)^{1\times M}$, $Q \in (0, 1)^{M\times K}$, and z is the one-hot coding of the exercises.

For the other optional factors, the knowledge concept difficulty vector of the test question is derived by multiplying the one-hot encoding of the exercise, z, employing a matrix that is amenable to training, B. Additionally, the one-hot coding of the exercise, z, is obtained by multiplying the one-hot coding of the exercise with the trainable matrix, D, to obtain the exercise differentiation vector, θ. The knowledge concept difficulty vector, t, and the exercise differentiation vector, θ, are each computed by the following formulas:

$$t = sigmoid(z \times B) \tag{5}$$

$$\theta = sigmoid(z \times D) \tag{6}$$

where $z \in (0, 1)^{1 \times M}$ is the one-hot encoding of the exercise and where $B \in R^{M \times K}$ and $D \in R^{M \times K}$ are trainable matrices.

Differentiation Matching Factor Calculation Module

Usually, the differentiation and difficulty of an exercise can indirectly reflect whether students can perform the exercise correctly. For an exercise with high differentiation and difficulty, the probability that a student with poor learning ability can do so correctly will be small [26]. Therefore, the relationship between the students' level and the difficulty and differentiation of the exercises can be considered by assigning different weights to the difficulty and differentiation of the exercises depending on the students' mastery of the knowledge concepts. Therefore, the α, t, and θ obtained from the embedding module are used as inputs to this layer to calculate the differentiation matching factor. Specifically, first, the Hadamard products of t, θ and α, θ are computed to obtain the differentiation difficulty vector as well as the familiarity difficulty vector, and next, the differentiation matching factor is obtained by multiplying the Euclidean paradigms of each of the differentiation difficulty vectors as well as the familiarity difficulty vector.

The differentiation difficulty vector m and the familiarity difficulty vector n are obtained via the following equation:

$$m = t \circ \theta \tag{7}$$

$$n = \alpha \circ t \tag{8}$$

Further computation yields the discriminant matching factor γ:

$$\gamma = ||m||_2 \times ||n||_2 \tag{9}$$

where $||m||_2$, $||n||_2$ denote the Euclidean paradigms that distinguish the difficulty vector m and the familiar difficulty vector n, respectively.

Predictive Modules

In the prediction module, by fusing the student proficiency vector α, the exercise difficulty vector t, the exercise differentiation vector θ, the knowledge concept correlation vector p, the hyperparameter η, and the differentiation matching factor γ, and thus predicting the student's performance in the exercises, the specific formula is as follows:

$$x = p \circ (\alpha - t) \circ \theta \times \eta \gamma \qquad (10)$$

Applying the three fully connected layers to the results of the interaction function yields the model's predicted score for the student on exercise y:

$$f_1 = \varphi\left(W_1 \times x^T + b_1\right) \qquad (11)$$

$$f_2 = \varphi(W_2 \times f_1 + b_2) \qquad (12)$$

$$y = \varphi(W_3 \times f_2 + b_3) \qquad (13)$$

where the sigmoid function is utilized as the activation function, denoted by φ. The matrices representing the weights of the network are indicated as W_1, W_2, and W_3, whereas the biases associated with these weights are denoted by b_1, b_2, and b_3. These components are crucial for the operational dynamics and learning efficacy of the network.

To augment the explicability of the model, the hypothesis of monotonicity is incorporated. This assumption posits that an increase in the probability of a student answering an exercise correctly correlates with a higher level of knowledge acquisition. To ensure that the monotonicity assumption is upheld during the training process, we restrict each element in W_1, W_2, and W_3 to be positive.

The loss function of the model is the cross-entropy between the output y and the true label r:

$$loss = -\sum_i r_i log y_i + (1 - r_i) log (1 - y_i) \qquad (14)$$

4 Experiments

To evaluate the validity and effectiveness of the DCDM model proposed in this paper, a series of experimental studies are conducted in this section. These include a comparative experiment to assess the performance of the DCDM model against other cognitive diagnostic models, an ablation study to investigate the impact of various components of the model, a hyperparameter experiment to explore the influence of the discriminative matching factor on the results, and an explanatory experiment to determine the reasonableness of the model's diagnostic outcomes.

4.1 Dataset Description

The empirical investigations were undertaken via datasets that are accessible to the general public, ASSISTments2009–2010 [27] and FrcSub [28]. ASSISTments2009–2010 are openly accessible and amassed by the ASSISTments virtual tutoring framework, which provides more than 4,000 student responses on more than 17,000 exercises on more than 324,000 responses on exercises covering 123 knowledge concepts. FrcSub represents a publicly accessible dataset that is extensively utilized in the domain of cognitive modeling and consists of test responses from examinees on fraction subtraction problems. It provides more than 10,720 responses from more than 536 students on more than 20 exercises whose exercises cover 8 knowledge concepts. Since students can submit their answers multiple times in the online learning system, the original dataset is not conducive to static cognitive diagnosis; for this reason, the dataset is preprocessed to use only the records submitted by the students for the first time. In addition, to ensure that each student has enough data from the exercises for the diagnosis, the student records with fewer than 15 logs are deleted. Table 1 presents the statistical information of the two datasets.

Table 1. Statistical data of the dataset.

Dataset	Number of students	Number of exercises	Number of knowledge concepts	Number of answer records	Average number of knowledge concepts per exercise
ASSIST	4163	17746	123	324572	1.19
FrcSub	536	20	8	10720	2.8

4.2 Experimental Setup

The experiment partitions the student response data from the ASSISTments2009–2010 and FrcSub datasets into training and testing subsets, with an 8:2 allocation for each individual's answer record. The fully connected layer consisted of neurons in the following configuration: 512 neurons in the first layer, 256 neurons in the second layer, and 1 neuron in the output layer. The activation function was a sigmoid function, and Xavier was used to initialize all the network parameters [29]. The model is based on PyTorch implemented in Python 3.7 and trained on a standalone NVIDIA RTX3090 with a learning rate of 0.001 and an optimizer of the Adam optimizer [30]. To prevent overfitting, the model was dropout, where $p = 0.1$.

4.3 Baselines and Assessment Criteria

Baselines
To assess the validity of the model, several traditional cognitive diagnostic methods are selected to perform comparative experiments with neural network-based methods on the same dataset.

- IRT [7]: A continuous cognitive diagnostic approach that models one-dimensional student and exercise characteristics through linear functions.

- MIRT [8]: The multidimensional extension of IRT allows for the modeling of multiple levels of student knowledge and exercise parameters.
- PMF [9]: A factorization method that maps students and exercises them to low-order latent factor spaces.
- DINA [10]: A discrete cognitive diagnostic approach to modeling students' knowledge levels through binary vectors.
- NCD [11]:Modeling higher-order and complex student practice interaction functions via neural networks.
- ACECD [31]: Augmentation of exercise concepts via attentional mechanisms.

Assessment Criteria

To measure the performance of the model, the area under the ROC curve (AUC) [32], RMSE [33], and ACC [11] metrics were used.

(1) Mean Square Error (RMSE)

The Mean Square Error (RMSE) quantifies the distance between the predicted and observed scores. The formula is as follows:

$$\text{RMSE} = \frac{1}{n} \sum_{i}^{n} (y_i - \widehat{y_i})^2 \tag{15}$$

where y_i represents the actual score of the student and where $\widehat{y_i}$ indicates the predicted score of the model.

(2) Accuracy ACC

$$\text{ACC} = \frac{\text{TP} + \text{TN}}{\text{TP} + \text{TN} + \text{FP} + \text{FN}} \tag{16}$$

where TP represents the number of questions where the model accurately forecasts that students will respond correctly—specifically, instances where the model's prediction aligns with the student actually answering correctly. Conversely, FP refers to instances where the model erroneously predicts a correct answer from students, despite the actual response being incorrect. The FN captures the number of questions where the model incorrectly anticipates an incorrect response from students, yet the students answer correctly. Finally, TN denotes the cases where the model correctly predicts that students will answer a question incorrectly, which is consistent with their actual incorrect responses.

4.4 Experimental Results

Comparison Experiments with Other Cognitive Diagnostic Models

Given the inherent challenge in directly assessing the true state of students' knowledge, cognitive diagnostic models typically derive their results from estimations of the extent to which students have mastered specific knowledge concepts. Consequently, the evaluation of these models is generally conducted by contrasting their diagnostic outcomes with the students' actual performance. To evaluate the efficacy of the DCDM model, we perform a comparative analysis with a baseline model using two publicly available datasets.

Table 2 shows the results of the predictive performance and evaluation metrics of all the models on ASSISTments 2009–2010 and FrcSub. As observed in Table 2, the neurocognitive diagnostic models differentiated by student proficiency, task difficulty, and differential factors, as proposed in this study, demonstrate a significant enhancement over traditional cognitive diagnostic approaches. This improvement is attributed to the incorporation of neural networks, which facilitate the learning of intricate interactions between students and tasks. Additionally, the model introduced in this paper outperforms the NCD model to some extent, as it more comprehensively accounts for the interplay between the student's proficiency level and the characteristics of the exercises and assigns different exercise diagnostic factor weights to students of different levels according to their levels. Moreover, ACECD is also improved compared with NCD because the attention mechanism is used to augment the exercise concepts with Q-matrix correction. The model proposed in this paper is also slightly improved compared with ACECD. Specifically, the DCDM model on the ASSISTments2009–2010 dataset improves the ACC and AUC over NCD by 0.41% and 0.82%, respectively, while the RMSE is reduced by 0.33%. For the FrcSub dataset, the ACC is improved by 0.66%, the AUC is improved by 0.65%, and the RMSE is reduced by 1.07%, which proves the effectiveness of this model.

Table 2. Results of the experiment on the prediction of students' performance.

Model	ASSIST2009			FrcSub		
	ACC	RMSE	AUC	ACC	RMSE	AUC
IRT[7]	0.6643	0.4594	0.6849	0.8028	0.3850	0.8676
MIRT[8]	0.6954	0.4517	0.7090	0.8195	0.3787	0.8858
PMF[9]	0.6713	0.4782	0.7295	0.8102	0.3865	0.8774
DINA[10]	0.6496	0.4678	0.6756	0.8257	0.3733	0.8906
NCD[11]	0.7294	0.4354	0.7531	0.8275	0.3731	0.8991
ACECD[28]	0.7332	0.4237	0.7601	0.8331	0.3703	0.9012
DCDM	**0.7335**	**0.4321**	**0.7613**	**0.8341**	**0.3624**	**0.9056**

Ablation Study

To assess the efficacy of the proposed differentiation alignment factor, DCDM was compared with a version of the model in which certain modules were removed, using both datasets. In Table 3, D-m considers only the relationship between students' proficiency and the difficulty of the exercises, and D-n considers only the relationship between the difficulty of the exercises and the level of differentiation.

From the experimental outcomes presented in Table 3, it is evident that solely considering the relationship between students' proficiency and exercise difficulty or independently accounting for the connection between task difficulty and differentiation results in

Table 3. Ablation test results of the model.

Model	ASSIST2009			FrcSub		
	ACC	RMSE	AUC	ACC	RMSE	AUC
DCDM	0.7335	0.4321	0.7613	0.8341	0.3624	0.9056
D-m	0.7327	0.4332	0.7610	0.8337	0.3629	0.9049
D-n	0.7321	0.4356	0.7602	0.8331	0.3687	0.9040

a decline in predictive performance. This finding substantiates the utility of the differentiation matching factor. Incorporating the relationship between students' proficiency and the exercises proves more effective in optimizing the model, as it allows for the allocation of varying weights to task difficulty and differentiation on the basis of the students' mastery of knowledge concepts. Furthermore, accounting for the interplay between exercise difficulty and differentiation enhances the diagnostic efficacy of these tasks. Specifically, on the ASSIST2009 dataset, considering only the relationship between student proficiency and exercise difficulty alone resulted in a 0.08% decrease in accuracy, and considering only the relationship between exercise difficulty and differentiation alone resulted in a 0.14% decrease in accuracy. For the dataset FrcSub, considering only the relationship between student proficiency and exercise difficulty alone resulted in a 0.04% decrease in accuracy, and considering only the relationship between exercise difficulty and differentiation alone resulted in a 0.1% decrease in accuracy. Therefore, it is necessary to consider both the student proficiency factor and the exercise diagnostic factor.

Hyperparametric Experiments

To further investigate the impact of the discriminative matching factor on the experimental outcomes, we set a hyperparameter η for the discriminative matching factor and observe the effect of the discriminative matching factor on the experimental results by adjusting the value of η. Figure 3 represents the effect of different values of η on the diagnostic results on ASSIST2009.

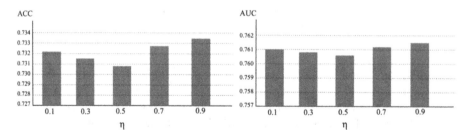

Fig. 3. Effect of η on the experimental metrics.

As shown in Fig. 3, at values of η greater than 0.5, the ACC and AUC increase with increasing values of η, which indicates that the greater the weight of the discriminant matching factor is, the better the accuracy of the final diagnostic results. For the value of η lower than 0.5, the ACC and AUC decrease with increasing η, which may be due to too much lowering of the weight of the discriminant matching factor, which reduces the influence of the exercise, a diagnostic factor, on the results.

Interpretability Analysis

To explain the interpretability of the assessment model, further experiments were performed on the ASSIST2009 dataset. From an objective concept of view, if a student demonstrates a superior comprehension of a particular knowledge concept in comparison to another student, he or she will have a greater probability of correctly answering the exercise questions about the knowledge concept c. Therefore, the degree of agreement [degree of agreement, DOA] [34] metric was used to assess the interpretability of the model. For knowledge concepts c, DOA(c) is as follows:

$$DOA(c) = \frac{1}{Z} \sum_{a=1}^{N} \sum_{b=1}^{N} \delta\left(F_{ac}^{s}, F_{bc}^{s}\right) \times \sum_{j=1}^{M} I_{jc} \frac{J(j, a, b) \wedge \delta\left(r_{aj}, r_{bj}\right)}{J(j, a, b)} \tag{17}$$

$$Z = \sum_{a=1}^{N} \sum_{b=1}^{N} \delta\left(F_{ac}^{s}, F_{bc}^{s}\right) \tag{18}$$

where F_{ac}^{s} represents student a's mastery of knowledge concept c. If student a exhibits a greater level of proficiency in the knowledge concept than student b does, then $\delta\left(F_{ac}^{s}, F_{bc}^{s}\right) = 1$; otherwise, $\delta\left(F_{ac}^{s}, F_{bc}^{s}\right) = 0$. If exercise j contains knowledge concept c, then $I_{jc} = 1$; otherwise, $I_{jc} = 0$. If both student a and student b perform the exercise, then $J(j, a, b) = 1$; otherwise, $J(j, a, b) = 0$. The diagnostic outcomes were evaluated on the basis of the mean value of the DOA (c) across all knowledge concepts.

Conventional cognitive diagnostic frameworks, exemplified by the DINA model, delineate a distinct relationship between latent traits and knowledge concepts. In contrast, the neural network-based NCD model incorporates a monotonicity assumption, thereby improving its interpretability. To evaluate the interpretability of the proposed DCDM model, a comparative analysis is conducted with the NCD, DINA, and random models, utilizing the degree of agreement (DOA) as a metric to assess students' proficiency in the knowledge concepts. The experimental results, presented in Fig. 4, demonstrate that the DCDM model not only improves the prediction accuracy but also retains interpretability.

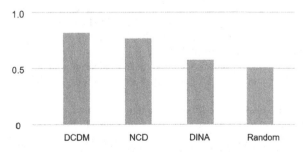

Fig. 4. DOA values of the model.

This is attributed to the incorporation of a monotonicity assumption, similar to that used in NCD, which ensures the interpretability of the DCDM model.

5 Conclusion

For students at different levels, exercises with different levels of difficulty and differentiation have a greater impact on whether they can answer the exercises, but the existing methods cannot accurately capture the relationships between students and exercise diagnostic factors. Therefore, this paper proposes a differentiated neurocognitive diagnostic model (DCDM) based on students' level, exercise difficulty and differentiation, which is divided into three modules: an embedding module, a differentiation matching factor computation module, and a prediction module. The embedding module encodes the students and exercises into embedding vectors for subsequent interactions, and the differentiation matching factor computation module assigns different weights to the difficulty and differentiation of the exercises on the basis of the students' different levels of mastery of knowledge. And differentiation according to the students' mastery of knowledge concepts, i.e., calculating the differentiation matching factor; finally, the prediction module fuses the vectors and the differentiation matching factor to obtain the final diagnostic results and simultaneously diagnoses the students' mastery of knowledge concepts in the process of training. Leveraging two empirical datasets and established benchmark models, this study demonstrates that the DCDM model exhibits superior diagnostic efficacy. Furthermore, the model ensures the interpretability of the cognitive diagnostic approach.

Acknowledgments. This work is supported by the National Natural Science Foundation of China (No. 62266054), the Major Science and Technology Project of Yunnan Province (202402AD080002), the Yunnan Fundamental Research Projects (No. 202401AT070122), the Yunnan International Joint Research and Development Center of China-Laos-Thailand Educational Digitalization (No. 202203AP140006) and the Scientific Research Foundation of the Yunnan Provincial Department of Education (No. 2023Y0534).

References

1. Carbonell, J.R.: AI in CAI: An artificial-intelligence approach to computer-assisted instruction. IEEE transactions on man-machine systems **11**(4), 190–202 (1970)
2. Liu, Q.,et al.: Fuzzy cognitive diagnosis for modeling examinee performance. ACM Transactions on Intelligent Systems and Technology (TIST), **9**(4), 1–26. (2018)
3. Leighton, J., Gierl, M.: Cognitive diagnostic assessment for education: Theory and applications. Cambridge University Press, (2007)
4. Liu, Q.,et al.: Exploiting cognitive structure for adaptive learning. In: Proceedings of the 25th ACM SIGKDD international conference on knowledge discovery & data mining, pp. 627–635, (2019)
5. Pinar, W.F.: Understanding curriculum: An introduction to the study of historical and contemporary curriculum discourses. Vol. 17. Peter lang, (1995)
6. Koren, Y., Bell, R., Volinsky, C.: Matrix factorization techniques for recommender systems. Computer **42**(8), 30–37 (2009)

7. Embretson, S.E., Reise, S.P.: Item response theory. Psychology Press, 2013
8. Chalmers, R.P.: Mirt: A multidimensional item response theory package for the R environment. Journal of statistical Software **48**, 1–29 (2012)
9. Jaeckels, J.M., Bae, M.S., Schauer, J.J.: Positive matrix factorization (PMF) analysis of molecular marker measurements to quantify the sources of organic aerosols. Environmental science & technology **41**(16), 5763–5769 (2007)
10. De La Torre, J.: DINA model and parameter estimation: A didactic. Journal of educational and behavioral statistics **34**(1), 115–130 (2009)
11. Wang, F.,et al .: Neural cognitive diagnosis for intelligent education systems. Proceedings of the AAAI conference on artificial intelligence **34**(04), 6153–6161 (2020)
12. Kocdar, S., Karadag, N., Sahin, M.D.: Analysis of the Difficulty and Discrimination Indices of Multiple-Choice Questions According to Cognitive Levels in an Open and Distance Learning Context. Turkish Online Journal of Educational Technology-TOJET **15**(4), 16–24 (2016)
13. Chan, W., Jaitly, N., Le, Q., Vinyals, O.: Listen, attend and spell: A neural network for large vocabulary conversational speech recognition. In: 2016 IEEE international conference on acoustics, speech and signal processing (ICASSP), pp. 4960–4964. IEEE, (2016)
14. Lawrence, S., Giles, C.L., Tsoi, A.C., Back, A.D.: Face recognition: A convolutional neural-network approach. IEEE transactions on neural networks **8**(1), 98–113 (1997)
15. Wen, H., Liu, Y., Zhao, N.: Longitudinal cognitive diagnostic assessment based on the HMM/ANN model. Frontiers in Psychology **11**, 2145 (2020)
16. Piech, C., et al.: Deep knowledge tracing. In: Advances in neural information processing systems, **28**, (2015)
17. Williams, R.J., Zipser, D.: A learning algorithm for continually running fully recurrent neural networks. Neural computation **1**(2), 270–280 (1989)
18. Tsutsumi, E., Kinoshita, R., Ueno, M.: Deep-IRT with Independent Student and Item Networks. In: International Educational Data Mining Society, ERIC (2021)
19. Tong, S., et al.: Incremental cognitive diagnosis for intelligent education. In: Proceedings of the 28th ACM SIGKDD conference on knowledge discovery and data mining, pp. 1760–1770 (2022)
20. Huang, J., et al.: Group-level cognitive diagnosis: A multitask learning perspective. In: 2021 IEEE International Conference on Data Mining (ICDM), pp. 210–219. IEEE (2021)
21. Zhou, Y., et al.: Modeling context-aware features for cognitive diagnosis in student learning. In: Proceedings of the 27th ACM SIGKDD conference on knowledge discovery & data mining, pp. 2420–2428. (2021)
22. Liu, Y., Zhang, T., Wang, X., Yu, G., Li, T.: New development of cognitive diagnosis models. Frontiers of Computer Science **17**(1), 171604 (2023)
23. Wang, S., Zeng, Z., Yang, X., Xu, K., Zhang, X.: Self-supervised graph learning for long-tailed cognitive diagnosis. Proceedings of the AAAI Conference on Artificial Intelligence **37**(1), 110–118 (2023). https://doi.org/10.1609/aaai.v37i1.25082
24. Wang, S., Zeng, Z., Yang, X., Xu, K., Zhang, X.: Boosting neural cognitive diagnosis with student's affective state modeling. Proceedings of the AAAI Conference on Artificial Intelligence **38**(1), 620–627 (2024)
25. Zhang, Z., et al.: Understanding and improving fairness in cognitive diagnosis. Science China Information Sciences **67**(5), 152106 (2024)
26. Kumar, M.K., et al.: Difficulty and Discriminative Ability of Core Versus Supplementary Questions—Can We Test for Competency and Excellence Simultaneously? Medical Science Educator **26**(4), 547–551 (2016). https://doi.org/10.1007/s40670-016-0329-5
27. Feng, M., Heffernan, N., Koedinger, K.: Addressing the assessment challenge with an online system that tutors as it assesses. User modeling and user-adapted interaction **19**, 243–266 (2009)

28. Ma, H., Huang, Z., Tang, W., Zhang, X.: Exercise recommendation based on cognitive diagnosis and neutrosophic set. In: 2022 IEEE 25th International Conference on Computer Supported Cooperative Work in Design (CSCWD), pp. 1467–1472. IEEE (2022)

29. Pandey, S., Srivastava, J.: RKT: relation-aware self-attention for knowledge tracing. In: Proceedings of the 29th ACM international conference on information & knowledge management, pp. 1205–1214, (2020)

30. Glorot, X., Bengio, Y.: Understanding the difficulty of training deep feedforward neural networks. In: Proceedings of the thirteenth international conference on artificial intelligence and statistics, pp. 249–256. JMLR Workshop and Conference Proceedings, (2010)

31. Yuan, D., Sun, C., Fu, P.: Concept-enhanced Cognitive Diagnosis Model Based on Attention Mechanism. Computer Science **50**(11), 241–247 (2023)

32. Kinga, D., Adam, J.B.: A method for stochastic optimization. In: International conference on learning representations (ICLR), vol. 5, p. 6. San Diego, California, (2015)

33. Pei, H., Yang, B., Liu, J., Dong, L.: Group sparse Bayesian learning for active surveillance on epidemic dynamics. In: Proceedings of the AAAI Conference on Artificial Intelligence, **32**(1). (2018)

34. Fouss, F., Pirotte, A., Renders, J.M., Saerens, M.: Random-walk computation of similarities between nodes of a graph with application to collaborative recommendation. IEEE Transactions on knowledge and data engineering **19**(3), 355–369 (2007)

Research on Strategies for Enhancing the Employment Competitiveness of Computer Science Graduates Under the School Enterprise Cooperation Model

Bing Wang[(⊠)] [iD], Ke Liang[iD], and Feng Yuan

Shandong Management University, Jinan, China
877357651@qq.com

Abstract. Employment is the foundation of people's livelihood. Graduates, as the main force in the annual job market, affect social stability. Given the rapid development of computer technology and increasingly fierce employment competition, to increase the competitiveness of computer graduates in employment, this article focuses on using the school enterprise cooperation model to help computer graduates find employment. This article analyzes the current employment situation in computer-related majors, providing insights into the employment difficulties faced by graduates. It dissects the needs of enterprises and, in combination with the school–enterprise cooperation model, develops targeted talent training strategies that align with the market demands in the computer field. This plan is implemented mainly through meeting the needs of enterprises, strengthening student participation in practical projects, optimizing course content, and establishing a school enterprise cooperation platform. The content of this study can effectively enhance the professional abilities of graduates and strengthen the core competitiveness of computer science graduates in employment.

Keywords: School Enterprise Cooperation · Computer Science Major · Employment Competitiveness · School Enterprise Cooperation Platform

1 Introduction

With the development of information technology, computer technology has become a cutting-edge force in social development. Graduates majoring in computer science, as active forces in the IT field, are influencing the development of information technology in society. However, with the rapid development of information technology, the theoretical knowledge that computer majors only learn in school cannot meet market demand, leading to difficulties in employment for such students. The employment quality of graduates directly reflects the education quality and social service ability of a university, and the university should effectively ensure the employment of students. To meet the rapidly changing demands of the times, school enterprise cooperation can effectively solve such problems. Xu Z noted that school enterprise cooperation plays an important role in the cultivation of computer professionals and that utilizing the training model of school enterprise cooperation can greatly increase students' employment competitiveness upon graduation [1]. Research by Chen F shows that university enterprise cooperation can enhance the synergistic effect of universities and promote their sustainable development [2]. However, the current school enterprise model relies mainly on enterprise personnel to give lectures and teach students simple training projects, which cannot integrate the educational resources of schools and the practical experience of enterprises deeply and cannot provide students with learning content that is more closely related to actual development work [1]. Hu B et al. reported that the depth of school enterprise cooperation in the current school enterprise training model is not sufficient and that the participation of enterprises is insufficient [3]. On this basis, this article is dedicated to researching strategies for enhancing the employment competitiveness of computer science graduates under the school enterprise cooperation model. The aim is to explore a scientific, effective, and realistic talent cultivation strategy through in-depth analysis of the current employment situation of computer science majors, the actual needs of enterprises, and the operation mode of the school enterprise cooperation model [4].

2 Analysis of the Employment Status of Computer Science Graduates

With the development of information technology and the digital economy, especially the acceleration of digital transformation, the demand for computer professionals continues to grow. The demand for professional talent with new technological capabilities, such as artificial intelligence, big data, and cloud computing, has surged in various industries. Although there is a high demand for computer talent in the recruitment market, relatively few computer talent meet the job requirements of enterprises, resulting in a mismatch between supply and demand.

According to the 2024 professional employment ranking data provided by multiple professional statistical agencies, the employment rate of computer-related majors has fallen out of the top five, and the employment rate of computer graduates has shown a downward trend. According to the analysis, this is due to the development of emerging technologies such as big data and artificial intelligence, and the knowledge that computer science students learn in school can no longer meet market demand. Therefore, except for some well-known universities, most computer science majors in universities face employment difficulties [5]. In response to this situation, some graduates majoring in computer science hold attitudes toward delayed employment, upgrading their education, changing industries, and taking civil service exams [6]. According to the "2024 Graduate Enrollment Survey Report", there will be approximately 10.84 million college graduates nationwide in 2024, with approximately 4.38 million applying for the master's degree examination. Nearly 40% of graduates choose to join the army of postgraduate entrance examination candidates.

On the one hand, graduates often encounter setbacks when searching for job positions closely related to their majors, and some students have to turn to fields unrelated to computer science for employment to find another way. On the other hand, some students choose to delay employment, hoping to compensate for their lack of knowledge and skills through further learning and improving their education, and some students, owing to factors such as employment pressure and uncertain industry prospects, have shown a negative attitude toward the job market, turning their attention to relatively stable career paths such as civil servants and public institutions, hoping to avoid employment risks by taking civil service examinations and civil service examinations [7].

3   Analysis of Demand in the Computer Employment Market

In the context of rapid development in today's society, enterprises are facing unprecedented efficiency and cost pressures, striving to achieve maximum returns with minimal investment in the shortest possible time. However, inexperienced graduates, owing to a lack of practical project development experience, contradict the demand of enterprises for immediate benefits. Therefore, when making decisions, enterprises often carefully consider the cost of human resource allocation, among which the training of new employees is seen as a task that requires time and resource investment, which may have a certain impact on the current operational efficiency of the enterprise. Therefore, when companies recruit graduates, they often not only evaluate their potential and long-term value but also weigh the cost-effectiveness ratio in the short term, explore how to effectively promote the rapid growth and integration of new employees while controlling costs, and ensure that the overall operation of the enterprise is not affected. This has led to the selection criteria for computer science graduates in enterprises far exceeding the level of pure professional knowledge mastery.

Although there are various forms of training courses in the market aimed at enhancing graduates' professional skills and competitiveness, these trainings often have difficulty replacing the valuable experience brought by real project development. Actual project development requires graduates not only to have solid professional knowledge but also to have comprehensive abilities such as problem-solving, adaptability, innovative thinking, and teamwork. The cultivation and exercise of these abilities can be fully reflected and improved only in a real project environment, which cannot be achieved through training. Enterprises are well aware that graduates who only have theory but lack practical experience often find it difficult to adapt quickly to the needs of their job positions.

According to the data provided in the "2024 Chinese Undergraduate Employment Report" by the Michelson Research Institute, undergraduate students majoring in electronic information have higher monthly incomes. As shown in the Table 1.

The data in the Table 1 indicate that electronic information majors almost dominate the top 7 in terms of monthly income rankings. However, compared with the income in 2019, the core majors of computer science and technology already exited the top 7 rankings in 2023. In addition, several majors, such as network engineering, digital media technology, information management and information systems, are outside the top 7. Moreover, artificial intelligence, big data, and electronics majors are among the top 7 majors in 2023. This shows that the current social demand is no longer a single development direction demand for computer science but rather more for the combination of computer science and high-tech majors.

Table 1. Income Ranking of Graduates in 2023 and 2019

Rank	2023		2019	
1	7756¥	Information Safety	Information Safety	7310¥
2	7151¥	Microelectronics Science and Engineering	Software Engineering	7123¥
3	7061¥	Software Engineering	Network Engineering	6857¥
4	7014¥	Data Science and Big Data Technology	Information Engineering	6798¥
5	7011¥	Electronic Science and Technology	Internet of Things Engineering	6671¥
6	6967¥	Internet of Things Engineering	Computer Science and Technology	6633¥
7	6966¥	Intelligent Science and Technology	Digital Media Technology	6267¥

4 The Problems of School Enterprise Cooperation in Computer Science Teaching

4.1 Lack of Depth in School Enterprise Cooperation

In the current situation of school enterprise cooperation in computer science, there is a common tendency toward short-term, order-based talent cultivation models. This model often leads to schools and enterprises acting independently, completing only established tasks, and lacking deep integration and communication. This cooperation model has obvious shortcomings in depth, making it difficult to truly and effectively enhance students' practical abilities.

Specifically, in terms of schools, teachers focus mainly on the development and teaching of basic theoretical courses. Although they have rich experience in the teaching field, they often find it difficult to integrate theoretical knowledge closely with practical applications due to a lack of practical project experience. In contrast, corporate teachers focus on teaching and developing practical courses. Enterprise teachers have rich practical experience, but there may be shortcomings in systematically understanding and imparting theoretical knowledge. In addition, the company has not leveraged its advantageous position. As direct participants in the computer talent market, enterprises can accurately grasp current cutting-edge and popular technologies as well as corresponding talent gaps. However, despite being well aware of these needs, companies are not direct participants in the education system or creators of talent development programs, which leads to the inability to transmit market demand. During the practical process, students may not have access to the real development projects of enterprises. Students can only participate in simulation projects, teaching cases, or simplified versions of projects. Although these projects can exercise students' skills to a certain extent, they cannot fully replicate the complexity, challenges, and uncertainties of real project development.

4.2   Lack of Breadth in School Enterprise Cooperation

In the school enterprise cooperation model, most universities choose to cooperate with SMEs, mainly local enterprises, resulting in a relatively narrow scope of school enterprise cooperation. Although local enterprises have certain convenience in terms of geography, they have many drawbacks in terms of talent cultivation. Large enterprises and industry leaders often have a grasp of the forefront of computer science, which is more advantageous for small enterprises in terms of mastering computer students' vocational skills, understanding the latest developments in computer science, and formulating career development plans. Schools can obtain the latest and most scientific talent demand information from large enterprises, making the connection between talent training and the market more close.

In the school enterprise cooperation model, most universities have the problem of relatively narrow selection of cooperative enterprises, which is manifested in the fact that a single major often only establishes cooperative relationships with one or two enterprises. Although this "one-on-one" or "few-to-one" cooperation model can achieve initial docking between universities and enterprises to a certain extent, in the long run, its cooperation has certain limitations. This type of school enterprise cooperation model often cannot fully cover the broad needs and diverse development directions of the professional field. As a discipline covering multiple directions, such as software development, network security, data analysis, and artificial intelligence, computer science requires diverse practical platforms and resource support for talent cultivation. Single enterprise cooperation has difficulty meeting the diverse needs of students in different technological paths and with career development, which limits their vision and potential.

4.3   Lack of School Enterprise Cooperation Platforms

The main reason for the disconnect between the talent cultivation goals of universities and the actual needs of enterprises is the lack of communication platforms between universities and enterprises. The foundation of cooperation between universities and enterprises is unstable, leaning toward task-based teaching, and communication between the two sides is not smooth, making effective management and practical docking difficult.

The computer science major still faces the lack of a comprehensive talent market demand analysis platform in school enterprise cooperation. The lack of this platform makes it difficult for schools and enterprises to accurately grasp market demand and technological development trends during the training process. The lack of a market demand analysis platform means that universities often rely on past experience or limited industry reports when developing teaching plans, course offerings, and practical training projects for computer majors, which may not reflect the latest changes in the market in a timely manner. This situation of information asymmetry not only leads to a disconnect between the knowledge learned by computers and the actual needs of enterprises but also makes students lack competitiveness in the job market.

5 Research on the Improvement Strategy of the School Enterprise Model

5.1 Enterprises Provide Real Practical Project Training

To meet market demand and enhance students' practical development experience, computer science students should enter into practical learning after completing theoretical courses to effectively train and improve their practical work skills and help them lay a solid foundation for development. In the school enterprise cooperation model, enterprises provide real or challenging development projects that are not core to the school, allowing students to participate under the guidance of mentors or technical personnel from the enterprise [8]. In this way, students can not only be exposed to cutting-edge technology in the industry but also accumulate practical project experience. When selecting projects, enterprises consider both the technical difficulty of the project and the level of students' abilities. Ensuring that the selected project showcases cutting-edge industry technologies while also presenting moderate challenges within the student's capabilities. In addition, enterprises and schools jointly customize and adjust projects, gradually increasing the difficulty of project practice as students grasp the progress of the project, making it more in line with market development needs [9].

5.2 Establishing a School Enterprise Cooperation Platform

The construction of the school enterprise cooperation platform mainly includes the school enterprise communication platform and the employment market demand analysis platform. Building and optimizing communication platforms in school enterprise cooperation not only requires universities to take initiative, strengthen their connections and cooperation with enterprises, and jointly develop talent training plans that meet market demand but also requires enterprises to actively participate, share industry resources, provide practical opportunities for computer students, and build communication platforms between universities and enterprises.

Using big data and artificial intelligence technology, a job market demand analysis platform is built to analyze massive amounts of recruitment information. By analyzing the names, job descriptions, and job requirements of recruitment positions, we can clearly understand the specific demand directions for computer professionals in the current market [10], such as front-end development, back-end development, artificial intelligence, big data analysis, cloud computing, network security, mobile development, and other more specific technical talent needs. The platform can reflect in real time the changes in demand and skill gaps of different technical positions in the computer industry, clearly indicating which technical talents are currently in short supply in the market and which technologies are being phased out and gradually losing competitiveness.

Through real-time data analysis, universities can quickly adjust their course offerings and teaching plans. For example, if there is a surge in demand for professional talent in fields such as artificial intelligence and big data analysis in the market, courses in these areas can be increased accordingly, or the content of existing courses can be optimized to better meet market demand. Moreover, for technologies with declining demand or imminent obsolescence, the proportion of relevant courses can be appropriately reduced to avoid resource waste and difficulties in students' future employment. Schools can also use these data to help students analyze their own strengths and market demands, guiding them to choose the technology direction that suits them for in-depth learning and development.

5.3   Benchmarking Market Demands and Optimizing Course Offerings

The connection between schools and enterprises should be strengthened, in-depth research on talent market demand should be conducted, talent market information should be analyzed, industry development trends and talent demand trends should be accurately grasped, popular cutting-edge technologies in the industry should be connected, core courses of such technologies should be incorporated into teaching plans, and students should master scarce technologies in the market. Exclude courses that are not directly related to employment or even majors and have redundant content, avoid wasting students' energy and teaching resources, and strive to provide strong support for students' employment in every course as much as possible. Taking computer science and technology as an example, in a talent training program, the main courses are focused on learning development languages, including C, Java, Python, and the web. Traditional computer development courses are too many and should adapt to the development of the times, introducing cutting-edge technology learning and even in-depth learning, such as big data, artificial intelligence and other technologies. These technologies can be seen in the "2024 China Undergraduate Employment Report" in that they are more popular among enterprises. Industry experts and corporate mentors should be invited to participate in lectures, practical project courses should be added, and students' understanding and ability to apply professional knowledge should be deepened. By optimizing and streamlining such courses, computer professionals with solid theoretical foundations and rich practical experience can be cultivated to meet the demand of enterprises for computer talent, thereby significantly enhancing students' employment competitiveness.

6   Summary

This article explores the use of improved school enterprise cooperation models to improve the employment quality of graduates majoring in computer science. By collaborating with enterprises, schools can accurately grasp market dynamics and business needs, thereby optimizing curriculum design and ensuring that teaching content covers both theoretical foundations and popular industry technologies. The school enterprise cooperation model enables students to accumulate real development experience in real work environments through joint project practices between schools and enterprises, effectively enhancing the professional competence and development ability of computer science graduates.

References

1. Xu, Z.: Research on the reform of school-enterprise cooperation teaching and education mode for computer majors. J. Contemp. Educ. Res. **8**(2), 144–150 (2024)

2. Chen, F.: Research on collaborative educational mechanism of school-enterprise cooperation in higher vocational colleges and universities based on deep learning. Appl. Math. Nonlinear Sci. **9**(1) (2024)
3. Hu, B., Zheng, J., Liu, Y.: The benefits and mode of enterprise participation in school-enterprise cooperation in vocational education. Int. J. Educ. Humanit. **8**(2), 68–71 (2023)
4. Ding, W., Wang, H.: Exploration on the talent training mode of the industry education integration and school enterprise cooperation of applied undergraduate majors. In: 2021 2nd Information Communication Technologies Conference (ICTC), pp. 348–352 (2021)
5. Qi, Mb.: Clustering mining method of college students' employment data based on feature selection. In: Liu, S., Ma, X. (eds.) Advanced Hybrid Information Processing, ADHIP 2021. LNICST, vol. 416, pp. 105–115. Springer, Cham (2022). https://doi.org/10.1007/978-3-030-94551-0_9
6. Liu, H.: Analysis and reconstruction of college students' attitude toward employment, from the perspective of university-enterprise cooperation. DEStech Trans. Soc. Sci. Educ. Hum. Sci., 342–350 (2020)
7. Shi, L., Pan, L.: Evaluation of college students' employment quality based on analytic hierarchy process. In: Proceedings of the 2020 3rd International Conference on E-Business, Information Management and Computer Science, vol. 257, pp. 02076–02079 (2020)
8. Yan, H., Yin, Q.: Research on the school enterprise cooperation training mode of big data professional engineering and technical talents. In: Proceedings of the 2021 1st International Conference on Control and Intelligent Robotics, pp. 731–735 (2021)
9. Lundberg, G.M., Krogstie, B.R., Krogstie, J.: Becoming fully operational: employability and the need for training of computer science graduates, pp. 644–651. IEEE (2020)
10. Li, W.L.: Research on personalized recommendation algorithm for college students' employment. Appl. Math. Nonlinear Sci. **8**, 1143–1154 (2023)

Research and Data Analysis of a Mobile Supervision Platform for the "Check, Protection and Promotion" of Trade Union Employees on the Basis of Big Data Management

Bing Bai$^{(\boxtimes)}$ ⓘ, Shengxian Xu ⓘ, and Feng Yuan

Shandong Management University, Jinan 250357, China
`bbingsdmu@126.com`

Abstract. Trade unions are committed to safeguarding the legitimate rights and interests of employees. The supervision of employee work safety can urge enterprises to implement safety measures, ensure that employees work in a safe environment, and reduce accident injuries. By inspecting and resolving safety hazards reported by employees in the workplace, the incidence of accidents can be reduced. The current way for union workers to check safety hazards is not real time, and related problems cannot be reflected in union staff in a timely and rapid manner, resulting in the low work efficiency of union staff. To solve the problems existing in the current way of workers checking safety hazards, this study developed a "Check, Protect and Promote" mobile supervision platform based on big data technology. The "Check, Protect and Promote" mobile supervision platform is an important means for union staff to solve safety hazards reported by employees. The platform integrates and processes the data uploaded by employees, uses big data technology to analyze the data, and finally, provides feedback on the problems so that union staff can promptly, clearly and quickly address safety hazards found in the workplace. It is an online smart platform. Existing safety hazards can be divided into several major categories. Employees who report problems can report them according to the response category, and the platform will also handle them according to the different problem categories. With the help of big data technology, the union supervision platform can speed up the resolution of problems reported by employees in real time through data integration, statistics, processing and analysis. In the future, the development of this mobile supervision platform can be widely used in the union system.

Keywords: Big Data Technology · "Check, Protect and Promote" mobile supervision platform · Data analysis · Union workers

1 Introduction

1.1 Research Background and Significance

The development of enterprises must keep pace with changes in social development, and the work of enterprise trade unions must also adapt to the requirements of the times [1]. Given the background of big data, there are still many drawbacks in the way

Chinese employees check for safety hazards. At present, the commonly used methods are registration forms or reports through WeChat public accounts, WeChat groups, QQ groups and other older methods. These methods cannot achieve real-time reporting and effective data processing, resulting in the inability to promptly and quickly reflect relevant problems to trade union staff, greatly reducing work efficiency and preventing existing problems from being solved in a timely and effective manner. WeChat public accounts and the ability to fill in registration forms have poor timeliness, which can easily lead to information transmission lags when dealing with safety hazards. There are also drawbacks in reporting hazards in WeChat groups and QQ groups. Messages are easily mixed into daily chat messages and ignored. If there are many members, the amount of information is large and complex, making it difficult for administrators to sort out information. In addition, members describe problems in different ways, and the information may be inaccurate and incomplete. Some descriptions are simple or lack key details, and some are vague, which creates obstacles to understanding and handling. These problems make it difficult to discover and report safety hazards in a timely manner, and supervision and rectification work are difficult to carry out effectively. In addition, owing to the disorderly information, it is impossible to comprehensively summarize and analyze the reported hazards, which is not conducive to the overall grasp of the hazard situation and affects the advancement of safety management.

To solve these problems, this study developed a mobile supervision platform called "Check, Protect and Promote" on the basis of big data technology [2]. This mobile client platform uses big data technology to supervise and manage safety hazards found by employees at work. It is specifically used for employees to report problems and for union staff to solve problems and provide feedback. The existing safety hazards can be divided into several categories. Employees who report problems can accurately report problems according to the corresponding categories. The statistical processing and analysis of data can accelerate the resolution of problems reported by employees in real time and improve the efficiency and level of solving safety hazards in the workplace.

1.2 Related Work

At present, various types of mobile supervision platforms are being developed, and their functions and target groups are more targeted so that problems arising at work can be solved more quickly and conveniently.

Author, Li. And others proposed a big data-driven comprehensive supervision platform framework to address the problem of mobile source supervision. By integrating multisource heterogeneous data and building a big data center, a closed-loop traceability supervision decision-making system for the entire life cycle was formed through business collaboration and data mining to improve the level of mobile source supervision [3]. With the help of technologies such as mobile smart terminal control and audio–visual data collection, Skyway designed a new generation of universal supervision platform to meet the needs of Android and iOS application dissemination statistics and program monitoring, effectively improving the efficiency of audio–visual program supervision in the mobile internet era [4]. Author L. and Author T. built a "blockchain + big data" supervision platform architecture and designed a scheme to address the three major problems existing in traditional food supervision. Through algorithm design, intelligent analysis and one-click alerts have been achieved, changing post event recovery to prevent warning, thus reducing food safety hazards [5].

Internationally, research on mobile monitoring platforms is based mainly on practical applications. Apte et al. demonstrated that mobile monitoring can generate insights into air pollution exposure, which can be externally verified by a variety of other analytical methods [6]. The system developed by Rodriguez-Valero Natalia et al. has been demonstrated to be a real-time monitoring platform for detecting symptoms that may exist in tropical imported diseases, especially arbovirus diseases, which helps to prepare for the introduction of vector-borne diseases in nonendemic countries [7]. Kuo, Chi-Cheng developed a mobile monitoring system with an embedded image capture rotating platform and a dedicated short-range communication (DSRC) transceiver for real-time monitoring of remote environments from a mobile terminal [8].

Therefore, this study developed a "Check, Protect and Promote" mobile supervision platform to enable employees to promptly report safety hazards in the workplace and to promote the efficiency of trade union staff in solving and handling problems reported by employees to better realize the trade union supervision function and facilitate the smooth progress of safe production.

2   Design

2.1   Platform Overview

The "Check, Protect and Promote" mobile supervision platform is based on big data technology and has built an efficient safety hazard handling mechanism. The platform is based on the big data processing process, including the collection and reporting of problem data, in-depth processing and classification integration, and finally feedback of the processing results to the reporting end. Its main purpose is to provide employees with a convenient and efficient way to report problems and ensure that safety hazards can be quickly and properly resolved.

As a real-time problem reporting system, this platform has shown significant advantages in problem discovery and reporting and has greater timeliness and convenience. The platform uses big data technology to classify common safety hazards and build a complete data classification system. When employees use the platform to report problems, they can make accurate choices on the basis of the preset problem type options. This design greatly facilitates back-end staff. Back-end staff can quickly start the corresponding processing process on the basis of the problem type, effectively improving the efficiency of problem solving.

In addition, the platform also has a reporting result query function, where employees can view relevant information about their previously reported problems, including the status of the problem, such as resolved, reported, or resolved. At the same time, the platform also has an information push function, which can push union news and provide union employees with a window to keep up to date with the latest union developments, further expanding the platform's application value and information dissemination function and allowing the platform to play a more comprehensive role in safety supervision and information exchange.

2.2   Data Collection and Preprocessing

Data preprocessing and calibration eliminate noise, outliers and redundant information in the data through cleaning, integration, transformation and other means to make the data more standardized, complete and consistent [9]. Given that the data collected by trade unions come from a wide range of sources, are complex and lack uniformity, data processing is challenging. Under big data technology, data problems need to be handled in a refined manner. For data deduplication, appropriate algorithms are used to compare key information such as hazard descriptions, locations, times, etc., one by one, identify and retain unique records, and avoid duplication of information interfering with subsequent analysis. For invalid data, reasonable screening rules are used, such as defining data with missing hazard types or discovery times as invalid and verifying or removing them to ensure that the data are complete and valid. For erroneous data, a data range and logical verification mechanisms are constructed to identify them. For example, if the discovery time is unreasonable or the hazard level label exceeds the limit, they are corrected or deleted after judgment.

After completing data cleaning, safety hazard data are classified by hazard type (electrical, fire protection, mechanical equipment and other safety categories) and danger level (high, medium, low), and in-depth analysis is carried out to count the number and proportion of safety hazards of different types and levels, analyze the distribution characteristics and trends, and fully explore the value of data to assist trade unions in safety management decision-making.

2.3   Security Issues of Sensitive Data on the Platform

To ensure the security of sensitive employee data on the platform, this study takes measures at both the technical and management levels. In terms of technology, the AES encryption algorithm is used to encrypt data storage and transmission to ensure the confidentiality of data in all links. Moreover, a data backup and recovery mechanism is established to prevent data loss. In terms of management, a strict data access permission system is formulated to clarify the access permissions of personnel at different levels, and only authorized personnel can access and process relevant data. For example, ordinary union staff can access and process only general hidden danger information, whereas senior management personnel can access and process data involving sensitive information.

2.4   K-means Cluster Analysis

We use the K-means clustering analysis algorithm [10] for the data collected via the "Check, Protect and Promote" mobile supervision platform. The K-means clustering analysis algorithm facilitates the analysis of the internal structure and patterns of data. It can group similar data into clusters, making it easier to analyze the characteristics and differences of each cluster. It helps to discover abnormal points or outliers in the dataset, providing direction for further in-depth analysis of uploaded security risks.

Randomly select K initial centroids:

$$C_1, C_2, \ldots, C_k \qquad (2\text{-}1)$$

Given a dataset:

$$X_1, X_2, \ldots, X_n \tag{2-2}$$

Euclidean distance: This calculates the distance between two points in Euclidean space:

$$D_{ed} = \sqrt{\sum_{k=1}^{m}\left(X_{ik} - X_{jk}\right)^2} \tag{2-3}$$

Objective function:

$$J = \sum_{i=1}^{n}\sum_{j=1}^{k} r_{ij}\left\|X_i - C_j\right\|^2 \tag{2-4}$$

where r_{ij} indicates whether X_i belongs to cluster j.

By assigning each data point to the nearest centroid to form K clusters and then calculating the centroid of each cluster, which is the average value of all the data points in the cluster, this operation is continuously iterated to classify the platform data.

3   Design

3.1   Demand Analysis

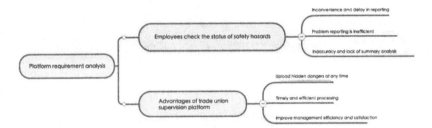

Fig. 1. Demand analysis diagram

At present, employees face many inconveniences in troubleshooting safety hazards, such as untimely reporting, which leads to low utilization rates of human, material and financial resources. Manual troubleshooting of safety hazards is inefficient; on the one hand, there is a certain degree of error, and on the other hand, there is a lack of effective summary analysis of reported hazards. In view of this, adopting a trade union supervision platform is highly important. Through this platform, employees can upload the problems they find or the existing safety hazards at any time, and then, the trade union management personnel will address them in a timely and efficient manner according to the type of problem. With the help of such an intelligent manual supervision and management platform, the work efficiency of trade union management can be significantly improved, problems can be detected and solved in a timely manner, and employee satisfaction can be improved (Fig. 1).

3.2 Platform Features

The "Check, Protect and Promote" trade union supervision platform provides a convenient and fast service platform for employees to discover safety hazards, report problems in a timely manner, and effectively solve problems. This platform is a real-time problem reporting system. After users discover safety hazards, they promptly report them from the platform in a classified manner. Managers use the information reported in the background to hand over different types of hazards to personnel who specialize in handling such problems. This allows trade union staff to handle hidden dangers more quickly and efficiently. The mobile platform also provides news about the trade union, allowing users to understand the latest relevant information about the trade union. The three functional modules of problem reporting, reporting results, and trade union news provide users with a convenient user experience and improve the efficiency of problem solving (Fig. 2).

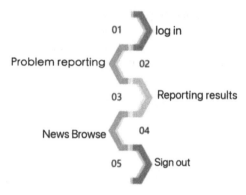

Fig. 2. Overview of main functions

Report a Problem

The problem reporting module includes problems related to unsafe behavior, rights protection, equipment, management, production, etc. The overall process is shown in Fig. 3. According to the type of problem that occurred, the corresponding problem is clicked, and then the event detail interface will appear. In this interface, the applicant needs to fill in the name of the problem, which should be concise and highlight the key points of the problem. The applicant and the reporting unit should fill in the name truthfully as a criterion. In the detailed description of the problem, it is necessary to write in detail the time, specific location, degree of urgency at the time, and surrounding environmental conditions of the problem. The content is clear and organized so that the backstage staff can respond as soon as possible. If the problem that occurs is not in the type of problem prompted, you can click the " + " sign in the upper right corner of the problem reporting interface and fill in the new application interface step by step according to the prompts.

Reporting Results

In the reporting result module, the processing results of the problem submitted by the

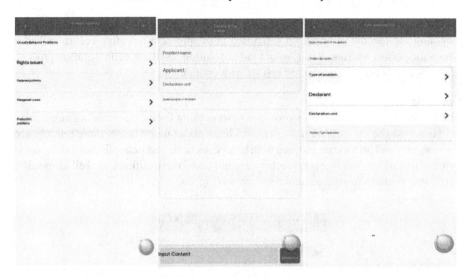

Fig. 3. Problem Reporting Process

user in the problem reporting module are displayed (as shown in Fig. 4). The results are displayed in the following three types:

1. This means that the background has received the information and that the relevant personnel are investigating the authenticity of the information.
2. This means that the investigators have determined the authenticity of the information and have made solutions to the problem. The user only needs to wait for the results.
3. This means that the problem has been handled in a timely manner and that there is no similar problem at present.

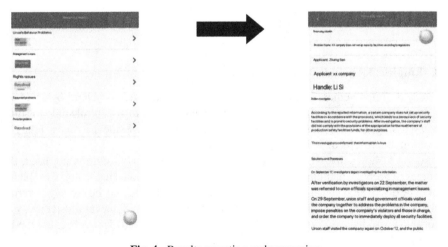

Fig. 4. Results reporting and processing

The corresponding processing situation is given in the processing result module, including the specific information submitted in the problem reporting before and adds who is the person who handles it, what kind of solution and the specific solution process. Thus, users can see the processing results with confidence.

Union News

The union news function mainly provides news reading for users, including news about unions across the country, so that users can learn about union deeds more quickly and conveniently and provide employees with timely, accurate and rich information. It covers union activities such as rights protection, training, and competitions, as well as industry trends and changes in policies and regulations (Fig. 5).

Fig. 5. Union News Interface

3.3 Empirical Analysis

To study the improvement in the efficiency of processing reported problems by using the K-means cluster analysis algorithm, this study conducted a group control study to study the processing time and accuracy before and after using the K-means cluster analysis algorithm, the results of which are shown in Fig. 6.

Figure 6 shows that when the K-means cluster analysis algorithm is not used, the accuracy of problem handling is low. This is because the traditional reporting of problems cannot be discovered and handled in a timely manner, and there may be message overlap in the group chat, resulting in a decrease in accuracy. After the K-means cluster analysis algorithm is used, the accuracy of problem handling is improved. This is because the K-means cluster analysis algorithm classifies safety hazards according to actual conditions and categories, making it easier for union employees to address related safety hazards in a targeted manner.

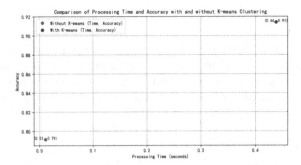

Fig. 6. Efficiency comparison before and after use

We use the probability of safety hazards as the horizontal axis and the risk of safety hazards as the vertical axis. We use the K-means cluster analysis algorithm to study the degree of harm of various safety hazards and improve the efficiency of union workers in solving various safety problems reported by enterprise employees through the algorithm. There are dozens of different safety hazard risks in the actual processing and receiving process, such as electrical safety hazards, mechanical equipment safety hazards, height operation safety hazards, chemical safety hazards, fire safety hazards, traffic safety hazards, and environmental safety hazards. However, to specifically demonstrate the effect of the K-means cluster analysis algorithm in solving various safety hazards, we take electrical safety risks, fire safety hazards, and mechanical equipment safety hazards as examples to demonstrate its effectiveness.

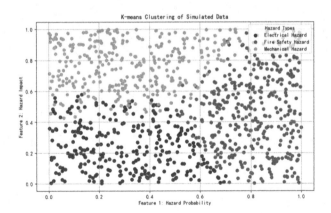

Fig. 7. K-means cluster analysis diagram

As shown in Fig. 7, the effect of using the K-means cluster analysis algorithm for classification is relatively good. Different safety hazard categories are classified in a targeted manner, which helps union employees to clearly address the safety hazard issues involved and promotes safe production.

4 Conclusion

In the process of project development, this study makes full use of big data technology, focuses on the problems currently faced by employees when investigating safety hazards, and classifies and processes relevant data. By building a reasonable data classification system in the platform, it aims to solve safety hazard-related problems more efficiently and with higher quality. On this basis, the "Check, Protect and Promote" mobile supervision platform was successfully developed.

Moreover, this study refers to the concise and refined design principles of social platforms such as WeChat and QQ. Given that the platform is aimed at a large group of employees, we are committed to making the application design simple and easy to understand to lower the threshold for employees to use it. In terms of interface design, we carefully planned and started from the perspective of visual aesthetics, hoping to present a delicate and beautiful interface effect and enhance the user experience.

In addition, this study will continue to improve the platform. On the one hand, we will pay close attention to new problems that may arise and optimize system functions in a timely manner; on the other hand, we will continue to improve the interactive interface and focus on enhancing the user's emotional experience during use, making them feel friendly and friendly, and finally creating a product with complete functions, a beautiful interface and excellent user experience.

Acknowledgments. This work is partially supported by Shandong Province Financial Application Key Research Project "Research on Financial Support for the Coordinated Development of Shandong Regional Spatial Layout and Rural Revitalization Strategy", Project No.: 2021-JRZZ-17.

References

1. Author, W.: Analysis on how to do a good job in trade union management under the new situation. In: Collection of Papers on Typical Cases of Excellent Party Building in the National Power Energy Industry, p. 1. Guoneng Shaanxi New Energy Power Generation Co., Ltd. (2024)
2. Author, L., Author, Z.: A review of big data technology research. J. Zhejiang Univ. (Eng. Sci.) **48**(06), 957–972 (2014)
3. Author, S.: Research on universal mobile audio-visual application supervision platform. Digit. Media Res. **39**(09), 70–76 (2022)
4. Author, L., Author, T.: Research on food safety supervision big data platform based on blockchain. Food Ind. **43**(05), 341–346 (2022)
5. Author, L., Author, L., Author, L., et al.: Research on the comprehensive supervision platform of mobile sources driven by big data. In: Chinese Society of Environmental Sciences. Proceedings of the 2020 Annual Conference of Science and Technology of the Chinese Society of Environmental Sciences, vol. 1, p. 5. Guangzhou Yunjing Information Technology Co., Ltd. (2020)
6. Apte, J.S., et al.: Scalable multipollutant exposure assessment using routine mobile monitoring platforms. Res. Rep. (Health Eff. Inst.) **2024**, 216 (2024). 51–54

7. Rodriguez-Valero, N., et al.: Mobile based surveillance platform for detecting Zika virus among Spanish Delegates attending the Rio de Janeiro Olympic Games. PLoS ONE **13**(8), e0201943 (2018)
8. Kuo, C.C., Weng, W.L., Li, P.R., Tsai, K.C., Mar, J.: A mobile surveillance system implemented with an embedded image capturing rotation platform and dedicated short range communications system. Adv. Sci. Lett. **8**(1), 469–473 (2012)
9. Author, L., Author, Z., Author, W., et al.: Research on data preprocessing and calibration analysis methods based on cloud model theory. In: Systems Engineering - Theory and Practice, pp. 1–19, 27 October 2024
10. Zhimin, H., Chengdong, L.: Grade evaluation data analysis based on K-means clustering algorithm. Electron. Qual. **2023**(12), 40–44 (2023)

Research on the Investigation and Cultivation of Online Autonomous Learning Abilities Among Students Majoring in Russian in Higher Vocational Education

Mian Zhao[✉], Yu Yan, and Lingxu Xiao

Sanya Aviation and Tourism College, Sanya 572000, Hainan, China
330733524@qq.com

Abstract. In the context of the information age, nurturing the online autonomous learning abilities of students majoring in Russian is crucial for enhancing the Russian language application skills of students in higher vocational education. Through a questionnaire survey, this paper explores the status of online autonomous learning in Russia among first- and second-year students in the Russian department of a higher vocational college. It analyzes the existing problems and offers targeted suggestions for teachers to cultivate students' autonomous learning abilities in their instruction.

Keywords: Online study · Higher Vocational Russian major students · Self-learning in Russian · Learning strategies

1 Introduction

Compared with students from undergraduate institutions, vocational college students majoring in Russian generally have weaker self-learning abilities. Due to the limitations of the academic system, their on-campus learning time is short, and most students start with no prior knowledge of Russian. As a result, achieving the level required to pass the Russian Public Level 4 exam within less than three years has always been a challenge in vocational Russian education. In the era of "Internet+" education, computer-assisted teaching has further expanded educational pathways from the perspective of "external environments." [1] Classroom instruction by teachers is no longer the only way for students to learn. Students can access abundant Russian learning resources online, unrestricted by time and space, to acquire language knowledge and improve their language skills. Teaching practice has shown that guiding students to use online resources during the learning process can indeed change their attitudes toward learning, transforming them from passive to active learners. [2] Therefore, cultivating students' habits and abilities for autonomous online learning of Russian is of great significance for improving their language proficiency, enhancing their overall quality, and raising the quality of talent cultivation.

This study targets first- and second-year students from the Russian department of a certain higher vocational college, aiming to comprehensively understand the situation of autonomous online Russian learning among higher vocational Russian students. It analyzes existing problems and proposes corresponding countermeasures. The goal is to offer constructive suggestions for the teaching of higher vocational Russian teachers, thereby consciously and purposefully cultivating the online autonomous learning abilities of students majoring in Russian in higher vocational education.

2 Research Design

2.1 Survey Design

This study is based on constructivist learning theory and humanistic psychology theory. After reviewing relevant domestic and international research papers on autonomous learning, the questionnaire on the current situation of autonomous English learning abilities among secondary vocational business English students in the "Internet + Education" context, compiled by Liao Jinlian, was reviewed. This questionnaire is adjusted according to the actual situation of Russian major students at our school. The main body of the questionnaire consists of 26 questions covering six dimensions: the learning environment, learning objectives, learning resources, learning strategies, learning monitoring, and learning evaluation. The score is based on a 5-point Likert scale ranging from "never like this," "rarely like this," "sometimes like this," "often like this," to "always like this," with "never like this" scored as 1 and "always like this" scored as 5.

2.2 Survey Participants

The participants were first- and second-year students from the Russian department of a certain higher vocational college. The questionnaires were completed during class and collected on the spot. A total of 130 students participated in the survey. After excluding some invalid questionnaires, 100 valid questionnaires were obtained, including 51 from first-year students and 49 from second-year students.

2.3 Reliability and Validity Analysis of the Survey Questionnaire

This study conducted reliability and validity analyses of the collected questionnaires via SPSS to determine whether the results of the questionnaire were reliable and stable, thereby ensuring the reliability and validity of the questionnaire.

Reliability Analysis. This study used Cronbach's alpha coefficient as the reliability indicator. Cronbach's alpha is widely used in academia as an indicator to evaluate the internal consistency reliability of a questionnaire. Its formula is as follows:

$$\alpha = \frac{k}{k-1}\left(1 - \frac{\sum S_i^2}{S_X^2}\right)$$

The value range of Cronbach's alpha is $0 \leq \alpha \leq 1$. A higher value of (α) indicates a higher degree of interitem correlation and better internal consistency reliability. In practice, $\alpha \geq 0.9$ generally indicates an extremely high level of internal consistency for the questionnaire, $\alpha \geq 0.7$ indicates a good level of internal consistency, $0.5 \leq \alpha \leq 0.7$ suggests that the questionnaire is valuable and acceptable but should undergo significant modifications, whereas $\alpha \leq 0.5$ indicates poor internal consistency, suggesting that the questionnaire is of low value and should be rejected.

The survey questionnaire was divided into six dimensions: external conditions, learning objectives, learning resources, learning strategies, learning monitoring, and learning evaluation. The Cronbach's alpha values for each dimension of the questionnaire, as analyzed through SPSS, are shown in Table 1.

Table 1. Cronbach's α value of internal consistency in the questionnaire for autonomous Russian language learning on the internet.

Projects	Cronbach's alpha value	Number of items	Sample
External conditions	0.859	5	100
Learning Objectives	0.950	3	100
Learning Resources	0.644	3	100
Learning Strategies	0.965	9	100
Learning to Monitor	0.911	3	100
Learning Evaluation	0.935	3	100
Overall Assessment	0.965	26	100

Validity Analysis. Validity refers to the extent to which the differences in measured values among the subjects surveyed reflect the true differences in values; that is, it reflects the effectiveness of the questionnaire.

The validity of the questionnaire focuses mainly on the analysis of construct validity. Construct validity evaluates whether the correlations among observable variables are consistent with theoretical predictions, and it is generally considered the most robust indicator of validity. Through SPSS analysis, the construct validity of this questionnaire is shown in Table 2.

Table 2. KMO and Bartlett's tests

Sampling sufficient KMO metric		0.924
Bartlett's test for sphericity	Approximate cardinality	3159.884
	df	325.000
	Sig.	0.000

Exploratory factor analysis revealed that the KMO value is 0.924, which is significantly greater than 0.6. The Sig value (i.e., P value) corresponding to Bartlett's test of sphericity is 0.000, which is less than 0.05. The results of Bartlett's test of sphericity indicate that the data meet the criteria for factor analysis, suggesting that the construct validity of this questionnaire is good.

In summary, the survey questionnaire used in this study has good reliability and validity.

3 Survey Results Analysis

3.1 External Conditions

Carrying out online autonomous learning requires good hardware and software facilities, as well as effective guidance from teachers. According to the survey results, as mobile phones and the internet are now widely available, the hardware facilities for online self-learning can generally be guaranteed, and students have basic information-searching capabilities. However, the use of information technology teaching platforms in teachers' instruction is not sufficient, and there is a lack of guidance for students in the use of the internet for autonomous Russian language learning (Table 3).

Table 3. External conditions

Question	Sample size	Average value	Standard deviation
1. I have smooth-running internet devices	100	4.160	0.820
2. I am familiar with the basic operations of the internet and can easily search for the required information	100	3.890	0.737
3. I can easily access the internet at school, home, and public places	100	3.850	0.892
4. Our teachers often recommend online Russian learning resources to us	100	2.780	0.799
6. All of our teachers use information technology teaching platforms such as Smart Vocational Education during class, upload Russian learning materials, and interact with students on the platform	100	2.840	0.884

3.2 Learning Goals

Humanistic teaching theory posits that the first step in autonomous learning should be setting reasonable learning objectives to help students meet their needs for self-actualization. Clear and reasonable objectives are the premise for effective learning. From the perspective of learning objectives, the responses to Q7 and Q8 are close to

Table 4. Learning Objectives

Question	Sample size	Average value	Standard deviation
7. Before studying online, I have clear self-learning content, learning progress, and time arrangement	100	2.480	0.847
8. Even when I have started learning Russian on the internet, I still have clear learning goals	100	2.440	0.857
9. I can set short-term or long-term Russian learning goals	100	3.380	0.885

"rarely like this," and the response to Q9 tends to "sometimes like this," indicating that students' goals for autonomous Russian language learning are not sufficiently clear and defined (Table 4).

Regarding the question "What are your reasons for autonomously learning Russian in an online environment?" The options most selected by the students were "expanding knowledge" (71%), "Exam requirements" (59%), "creating a language environment, improving language skills" (54%), and "completing tasks assigned by teachers" (53%). This finding indicates that students have a demand for autonomous Russian language learning online and possess certain motivations, but their learning objectives are still not clear and precise.

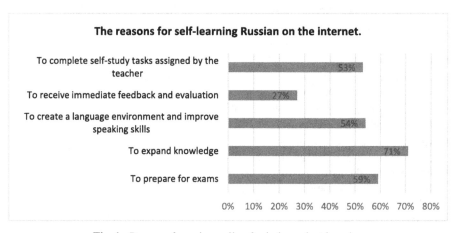

Fig. 1. Reasons for going online for independent learning

3.3 Learning Resources

In terms of learning resources, students are aware that many resources are available online and possess a certain ability to search for them. However, the ability to obtain useful resources from the vast amount of information on the internet and to fully utilize these resources still needs to be improved (Table 5).

Table 5. Learning Resources

Question	Sample size	Average value	Standard deviation
5. I think there are many Russian learning resources online, and they are updated quickly	100	3.520	0.822
10. I like to use online resources such as songs, movies, short videos, and online courses to learn Russian	100	2.470	0.846
11. Too much online information can hinder me from finding the online learning resources I want	100	3.200	0.829
12. I am able to filter useful information from the vast and disordered internet according to my needs, obtain materials related to specific topics, and make full use of the resources obtained	100	2.070	0.913

With respect to the question "Which internet software or platforms have you used to learn Russian," the most selected option by students is online dictionaries (86%), which are primarily used for vocabulary lookup and translation, followed by short video platforms such as TikTok (51%). The use of other online resources is relatively limited.

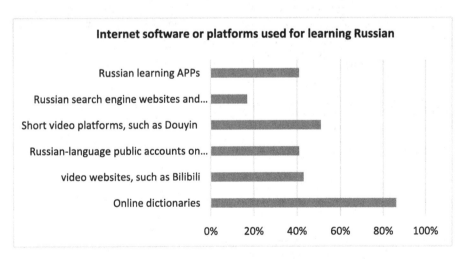

Fig. 2. Internet platforms and software used to learn Russian

3.4 Learning Strategies

This section incorporates questions designed on the basis of the foreign language learning strategies proposed by Rebecca L. Oxford. Oxford categorizes foreign language learning strategies into direct strategies and indirect strategies, with direct strategies including memory strategies, cognitive strategies, and compensation strategies and indirect strategies including metacognitive strategies, affective strategies, and social strategies [3].

The survey questionnaire, which was tailored to the actual situation of the students, selected memory strategies, cognitive strategies, metacognitive strategies, and social strategies as the objects of investigation. Memory strategies refer to effectively storing language information through the use of association, imagery, recording, and other

Table 6. Learning Strategies

Learning Strategies	Question	Sample size	Average value	Standard deviation
Memory Strategies	14. I increase my vocabulary through Russian internet resources	100	2.53	0.797
Cognitive Strategies	15. I practice listening through Russian language resources on the internet	100	2.45	0.833
Cognitive Strategies	16. I practice speaking and improve language expression through online Russian learning resources	100	2.42	0.843
Cognitive Strategies	17. I subscribe to and watch online Russian language videos to reinforce what I have learned in class and to expand my knowledge	100	2.46	0.797
Cognitive Strategies	21. I read short Russian texts on the internet to improve my reading	100	2.42	0.855
Metacognitive strategies	18. I use online learning channels to help myself find ways to learn Russian well	100	2.55	0.809

(continued)

Table 6. (*continued*)

Learning Strategies	Question	Sample size	Average value	Standard deviation
Metacognitive strategies	19. I take the initiative to find Russian language learning resources through online channels	100	2.54	0.797
Social Strategy	20. I ask my teacher or classmates to recommend good websites or materials for learning Russian	100	3.46	0.892

skills; cognitive strategies involve practicing, receiving, and transmitting information, analyzing and reasoning, and establishing corresponding rules for the input and output of information; metacognitive strategies include setting learning priorities, arranging, planning, and evaluating the learning process and outcomes; and social strategies involve asking questions and collaborating with others.

According to the survey results, students seldom use learning strategies in autonomous Russian language learning online, mainly falling into the categories of "sometimes like this" or "rarely like this" (Table 6).

By conducting an independent sample t test on first-year and second-year students, the results show that there is no significant difference in learning strategies between the two grades. Overall, students lack awareness of learning strategies, and teachers should provide more guidance in this area.

Table 7. Independent sample t test for first- and second-year students

Learning Strategies	Question	What grade level are you in? (Mean ± Standard Deviation)		t	p
		Second Year	First Year		
Memory Strategies	13. I will increase my vocabulary through Russian internet resources	2.75 ± 0.89	2.44 ± 0.75	1.739	0.085
Cognitive Strategies	14. I will practice listening through Russian language resources on the internet	2.46 ± 1.04	2.44 ± 0.75	0.092	0.927

(*continued*)

Table 7. (*continued*)

Learning Strategies	Question	What grade level are you in? (Mean ± Standard Deviation)		t	p
		Second Year	First Year		
Cognitive Strategies	15. I will practice speaking and improve language expression through online Russian learning resources	2.46 ± 1.04	2.40 ± 0.76	0.286	0.777
Cognitive Strategies	16. After school, I subscribe to and watch online Russian language videos to reinforce what I have learned in class and to expand my knowledge	2.57 ± 0.84	2.42 ± 0.78	0.871	0.386
Cognitive Strategies	17. I will use online learning channels to help myself find ways to learn Russian well	2.61 ± 0.88	2.53 ± 0.79	0.439	0.662
Metacognitive strategies	18. I will take the initiative to find Russian language learning resources through online channels	2.61 ± 0.88	2.51 ± 0.77	0.524	0.602
Metacognitive strategies	19. I will ask my teacher or classmates to recommend good websites or materials for learning Russian	3.57 ± 0.92	3.42 ± 0.88	0.777	0.439
Social Strategy	20. I will read short Russian texts on the internet to improve my reading	2.61 ± 0.96	2.35 ± 0.81	1.371	0.173

3.5 Learning Monitoring and Evaluation

Rogers' humanistic teaching theory proposes that the main steps of autonomous learning include setting goals, making plans and choosing strategies, and monitoring and evaluating the implementation of learning. According to the survey results, for questions related to learning monitoring and evaluation, students' responses tend to be "rarely like this." It is evident that students lack effective monitoring and evaluation when engaging in autonomous Russian language learning online, struggle to persist with their goals in the long term, rarely evaluate and reflect on their learning, and do not establish closed-loop management for online autonomous learning, making their online autonomous learning rather arbitrary (Table 8).

Table 8. Learning monitoring and evaluation

Project	Question	Sample size	Average value	Standard deviation
Learning Monitor	21. In the process of independent study of Russian online, I will adjust my study plan according to the actual needs of the learning situation	100	3.410	0.877
	22. I will evaluate my learning of Russian in the online environment and identify weaknesses and measures for improvement	100	2.450	0.796
	23. When I find that my current study method is not appropriate, I will adjust it in time	100	2.510	0.759
	24. After setting goals and plans for independent study of Russian online, I will put them into action and stick to them for a long time	100	2.440	0.795

(continued)

Table 8. (*continued*)

Project	Question	Sample size	Average value	Standard deviation
Learning Evaluation	25. I will summarize my learning at a certain stage and reflect on my progress and shortcomings	100	2.490	0.798
	26. I will regularly participate in the internet learning assessment system to evaluate the effectiveness of my independent study of Russian online	100	2.470	0.861

4 Teaching Suggestions

Owing to the lack of motivation among vocational students and the overwhelming amount of information available online, there are many issues with independent professional learning through the internet in the absence of effective guidance. These issues include unclear learning objectives, low resource acquisition and utilization, a lack of learning strategies, insufficient self-monitoring, and a lack of reflection and evaluation in learning. As a result, relying solely on students to learn aimlessly online makes it difficult to ensure effective learning outcomes. This situation requires teachers to consciously guide and supervise students in using online resources and AIGC tools to reinforce and expand their knowledge, thereby compensating for insufficient classroom teaching hours and cultivating students' self-directed learning abilities and lifelong learning skills. Therefore, the following suggestions are made for teachers in their teaching practices:

4.1 Focus on Student-Centered Classroom Teaching to Foster Students' Initiative in Learning

It is essential to adhere to a student-centered approach by employing methods such as task-driven activities and flipped classrooms to engage in exploratory learning. This approach mobilizes students' subjective initiative, allowing them to discover and create knowledge and expand their capabilities through their own subjectivity, initiative, and independence. The goal is to transform the traditional "I am taught" into "I want to learn," shifting the acquisition of knowledge from teacher-led instruction to student-led discovery and construction.

4.2 An Online Learning Resource Library is Built to Cultivate Information Retrieval and Utilization Skills

Teachers should integrate information technology with curriculum teaching more extensively, making full use of online educational platforms such as Yunbanke, Zhihuizhijiao (ICVE), and Zhihuishu (Treenity) to establish online learning resource libraries. These libraries should include recorded teaching videos, presentations, exercises, tests, and links for further knowledge expansion. By adopting a blended "online and offline" teaching approach, students can be trained to independently use the resource library and develop their information retrieval and utilization skills.

4.3 Adhere to Goal Orientation to Guide and Assist Students in Setting Effective Learning Goals and Plans

At the beginning of each semester, students assess their Russian language proficiency, including vocabulary, grammar, reading, listening, and speaking skills. Teachers should guide students to set realistic learning goals and plans on the basis of their actual Russian language levels, including independent study plans. Students should utilize their spare time to fully leverage the resources available on learning platforms and online, addressing weaknesses in their Russian language skills.

4.4 Focus on Monitoring and Evaluation to Enhance the Effectiveness of Online Independent Learning

Teachers should effectively utilize the monitoring and evaluation functions of information-based teaching platforms to oversee students' independent online learning. This involves understanding and tracking students' progress and learning status with resources, enhancing communication and interaction with students on the platform, promptly addressing their questions, and providing timely evaluations of their learning outcomes. Additionally, teachers can guide students in the use of popular generative AI tools for interactive learning. AIGC possesses intelligent Q&A and natural language processing capabilities, enabling it to answer students' questions in real-time both during and after class. [4] Generative AI can offer instant feedback; point out errors in pronunciation, grammar, or comprehension; and provide suggestions for improvement, making it an ideal tool for self-assessment, reflection, and monitoring in learning.

4.5 Interest Groups Should Be Organized for Learning to Foster a Cooperative Spirit in Online Self-Directed Learning

Learning interest groups are a distinctive "second-classroom" activity at our school. By conducting a series of related learning interest activities led by subject teachers during spare time, students' enthusiasm for learning, creativity, and team cooperation can be enhanced. Therefore, it is beneficial to fully utilize learning interest groups to carry out online self-directed learning activities, such as adding subtitles to videos, dubbing videos, shooting Russian language videos, and establishing and maintaining Russian language learning social media accounts. This fully mobilizes students' team cooperation spirit, collectively utilizing online resources to learn Russian.

Acknowledgments. Project supported by the Education Department of Hainan Province A study on the policy and practice of English curriculum thinking in higher vocational education based on the SPOC mixed teaching model, Project number: Hnjgzc2022−112.

References

1. Zhu, G., Tong, W.: Research on autonomous learning models for German as a foreign language learners in the internet context. J. Zhejiang Ocean Univ. (Humanit. Soc. Sci. Ed.) **38**(6), 81–86+90 (2021)
2. Zhang, Y.: Utilizing online resources to cultivate students' self-learning abilities in Russian language teaching. J. Jilin Prov. Educ. Coll. **25**(10), 86–87 (2009)
3. Liao, J.: Investigation and study on the English independent learning ability of middle-level business English students in the context of "Internet+ education". Jilin University of Foreign Studies (2022). https://doi.org/10.27833/d.cnki.gjlhw.2022.000034
4. Sun, J.: AIGC empowers teaching reform in application-oriented undergraduate classrooms: A case study of the "Principles and Applications of Big Data Technology" course. Off. Autom. **29**(19), 45–47 (2024)

A Study on the Use of Fitness Apps for Extracurricular Physical Exercise Among Chinese University Students: A Case Study of a University in Yunnan

Jian Cai[1], Qingling Wang[2(✉)], and Qingyu Yang[1]

[1] School of Education, Yunnan College of Business Management,
Kunming 650106, Yunnan, China
[2] School of Foreign Languages, Yunnan Normal University, Kunming 650500, Yunnan, China
2316207767@qq.com

Abstract. To improve the physical fitness of college students, the government has implemented a series of measures, including the promotion of "Sunshine Sports" and physical fitness testing. This study investigates the usage of fitness and exercise apps among college students in Yunnan, explores their motivations for using these apps or their reasons for not using them, and identifies issues encountered by students in the process. Using methods such as a literature review, questionnaire surveys, and statistical analysis, this study surveyed 412 university students (from freshmen to seniors) at a university in Yunnan. The findings indicate a high adoption rate of fitness apps among students, who are primarily used for fitness improvement, weight loss, and exam preparation. However, most students engage in extracurricular sports activities infrequently; academic workload and lack of willpower are primary barriers to their participation in sports activities. Additionally, many students lack awareness of the importance of warm-up and cooldown routines. The most frequently used features include exercise planning, step counting, and GPS tracking. However, inaccuracies in GPS positioning and feedback data are common issues faced by students. This study suggests that universities should encourage students to engage in physical activities and that teachers can promote sports safety awareness and integrate fitness apps into physical education curricula. Students may learn to manage their time effectively to balance academics and exercise, and developers should enhance GPS reception and optimize app functionalities, incorporating more innovative features.

Keywords: Use of Fitness Apps · Extracurricular Physical Exercise · University Students

1 Introduction

To improve the physical fitness of university students, the Chinese government has implemented a series of measures. In 2007, the General Administration of Sport of China and the Ministry of Education jointly issued the "National Sunshine Sports Program for

K. Zhang et al. (Eds.): CSEI 2024, CCIS 2447, pp. 135–150, 2025.
https://doi.org/10.1007/978-981-96-3735-5_11

Millions of Students," which requires all levels of government to carry out sunshine sports activities and ensures that 85% of students engage in at least one hour of exercise daily, thereby encouraging them to participate in physical activities and improve their health [1]. In 2014, the Ministry of Education issued the "National Student Physical Health Standards (Revised 2014)," which mandated physical fitness tests for all enrolled undergraduate students and stipulated that only those who passed the fitness test were eligible to receive their graduation certificate [2]. To meet the annual fitness test standards, students choose various ways to engage in physical exercise. In recent years, fitness applications (apps) have become among the most popular methods of exercise among students.

This study aims to survey the basic usage of fitness apps among university students in Yunnan, explore the motivations behind their use as well as the reasons for not using fitness apps, and identify the problems encountered by students during the use of fitness apps. The goal is to provide more scientific and convenient exercise methods for university students in Yunnan, improve their physical fitness and health levels, and deepen the reform of physical education in universities.

2   Literature Review

In recent years, with the increasing use of fitness apps for physical exercise among university students, scholars have also conducted research in this area. The relevant studies have focused on how fitness apps cultivate healthy lifestyles among university students, how such apps promote their physical fitness, and how they manage their health behaviors.

2.1   Fitness Apps Promote Healthy Living Habits Among University Students

Research on university students' use of mobile fitness apps and their relationships with healthy lifestyles has received some attention. Guo and Choi, through their research on university students' extracurricular activities, noted that most students use fitness apps to help achieve their fitness goals and that these apps play an important role in shaping healthy lifestyles among university students [3]. Ma et al. reached a similar conclusion: Chinese university students have a high usage rate of mobile fitness apps, and the use of these apps is positively correlated with their healthy lifestyles [4]. However, Mollee et al. reported that most students track and socially share fitness results. Other features are used less frequently, and designers should further improve the apps to meet the personalized and diverse needs of university students, thereby promoting the development of healthy lifestyles [5].

2.2   Fitness Apps Promote University Students' Health

Jabour et al. reported that students in health-related colleges primarily use apps for fitness and calorie tracking. Younger users are more likely to continue using and promoting these health apps, considering the large-scale promotion of such apps among young people an effective strategy for preventing obesity and diabetes [5]. Through experiments, Gianluca et al. discovered that university students who engage in daily exercise via fitness apps have significantly better cardiopulmonary function than those who do not use these apps do, demonstrating the positive impact of these apps on physical health [6].

2.3 The Role of Fitness Apps in Managing University Students' Health Behaviors

Lin CT et al.'s research further confirmed that fitness apps can effectively manage individual physical activities by encouraging individuals to participate in exercise and thus influencing their health behaviors [7]. Güner et al. noted that the widespread use of tablets and smartphones may facilitate the adoption of fitness apps, helping to regulate personal lifestyles, diet, and exercise behaviors. This is particularly beneficial for patients who need lifestyle changes, as the frequent use of these apps can improve their adherence and enhance health behavior outcomes [9].

In summary, more studies have focused on fitness apps in relation to university students' health and lifestyles, on the functionality of fitness apps and their role in improving and managing physical health. Studies indicate that fitness apps play a positive role and have great potential in promoting health and managing health behaviors, and they are widely adopted among university students. However, the use of app features remains imbalanced, highlighting the need for continuous optimization and innovation.

A literature search revealed no specific studies on the use of fitness apps among university students in the border province of Yunnan, China. Yunnan has unique geographical characteristics, with diverse topographies, primarily consisting of plateaus, rich ethnic cultures, and distinctive climatic conditions, which provide new scenarios and challenges for the daily application of fitness apps. Additionally, there is a lack of research focusing on the problems users encounter when using fitness apps, leaving room for further study. Thus, the study of the motivation and problems of sports apps among university students in Yunnan Province can offer new perspectives and ideas for research in this area.

3 Methodology

3.1 Research Participants

A total of 379 university students, ranging from freshmen to seniors, participated in the study, which focused on the use of fitness apps at a university in Yunnan. All participants were undergraduates of nonphysical education majors, the majority of whom were aged between 18 and 24. Over half of the participants (62.27%) were female, whereas the remaining 37.73% were male. Among the students, 68.87% were Han Chinese, and 31.13% were ethnic minorities. Additionally, all the participants owned at least one smartphone (Tables 1 and 2).

3.2 Research Method

This study employs a questionnaire survey method. The questionnaire "Survey on the Usage of Fitness Apps for Extracurricular Sports Activities among Undergraduates",

Table 1. Survey Results of the Basic Information of the Students (N = 379)

Gender	Participants	Percentage
Male	143	37.73%
Female	236	62.27%
Total	379	100%

Table 2. Survey Results of the Students' Basic Information (N = 379)

Ethnicity	Participants	Percentage
Han	261	68.87%
Ethnic Minorities	118	31.13%
Total	379	100%

which starts with basic information and progressively delves into students' usage of fitness apps, exercise habits, workout effectiveness, and user feedback, was designed. The questions are designed from closed-ended questions (multiple choice) to open-ended questions, gradually guiding users to express more specific opinions and feelings. The questions in the questionnaire cover various aspects, including user background, usage patterns, exercise habits, workout effectiveness, and student feedback, which helps to comprehensively understand the usage of fitness apps. A total of 412 questionnaires were distributed to freshmen through senior students at a university in Kunming, Yunnan, via Sojump, with a total of 412 questionnaires collected, resulting in a response rate of 100%. Among these, 379 were valid responses, resulting in a validity rate of 91.99%.

Mathematical statistics, descriptive statistics and cross-analyses were conducted through Sojump to obtain data analysis results, which provide accurate and effective data support for investigating university students' use of fitness apps for extracurricular physical exercise, their motivations, influencing factors, and existing problems.

3.3 Reliability and Validity Tests of the Questionnaire

This study used the test-retest reliability method by distributing the questionnaire "Survey on the Use of Fitness Apps in Undergraduate Extracurricular Physical Exercise" to a randomly selected sample of 30 university students. Four weeks later, the same questionnaire was distributed again to the same group of students. The results from both tests were analyzed via SPSS 22.0, yielding R = 0.82 (P < 0.05), indicating that the questionnaire has good reliability.

To ensure the rationality and validity of the "Survey on the Use of Fitness Apps in Undergraduate Extracurricular Physical Exercise" questionnaire, nine expert professors were invited to evaluate the questionnaire. On the basis of their suggestions, revisions were made to the questions, and the final version of the questionnaire was established.

Table 3. List of Expert Professors for Questionnaire Validity Evaluation (N = 9)

Title	Professor	Associate Professor	Lecturer
Participants	3	5	1

Table 4. Expert validity evaluation form (N = 9)

Is the questionnaire reasonable	Very reasonable	Fairly reasonable	Reasonable	Unreasonable	Very unreasonable
Questionnaire Content Design Evaluation	0	0	9	0	0
Questionnaire Structure Design Evaluation	1	1	7	0	0
Questionnaire Logical Structure Evaluation	0	3	6	0	0
Overall Design Evaluation	0	2	7	0	0

Table 3 lists the expert panel members who evaluated the validity of the questionnaire. Table 4 shows the evaluation form used to assess the questionnaire's validity. This questionnaire strictly followed the basic requirements of sports research and was repeatedly revised on the basis of suggestions from the expert panel. The final evaluation results from the experts indicate that the questionnaire has good validity.

4   Results and Suggestions

4.1   Results

Usage of Fitness Apps Among University Students in Yunnan
Number of Students Using Fitness Apps (Table 5 and Fig. 1)
The survey results shown in the table indicate that 308 students, accounting for 81.27%, use fitness apps for extracurricular physical exercise, whereas 71 students, accounting for 18.73%, do not use fitness apps for this purpose. This indicates that fitness apps have a relatively high rate of adoption and acceptance among the student population (Table 6 and Fig. 2).
Sports Activities Students Engage in Using Fitness Apps

Table 5. Survey Results of the Number of Students Using Fitness Apps (N = 379)

Do you use fitness apps for extracurricular physical exercise?	Participants	Percentage
Yes	308	81.27%
No	71	18.73%
Total	379	100%

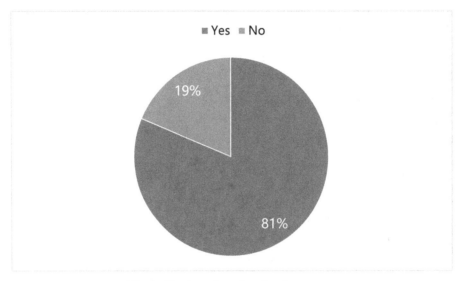

Fig. 1. Number of people using fitness apps

Table 6. Statistics of Sports Activities Students Engage in Using Fitness Apps (N = 308)

Activities	Participants	Percentage
Running	277	89.94%
Ball Sports	88	28.57%
Fitness	97	31.49%
Dance	28	9.09%
Yoga	29	9.42%
Martial Arts	20	6.49%
Jump Rope	70	22.73%
Cycling	61	19.81%
Others	74	24.03%

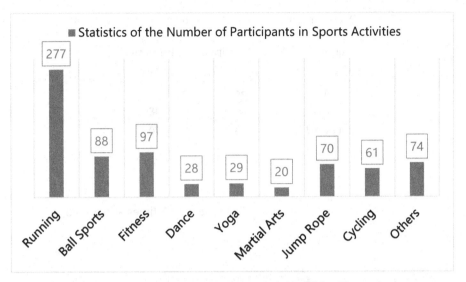

Fig. 2. Number of Participants in Sports Activities Using Fitness Apps

The data in the table clearly indicate that running is the most popular activity, with 277 participants, accounting for 89.94% of the total. Running is favored by students because of its simplicity, lack of special equipment requirements, and suitability for all ages and fitness levels. In addition to running, other sports also demonstrate a high degree of diversity in terms of participation. Ball sports, fitness, jump rope, and cycling each have a significant number of student participants, indicating that students value diversity and fun in their exercise routines. Ball sports and fitness have similar participation rates, with rates of 28.57% and 31.49%, respectively. Students who enjoy ball sports tend to use the app to watch training videos, technique analysis, and match information, whereas fitness enthusiasts use the app to learn workout techniques, create personalized fitness plans, receive dietary advice, and track progress. Jump rope and cycling, as aerobic exercises, attracted 22.73% and 19.81% of the students, respectively. Students use fitness apps to accurately record various data, such as the number of jumps, duration, and number of calories burned, as well as cycling speed, distance, and elevation. On the basis of the recorded data, students can assess their performance and adjust their exercise plans for better results. Although activities such as dance, yoga, and martial arts have fewer participants, a considerable number of students choose them. Through the app's community features, students share their training experiences, achievements, and knowledge, making connections with like-minded individuals. Additionally, 24.03% of the students chose "Other," which includes less commonly listed activities, highlighting the wide range and personalization of students' exercise choices (Table 7 and Fig. 3).

Frequency of University Students' Use of Fitness Apps

According to the "Basic Standards for Physical Education in Higher Education Institutions," universities should organize that students participate in extracurricular physical activities at least three times a week, ensuring that students engage in one hour of exercise each day. The data in the table indicate that 23.70% of the students exercised five

Table 7. Weekly frequency of students' use of fitness apps (N = 308)

Frequency	Participants	Percentage
0 times	37	12.01%
1–2 times	138	44.81%
3–4 times	60	19.48%
5 times and above	73	23.70%
Total	308	100%

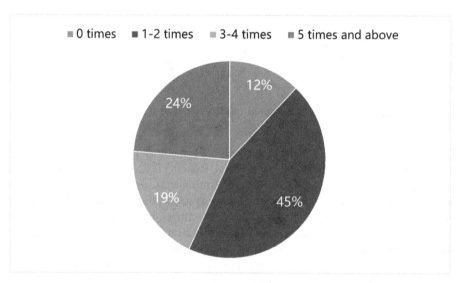

Fig. 3. Weekly frequency of students' use of fitness apps

or more times per week, whereas 19.48% exercised 3–4 times per week. More than half of the students failed to meet the standard of participating in extracurricular physical activities at least three times per week, with the highest percentage of students exercising only 1–2 times per week. This shows that although most students are aware of the importance of physical exercise, relatively few consistently engage in extracurricular physical activities three or more times per week. Despite their recognition of the importance of exercise, the actual percentage of students who follow through on this knowledge is quite low, indicating that the participation rate in extracurricular physical activities among university students is far from ideal. Clearly, under such circumstances, students' weekly exercise levels are insufficient, and many have not yet developed good exercise habits (Fig. 4).

Functions of Fitness Apps Used by Students

As shown in Table 8, exercise plans are the most frequently used feature of fitness apps, accounting for 57.47% of the total valid responses. This is followed by step counting and GPS tracking, which have relatively high usage rates of 50.65% and 50.32%, respectively.

Table 8. Statistics of functions used by students in fitness apps (N = 308)

Functions	Participants	Percentage
GPS Tracking	155	50.32%
Event Notifications	39	12.66%
Step Counting	156	50.65%
Exercise Plans	177	57.47%
Diet Plans	61	19.81%
Video Tutorials	69	22.40%
Calorie Consumption Tracking	126	40.91%
Others	38	12.34%

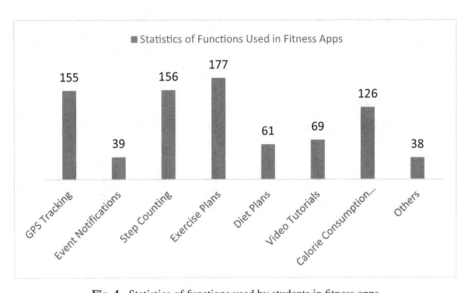

Fig. 4. Statistics of functions used by students in fitness apps

Calorie consumption tracking and video tutorials are used by 40.91% and 22.40% of the students, respectively, whereas diet plans and event notifications have lower usage rates, at 19.81% and 12.66%, respectively. This finding indicates that most students use fitness apps to encourage themselves to maintain regular physical activity and to track their exercise data (Table 9 and Fig. 5).

Factors Influencing the Use of Fitness Apps among University Students in Yunnan
Analysis of Students' Motivation for Using Fitness Apps
The data in the table indicate that the top motivation for students using fitness apps is to enhance physical fitness, accounting for 71.43% of the total. This shows that most students have a reasonable purpose for participating in physical exercise, with improving physical health as their primary goal. The second most common motivation was

Table 9. Survey results of students' motivation for using fitness apps (N = 308)

Motivation	Participants	Percentage
Enhance Physical Fitness	220	71.43%
Weight Loss and Body Shaping	153	49.68%
Exam Requirements	132	42.86%
Hobbies and Interests	122	39.61%
Exercise for Stress Relief	105	34.09%
Recreation and Entertainment	60	19.48%
Others	35	11.36%

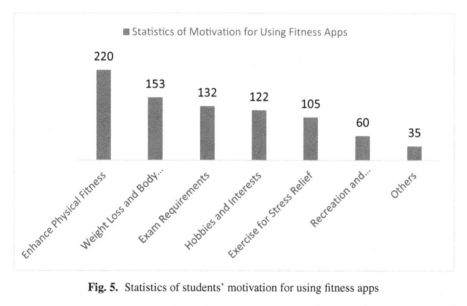

Fig. 5. Statistics of students' motivation for using fitness apps

weight loss and body shape, accounting for 49.68%. As students' aesthetic awareness increases during their university years, some begin to realize the importance of fitness and body shaping, making extracurricular physical exercise a key way for them to achieve better body appearance. Weight loss and body shape thus become among the main driving forces for their participation in physical activities. The third-ranked motivation is exam requirements, accounting for 42.86%. According to the "National Student Physical Health Standards (Revised 2014)" issued by the Ministry of Education, university students must meet the physical fitness standards and complete the required physical education credits to be eligible for graduation. This regulation has prompted many students to actively engage in extracurricular physical exercise in hopes of achieving excellent results in fitness tests. Hobbies and interests ranked fourth, accounting for 39.61%, with some students using these apps simply because they enjoy sports. They take pleasure in the fun that exercise brings or use the apps to explore new ways of exercising and challenges. The fifth is exercise for stress relief, accounting for 34.09%. Given the increasing "involution" phenomenon in China, university students face tremendous pressure in their studies, lives, and thoughts. To alleviate this anxiety and tension, many students choose physical exercise as a positive coping mechanism. Finally, recreation and entertainment, as well as other reasons, account for 19.48% and 11.36%, respectively. Regardless of the reason students engage in physical exercise, the result is improved physical fitness and health (Table 10 and Fig. 6).

Key Factors Limiting Students' Use of Fitness Apps for Extracurricular Physical Exercise

Table 10. Statistics of factors limiting students' use of fitness apps for extracurricular physical exercise (N = 308)

Influencing factor	Participants	Percentage
Heavy Academic Workload	148	48.05%
Lack of Equipment and Facilities	87	28.25%
Personal Equipment Limitations	77	25.00%
Lack of Willpower	180	58.44%
Lack of Exercise Atmosphere	122	39.61%
Lack of Encouragement	98	31.82%
Influence of Online Games	63	20.45%
Others	49	15.91%

The data presented in the table clearly reveal that multiple factors affect students' participation in extracurricular physical exercise. The main factors include a heavy academic workload, lack of willpower, absence of an exercise-friendly atmosphere, lack of encouragement, limitations in equipment and facilities, and personal equipment constraints. Among the objective factors, the most significant is heavy academic workload, accounting for 48.05%. Among the subjective factors, the highest is the lack of willpower, accounting for 58.44%, with the absence of an exercise-friendly atmosphere also accounting for a considerable proportion.

Heavy academic workload and a lack of willpower are the main obstacles preventing students from participating in extracurricular physical activities. As educational competition intensifies and course content increases, students need to spend significant time

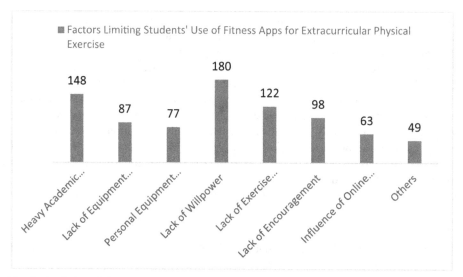

Fig. 6. Statistics of factors limiting students' use of fitness apps for extracurricular physical exercise

and effort on their studies, which often takes away from the time available for exercise. Although many students are aware of the importance of physical exercise, they lack sufficient self-discipline and willpower to maintain a regular exercise routine. They lack clear exercise goals and self-discipline and are easily distracted by other temptations.

Ultimately, the true factor affecting students' participation in physical exercise is their will. If students have enough willpower and self-discipline and set achievable exercise goals, regardless of how demanding their academic workload is or how limited their space and equipment may be, they will still be able to utilize fragmented time and limited space to engage in physical activities.

Analysis of Issues Faced by University Students While Using Fitness Apps

Table 11. Students' Warm-up Routine Before Exercising with Fitness Apps (N = 308)

Do you warm up before exercising?	Participants	Percentage
Yes	114	37.01%
No	194	62.99%

From the data analysis in Table 11, it is evident that 62.99% of the students did not perform an adequate warm-up before exercising with fitness apps, whereas only 37.01% of the students did. Warm-up is a crucial step before exercise, as it increases the temperature of muscles and joints, making them more flexible and reducing the risk of muscle strains, ligament injuries, and other exercise-related injuries. It also helps relax muscles,

Table 12. Students' Stretching and Relaxation Routine After Exercising with Fitness Apps (N = 308)

Do you stretch after exercising?	Participants	Percentage
Yes	92	29.87%
No	216	70.13%

improves blood circulation, and reduces the load on muscles, effectively minimizing postexercise muscle soreness.

According to the data in Table 12, 70.13% of the students do not perform adequate cool-down and stretching after exercising with fitness apps, whereas only 29.87% of the students indicate that they stretch and relax after exercising. Performing proper cool-down and stretching postexercise is also very important, as it speeds up blood circulation, helps disperse lactic acid, and reduces muscle soreness and fatigue. It can also prevent muscle cramps and localized injuries, reducing discomfort after exercise. Additionally, it helps decrease muscle adhesion, improves muscle function, and prevents exercise-related injuries.

In summary, more than half of the students lacked awareness of the importance of warm-up and stretching before and after exercising with fitness apps. This increases the likelihood of students experiencing exercise-related injuries during workouts and muscle soreness afterward (Fig. 7).

Analysis of Issues with Fitness Apps During Student Use

Table 13. Issues encountered with fitness apps during student Use (N = 308)

Issues	Participants	Percentage
Poor Interaction Between the Software and User	108	35.06%
Inaccurate Feedback Data	123	39.94%
Inaccurate GPS Positioning	137	44.48%
Low Efficiency in Resolving App Issues	97	31.49%
Others	70	22.73%

Students encounter various issues to some extent while using fitness apps. According to the data analysis in Table 13, the most common issue is inaccurate GPS positioning, accounting for 44.48%, followed by inaccurate feedback data, accounting for 39.94%. The third most reported issue is poor interaction between the software and the user, accounting for 35.06%, and last, low efficiency in resolving app issues, at 31.49%.

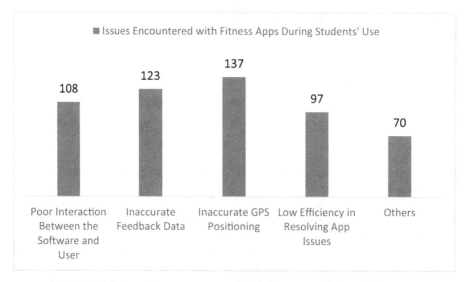

Fig. 7. Statistics of issues encountered with fitness apps during student use

4.2 Suggestion

On the basis of the survey of students' use of fitness apps for physical exercise and the analysis of related issues and causes, the following recommendations are proposed:

To motivate students to engage in physical exercise through reward mechanisms or sports competitions, schools should regularly organize various sporting events, fitness challenges, and sports festivals to inspire student participation. By encouraging competition, students can be motivated to actively engage in physical activities, ultimately developing the habit of exercising at least three times a week.

Enhance awareness of sports safety in physical education courses: Teachers should emphasize the importance of warm-ups, cool-downs, and other essential safety knowledge in sports to help students develop good exercise habits and reduce the risk of injuries.

Fitness apps can be incorporated into physical education curricula: teachers can introduce and use fitness apps in class, guiding students in how to use these apps to create workout plans, record exercise data, and analyze progress. This will help make fitness apps valuable tools for both in-class and extracurricular activities.

Learn to manage time effectively and balance academics with physical exercise: Students should make the most short breaks, lunch hours, or evenings for simple exercise. By setting clear academic and exercise goals and managing time wisely, students can use fitness apps to plan and monitor their fitness routines.

Set clear fitness goals: Students can use fitness apps to set personalized goals, such as daily running distances or calorie consumption, on the basis of their physical condition and fitness needs. These apps can help monitor and track progress, boosting a sense of achievement and motivation for long-term exercise.

Optimize app functionality: Improving the user experience by enhancing technical precision, app interactivity, and problem-solving efficiency. Key features such as workout plans, step counting, and GPS tracking should be optimized to ensure data accuracy and ease of use.

A GPS signal reception module is developed to increase the GPS signal reception capability, advanced positioning technologies are used, and auxiliary tools such as Wi-Fi positioning are incorporated to improve accuracy and reliability. The positioning algorithm is refined, and the app and its map data are regularly updated.

Introduce more innovative features: Develop more personalized content in fitness apps, such as customized workout recommendations, dietary advice, progress tracking, social interaction, and event notifications.

5 Conclusion

This study provides an in-depth understanding of the use of fitness apps among university students at a certain university in Yunnan. It was found that fitness apps have a high adoption rate among students, with running being the most popular activity. Other sports, such as ball games, fitness training, jump rope, and cycling, also had significant effects, indicating students' need for diverse exercise options. The main motivations for students to use fitness apps were to increase their physical fitness, lose weight, and meet exam requirements, reflecting their strong focus on health, appearance, and academic demands. However, most students did not exercise three or more times per week, indicating that although they are aware of the importance of physical exercise, their actual participation in extracurricular physical activities remains low and requires further guidance.

Heavy academic workload and a lack of willpower are the main factors hindering students from engaging in extracurricular physical activities, highlighting challenges related to academic pressure and self-discipline. Most students lack awareness of the importance of warming and cooling before and after exercise, which may increase the risk of injuries and muscle soreness, necessitating enhanced education on these topics. The most frequently used features were workout plans, step counting, and GPS tracking, reflecting students' need for fitness data monitoring and personalized fitness plans. Issues with inaccurate GPS positioning and feedback data were common, suggesting that there is room for improvement in terms of the app's technical precision and user experience.

Universities are recommended to stimulate students' enthusiasm for participating in physical exercise through reward systems or sports competitions. Teachers should strengthen safety awareness in physical education classes and consider incorporating fitness apps into the curriculum. Students should learn to plan their time reasonably, balance academics and physical exercise, and set clear workout goals. Developers are advised to improve GPS signal reception, optimize app functionality, and introduce more innovative features.

The data and conclusions above were derived from a study conducted at a single university, so there may be certain limitations.

References

1. Ministry of Education, General Administration of Sport of China, Communist Youth League Central Committee. Notice on Fully Launching the National Sunshine Sports Program for Millions of Students (Document No. 6 of the Ministry of Education, 2006), 12 (2006)

2. Ministry of Education. Notice on the Issuance of the "National Student Physical Health Standards (Revised 2014)" (Document No. 5 of the Ministry of Education, 2014), 7 (2014)
3. Guo, Q., Choi, K.: A study on the role of sports APP in building a healthy lifestyle of college students. In: 4th International Conference on Culture, Education and Economic Development of Modern Society (ICCESE2020) (2020)
4. Ma, G., Shi, Y., Ju, H., et al.: Usage of mobile fitness apps among university students and its relationship with healthy lifestyles. Chin. J. Sch. Health **45**(08), 1131–1135 (2024)
5. Mollee, J., Middelweerd, A., Kurvers, R., et al.: What technological features are used in smartphone apps that promote physical activity? A review and content analysis. Pers. Ubiquit. Comput. **21**, 633–643 (2017)
6. Jabour, A.M., Rehman, W., Idrees, S., et al.: The adoption of mobile health applications among university students in health colleges. J. Multidiscip. Healthc., 1267–1273 (2021)
7. Rospo, G., et al.: Cardio respiratory improvements achieved by American college of sports medicine's exercise prescription implemented on a mobile app. JMIR mhealth and Health **4**(2) (2016)
8. Lin, C.T., Shen, C.C., Mao, T.Y., et al.: Empirical investigation of sports management, behavior growth and usage of sports APP: new learning perspective. Polish J. Manag. Stud. **19**(1), 225–234 (2019)
9. Güner, P.D., Bölükbaşı, H., Kokaçya, S.H., et al.: Mustafa Kemal University students' use of mobile health applications. Konuralp Med. J. **10**(3), 264–268 (2018)

A Study on a Blended Learning Assessment Model in the Context of the Digital Transformation of Education a Case Study of a "University Computer Fundamentals" Course at Yunnan Normal University

Fei Ren[1], Juan Chen[2(✉)], and Tianyu Xie[1]

[1] Key Laboratory of Educational Informatization for Nationalities, Yunnan Normal University, Kunming, China
[2] School of Information Science and Technology, Yunnan Normal University, Kunming, China
2752208074@qq.com

Abstract. The digital transformation of education has driven the exploration of innovative assessment models for Blended Learning. This study aims to develop a comprehensive Blended Learning evaluation model based on Blockchain Technology to enhance student learning assessment and secure data management. Using the University Computer Fundamentals course at Yunnan Normal University as a case study, this model evaluates Blended Learning across three stages: pre-class, in-class, and post-class. It integrates multiple dimensions, including teaching effectiveness, satisfaction, and learning outcomes, providing a transparent and multidimensional assessment framework. Key findings indicate that the proposed model improves the efficiency, accuracy, and security of learning assessments in Blended Learning. This study contributes to the digital transformation of educational assessments, suggesting future research directions to further refine Blended Learning evaluation methods.

Keywords: Digital transformation in education · blended learning · evaluation of learning · blockchain

1 Introduction

The rapid digital transformation in education has introduced cloud computing, artificial intelligence, and blockchain into instructional methods and assessments, reshaping educational practices globally. In recent years, the integration of Blended Learning has grown, blending face-to-face and online teaching methods to enhance accessibility and engagement. However, current Blended Learning evaluation models often face challenges, including a lack of comprehensiveness, insufficient real-time feedback, and limited accuracy and transparency.

This study aims to address these issues by leveraging Blockchain Technology to create a transparent, secure, and decentralized Blended Learning evaluation model.

Using the University Computer Fundamentals course at Yunnan Normal University as an example, the model evaluates Blended Learning outcomes through multiple dimensions, including teaching effectiveness, student and teacher satisfaction, and knowledge mastery rates. This approach not only strengthens the reliability and traceability of educational assessments but also improves the efficiency and accuracy of student learning evaluations.

By focusing on a practical application, this study contributes to the advancement of Blended Learning evaluation practices, providing a reference model for enhancing educational assessments in the digital era.

2 Related Research Work

2.1 Background of the Study

In recent years, technologies such as blockchain, big data and cloud computing have brought about significant changes to human production, life and ways of thinking, and have also affected the development of the education system, with the education sector shifting from the traditional models of paper-based textbooks, blackboard lectures and face-to-face tutorials to a more convenient, mobile and digitalised one. Based on this, countries have developed policy documents to promote the digital transformation of education, and put forward visions and strategies for the development of education. The Education 2030 Agenda, which was established by UNESCO in 2015 to set goals and guidelines for global education development, states that "the focus should be on the quality of education and learning", with the core objective of promoting the digital transformation of education in order to advance education equitable, inclusive and sustainable development [1]. The Ministry of Education in China released the Education Informatization 2.0 Action Plan in 2018, which proposes specific tasks such as promoting the development of hybrid education, exploring innovative education evaluation and strengthening the construction of digital education platforms to promote the digital transformation of education [2]. Thus, the context of digital transformation of education is formed by a number of factors and is an important initiative of China's education reform. "The digitalization of education can be seen as the digital leap of the informatisation process," claims domestic scholar Zhu Zhiting [3]. The digital transformation of education is about using digital technology and the Internet to break down the constraints of time and space and to provide the conditions and support for Blended Learning. The current phase of Blended Learning is significantly different from the Blended Learning model of the 1990s, which integrated face-to-face and online learning interactively and put the student at the center of the teaching [4]. Research on digital transformation and Blended Learning assessment models has become a focus of education policy implementation globally.

2.2 Rationale for Blended Learning

Blended Learning describes an educational approach that integrates both in-person teaching and online learning components [5]. Students gain from valuable learning experiences that align with the principles of higher education and enhance their effectiveness in learning [6]. A Blended Learning environment combines face-to-face instruction with technology [7]. In order to improve teaching and learning effectiveness, it combines the strengths of both learning modes. Blended Learning has a solid foundation in learning theories including Constructivist and Behaviourist Learning Theories, Cognitive Learning Theories, Social Learning Theories, etc. [8]. Merrill's 'primary teaching principle' suggests that effective learning occurs when learners work on tasks that suit them [9]. There are also studies that show that different learning theories apply to different target levels and contexts of learning, and therefore to different audience and content contexts [10]. The paper uses University Computer Fundamentals, offered by Yunnan Normal University, as an example of blended teaching.

3 Existing Blended Learning Evaluation Frameworks and Issues

Evaluation is an integral part of education, as continuous improvement of Blended Learning and curriculum can only be achieved based on evaluation data. Efficacious evaluation is based on systematic and long-term collection of evaluation data [11, 12]. In practice, most institutions have not yet established effective evaluation mechanisms for Blended Learning due to the variability of objects, platforms, and data [4]. Although there are many scholars both at home and abroad who have conducted a lot of research on Blended Learning, some scholars have tried to evaluate Blended Learning from multiple perspectives, such as: student engagement and interaction [13]. Problem-based learning frameworks and more [14] Fang Qimei et al. showed that the most established and widely used framework for blended instructional evaluation through comparative analysis is the Community of Inquiry Theory (CoI model) [15]. A summary of several papers concludes that the current problems of Blended Learning evaluation are mainly in the following areas:

- The assessment model is not comprehensive enough: traditional education assessment mainly focuses on students' knowledge mastery and understanding, while Blended Learning emphasizes the comprehensive ability to solve practical problems and actual situations, requiring consideration of multiple dimensions, including knowledge, practical skills, and comprehensive problem-solving skills.
- Assessment content is not close enough to reality: the assessment content does not match the learning content, and the assessment results do not have enough practical application value. The assessment results do not reflect practical application skills, which limits the effectiveness of Blended Learning assessment and also restricts the development of students' comprehensive skills.
- Evaluation methods are not sufficiently timely and accurate: traditional educational evaluation focuses on the evaluation of basic indicators such as manual scoring, time and the number of clicks to view. Blended Learning assessment requires the use of more advanced technology to improve the scientific and accuracy of assessment methods, such as artificial intelligence and big data and other technical means to make the results more objective and accurate.
- Evaluation standards are not uniform: Blended Learning scenarios cannot be evaluated through uniform and standardized rubrics, and the lack and inconsistency of evaluation standards make the evaluation results of students lack comparability.

The above problems need to be solved by using advanced technology, by giving applicants the ability to view relevant information and by setting realistic evaluation content.

4 Building a Hybrid Teaching Evaluation System Supported by Educational Blockchain Technology

4.1 Blended Learning Holistic Design

Theory and practice of Blended Learning both require instructional design. As shown in Fig. 1, the author composes the blended teaching process based on Huang Ronghuai's "Blended Learning Curriculum Design Framework."

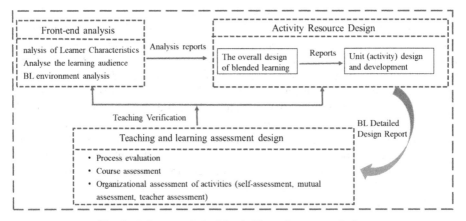

Fig. 1. A framework for Blended Learning course design

- Blended Learning front-end analysis and design: design of teaching objectives based on learner characteristics and Blended Learning environment features.
- Activity resource design: involves multiple evaluators, online and offline evaluation data, and multiple learning resources in Blended Learning.
- Blended Learning overall assessment design: This paper builds a comprehensive assessment system using Blockchain Technology, considering the shortcomings of existing assessment models. It explores whether making the assessment process data directed and public will improve students' motivation to learn.

4.2 Blockchain-Based Blended Learning Assessment Research

The digital transformation of education has proliferated education data, and hybrid teaching data has many users, complex information systems, multiple evaluation criteria, large amounts of data, and weak supervision. This has made education data an important target for unlawful elements to attack, leading to a series of leakage incidents [16]. Teachers and students' personal information has been stolen, which has seriously affected daily life and even threatened national security. To manage education data effectively, Blockchain Technology, which is decentralised, transparent, secure, and traceable, should be relied upon. Recently, blockchain has gained popularity in China's education sector: a credible and traceable lifelong learning growth profile, a flexible, open, and dynamic formative education evaluation platform [17].

4.3 A Blockchain Technology-Based Evaluation Model for Course Case Teaching

4.3.1 Design of the Model

The hybrid teaching evaluation model based on Blockchain Technology includes four main parts: evaluation object, evaluation index, evaluation process and evaluation result. The whole teaching is divided into before, during and after class. Before the lesson, the teaching is designed according to the characteristics of the course and students, and students learn through self-learning resources and feedback learning data; during the lesson, through independent inquiry and cooperative learning, students solve problems, explain important and difficult points, and complete learning tasks. After the lesson, all teaching data is collated. The whole process is carried out throughout with the flow of learning data to the blockchain platform (Fig. 2).

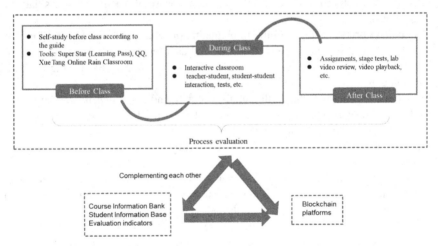

Fig. 2. A Blended Learning assessment model based on Blockchain Technology

4.3.2 Basis for Model Implementation

The following technologies are required for implementing a Blended Learning assessment model based on Blockchain Technology (Fig. 3).

- Blockchain Technology: this technology is decentralised, distributed and tamper-evident. Blockchain-based technology can be used to collect, store, encrypt and verify data related to the teaching practice of course cases for the implementation of

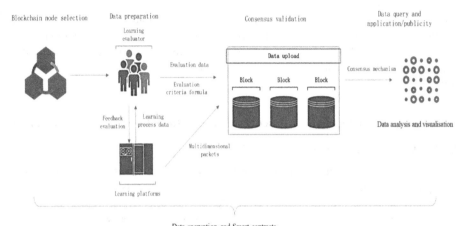

Fig. 3. Blockchain Technology based model implementation platform technology layer

Blended Learning evaluation models. Furthermore, it ensures data security and trustworthiness. By identifying the evaluators and the targets for the publication of the results and selecting the nodes, the targeted disclosure of teaching process data can be achieved.

- Data collection technology: In the implementation of the Blended Learning evaluation model, learning data, evaluation data, and user feedback information, etc. Data support for the evaluation model requires collecting and storing data through multiple technologies.
- Encryption technology: the confidentiality of data and data integrity can be guaranteed. The use of encryption in the implementation of Blended Learning evaluation models protects data from tampering and malicious attacks.
- Smart Contract Technology: smart contracts written in a language can manage transactions without the need for an intermediary, secure transactions and produce transaction results. In a Blended Learning evaluation model implementation, after determining the weighting of evaluation metrics, smart contracts can automate functions such as evaluating, distributing rewards and handling disputes.
- Data Analysis and Visualisation Techniques:the analysis and visualisation of data collected during the teaching and learning process is an important part of the implementation of Blended Learning assessment models. The aim is to generate detailed student learning records and assessment reports, to analyse students' strengths and weaknesses in knowledge, and to improve data support and decision-making for teachers. Data analysis and visualisation techniques can also help to assess the effectiveness of the model's operation and to improve it based on the results.

5 An Empirical Study Based on the "University Computer Fundamentals" Course at Yunnan Normal University

5.1 Basic Course Information

For this study, the course "University Computer Fundamentals", which is offered to undergraduate students at Yunnan Normal University, was used, which is divided into a theory class and a laboratory (hands-on) class. Through a hybrid online and offline classroom design teaching, 50 students in the class were surveyed by designing a pre-course questionnaire, in which the results of students' self-assessment of their computer technology level are shown in Fig. 4 below. 80% of students consider their theory and operation level to be average, so when teachers conduct Blended Learning, they should collect problems left by students during pre-course learning and solve them in class. The second section of Unit 5 of the course was used to create a guided learning sheet. By uploading their learning difficulties before class, teachers were able to survey their learning ability based on the Cognitive Load (Fig. 5).

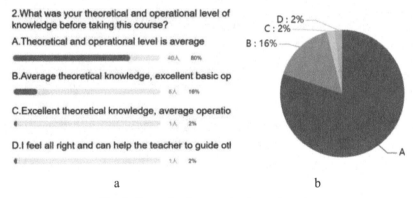

a   b

Fig. 4. Example of a pre-school questionnaire

5.2 Course Evaluation Model Design

As a result of the aforementioned basic research, the Blockchain Technology-based case study teaching evaluation model (see Fig. 6) includes the following factors:

1) Evaluation target: the model evaluates teaching objectives, teaching contents, teaching methods and teaching effects for first-year students receiving higher education.
2) Evaluation indicators: the basic elements and practical process of teaching course cases, the quality of learning resources, etc., reflecting various teaching links and student feedback.
3) Data collection: implemented with Blockchain Technology, mainly including video, audio, text, interactive links, feedback of students, teacher evaluation, and other data in the course of case teaching.

5.2 excel guided learning sheets		
Study Guides	The Goals	1.Understanding the "before and after" and composition of the spreadsheet 2.Students master the basic operation of the spreadsheet, the use of common functions 3.Can use the knowledge learned EXCEL to solve practical problems 4.Strengthen the analysis, thinking and problem-solving skills
	Resources and methods	Learning methods 1. Independent learning 2. Collaborative learning	Learning resources: Learning Cloud, Learning Pass corresponding chapter videos, classroom PPTs, discussion boards
	Preview of the classroom learning format	Using a task-driven blended teaching model Theory classes: answering and explaining questions; conducting accompanying quizzes; Practical classes: completion of tasks and submission of work.
Study Tasks	Task 1	1.Observation to understand the composition of the Excel window	Note: Students need to consult relevant materials such as Baidu terminology, B-site video presentations and textbooks when understanding a concept or a table formula that has not been explained for analysis.
	Task 2	2.Master the basic operation of the table
	Task 3	3.Try to build your own data experience
Learning Advice	Study guides	1. Record self-learning difficulties 2. Practice based on resources 3. Thinking • Talk about the application of spreadsheets in relation to the profession studied. • Briefly describe the data processing process and the purpose of data processing.
	Learning Confusion	1. Upload questions to the excel topic discussion board

Fig. 5. Pre-course Learning Guide Sheet

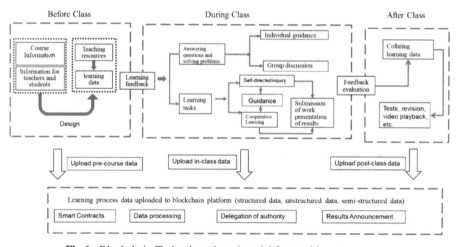

Fig.6. Blockchain Technology-based model for teaching course cases

Based on the above model design, a future-oriented teaching evaluation model can be established in the practice of course case teaching, and Blockchain Technology can be used to manage and evaluate teaching data, build a quality assurance mechanism for course case teaching, stimulate students' interest in participating in learning, and improve teaching quality and effectiveness. Blockchain Technology provides technical support and guarantee for the generation of evaluation results of course case teaching, and can ensure the authenticity of evaluation results and the integrity of data. The evaluation results are generated and visualised through the analysis of the collected data.

The evaluation results reflect the actual effect of the course case teaching, including teaching results, student feedback, teaching improvement and teaching quality assurance. The evaluation results also provide strong support and reference for subsequent teaching improvement and decision-making.

5.3 Research Conclusion

By analysing the student learning data, the actual effect of Blended Learning can be derived in general, and the teaching realisation is discussed separately in relation to the research objectives and content. Based on the results of the teaching session evaluation and the comprehensive evaluation, it can be seen that the Blended Learning evaluation model based on Blockchain Technology can give full play to Blended Learning in the context of digital transformation of education, and solve most of the problems that exist in the original Blended Learning evaluation.

The model has the following advantages: ① High data security and credibility: the decentralised and distributed features of Blockchain Technology can ensure the integrity and authenticity of the data, making the evaluation results more accurate and reliable. ② Student privacy is protected: By using Blockchain Technology to encrypt student data, student privacy is strongly protected. ③ Automation of evaluation results: The use of smart contract technology for evaluation can automate the generation of evaluation results and reduce human intervention and errors. ④ Visualisation of teaching effects: Data analysis and visualisation technology can visually reflect students' learning and teaching effects, providing teachers with better teaching feedback and guidance. ⑤ Promoting student engagement: Adopting Blockchain Technology to track and reward students' learning outcomes can motivate students to participate more actively in the interactive aspects of Blended Learning.

But the evaluation model needs to be optimised: many technical operations need to be simplified, and there is a need for national social support to find low-cost and high-yield ways of doing this.

6   Conclusions and Outlook

6.1   Conclusion

The ultimate goal of this study is to construct a Blended Learning evaluation model based on Blockchain Technology, and to verify the application value of the model by applying it to practical teaching, and to discover and summarise the future development trend of Blended Learning evaluation. Through the analysis of the experimental results, this study has successfully achieved the research objectives, established a feasible Blended Learning evaluation model, and provided new ideas and methods for improving teaching quality and creating smart education. The study relies on various technical tools such as Blockchain Technology, data collection technology, encryption technology, smart contract technology and data analysis and visualisation technology to achieve the construction and application of a Blended Learning evaluation model. Together, these technological tools support the complete implementation of the Blended Learning assessment model, and also provide new ideas and methods for the exploration of Blended Learning assessment systems.

The educator Dewey has advocated that assessment should be based on the actual performance of students, so how can assessment in a digital context ensure the fairness of the target audience, the reliability of the assessment process and the objectivity of the assessment findings? How can the interference of factors such as race, gender and geography in assessment be eliminated or minimised in a digital assessment approach? These are questions that cannot be resolved at present. This study can only try to ensure the fairness of assessment from the perspective of multiple evaluators, multi-dimensional assessment data and multi-level assessment, in the hope that it can truly reflect the actual performance and potential of students and promote the democratisation and development of education.

6.2 Research Outlook

In the current era of digital transformation in education and with the emergence of the latest app - ChatGPT - which allows students to commit academic fraud and plagiarism in their assignments, etc. occur repeatedly. Looking ahead to future research directions and challenges in Blended Learning assessment models, Blockchain Technology is needed to improve strategies and methods with a view to providing references and lessons for Blended Learning teaching practice and theoretical research. To summarise future research can also be conducted in the following areas:

① Extension and application of the model: extend the Blended Learning evaluation model to more courses, expand the scope of application and assess the practicality and feasibility of the model.
② Optimization of evaluation indicators: further improve the evaluation indicator system and improve the accuracy and validity of evaluation results on the premise of ensuring data security and student privacy.
③ Combination of models and artificial intelligence technology: Combine Blended Learning evaluation models and artificial intelligence technology to further improve the automation level and efficiency of the models.
④ Monitoring and improvement of teaching quality: the Blended Learning assessment model enables timely feedback on student learning and teaching effectiveness, and teachers can target their teaching strategies and improve teaching quality.

Acknowledgements. I would like to thank the university for its assistance and support. This paper is part of the Yunnan Provincial Key Laboratory for Smart Education project. Special thanks to The Steering Committee for Teaching Computer Courses in Universities, Ministry of Education, "The Steering Committee for Teaching Computer Courses in Universities, Ministry of Education, for its support of the Teaching and Learning Reform Project 2022. I would like to express my gratitude to Yunnan Society of Computer Education for the support of the Teaching Research Project 2022 (Yungao Jijiao 202203), Research on the design and application of hybrid teaching evaluation mechanism based on Fabric blockchain (M-B133), Research on Learning Emotions in Primary School English Specialized Classes (M-B123). And my teachers and friends for their guidance in writing the thesis and help in data collection.

References

1. unesco. https://www.unesco.org/en. Accessed 10 June 2024
2. Ministry of Education: Notice on Printing and Distributing the "Education Informatization 2.0 Action Plan". http://www.moe.gov.cn/srcsite/A16/s3342/201804/t20180425_334188.html. Accessed 1 July 2024
3. Zhu, Z., Hu, J.: Exploring the nature of digital transformation in education and research outlook. China Educ. Technol. (4), 1–8+25 (2022)
4. Feng, X., Wang, R., Wu, Y.: A review of the current state of research on blended learning and teaching at home and abroad - an analytical framework based on blended learning and teaching. J. Distance Educ. **36**(3), 13–24 (2018)
5. Lai, L., She, L., Li, C.: Online teaching model in the context of blended learning environment: experiential learning and TAM. Educ. Inf. Technol. **29**, 17235–17259 (2024)
6. Kapo, A., Milutinovic, L.D., Rakovic, L., et al.: Enhancing e-learning effectiveness: analyzing extrinsic and intrinsic factors influencing students' use, learning, and performance in higher education. Educ. Inf. Technol. **29**, 10249–10276 (2024)
7. Graham, C.R.: Blended Learning Systems: The Handbook of Blended Learning: Global Perspectives, Local Designs, pp. 3–21 (2006)
8. Alcaraz, R., Martínez-Rodrigo, A., Zangróniz, R., Rieta, J.J.: Blending inverted lectures and laboratory experiments to improve learning in an introductory course in digital systems. IEEE Trans. Educ. **63**(3), 144–154 (2020)
9. Merrill, M.D.: First principles of instruction. Educ. Technol. Res. Dev. **50**(3), 43–59 (2002)
10. van der Stap, N., van den Bogaart, T., van Ginkel, S., Rahimi, E., Versendaal, J.: Towards teaching strategies addressing online learning in blended learning courses for adult-learners. Comput. Educ. **219**, 105103 (2024)
11. Nikolopoulou, K.: Self-regulated and mobile-mediated learning in blended tertiary education environments: student insights from a pilot study. Sustainability **15**(16), 12284 (2023)
12. Toth, M., Foulger, T.S., et al.: Post -lmplementation lnsights about a hybrid degree program. Techtrends Link. Res. Pract. lmprove Learn. **3**, 76–80 (2008)
13. Aspden, L., Helm, P.: Making the connection in a blended learning environment. Educ. Media lnt. (3), 245–252 (2004)
14. Hassoulas, A., de Almeida, A., West, H., et al.: Developing a personalised, evidence-based and inclusive learning (PEBIL) model of blended learning: a cross-sectional survey. Educ. Inf. Technol. **28**, 14187–14204 (2023)
15. Bayram, A., Bayram, S.B., Özsaban, A.: Using the online education planned based on Anderson's theory to facilitate the practice learning experiences of nursing students: a phenomenological study. Educ. Inf. Technol. (2024)
16. Hong, W., Ren, J., Xu, L., et al.: Classification of educational data under the background of data security law. Chin. J. ICT Educ. **28**(3), 41–50 (2022)
17. Lan, L., Wu, F., Shi, R., et al.: A visual analysis of "blockchain+education" research in China: a sample of 160 core journal papers related to "blockchain+education". Mod. Educ. Technol. **31**(10), 23–31 (2021)

A Study on Students' Cross-Cultural Communication Competence in Higher Vocational English Courses in the Context of Smart Education

Xuemin Du[✉]

Sanya Aviation and Tourism College, Fenghuang Road 218#, Sanya, China
minxuedu@163.com

Abstract. This research focuses on exploring the relationship between smart education and cross-cultural communication ability. This paper deeply explores the internal relationship between smart education and intercultural communication ability; innovatively analyzes the knowledge, awareness, and skills of cross-cultural communication of higher vocational students; and then explores the unique paths and strategies for improving cross-cultural communication ability in English courses against the background of smart education, including the optimization of the smart education environment and resources to create a high-quality cross-cultural communication atmosphere. It provides new strategies and methods for improving English teaching and cross-cultural communication ability from a new perspective, which indicates significant novelty and innovation.

Keywords: Smart education · higher vocational English courses · cross-cultural communication

1 Introduction

In the context of free trade ports and the "Belt and Road Initiative", vocational students must possess strong cross-cultural communication competence to adapt to increasingly frequent international exchanges and cooperation. This requires the cultivation of international talent who are familiar with international practices and understand the differences in traditions, customs, and concepts among different cultures. The traditional English course education model has certain limitations in cultivating cross-cultural communication. The traditional teaching model will prove incapable of fulfilling the requirements of industrial development. This paper aims to investigate the correlation between students' cross-cultural communication capabilities and smart education.

K. Zhang et al. (Eds.): CSEI 2024, CCIS 2447, pp. 162–182, 2025.
https://doi.org/10.1007/978-981-96-3735-5_13

2   Implications for the Study

This study explores the knowledge, awareness and competence of cross-cultural communication. It also looks into approaches and strategies to enhance students' cross-cultural communication ability in the context of smart education. The research results can provide theoretical guidance for higher vocational English education, making the curriculum and teaching methods more in line with talent cultivation needs in China.

3   Research Status of Smart Education and Cross-Cultural Communication Ability

3.1   Smart Education

Smart education is an educational model supported by modern information technology. It centers on students and aims to cultivate their innovative spirit, practical ability, and comprehensive quality. By deeply integrating educational information with education, it builds an intelligent and personalized learning environment to meet students' diverse and differentiated development needs. Currently, smart education in China has advanced rapidly. In this situation, smart education is anticipated to offer robust support for the advancement of higher vocational students' English communication ability.

In the smart learning environment, students are good at using information technology tools, such as online courses and the mobile internet, to expand the learning channels for cross-cultural communication. Additionally, smart education can achieve personalized, intelligent, and real-time education and teaching, which is beneficial for targeted tutoring of students' cultural communication ability. Thus, the ability and literacy of vocational students in cross-cultural communication will be enhanced. With the assistance of high-level technologies such as the internet, big data, and artificial intelligence, teachers employ smart teaching concepts to construct an efficient, interactive, and intelligent teaching environment and promote individualized, independent, and active learning among students.

3.2   Cross-Cultural Communication Competence

Since the start of the 21st century, the research of foreign researchers on cross-cultural communication competence has shifted from emphasizing the "complexity" and "hybridity" of culture to concentrating on intercultural communication competence. Scholars have proposed two-factor, three-element, four-element, and multifactor theories. However, the three-element theory of intercultural communication competence proposed by Brian H. Spitzberg (1985) and William R. Cupach (1985) is more influential. The three elements consist of motivation, skills, and knowledge. Byram (2001) suggested that to enhance students' intercultural competence, actively encouraging and promoting "the development of a critical sense of reflection" should be performed.

The research outcomes in China have focused mainly on cross-cultural communication and language teaching. Hu Wenzhong (2013) combined the viewpoints of both domestic and foreign scholars regarding the components of cross-cultural communication competence and summarized it into three competence levels: cognition, emotion, and behavior. Zhang Hongling (2012) suggested integrating the cultivation of cross-cultural communication competence with the development of students' language skills. Ge Chunping and Wang Shouren (2016) proposed cultivating students' intercultural communication ability through four means: strengthening teacher construction, improving teaching materials, fostering awareness, and attaching importance to practical training.

3.3 The Relationship Between Smart Education and Intercultural Communication Competence

As the research on the theoretical and practical facets of smart education has deepened, scholars have engaged in thorough discussions regarding the combination of smart education and cross-cultural communication competence. They contend that by integrating advanced information technology and educational notions, smart education can supply more plentiful, three-dimensional, and personalized learning resources and environments for nurturing cross-cultural communication competence. Currently, research on smart education focuses mainly on the development of a cross-cultural teaching model in smart education, and numerous studies have demonstrated that smart education has a significant influence on the development of cross-cultural communication. Through the utilization of online digital resources, digital platforms, big data, artificial intelligence, and other modern information technologies, students' learning situations are analyzed, the learning differences among students are accurately grasped, teaching content is adjusted promptly, and teaching objectives and processes are formulated scientifically. The past classroom teaching mode based on teacher instruction has changed, and a new learning mode based on smart education has become the principal learning mode for students. With the advancement of information technology, teaching and learning transcend the constraints of classrooms and class periods, and students can fully exploit "fragmented" time for learning anytime, anywhere, and as demanded.

4 Research on the Cross-Cultural Communication Ability of Students in Higher Vocational English Courses

4.1 Purpose of the Study

This research aims to assess the influence that smart education has on the transcultural communication capabilities of students in colleges and explore ways to increase how cross-cultural communication ability can be enhanced through English courses in the context of smart education.

4.2 Research Content

The specific research elements include the following:

1. Analyze the inherent connection between smart education and transcultural communication and elaborate on the current status and issues of higher vocational English courses;

2. Targeted methods for enhancing transcultural communication ability are proposed to facilitate the advancement of students' ability to communicate with people from different cultures.

4.3 Research Objects

This study takes the students of S College as subjects. This college is a comprehensive vocational institution offering a total of 32 majors and having approximately 10,000 students. For the sample selection of this study, the principle of random sampling was adopted, and the subjects were chosen randomly. To facilitate the sending, receiving, and analysis of questionnaires, the majors are categorized into three types: civil aviation transportation, railway transportation, and art majors. The participants' ages ranged from 18 to 25 years, and 207 males and 253 females were included. There are 242 first-year students, 195 sophomores, and 23 juniors. These students come from diverse majors, with 216 from civil aviation transportation majors, 120 from railway transportation majors, and 124 from art majors.

4.4 Purpose of the Survey

This paper aims to address the following questions: (1) What is the current state of cross-cultural communication ability in smart education? (2) Are there disparities in students' ability with respect to cross-cultural communication when backgrounds are variable? (3) What primary factors influence cross-cultural communication ability?

4.5 Research Methodology

In accordance with the research theme and objectives, this study adopts the literature method, the survey method, and the case analysis method for conducting the research.

Documentary Method. In the preparatory stage of the research, the literature method was utilized to organize the existing research outcomes related to "smart education", "higher vocational English courses", and "cross-cultural communication ability". Through the collection and analysis of relevant literature via renowned data platforms and large resource databases, an understanding of the historical development and research status in this field is gained. The research results are drawn upon to undertake this study, thereby offering a theoretical basis for subsequent strategies for enhancing cross-cultural communication competence.

Survey method. The necessary data are gathered, processed, and analyzed via the survey method. On the basis of the scale and self-compiled questionnaire used in existing research and in line with the requirements of this study, the indicators were eliminated and revised through trial testing to constitute the formal questionnaire used in this study. The interview survey method adopts the form of semiopen dialog to collect information related to students' ability to communicate across cultures, which is conducive to further excavating the questionnaire data.

Case Study Method. A vocational college that has fully implemented smart education was chosen as a case study to examine the school's measures in smart education, such as the introduction of intelligent learning platforms and the allocation of multimedia teaching resources. Students' intercultural communication competence within this context was observed, and the variations in these students' intercultural communication competence were analyzed.

Through case analysis, the results obtained via the literature method and the survey method are mutually verified. The relationship between the smart education environment and the various elements of cross-cultural communication ability is understood more comprehensively and profoundly, providing a rich and detailed practical basis for proposing strategies to enhance cross-cultural communication ability.

4.6 Questionnaire Design

This questionnaire comprises 3 sections: the basic information of the testees, English learning, and the students' cross-cultural communication competence. Taking into account the higher vocational students' learning characteristics, their own learning experiences, and the possible understanding of the connotation of each constituent element, the content of each dimension is described as precisely as possible. Excluding basic information, there are 42 questions regarding smart education and English learning and cross-cultural communication ability. The test takers are required to directly type ($\sqrt{}$) in the space where the corresponding row and column intersect on the basis of the description (row) of each question and the degree (column) that aligns with them.

The first section involves the collection of students' basic information. It is used for cross-analysis of students' gender, grade, major, and intercultural communication ability to obtain the degree of influence of the above factors on students' intercultural communication ability.

The second section is a survey on the relationship between smart education and students' English learning. The questionnaire offers 5 options on the basis of different levels of agreement. To facilitate statistics and analysis, the question options are assigned as follows: 10% and below, approximately 30% conformity, approximately 55% conformity, approximately 80% conformity, and more than 90% conformity. In this study, the questions related to students' English learning are presented on a five-point scale, with "not at all", "not quite agree", "not sure", "somewhat agree", and "completely agree" designated as 1, 2, 3, 4, and 5, respectively. Questions 4 to 7 pertain to the use of digital platforms and digital resources. Questions 8 to 17 pertain to students' English learning.

The third section is the survey of cross-cultural communication ability. This study developed a questionnaire on three aspects: knowledge, attitudes, and skills. This knowledge encompasses two dimensions, domestic culture and foreign culture, and sets up questions, including history, society, and values. Intercultural competence attitudes cover global awareness, language and cultural awareness, and communicative motivation and include questions about cultural differences, different cultural perspectives, and the willingness to communicate. Intercultural competence skills cover all aspects, including skills, strategies, language, reflection, resilience, and other issues. The questionnaire result options are divided into five options on the basis of the degree to which the students consider the question description to be consistent with themselves. For the convenience of statistics and analysis, the question options are assigned values and divided into 10% and below, approximately 30%, approximately 55%, approximately 80%, and more than 90%. In this study, students' intercultural communication competence is divided into three dimensions, namely, attitudes, knowledge, and skills, and the questions are presented on a five-point scale, with "not at all agreeing", "not quite agreeing", "not sure", "somewhat agreeing", and "completely agreeing", with scores of 1, 2, 3, 4, and 5, respectively. Questions 18 to 27 belong to the survey of cross-cultural communication skills. The larger the total score is, the better the students' communication skills are in terms of cross-cultural knowledge. Questions 40 to 45 pertain to the awareness of cross-cultural communication skills. The average score of all the questions in this section represents the student's score on intercultural communication ability. The higher the score is, the better the student's intercultural communication ability. The specific assignments to the question titles are shown in Table 1.

Table 1. Question option assignments

Options	10%	30%	55%	80%	90%
4–45	10% and below	30% about	55% about	80% about	90% and above

4.7 Survey Results and Analysis

In this study, data were collected via the self-developed "Questionnaire on cross-cultural Communication Competence of Students in Higher Vocational English Courses in the Context of Smart Education", and the questionnaire was sent and received through Wenjuanxing. Students participated in the questionnaire survey, resulting in 460 valid questionnaires, with an effective rate of 100%. The statistical software SPSS 22.0 was used to organize and score the data.

According to the results, 45% of the total respondents were male, and 55% were female. With respect to majors, 47% were in civil aviation transportation, 26% were in railway transportation, and 27% were in art (Table 2).

4.7.1 Reliability Analysis

According to the above table, the reliability coefficient value is 0.979. This implies that the reliability of the research data is extremely high. With respect to the "CITC value", all the CITC values of the analysis items surpassed 0.4, indicating that there was a favorable correlation among the analysis items and a high level of reliability (Table 3).

4.7.2 Validity Analysis

The KMO values lie within the range of 0–1. The above table shows that the KMO value was 0.970, and the significance was less than 0.005, indicating that the questionnaire validity was extremely good (Table 4).

Table 2. Sample Composition of the Actual Survey

Question	Option	Frequency (person)	Percentage (%)
Gender	Male	207	45%
	Female	253	55%
Grade:	Freshman	242	52.6%
	Sophomore	195	42.3%
	Juniors	23	5%
Major	Civil Aviation Transport related majors	216	47%
	Rail transport related majors	120	26%
	Art majors	124	27%

Table 3. Cronbach's Alpha Reliability Analysis

Number of Items	Sample Size	Cronbach α Coefficient
42	460	0.979

Table 4. Results of Validity Analysis

KMO value		0.970
Bartlett Sphericity Test	Approximate chi-square	21527.804
	df	861
	p-value	0.000

4.7.3 Descriptive Analysis

Basic information of English courses in vocational colleges

The assignment of questions is categorized into 5 levels. A score of 1 is given when 10% or less agrees, a score of 2 when approximately 30% agrees, a score of 3 when approximately 55% meets the score, a score of 4 when approximately 80% meets the score, and a score of 5 when more than 90% meets the score. A median value of 2.5 points implies that the role of smart education in students' English learning is at a medium level. Therefore, in this study, 3 points are taken as a better reference point for the role of smart education in students' English learning. A score higher than 3 points indicates that the richer the digital platform and digital resources are, the better the students' English learning effect.

Table 5 indicates that the digital platforms and digital resources of higher vocational college English courses are relatively abundant, the update speed is quicker, and the learning effect of English is improved.

Table 5. Descriptive Statistics of Several Indicators of English Courses in Vocational Colleges (n = 460)

Items	Sample Size	Min	Maximum	Mean	Standard Deviation	Median
Use of Digital Platforms and Digital Resources	460	1.000	5.000	3.759	0.929	4.000
Student English Learning	460	1.000	5.000	3.725	0.874	3.900

The results of the questionnaire for higher vocational English courses are presented in Table 6.

Case: An answer to the question of whether a college has a good environment for smart education

Interview time: August 29, 2024

Location: S college

Interviewee: WSQ

Interviewee information: Freshman, flight attendant major

Question: Does the infrastructure of a college meet the needs of English learning for students?

Answer: Our classes are all held in the multimedia classroom, and the network speed is very fast. The teacher uses a computer or mobile phone to interact with us in class, such as by providing culturally relevant teaching video resources or asking us to complete certain exercises. Teachers provide feedback on our learning on the smart learning platform. However, the computer configuration in the classroom sometimes crashes or crashes when some complex teaching software is running.

Q: What are your school's learning resources for improving intercultural communication?

Answer: Teachers use relevant resources on the smart learning platform so that we can learn, and the resources are relatively rich. In addition, the teachers also recommended some apps to encourage everyone to use AI technology to practice communication ability in culture.

According to the analysis of the interview and questionnaire data, the digital platforms and digital resources employed in higher vocational English courses are relatively abundant. The resources are updated at a faster pace, and the digital platforms have more functions, which can better fulfill the English learning requirements of the participants. Resources and the utilization of technology offer significant assistance in learning English.

Table 7 reveals that the average value of the 10 items related to the intercultural communication competence knowledge of higher vocational students ranges from 3.241–4.083, and the standard deviation is in the range of 0.838--130. This finding indicates that there is a statistically significant difference in the items related to cross-cultural communication competence knowledge. For the questions with an average score of more than 4, namely, "I know my country's social norms" and "I know my country's values",

Table 6. Descriptive Statistics of Some Indicators of Higher Vocational English Courses (n = 460)

	Sample Size	Min	Maximum	Mean	Standard Deviation	Median
There are abundant of digital English learning resources that can help me learn English better	460	1.000	5.000	3.689	1.065	4.000
The English learning resources provided by the digital platform are updated quickly	460	1.000	5.000	3.717	1.028	4.000
Taking advantage of digital resources can help me learn English anytime, anywhere	460	1.000	5.000	3.813	0.997	4.000
When I search for resources online, I always find websites or features that can help me learn English	460	1.000	5.000	3.815	0.985	4.000
I am proficient in using commonly used digital learning devices (e.g. laptops, pads, etc.) and learning software for English learning	460	1.000	5.000	3.759	1.021	4.000
I use digital platforms to self-control and evaluate the quality of the English learning process	460	1.000	5.000	3.680	1.001	4.000

(continued)

Table 6. (*continued*)

	Sample Size	Min	Maximum	Mean	Standard Deviation	Median
I consciously use other features of digital learning tools to help with English learning	460	1.000	5.000	3.733	1.001	4.000
I try to combine different digital learning tools and apply them to English learning	460	1.000	5.000	3.665	1.029	4.000
I often use digital teaching platforms to access English learning resources	460	1.000	5.000	3.713	1.012	4.000
I prefer the teacher use digital resources for English lessons	460	1.000	5.000	3.713	1.001	4.000
The use of digital tools is a great way to communicate with each other	460	1.000	5.000	3.776	0.963	4.000
I have a strong sense of learning when I use digital resources to learn	460	1.000	5.000	3.720	0.969	4.000
I think "digital education" resources and the use of technology are very helpful for learning English	460	1.000	5.000	3.770	0.974	4.000

the majority of the participants believed that they were highly aware of their country's social norms and values.

Table 8 indicates that the mean value of the six items regarding higher vocational students' attitudes toward intercultural communication competence ranges from 3.776–4.013, and the standard deviation lies between 0.873 and 0.916. For the question "Willingness to respect the ways and customs of foreigners", with a mean greater than 4, the majority of the participants felt highly willing to respect people from different cultural backgrounds.

Table 9 reveals that the average value of the 12 items of the intercultural communication competence of higher vocational students ranges from 3.365–4.072. The standard deviation lies between 0.870 and 1.269. This shows that there is a significant difference in the items related to the intercultural communication competence of higher vocational students. For the question "Ability to reflect and learn when cross-cultural conflicts and

Table 7. Descriptive Statistics of Some Indicators of Cross-Cultural Communication Competence Knowledge of Higher Vocational Students (n = 460)

Items	Sample Size	Min	Maximum	Mean	Standard Deviation	Median	Coefficient of variation
I know the history of my country	460	1.000	5.000	3.907	0.921	4.000	23.565%
I know a lot about the social norms of my country	460	1.000	5.000	4.061	0.838	4.000	20.635%
I know the values of my country	460	1.000	5.000	4.083	0.894	4.000	21.898%
I know a lot about the history of foreign countries	460	1.000	5.000	3.298	1.128	3.000	34.209%
I am very knowledgeable about the social norms of foreign countries	460	1.000	5.000	3.274	1.112	3.000	33.963%
I am very knowledgeable about foreign values	460	1.000	5.000	3.263	1.121	3.000	34.366%
I am very familiar with the cultural taboos of foreign countries	460	1.000	5.000	3.241	1.130	3.000	34.866%
Understand the knowledge of foreigners' speech and behavior	460	1.000	5.000	3.283	1.100	3.000	33.506%

(continued)

Table 7. (*continued*)

Items	Sample Size	Min	Maximum	Mean	Standard Deviation	Median	Coefficient of variation
Understand the basics of concepts such as intercultural communication and communication	460	1.000	5.000	3.496	1.045	4.000	29.887%
I know some strategies and tips for successful cross-cultural communication	460	1.000	5.000	3.493	1.053	4.000	30.143%

misunderstandings arise and find appropriate solutions", with an average value greater than 4, the majority of the participants believed that they had an excellent ability to handle cross-cultural conflicts and misunderstandings.

Taking gender as the independent variable and higher vocational English courses and students' intercultural communication ability as the dependent variables, a t test was carried out to explore whether there were significant differences in the intercultural communication ability of higher vocational English courses and students of different genders. The results of the analysis are presented in Table 10.

The above table shows that different genders did not significantly affect one item of higher vocational English courses (P > 0.05). This implies that different genders exhibit consistency and no disparity in all higher vocational English courses. Additionally, gender had a significant effect on students' intercultural communication ability (P < 0.05). This finding indicates that gender had a significant effect on students' intercultural communication ability (T = 2.116, P = 0.035). Specifically, the comparison revealed that the average value for males (3.80) was significantly greater than that for females (3.66).

To better describe the variations in the knowledge, skills, and attitudes of students of different genders in terms of cross-cultural communication ability, an independent sample t test was employed to compare the cross-cultural communication ability of students of different genders and the average of each dimension.

The statistical results of the difference test are presented in Table 11.

The above table shows that the samples of different genders were consistent in terms of all students' awareness of cross-cultural communication competence, and no difference was present (P > 0.05). The gender sample presented a significant difference in the two items of students' cross-cultural communication competence skills (P < 0.05), indicating that there were disparities in students' knowledge of intercultural communication

Table 8. Results of Descriptive Statistical Analysis of Higher Vocational Students' Attitudes towards Cross-Cultural Communication Ability

Items	Sample Size	Min	Maximum	Mean	Standard Deviation	Median	Coefficient of variation
Be aware of the cultural similarities and differences that exist when communicating with foreigners	460	1.000	5.000	3.793	0.902	4.000	23.776%
Be aware of the differences in cultural identities when interacting with foreigners	460	1.000	5.000	3.776	0.905	4.000	23.967%
Be aware of the need to look at cross-cultural communication scenarios from different cultural perspectives	460	1.000	5.000	3.811	0.908	4.000	23.830%
Willing to communicate and learn from foreigners from different cultures	460	1.000	5.000	3.854	0.916	4.000	23.769%
Willing to respect the lifestyle and customs of foreigners	460	1.000	5.000	4.013	0.873	4.000	21.757%
Willing to learn foreign language Chinese culture well	460	1.000	5.000	3.887	0.924	4.000	23.779%

skills. There was a significant gender difference at the 0.05 level for students' intercultural communication skills ($t = 2.099$, $p = 0.036$), and the average value for males (3.86) was significantly greater than that for females (3.70). There was a significant gender difference at the 0.01 level for students' knowledge of intercultural communication skills (t = 3.156, p = 0.002), and the average value for males (3.67) was significantly greater than that for females (3.43) (Table 11).

Table 9. Descriptive Statistics of Several Indicators of the Cross-Cultural Communication Competence of Higher-vocational Students (n = 460)

Item	Sample Size	Min	Maximum	Mean	Standard Deviation	Median	Coefficient of variation
In intercultural communication, I was able to adjust my behavior so that the communication would go on properly	460	1.000	5.000	3.602	1.012	4.000	28.098%
When you have a language communication disorder, you can communicate with body language or other nonverbal means	460	1.000	5.000	3.759	0.931	4.000	24.781%
I can use a foreign language to communicate successfully with people from different social-cultural backgrounds and fields	460	1.000	5.000	3.365	1.107	3.000	32.900%
I treat foreigners politely when I communicate with them	460	1.000	5.000	3.987	0.910	4.000	22.819%
Try to avoid offending foreigners with inappropriate language and behavior when communicating with them	460	1.000	5.000	3.928	0.966	4.000	24.600%

(*continued*)

Table 9. (*continued*)

Item	Sample Size	Min	Maximum	Mean	Standard Deviation	Median	Coefficient of variation
The ability to try to avoid prejudice against foreigners when communicating with them	460	1.000	5.000	3.946	0.890	4.000	22.559%
When communicating with foreigners, they avoid talking about their privacy topics	460	1.000	5.000	3.950	0.917	4.000	23.212%
Sensitivity to cross-cultural differences	460	1.000	5.000	3.602	0.957	4.000	26.562%
When looking at events in other countries, we look at them from the other side's culture and from multiple perspectives	460	1.000	5.000	3.824	0.874	4.000	22.860%
Acquire knowledge related to intercultural communication directly through contact with foreign nationals	460	1.000	5.000	3.613	1.009	4.000	27.921%
Ability to use a variety methods, techniques and strategies to help learn foreign languages and cultures	460	1.000	5.000	3.657	0.956	4.000	26.152%
Ability to reflect and learn from cross-cultural conflicts and misunderstandings and to find appropriate solutions	460	1.000	6.000	4.072	1.269	4.000	31.155%

Table 10. T Test Analysis Results

	Gender: (mean ± standard deviation)		t	p
	Male (n = 207)	Female (n = 253)		
Intercultural communication skills	3.80 ± 0.78	3.66 ± 0.70	2.116	0.035*
Intercultural competence Higher Vocational English Courses	3.78 ± 0.94	3.71 ± 0.78	0.846	0.398

* p < 0.05 ** p < 0.01.

Table 11. Analysis of Gender Differences in Students' Intercultural Communication Competence

	Gender: (mean ± standard deviation)		t	p
	Male(n = 207)	Female(n = 253)		
Students' intercultural communication awareness	3.87 ± 0.84	3.84 ± 0.73	0.455	0.650
Students' intercultural communication skills	3.86 ± 0.86	3.70 ± 0.72	2.099	0.036*
Students' intercultural communication knowledge	3.67 ± 0.84	3.43 ± 0.81	3.156	0.002**

* p < 0.05 ** p < 0.01.

Table 12. Analysis of the Variance of Higher Vocational English Courses and Students' Intercultural Communication Competence and Grades

	Grade: (mean ± standard deviation)			F	p
	Freshman(n = 242)	Sophomore(n = 195)	Junior(n = 23)		
Higher Vocational English Courses	3.68 ± 0.80	3.79 ± 0.93	4.00 ± 0.74	2.036	0.132
Intercultural Communication Ability	3.63 ± 0.70	3.80 ± 0.75	4.03 ± 0.87	4.885	0.008**

* p < 0.05 ** p < 0.01.

There was a significant 0.01 level of intercultural communication ability for each grade (F = 4.885, p = 0.008), and the comparison differences revealed that the average scores of the groups with notable differences demonstrated that among all the grades, the third-year students had the best cross-cultural communication ability (M = 4.03), followed by the sophomores (M = 3.80) and then the freshmen (M = 3.63).

The above table shows that the samples of different majors did not exhibit any significant differences in terms of higher vocational English courses or students' intercultural communication ability (P > 0.05) (Table 13).

Table 13. Analysis of Variance between Higher Vocational English Courses and Students' Intercultural Communication Competence and Majors

	Specialty: (mean ± standard deviation)			F	p
	Majors related to Civil Aviation services(n = 216)	Majors related to railway services(n = 120)	Majors related to Art(n = 124)		
Higher Vocational English Courses	3.76 ± 0.87	3.64 ± 0.86	3.81 ± 0.83	1.427	0.241
Intercultural Communication Ability	3.75 ± 0.79	3.60 ± 0.64	3.79 ± 0.72	2.332	0.098

* p < 0.05 ** p < 0.01.

Correlation between higher vocational English courses and other factors (Table 14).

Table 14 shows that there is a strong positive correlation between English courses and students' cross-cultural communication knowledge, a notable positive correlation between higher vocational English courses and students' cross-cultural communication skills, and a significant positive correlation between higher vocational English courses and students' cross-cultural communication awareness.

5   Ways to Cultivate Cross-Cultural Communication Competence in Cigher-Vocational English Courses

5.1   Schools: Optimizing the Environment and Resources for Smart Education and Creating and Optimizing an Atmosphere of Cross-Cultural Communication

Optimizing the Environment and Resources for Smart Education
College needs to optimize the smart education environment and resources. This approach enables better collection and data analysis of teacher–student interaction data and student status data, real-time evaluation, three-dimensional communication and interaction, and a precise push of resources. By gathering high-quality cross-cultural communication teaching resources at all levels, schools can establish a school-based digital resource library for students to improve their cross-cultural communication competence. Moreover, schools can connect multiple subjects to conduct the coconstruction

Table 14. Partial Correlation Coefficients between Higher Vocational English Courses and Knowledge, Competence, and Awareness of Cross-Cultural Communication

Analytical Items	Mean	Standard Deviation	Higher Vocational English Course	Students' Knowledge of Intercultural Communication competence	Students' Intercultural Communication competence	Students' awareness of intercultural communication competence
Higher Vocational English Course	3.742	0.855	1			
Students' Knowledge of Cross-cultural Communication competence	3.540	0.836	0.682**	1		
Students' Cross-cultural Communication competence	3.775	0.790	0.671**	0.752**	1	
Students' awareness of Cross-cultural communication competence	3.856	0.782	0.617**	0.667**	0.864**	1

* $p < 0.05$ ** $p < 0.01$.

of interdisciplinary project-based learning resources and large-unit theme-based learning resources. Appropriate digital resources should be screened, effective information tools should be selected, and group or individual learning data should be integrated to increase the effectiveness and efficiency of cross-cultural communication teaching. Additionally, by optimizing the smart education platform and collecting students' multimodal data, teachers can comprehensively and dynamically understand the English learning status, learning problems and learning habits of classes and individual students and adjust teaching strategies and teaching content accordingly. They can also carry out group interventions or personalized interventions for classes or individual students.

Taking S College as an example, the college has made significant investments in hardware construction and created numerous smart classrooms and multimedia classrooms with air tourism characteristics. The classrooms are equipped with the latest VR and AR equipment, as well as high-definition large-screen display systems. For example, in the intercultural communication course of the aviation service major, teachers utilize VR equipment to immerse students in the ground handling processes and cultural scenes of airports in different countries. Students can interact with virtual passengers in simulated airports and aircraft cabins, understand the needs and communication styles of passengers from different cultures, and provide data support for analyzing students' learning status.

Creating and Optimizing an Atmosphere of Intercultural Communication

The atmosphere is also one of the factors influencing cross-cultural communication ability. Thus, schools need to create and optimize an intercultural communication atmosphere as well.

Extracurricular activities constitute one of the crucial means for vocational colleges to cultivate English cross-cultural communication competence. Generally, through the second class or practice, students are organized to take part in various English competitions, lectures, or conferences, thereby creating a favorable cross-cultural communication atmosphere and providing students with cross-cultural communication experiences. A school builds a cross-cultural communication platform for students that combines virtual elements. The utilization of extracurricular theme activities, the enrichment of extracurricular practical activities, placing students in real cross-cultural communication interactions, leading students onto a virtual cross-cultural communication platform, or the use of chat app social software to enable students to directly engage in cross-cultural real-time interaction.

The S college integrates a rich digital library in air tourism. First, it collects the training materials of flight attendants from major airlines worldwide, including service etiquette norms and cultural taboo cases in different countries and regions. When studying international hospitality courses, students can use the resource library to check the dining habits and accommodation preferences of hotel guests from different countries and analyze the problems that might be encountered in cross-cultural hospitality by watching practical case videos. Additionally, teachers and students are encouraged to independently create cross-cultural communication learning resources, such as the short video series "Interesting Facts about Tourism Culture in Various Countries" produced by students, which are widely disseminated on the smart learning platform on campus, creating a cross-cultural communication atmosphere and further enriching the diversity of resources.

5.2 Teachers: Strengthening the Concept of Smart and Improving Digital Literacy and Cross-Cultural Communication Literacy

First, teachers should proactively enhance their cross-cultural communication literacy through self-study and training, summarize the experience of intercultural communication, and be capable of communicating and sharing their feelings with students.

Second, English teachers need to constantly update their knowledge structure and maintain a high degree of sensitivity to new things and knowledge.

Finally, teachers should reinforce the concept of smartness; improve their own information-based teaching ability and technical literacy, including the ability to integrate teaching resources and teaching ability; and enhance their teaching level and cross-cultural communication ability to better guide students.

Taking S college as an example, the school encourages and provides resources and training for teachers in terms of policies, resources, and funds to assist teachers in improving their abilities in smart education and cross-cultural communication ability training, encourages teachers to take part in digital resource construction and competitions, and achieves good results in several competitions.

The college has introduced powerful smart teaching platforms, such as Smart Vocational Education, the Blue Ink Cloud, Wisdom Tree, etc., to achieve comprehensive teaching data collection and analysis. In classroom teaching, teachers post interactive topics, group tasks, and other teaching activities through the platform. For example, in the Civil Aviation English course, the teacher publishes a discussion on the topic of "how to provide meals for different passengers to introduce Chinese characteristics and culture", and the platform records the students' participation in the discussion in real time, including the content of the speech, the time of the speech, the cultural knowledge points cited, and other data.

6 Conclusion

Within the context of smart education, optimizing English courses is a crucial means to increase their cross-cultural communication capabilities. Research data indicate that developing students' intercultural competence is a dynamic and long-term task that needs to be accomplished by teachers, educational administrators, and students themselves. On this basis, this paper proposes methods for students to improve their intercultural communication: schools should optimize the environment and resources of smart education; create and optimize the atmosphere of cross-cultural communication; strengthen the concept; improve digital literacy and cross-cultural communication literacy; and enhance students' cross-cultural awareness, reflection and improvement, thus increasing their cross-cultural communication ability.

References

Byram, M., Nichols, A.: Developing Intercultural Competence in Practice. Multilingual Matters, Clevedon (2001)

Ge, C., Wang, S.: Cross-cultural communication ability cultivation and college English teaching. Foreign Lang. Foreign Lang. Teach. (02), 79–86+146 (2016)

Hu, W.: How to position cross-cultural communication ability in foreign language teaching. Foreign Lang. World (06), 2–8 (2013)

Spitzberg, B.H., Cupach, W.R.: Conversational skill and locus of perception. J. Psychopathol. Behav. Assess. 7(3), 207–220 (1985)

Zhang, H., Wu, S.: Development of a reference framework for cross-cultural competence teaching in foreign language education. Foreign Lang. World (05), 2–11 (2022)

Design and Implementation of an Explainable Course Recommendation Algorithm Based on Causal Inference

Xinpeng Chen, Zhengzhou Zhu$^{(\boxtimes)}$, and Yizhen Xie

Peking University, Beijing 100871, China
zhuzz@pku.edu.cn

Abstract. To solve the problem of insufficient personalization and interpretability of the MOOC platform recommendation system, the user behavior data and course characteristics were analyzed, and an interpretable course recommendation algorithm CountERText based on causal inference, was proposed. This algorithm uses counterfactual reasoning to generate intuitive recommendation explanations, enhances users' understanding of recommendation logic, optimizes the learning experience, and is of great significance in promoting the intelligent transformation of the education field.

Keywords: Causal inference · interpretability · recommendation algorithm · course recommendation · MOOC

1 Introduction

In the process of promoting the informatization of educational modernization, Massive Open Online Courses (MOOCs) as an innovative education model, have greatly improved the efficiency of knowledge dissemination. However, the lack of personalized recommendations and interpretability is still a challenge facing MOOCs. In response to these challenges, this paper makes the following contributions:

We constructed and pre-processed a dataset called ICourseData, which contains over 2,000 courses and more than 350,000 user interaction data, providing resources for personalized recommendation research.

We designed and implemented an explainable course recommendation algorithm called CountERText, which is based on causal inference. By generating counterfactual samples, the algorithm reveals the causal relationships underlying the recommendation decisions, thereby enhancing the explainability of the recommendation results.

The experimental results show that the CountERText algorithm has significant advantages in improving the explainability and accuracy of the recommendation system. It provides an effective personalized recommendation solution for MOOC platforms and has driven the development of recommendation technology in the education domain.

K. Zhang et al. (Eds.): CSEI 2024, CCIS 2447, pp. 183–199, 2025.
https://doi.org/10.1007/978-981-96-3735-5_14

2 Research Background and Significance

2.1 Background

As artificial intelligence has been increasingly applied in the education domain [1], Massive Open Online Courses (MOOCs), as a key components of educational modernization, have facilitated the widespread dissemination of educational resources. However, they face challenges such as a lack of personalization and low course completion rates. The application of personalized recommendation algorithms in education, especially on MOOC platforms, has been limited due to the lack of explainability.

This research aims to enhance the explainability of course recommendations through a causal inference-based algorithm. By improving the transparency of the recommendation process, the proposed approach can enhance user understanding and trust in the recommendations, driving the intelligent transformation of the education sector and enabling the organic integration of scalable education and personalized learning.

2.2 Current Research Status at Home and Abroad

Explainable Course Recommendation Algorithm. In recent years, researchers have proposed various algorithms to improve the accuracy, personalization, and explainability of recommendation systems for Massive Open Online Courses (MOOCs). These algorithms have focused primarily on the following areas:

Knowledge Graph-Based Recommendations. Researchers such as Alatrash R [4], Ma T [5], and Klasnja-Milicevic A [6] have leveraged techniques such as path reasoning, meta-paths, graph convolutional networks, contrastive learning, and attention mechanisms to model complex course relationships and knowledge structures.

Deep Learning-Based and NLP. Researchers such as Gu H [7] have leveraged deep learning and natural language processing techniques to increase the interpretability of MOOC recommendation systems.

Statistical and Machine Learning Models. Researchers such as Erkan E R [8] have leveraged techniques like SHAP (Shapley Additive Explanations) to enhance the explainability of MOOC recommendation systems.

Symbolic Logic-based and Reinforcement Learning. Researchers such as Gong J [9] have integrated symbolic logic and reinforcement learning techniques to develop highly explainable MOOC recommendation systems. Gong et al. proposed approaches that combine unified skill-based frameworks, reinforcement-based knowledge graph reasoning, and coarse-to-fine grain neuro-symbolic reasoning (CAFE). These techniques enable the generation of logically rigorous and multi-layered explanations for the recommended courses.

Causal Inference Methods. Traditional recommendation algorithms often overlook the underlying causal mechanisms that drive the relationships between user history, user attributes, and item content. As a result, recommendation systems may suffer from various issues, such as bias, unfairness, instability, lack of explainability, and feedback loops. In recent years, researchers have started to explore the incorporation of causal inference into recommendation systems to address these problems. This paper reviews the existing literature on the applications of causal reasoning in recommendation systems, which can be categorized as shown in Table 1.

Table 1. Examples of Causal Inference Algorithms

Algorithm Categories	Algorithm	Introduction
Causal Effect Estimation [10]	Inverse Probability Weighting (IPW)	The CountERText algorithm addresses issues of popularity bias and clickbait bias by simulating the user behavior distribution under intervention conditions through adjusting the weights of different behaviors in the observed data
	Potential Outcomes Framework(PO)	Based on the Rubin Causal Model, the algorithm estimates causal effects by comparing the potential outcomes under the intervention and non-intervention states
	Structural Causal Model (SCM)	Utilizing Graphical Models to Represent Causal Relationships and Infer Causal Effects
Counterfactual Reasoning	PRINCE [11]	Comparing Factual and Counterfactual Scenarios to Generate Minimal Edit Explanations for Recommendation Decisions
	CountER [12]	The algorithm takes the approach of finding the minimal feature changes required to precisely reverse the recommendation decision, and then provides counterfactual explanations
Causal Discovery [13]	Causal Discovery through Search-Based Methods	The algorithm leverages reinforcement learning techniques to discover the optimal causal graph, which can reveal the causal relationships between user behaviors and the recommendation outcomes
	Knowledge Graph-Based Causal Pathway Reasoning	The algorithm incorporates the use of knowledge graphs to enable explicit causal pathway reasoning, which further enhances the explainability

3 Experimental Data Description

The data for this study were obtained from the Chinese University MOOC (CMOOC) platform, which aggregates high-quality course resources from various universities across China and has a rich collection of user behavior records and course attribute information. Through web crawling techniques, the researchers were able to access the anonymized course interaction data. The final dataset, named ICourseData, includes 2,208 courses, 110,500 users and 3,504,028 "student-course" interaction records. The researchers performed data preprocessing to prepare the ICourseData dataset for their analysis and experiments on explainable MOOC recommendations.

0	1	2	3	4	5	6	7	8	9	10	11
课程id	课程名称	课程类别	教师	用户名	用户主页	用户id	评论内容	时间	点赞数	第几次课程	评分
BIT-20017	微积分（一）	国家精品 理学	翠哲 副教授	adnaninthe ja	org/home.htm?	1387344235	，真就看完就	2019-03-23	48	第5次开课	5
BIT-20017	微积分（一）	国家精品 理学	翠哲 副教授	1120163660--	org/home.htm?	1020229260	利用这里的资	2018-07-19	12	第3次开课	5
BIT-20017	微积分（一）	国家精品 理学	翠哲 副教授	IT-112018088	org/home.htm?	1146021412	足的是有时候明	2018-10-13	11	第5次开课	4
BIT-20017	微积分（一）	国家精品 理学	翠哲 副教授	020900206张雯	org/home.htm?	1027899769	长的视频，现	2019-07-03	10	第5次开课	5
BIT-20017	微积分（一）	国家精品 理学	翠哲 副教授	mooc083521	org/home.htm?	1146256015	课也太棒了叭	2019-06-24	4	第5次开课	5
BIT-20017	微积分（一）	国家精品 理学	翠哲 副教授	CCNU 夏雨	org/home.htm?	1144797104	点例子然后希	2018-09-12	4	第5次开课	4
BIT-20017	微积分（一）	国家精品 理学	翠哲 副教授	Mercury77777	org/home.htm?	1478261614	为什么感觉	2021-12-10	3	第8次开课	5
BIT-20017	微积分（一）	国家精品 理学	翠哲 副教授	012007-11202	org/home.htm?	1440709486	非常好非常好	2021-01-18	3	第7次开课	4
BIT-20017	微积分（一）	国家精品 理学	翠哲 副教授	药2001谌乐大	org/home.htm?	1444600700	自家学校的好	2021-01-03	3	第7次开课	5
BIT-20017	微积分（一）	国家精品 理学	翠哲 副教授	352030895591	org/home.htm?	1445707190	看完就会太神了	2020-10-14	3	第7次开课	3
BIT-20017	微积分（一）	国家精品 理学	翠哲 副教授	fykt14888407	org/home.htm?	1024828286	有点小，内容	2018-10-25	3	第5次开课	4
BIT-20017	微积分（一）	国家精品 理学	翠哲 副教授	ok鲜	org/home.htm?	1464966511	适合解决课外的	2021-10-10	2	第8次开课	5
BIT-20017	微积分（一）	国家精品 理学	翠哲 副教授	1332864028-	org/home.htm?	1482521473	老师！课程讲的	2021-09-28	2	第8次开课	5
BIT-20017	微积分（一）	国家精品 理学	翠哲 副教授	082822566771	org/home.htm?	1482634030	超级超级棒	2021-09-25	2	第8次开课	4
BIT-20017	微积分（一）	国家精品 理学	翠哲 副教授	-2119-112021	org/home.htm?	1478282411	讲解很清晰	2021-09-19	2	第8次开课	5
BIT-20017	微积分（一）	国家精品 理学	翠哲 副教授	jutooy	org/home.htm?	1033628938	长，甚至拆成	2022-03-05	1	第6次开课	1
BIT-20017	微积分（一）	国家精品 理学	翠哲 副教授	FangFragrance	org/home.htm?	1447273845	课的练习题很	2022-01-07	1	第8次开课	5
BIT-20017	微积分（一）	国家精品 理学	翠哲 副教授	隐隐野	org/home.htm?	1501975906	很是受益！！	2021-12-29	1	第8次开课	4
BIT-20017	微积分（一）	国家精品 理学	翠哲 副教授	25金诗涵 1120	org/home.htm?	1482692627	程很棒，值得学	2021-12-28	1	第8次开课	4
BIT-20017	微积分（一）	国家精品 理学	翠哲 副教授	娜你有度	org/home.htm?	1493411338	容全面讲解清	2021-12-14	1	第8次开课	5
BIT-20017	微积分（一）	国家精品 理学	翠哲 副教授	极光学徒	org/home.htm?	1489896676	得很易懂，由浅	2021-11-25	1	第8次开课	5
BIT-20017	微积分（一）	国家精品 理学	翠哲 副教授	2022102131刘	org/home.htm?	1447098516	推荐的啊，我	2021-11-15	1	第8次开课	4
BIT-20017	微积分（一）	国家精品 理学	翠哲 副教授	1120212360吴	org/home.htm?	1482729786	好好好好好好	2021-09-17	1	第8次开课	5
BIT-20017	微积分（一）	国家精品 理学	翠哲 副教授	叁柒柒柒柒	org/home.htm?	1445607263	棒，用来课后复	2021-01-15	1	第7次开课	5
BIT-20017	微积分（一）	国家精品 理学	翠哲 副教授	黄梓颖112020	org/home.htm?	1442200248	真的很不错	2021-01-09	1	第7次开课	5
BIT-20017	微积分（一）	国家精品 理学	翠哲 副教授	1120201352李	org/home.htm?	1444224196	很好呀太好了	2021-01-05	1	第7次开课	5
BIT-20017	微积分（一）	国家精品 理学	翠哲 副教授	2010于笑涵112	org/home.htm?	1443870100	科数分，有点	2020-12-15	1	第7次开课	5
BIT-20017	微积分（一）	国家精品 理学	翠哲 副教授	2001-11202013	org/home.htm?	1445586705	简直太棒了！	2020-11-28	1	第7次开课	5
BIT-20017	微积分（一）	国家精品 理学	翠哲 副教授	BIT1120202876	org/home.htm?	1443822664	，对我很有帮	2020-11-24	1	第7次开课	5
BIT-20017	微积分（一）	国家精品 理学	翠哲 副教授	120202827 何	org/home.htm?	1445387524	巩固知识，很	2020-11-22	1	第7次开课	5
BIT-20017	微积分（一）	国家精品 理学	翠哲 副教授	1120201693张	org/home.htm?	1444603201	好的，有所收	2020-11-20	1	第7次开课	5
BIT-20017	微积分（一）	国家精品 理学	翠哲 副教授	付光明 112020	org/home.htm?	1442871399	棒棒棒棒棒棒	2020-11-20	1	第7次开课	5
BIT-20017	微积分（一）	国家精品 理学	翠哲 副教授	1120200670蒋	org/home.htm?	1444966288	真好 真真	2020-11-18	1	第7次开课	5
BIT-20017	微积分（一）	国家精品 理学	翠哲 副教授	Michael Han	org/home.htm?	1443316643	的都很好，重点	2020-11-16	1	第7次开课	5

Fig. 1. Excerpt of the ICourseData Dataset

As shown in Fig. 1, the ICourseData dataset includes user personal information, course information, and user course selection records. The data collection process strictly adhered to relevant laws, regulations, and ethical guidelines to ensure the full protection of user privacy. In addition to supporting the explainable recommendation research presented in this paper, the ICourseData dataset has been made publicly available to the research community. This open-source initiative aims to facilitate the development of AI-assisted education, a rapidly evolving field.

4 Algorithm Design

4.1 Algorithm Design Approach

To improve the explainability of MOOC platform recommendation systems, this paper proposes the CountERText algorithm, which includes the following key steps:

The algorithm uses a genetic algorithm to perform feature selection, identifying the most critical features that contribute to predicting user preferences.

The approach employs Gumbel-Softmax techniques to integrate different types of features. It also learns the relative importance of these features during model training.

The algorithm develops a deep learning model that learns user behavior patterns and the model is used to predict user interest in courses and generate personalized recommendations.

The CountERText algorithm modifies the text features to demonstrate their impact on the recommendation results and provides intuitive explanations for the suggested courses, offering transparent justifications.

Finally, the algorithm provides an integrated module that includes the recommended courses and their explanations, aiming to increase user satisfaction and increase user engagement and retention on the MOOC platform. The framework design of the algorithm is shown in Fig. 2.

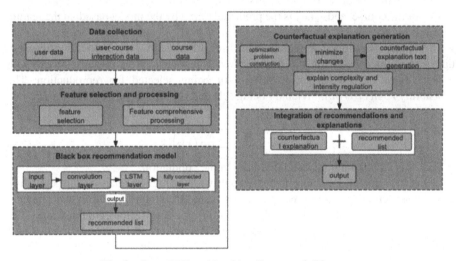

Fig. 2. CountERText Algorithm Framework Diagram

4.2 Feature Selection

In the ICourseData dataset, which contains extensive user and course information, including user personal characteristics, course attributes, and interaction data between users and courses, we aim to increase the accuracy and interpretability of the recommendation system. This paper conducts an in-depth analysis of all available features to identify which features have the greatest impact on the recommendation results. In this section, we utilize a genetic algorithm for feature selection and optimization. A genetic algorithm is a global search optimization method that simulates the process of biological evolution. This step helps the model identify the most critical features for the recommendation results and improves the model's predictive accuracy. The specific implementation steps are as follows:

Initialize the population. Randomly select a subset of features from the ICourseData dataset to form the initial population. The initial population $P0$ consists of a set of feature vectors representing user behavior and course attributes. Each feature vector x_i is represented using binary encoding, where $x_{ij} \in \{0, 1\}$ indicates whether the j-th feature is selected for the recommendation model.

Fitness evaluation. The fitness function $f(x_i)$ is used to measure the effectiveness of the feature subset x_i in the recommendation model. In this paper, the fitness is calculated using the accuracy $Acc(x_i)$, which reflects the consistency between the predicted user course preferences and the actual preferences of the recommendation model:

$$Acc(x_i) = \frac{1}{|V|} \sum_{v \in V} [r_v = \hat{r}_v(x_i)] \tag{1}$$

Where V is the set of user-course pairs in the validation set, r_v is the actual rating of user v for the course, and $\hat{r}_v(x_i)$ is the predicted rating by the model based on the feature subset xi.

Selection operation. The roulette wheel selection method is used to allocate selection probabilities based on the fitness of each feature subset. Feature subsets with higher fitness have a higher probability of being selected for reproduction. The probability $Pselect(i)$ of individual i being selected is proportional to its fitness:

$$P_{select}(i) = \frac{f(x)}{\sum_{j=1}^{N} f(x_j)} \tag{2}$$

Where N is the total number of individuals in the population.

Crossover operation. Select the individuals with the highest fitness in the population and perform crossover with other individuals using the single-point crossover method to generate new offspring. This helps to retain excellent feature combinations. The single-point crossover operation generates new feature subsets by randomly selecting a crossover point and exchanging information between the parent individuals.

$$x_{i'} = (x_{i1}, \ldots, x_{il}, x_{jl+1}, \ldots, x_{jL}) \tag{3}$$

$$x_{j'} = (x_{j1}, \ldots, x_{jl}, x_{il+1}, \ldots, x_{iL}) \tag{4}$$

Where $x_{i'}$ and $x_{j'}$ are the new individuals generated through crossover.

Mutation operation. To introduce new variations, this paper randomly selects some bits in the feature subsets for flipping, thereby exploring new feature combinations:

$$x'_{ij} = \begin{cases} 1, & with\ probability\ P_m \\ x_{ij}, & otherwise \end{cases} \tag{5}$$

Where Pm is the mutation probability.

New generation population. Through selection, crossover, and mutation operations, this paper generates a new generation population $P1$ and replaces the older individuals with lower fitness.

Iterative optimization. This process is repeated until the predetermined number of iterations G is reached or the fitness no longer shows significant improvement (i.e., convergence). Ultimately, this paper obtains an optimal set of feature subsets $x*$.

Figure 3 is the flowchart of the feature selection algorithm.

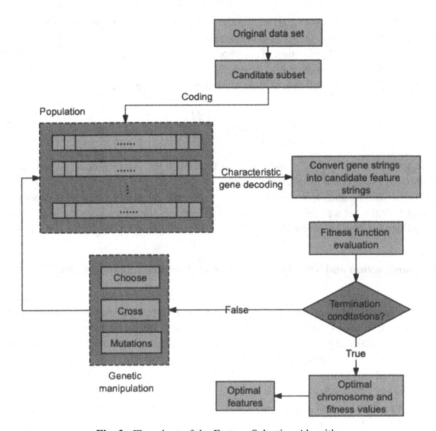

Fig. 3. Flowchart of the Feature Selection Algorithm

4.3 Comprehensive Feature Processing

In the course recommendation system of the MOOC platform, users' behaviors and preferences can be represented by various types of data, such as users' viewing history, ratings, course difficulty levels, and users' review texts. To integrate these different types of features and enable the model to simultaneously consider their impact on the recommendation results, this paper employs the Gumbel-Softmax technique. The specific implementation steps are as follows:

Feature representation and preprocessing. For numerical features, such as the total duration of courses watched by the user, this paper performs normalization to eliminate the impact of different scales. The original value x is converted to a value within the range [0, 1]. The calculation formula is as follows:

$$x_{norm} = \frac{x - min(X)}{max(X) - min(X)} \tag{6}$$

Where X represents the set of all numerical features, and min(X) and max(X) are the minimum and maximum values of this set, respectively.

Gumbel-Softmax Application. This paper applies the Gumbel-Softmax function to the feature vector, converting it into a probability distribution. For a feature vector z, the output probability distribution p of the Gumbel-Softmax can be expressed as:

$$p_i = \frac{\exp\left(\frac{z_i}{\tau}\right)}{\sum_{j=1}^{k} \exp\left(\frac{z_j}{\tau}\right)} \tag{7}$$

Where τ is the temperature parameter, used to control the "smoothness" of the output distribution, and k is the number of features.

Model Training and Optimization. During the model training process, this paper uses Gumbel-Softmax as a regularization term to help the model automatically identify the most influential features when dealing with multiple features.

4.4 Construction and Training of Black-Box Recommendation Model

In this subsection, we construct a model capable of accurately predicting user preferences for MOOC courses. This model leverages the rich feature set obtained during the data preprocessing and feature extraction stages and learns user behavior patterns to generate personalized course recommendations. This lays the groundwork for generating counterfactual explanations in subsequent algorithms. The following is a detailed explanation of this part:

The vector x_u includes the user's historical behavior data, such as course completion status, rating history, and browsing records, as well as personal information, such as age, gender, and educational background. The course feature vector x_c contains the course metadata, such as course category, difficulty level, instructor rating, and other course-related information.

Embedding Layer (for Text Data). Text data, such as user reviews and course descriptions, are first transformed into dense vectors e through the embedding layer. This is achieved using a pre-trained word embedding model (Word2Vec), which maps each word or phrase in the text to a continuous vector space, thereby capturing the semantic information of the text.

Convolutional Layer. The convolutional layer is used to extract key features from the text data. The convolution operation can be represented as $(f^*X)_j = \sum_{i=1}^{n} f_{i,j} \cdot x_i$, where f is the convolutional kernel used to extract features within a local region. n is the width of the convolutional kernel, and j is the index of the output feature map. This helps to identify key phrases or patterns in the text that may indicate user preferences.

LSTM Layer [26] for user behavior sequences, such as the order of course visits and timestamps, the LSTM layer can capture temporal dependencies. The hidden state update of an LSTM can be represented as $h_t = f_{LSTM}(x_t, h_{t-1}, c_{t-1})$, where ht is the hidden state at the current time step, x_t is the input at the current time step, h_{t-1} is the hidden state from the previous time step, and c_{t-1} is the cell state from the previous time step.

Fully Connected Layer and Output Layer. The fully connected layer receives features from both the convolutional layer and the LSTM layer and integrates them into a unified feature representation. This is followed by a non-linear transformation using an activation function (ReLU [20]), which enhances the model's expressive power.

The black-box recommendation model is illustrated in Fig. 4.

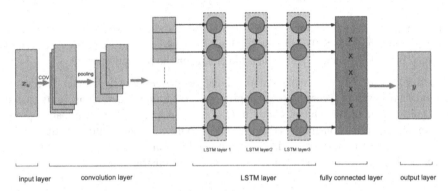

Fig. 4. Black-Box Recommendation Model Diagram

4.5 Counterfactual Explanation Generation

Based on the CountER method by Tan J [11], this paper proposes a causal inference method named CountERText. This method aims to demonstrate how changes in key input features, especially text features, affect the final recommendation results by modifying these features during the recommendation process. Through this approach, users can not only receive recommended courses but also understand why these courses were recommended to them and how the recommendation results would change if certain conditions were altered. In the following subsections, this paper will explore in detail how to generate these counterfactual explanations using the CountERText algorithm.

Optimization Problem Formulation. In the research on constructing a causality-based explainable course recommendation system, formulating the optimization problem is a crucial step. It not only determines the process of generating counterfactual explanations but also directly impacts the quality and practicality of the explanations. The detailed steps are as follows:

Objective Function Design. The goal of the optimization problem is to find a feature change vector Δ that can alter the recommendation result with the minimal amount of modification. To achieve this goal, it is necessary to design an objective function that can quantify both the size of the feature changes and their impact on the recommendation result. The objective function typically consists of two main components: the size of the feature changes and the extent of the change in the recommendation result.

The size of the feature changes can be measured using the L1 norm or L2 norm. The L1 norm tends to produce sparse solutions, meaning that only a few key features are modified, while the L2 norm tends to produce smoother changes. In this paper, we choose the L1 norm to emphasize the simplicity and interpretability of the explanations. The extent of the change in the recommendation result can be measured by comparing the predicted scores before and after the modification. Therefore, the objective function can be expressed as:

$$\min_{\Delta}\{\lambda_1||\Delta||_1 + \lambda_2(S(\Delta) - S(0)\} \tag{8}$$

Where Δ is the feature change vector, $S(\Delta)$ is the prediction scoring function after applying the change Δ, $S(0)$ is the original prediction score, and $\lambda 1$ and $\lambda 2$ are weight parameters used to balance sparsity and the change in the prediction score.

Constraint Setting. To ensure that the found feature changes effectively alter the recommendation result, it is necessary to set appropriate constraints. These constraints ensure the legality of the feature changes and limit the solution space of the optimization problem. In this paper, the constraint is that the change in the recommendation result must be significant enough to remove or add the recommended course from the recommendation list. Specifically, for user i and course j, the following constraints are set:

$$S(\Delta) = s_{ij}^{\Delta} \leq s_{ij}^{K+1} \tag{9}$$

Where s_{ij}^{Δ} is the predicted score for user i and course j after applying the change Δ, and s_{ij}^{K+1} is the score of the marginal item (the course ranked K + 1 on the recommendation list). This constraint ensures that course j will be removed from the recommendation list only if its score after the change is lower than the score of the marginal item.

Solving the Optimization Problem. To solve the above optimization problem using the gradient descent method, the feature change vector Δ needs to be continuously adjusted until all constraints are satisfied and the objective function is minimized. During the solution process, it is essential to consider the algorithm's convergence and stability to ensure that the global optimum is found.

Minimize changes. The core idea of minimizing changes is to identify those key features whose slight modifications are sufficient to alter the recommendation results. This approach is based on the principles of causal inference, where changes in specific factors within the input data can lead to observable changes in the output results. In the CountERText algorithm, an optimization framework is employed that achieves this goal by minimizing the L1 norm of feature changes. The L1 norm is known for producing sparse solutions, which means that only a few key features are modified in the generated counterfactual explanations. Compared to CountER, CountERText has made significant improvements in minimizing changes. CountER primarily focuses on identifying key features that impact recommendation results, whereas CountERText further optimizes this process by introducing the L1 norm to ensure the sparsity of feature changes. This approach not only reduces the number of features included in the generated explanations but also enhances the readability and comprehensibility of the explanations.

Counterfactual Explanation Text Generation. After the optimization problem is solved, the original text is modified based on the solution Δ∗ to generate the counterfactual explanation text. This step is the most critical part of generating explanations because it directly affects the quality of the explanations and user acceptance. The CountERText algorithm employs natural language processing techniques, specifically a text editing model based on Gumbel-Softmax, to generate the modified text. This approach not only captures the semantic information of the text but also maintains its coherence and fluency. Specifically, the modification of each word w can be expressed as:

$$\tilde{w} = GumbelSoftmax(\Theta_{\mathrm{w}}, T) \tag{10}$$

Here, Θ_w is the parameter matrix associated with the word w, and T is the temperature parameter, which controls the smoothness of the distribution. In this way, the generated text can be semantically similar to the original text but differ in key features, producing counterfactual text.

5 Experimental Results and Analysis

5.1 Baseline Model

The model in this paper is compared with explainable recommendation models perceived from three aspects, and also includes a random explanation baseline to show the overall difficulty of the evaluation task.

EFM [22]: Explicit Factor Model. This work combines matrix factorization with sentiment analysis techniques, integrating latent factors with explicit factors. In this way, it can predict user aspect preference scores and item aspect quality scores. The top-1 aligned aspects are used to construct aspect-based explanations.

MTER [23]: Multi-task Explainable Recommendation Model. This work predicts a tensor $X \varepsilon R m \times n \times (r + 1)$, which represents the affinity scores between users, items, and aspects, as well as an additional dimension for the overall rating. The tensor X is obtained through Tucker decomposition [33, 34]. Since user ratings for items are predicted through decomposition in the additional dimension rather than directly through explicit aspects, this method is not suitable for model-oriented evaluation. Therefore, this paper only reports the explanation performance of this model in user-oriented evaluation.

A2CF [24]: Attribute-aware Collaborative Filtering. This method uses a residual feedforward network to predict the missing values in the user aspect matrix X and the item aspect matrix Y. Initially, this method considered user-item preferences and item-item similarities to generate explainable alternative recommendations. We removed the item-item factors to make it compatible with our problem setting, enabling the generation of explanations for any item. Similar to EFM, Top-1 aligned aspects will be used for explanations.

Random: For each item recommended to the user, this paper randomly selects one or more aspects from the space and generates explanations based on them. The evaluation scores of the random baseline can indicate the difficulty of the task.

5.2 User-Oriented Evaluation

As mentioned earlier, to measure the effectiveness of user-oriented evaluation, this paper employs Precision, Recall, and F1-score as the primary evaluation metrics for user-oriented assessment. These metrics reflect the consistency between the generated explanations and the actual user preferences. The user-oriented evaluation results for CountERText and the baseline models are shown in Table 2 and Table 3.

Table 2. User-oriented Evaluation Metrics (Single-faceted Explanations)

Model	Precision (%)	Recall (%)	F1 (%)
Random	1.76	1.33	1.45
EFM	39.25	34.37	35.96
MTER	31.23	27.31	28.54
A2CF	39.38	35.30	36.59
CountERText	40.45	35.71	37.24
CountERText (mask)	40.94	36.19	37.73

Table 3. User-oriented Evaluation Metrics (Multi-faceted Explanations)

Model	Precision (%)	Recall (%)	F1 (%)
Random	1.59	1.75	1.74
EFM	30.47	85.81	43.39
MTER	12.93	41.16	20.90
A2CF	31.86	80.44	43.27
CountERText	28.79	87.07	40.68
CountERText (mask)	32.24	84.20	45.57

Through experiments, it can be noted that the random baseline (Random) performs poorly in both evaluations, indicating the difficulty of the task. Additionally, randomly selecting aspects as explanations almost fails to reveal the reasons behind the recommendations.

Evaluation Results of Single-Faceted Explanations. As shown in Table 2, the CountERText model outperforms other baseline models in terms of precision, recall, and F1-score. Specifically, the precision of the CountERText model is 40.45%, which is 1.2% points higher than the highest baseline model, EFM. The recall is 35.71%, which is 1.34 percentage points higher than EFM. The F1-score is 37.24%, also slightly higher than EFM's 35.96%. This result indicates that the CountERText model can effectively identify users' actual preferences and generate explanations consistent with those preferences.

Evaluation Results of Multi-faceted Explanations. As shown in Table 3, the CountERText model also demonstrates superior performance. Although its precision slightly decreases to 28.79%, the recall significantly increases to 87.07%, and the F1-score reaches 40.68%. This indicates that when generating explanations that include multiple aspects, the CountERText model can more comprehensively cover user preferences, even though this may result in some aspects of the explanations not being a direct reflection of the user's actual preferences.

5.3 Model-Oriented Evaluation

As mentioned earlier in this paper, to measure the effectiveness of model-oriented evaluation, we employ Probability of Necessity (PN) and Probability of Sufficiency (PS) as the primary evaluation metrics. The PN metric measures the necessity of a feature in the recommendation decision, that is, whether the recommendation result would change without this feature. The PS metric measures the sufficiency of a feature, that is, whether this feature alone is enough to sustain the recommendation decision. Additionally, this paper calculates the harmonic mean of PN and PS (FNS) to comprehensively evaluate the necessity and sufficiency of the explanations.

The model-oriented evaluation results for CountERText and the baseline models are shown in Table 4 and Table 5.

Table 4. Model-oriented Evaluation Metrics (Single-faceted Explanations)

Model	PN (%)	PS (%)	FNS (%)
Random	3.56	2.75	2.94
EFM	6.01	74.84	11.12
A2CF	25.66	65.53	36.88
CountERText	34.37	41.50	37.60
CountERText (mask)	35.49	46.91	40.35

Table 5. Model-oriented Evaluation Metrics (Multi-faceted Explanations)

Model	PN (%)	PS (%)	FNS (%)
Random	5.81	8.80	6.66
EFM	51.72	90.33	70.01
A2CF	53.48	87.89	65.71
CountERText	65.00	79.50	70.82
CountERText (mask)	60.40	81.30	69.30

Evaluation Results of Single-Faceted Explanations. According to the data in Table 4, the CountERText algorithm achieves 34.37% on the PN metric, surpassing other baseline models. This indicates that the features included in the explanations generated by the CountERText algorithm play a necessary role in the recommendation results in most cases. In other words, without these features, the recommendation results are likely to change. This result highlights the ability of the CountERText algorithm to identify key factors in recommendations. For the PS metric, the CountERText algorithm scores 41.50%, which is slightly lower than the EFM model's 46.91%. However, it still demonstrates the algorithm's ability to sustain the recommendation decision on the basis solely of the generated explanations in certain cases. This means that the CountERText algorithm also has a considerable advantage in terms of its ability to explain the recommendation results.

Evaluation Results of Multi-faceted Explanation. In the evaluation of multifaceted explanations, as shown in Table 5, the CountERText algorithm achieves 65.00% on the PN metric. This result is significantly higher than that of other baseline models, indicating that the CountERText algorithm can more comprehensively cover the necessary factors in the recommendation decision in multi-faceted explanations. This further confirms the algorithm's advantage in providing comprehensive explanations. For the PS metric, the CountERText algorithm scores 79.50%, which is slightly lower than the EFM model's 87.89%. This result may suggest that in multi-faceted explanations, the CountERText algorithm might require more features to jointly sustain the recommendation decision. This could also reflect the algorithm's conservativeness in generating explanations, as it tends to include more features to ensure the comprehensiveness of the explanation. For the FNS metric, our algorithm also outperforms the baseline models. This indicates that our algorithm not only identifies aspects that significantly impact the recommendation results but also shows that these aspects are often the key factors for the recommendation. These results demonstrate that our algorithm effectively reveals the decision logic of the recommendation model, providing meaningful explanations for users. Additionally, in model-oriented evaluations, the masking limits the ability of the CountERText explanation model's behavior.

5.4 Explanation Complexity and Intensity

Through the theoretical framework presented in this paper, it can be seen that the difficulty of removing different items from the Top-K list varies. Suppose for a particular user, the recommendation system generates the top-K recommended items on the basis of their ranking scores as v_{j1}, v_{j2}, ..., v_{jk}. Intuitively, removing v_{j1} from the list is more difficult than removing v_{jk}. The reason is that to remove v_{j1}, the explanation intensity must be at least $\epsilon = s_{i,j1} - s_{i,jK+1}$, which is greater than the intensity required to remove v_{jk}, i.e., $\epsilon = s_{i,j1} - s_{i,jK+1}$. Therefore, the explanations generated for items in higher positions on the list may have greater explanation complexity because the reasoning model must apply larger changes or more aspects to generate high-intensity explanations. In the experiments, this paper demonstrates the average explanation complexity of items at different positions to verify the above discussion.

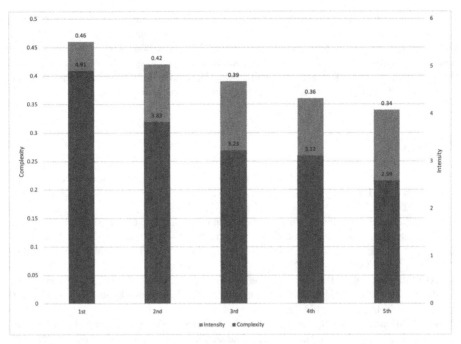

Fig. 5. Average Explanation Complexity/Intensity for Items at Different Positions

As shown in Fig. 5, the average complexity and explanation intensity for removing items from different positions (i.e., from the first to the fifth) are illustrated. Generally, removing the item in the first position from the recommendation list requires, on average, 1.59 more aspects than removing the item in the fifth position. This is because stronger changes are needed to remove it, which aligns with the fact that highly recommended items have more reasons for recommendation.

6 Conclusion

This paper addresses the challenges of personalization and explainability in MOOC recommendation systems by proposing a causal inference-based explainable course recommendation algorithm. The algorithm deeply analyzes user behavior data to generate counterfactual samples, revealing the underlying reasons for user course selection. This enhances the explainability and persuasiveness of the recommendation approach, as validated by the experimental results.

In the future, the researchers plan to further integrate educational psychology, explore cross-platform collaborative recommendations, and develop dynamic adaptive algorithms. The goal is to construct a more intelligent and equitable online education ecosystem that supports the modernization of education and the lifelong learning needs of society.

Acknowledgments. This paper is supported by the Humanities and Social Sciences Research Planning Fund Project of the Ministry of Education: "Research on Metacognitive Diagnosis Theory and Technology Driven by Multimodal Learning Data" (23YJA880091) and The Fun-damental Research Funds for the Central Universities. Additionally, we would like to acknowledge the Undergraduate Teaching Reform Project of Peking University in 2024: "Gamified Interactive Experimental Teaching in Software Engineering" (Project No. 7100903145).

References

1. Cui, J., Ma, Y.: Research progress and prospects of artificial intelligence education in my country. Coll. Educ. Manag. **17**(06), 31–39 (2023). https://doi.org/10.13316/j.cnki.jhem.202 31102.004
2. Zhu, X.: Looking forward to the future based on research on the current situation of blended teaching at home and abroad. Educ. Sci. Forum (08), 75–80 (2024)
3. Yu, H.: Educational equity: a rational order under the digital transformation boom. Educ. Theory Pract. **43**(25), 59–64 (2023)
4. Alatrash, R., Chatti, M.A., Ain, Q.U., et al.: ConceptGCN: knowledge concept recommendation in MOOCs based on knowledge graph convolutional networks and SBERT. Comput. Educ. Artif. Intell. **6**, 100193 (2024)
5. Ma, T., Huang, L., Lu, Q., et al.: KR-GCN: knowledge-aware reasoning with graph convolution network for explainable recommendation. ACM Trans. Inf. Syst. **41**(1), 1–27 (2023)
6. Klasnja-Milicevic, A., Milicevic, D.: Top-N knowledge concept recommendations in MOOCs using a neural co-attention model. IEEE Access (2023)
7. Gu, H., Duan, Z., Xie, P., et al.: Modeling balanced explicit and implicit relations with contrastive learning for knowledge concept recommendation in MOOCs. arXiv preprint arXiv: 2402.08256 (2024)
8. Erkan, E.R.: An explainable machine learning approach to predicting and understanding dropouts in MOOCs. Kastamonu Eğitim Dergisi **31**(1), 143–154 (2023)
9. Gong, J., Wan, Y., Liu, Y., et al.: Reinforced moocs concept recommendation in heterogeneous information networks. ACM Trans. Web **17**(3), 1–27 (2023)
10. Xu, S., Ji, J., Li, Y., et al.: Causal inference for recommendation: foundations, methods and applications. arXiv preprint arXiv:2301.04016 (2023)
11. Tan, J., Xu, S., Ge, Y., et al.: Counterfactual explainable recommendation. In: Proceedings of the 30th ACM International Conference on Information & Knowledge Management, pp. 1784–1793 (2021)
12. Ghazimatin, A., Balalau, O., Saha Roy, R., et al.: PRINCE: provider-side interpretability with counterfactual explanations in recommender systems. In: Proceedings of the 13th International Conference on Web Search and Data Mining, pp. 196–204 (2020)
13. Gao, C., Zheng, Y., Wang, W., et al.: Causal inference in recommender systems: a survey and future directions. ACM Trans. Inf. Syst. **42**(4), 1–32 (2024)
14. Zhu, X., Zhang, Y., Yang, X., et al.: Mitigating hidden confounding effects for causal recommendation. IEEE Trans. Knowl. Data Eng. (2024)
15. Zhu, Y., Ma, J., Li, J.: Causal inference in recommender systems: a survey of strategies for bias mitigation, explanation, and generalization. arXiv preprint arXiv:2301.00910 (2023)
16. Pearl, J.: Causal inference in statistics: an overview (2009)
17. Guo, C., Sablayrolles, A., Jégou, H., et al.: Gradient-based adversarial attacks against text transformers. arXiv preprint arXiv:2104.13733 (2021)

18. Yu, Y., Si, X., Hu, C., et al.: A review of recurrent neural networks: LSTM cells and network architectures. Neural Comput. **31**(7), 1235–1270 (2019)

19. Grigsby, E., Lindsey, K., Rolnick, D.: Hidden symmetries of ReLU networks. In: International Conference on Machine Learning, pp. 11734–11760. PMLR (2023)

20. Ranjbar, N., Momtazi, S., Homayoonpour, M.M.: Explaining recommendation system using counterfactual textual explanations. Mach. Learn., 1–24 (2023)

21. Aizawa, A.: An information-theoretic perspective of TF–IDF measures. Inf. Process. Manag. **39**(1), 45–65 (2003)

22. Wang, N., Wang, H., Jia, Y., et al.: Explainable recommendation via multi-task learning in opinionated text data. In: The 41st International ACM SIGIR Conference on Research & Development in Information Retrieval, pp. 165–174 (2018)

23. Karatzoglou, A., Amatriain, X., Baltrunas, L., et al.: Multiverse recommendation: n-dimensional tensor factorization for context-aware collaborative filtering. In: Proceedings of the Fourth ACM conference on Recommender Systems, pp. 79–86 (2010)

The Role of Teaching Gestures in Enhancing Student Involvement: An Experimental Study Based on a Continuous 600-Minute Video Analysis

Yiqiang Rao[1] , Zeyan Zhao[1,2] , Bo Zhao[1(✉)], and Chaojun Yang[1]

[1] Key Laboratory of Educational Informatization for Nationalities, Kunming 650500, China
ykzb63@126.com
[2] School of Information Science and Technology, Kunming 650500, China

Abstract. This experimental study investigates the impact of teaching gestures on student involvement in the classroom. The study analyzes the different impact of teaching gestures on student involvement by collecting and processing the data of teaching gestures, student involvement, and head-up rates. Specifically, this study conducted descriptive Statistics to explore the relationship between different types of teaching gestures and students' involvement. An Inferential Statistics conducted to analyze the mediating effect of teaching gestures between head-up rates and involvement. ANOVA analysis of variance was employed to determine whether there are significant differences in student involvement among various teaching gesture types. And then, through the calculation of Cohen's d to assess the impact size of teaching gestures on student involvement. The findings reveal a link between certain specific teaching gestures and increased student involvement, indicating that different teaching gestures strategic can effectively enhance students' attention. These discoveries underscore the importance of non-verbal communication in teaching. A deeper analysis of classroom data can provide a better understanding of how teachers can attract and maintain students' attention through gestures, thereby improving teaching quality and students' learning outcomes.

Keywords: Teaching gestures · Student involvement · Non-verbal communication

1 Introduction

Education is a complex human interaction that relies not only on verbal communication but also on the subtle non-verbal cues. Among these non-verbal elements, teaching gestures have emerged as a significant component of the pedagogical process, which have enhanced the learning experience by engaging students more effectively. Many researchers have repeatedly argued for the importance of teaching gestures in the teaching and learning process. Research has consistently shown the significant role of gestures in teaching and learning. Matsumoto (2017) found that both teachers and students

K. Zhang et al. (Eds.): CSEI 2024, CCIS 2447, pp. 200–209, 2025.
https://doi.org/10.1007/978-981-96-3735-5_15

use abstract deictic and metaphoric gestures in the ESL grammar classroom, which are important for instruction and assessment. Alibali (2013) demonstrated that students learn more when their teacher uses effective gestures, particularly in connecting ideas in mathematics instruction. Goldin-Meadow (2004) emphasized the crucial role of gestures in conveying information during problem-solving, both for children and teachers. Roth (2001) further underscored the importance of gestures in human communication and cognition, calling for more research on their role in education. While Nafisi (2010) highlighted the use of gestures as a pedagogic tool in singing lessons. Chue (2015) further emphasized the role of iconic gestures in science teaching, particularly in conveying abstract concepts. Novack (2015) expanded on this by discussing how learners' gestures can reveal their understanding and how teachers can use these gestures to support learning. These studies collectively underscore the importance of gestures in enhancing communication and learning in various educational contexts.

The primary concern of this research is to determine whether and how different types of teaching gestures influence student engagement in the classroom. Specifically, we aim to explore the correlation between various teaching gestures and the level of student involvement, as measured by observable metrics such as head-up rates and involvement levels. The purpose of this study is to provide empirical evidence that supports the hypothesis that certain teaching gestures can significantly increase student engagement. This study hope to contribute to the body of knowledge on effective teaching strategies and offer practical insights for educators seeking to enhance their pedagogical approaches. While this study aims to provide a comprehensive analysis of the impact of teaching gestures, it is important to acknowledge its scope and limitations. The study focuses on a specific educational context and may not be generalizable to all classroom settings. Additionally, the study's findings are based on a particular set of gestures and may not encompass the full spectrum of non-verbal communication in teaching.

2 Methodology

2.1 Definition and Classification of Teaching Gestures

A range of studies have explored the role of gestures in classroom teaching. Liu (2020) developed a taxonomy of teachers' gestures, finding that it can distinguish between novice and expert teachers. Lazaraton (2004) emphasized the importance of gestures as a form of input for second language learners. Zhang (2010) identified a variety of gesture classes in lecture videos, including pedagogical and traditional types. Solomon (2018) applied a gesture taxonomy to introductory computing concepts, suggesting its potential for understanding student knowledge in programming education. These studies collectively highlight the significance of gestures in the classroom and the potential for further research in this area. For the purposes of this study, teaching gestures are delineated into two principal categories: descriptive and indicative gestures. Descriptive gestures are employed by educators to vividly illustrate concepts, ideas, or scenarios, thereby enhancing the students' cognitive involvement and aiding in the visualization of abstract subjects. On the other hand, indicative gestures function as directional cues, guiding students' attention to specific elements within the learning environment or emphasizing particular points under discussion. To effectively contrast the impact of these gestures on student involvement, the study analyzes the distribution of descriptive gestures, indicative gestures, and instances without gestures in instructional videos. This quantitative approach allows for a systematic comparison of the prevalence and frequency of each gesture type across various teaching scenarios.

2.2 Data Sources and Statistical Methods

The data for this study was collect from the Smart Education Platform of our university. The platform records the teaching and learning process and provides a large number of indicators for evaluating teaching and learning. Specifically, this study extracted data on student classroom involvement and heads-up rates. In order to systematically document the usage of teaching gestures, the study implemented a time-stamped logging method. Teaching gestures were recorded at two-minute intervals throughout the lessons, mirroring the frequency of the engagement and head-up rate metrics. This synchronization ensures a temporal congruence between the observation of gestures and the measurement of student engagement, allowing for a more precise correlation analysis.

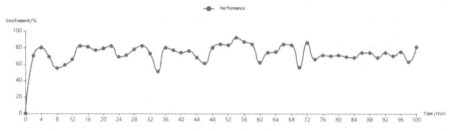

Fig. 1. Performance line of students

Figure 1 presents the performance line of students, graphically representing the classroom involvement levels at two-minute intervals. The y-axis of the graph denotes the involvement level, which is measured by the Smart Education Platform using a standardized metric that reflects the students' active participation and attentiveness. The x-axis represents the time progression of the class, with each unit corresponding to a two-minute segment. This temporal resolution allows for a detailed examination of the fluctuations in student involvement over the course. The classroom engagement level depicted in Fig. 1 is a composite metric derived from the analysis of specific student behaviors observed during class sessions. The specific behaviors considered in the calculation of student involvement include, Reading and Writing-Time spent on class tasks such as taking notes, completing exercises, or engaging with the material through writing. Raising Hands-Instances where students signal their willingness to participate by raising their hands, indicating a desire to contribute to the class discussion or ask questions. Listening-The attentiveness of students during lectures or when the teacher is providing information, demonstrated by focused body language and eye contact. Peer Interaction-The extent of collaboration and discussion among students, which is indicative of a collaborative learning environment. Responding-The frequency of student responses to teacher inquiries or prompts, reflecting the level of understanding and engagement with the material.

The involvement level is quantified through the Smart Education Platform, which employs algorithms to analyze classroom behavior data collected at two-minute intervals. The platform's smart system captures and weights these behaviors to produce a continuous performance line that reflects the flow of student involvement throughout the class. This method of calculation allows for a whole understanding of student involvement. Figure 2 shows an example of the percentage of teacher and student behaviors counted by the platform.

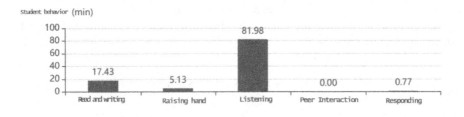

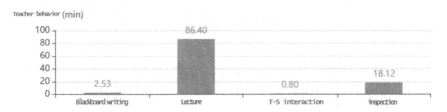

Fig. 2. Percentage of teacher-student behavior

The statistical approach of this study is designed to evaluate the relationship between the incidence of teaching gestures and student engagement metrics. Therefore, it is necessary to count the students' classroom engagement and head-up rate from the smart platform. However, there is no function in the system to recognize teaching gestures, so teaching gestures were counted by manual punching every two minutes. The data was analyzed using a combination of descriptive and inferential statistics. Descriptive statistics provided an overview of the distribution and frequency of teaching gestures and engagement metrics. Further, to examine the potential correlation between teaching gestures and student engagement, the study employed correlation analysis. This method quantifies the strength and direction of the relationship between variables, offering insights into whether the use of gestures is associated with increased student involvement. Additionally, to test the significance of observed correlations, inferential statistics, specifically the T-test, were utilized. The T-test is a robust statistical tool for comparing the means of two groups, which in this context, helps to determine if there are any statistically significant differences in student engagement levels corresponding to the presence or type of teaching gesture. The consistency of the data collection intervals for both teaching gestures and engagement metrics ensures that the statistical analysis is conducted on a comparable and aligned dataset, thereby enhancing the validity of the study's conclusions.

3 Data Analysis

3.1 Descriptive Statistics of Teaching Gesture

The descriptive statistics presented in this section serve as the foundation for understanding the basic features of teaching gestures and their potential impact on classroom dynamics. The detailed account of gesture usage provides a basis for further statistical analysis aimed at uncovering the relationship between teaching gestures and student involvement (Tables 1 and 2).

Table 1. Statistics on teaching gestures in involvement

gesture	count	mean	std	min	25%	50%	75%	max
0	191	0.57367	0.21733	0	0.46	0.62	0.73	0.92
1	61	0.54689	0.23083	0.05	0.34	0.62	0.73	0.84
2	54	0.53722	0.20948	0.07	0.325	0.61	0.7075	0.91

Table 2. Statistics on teaching gestures in head-up rate

gesture	count	mean	std	min	25%	50%	75%	max
0	191	0.23534	0.10579	0	0.16	0.23	0.31	0.57
1	61	0.24918	0.09202	0.11	0.18	0.23	0.31	0.54
2	54	0.25685	0.08211	0.04	0.1825	0.25	0.3275	0.4

The descriptive statistics for teaching gestures, categorized by type—0 for no gesture, 1 for indicative gestures, and 2 for descriptive gestures. With a sample size of 191, the mean involvement level is 0.574, suggesting a moderate degree of student involvement in the absence of gestures. The standard deviation is 0.217, indicating a fair amount of variability in engagement levels. The minimum engagement recorded is 0, and the maximum is 0.92, with the median at 0.62. The interquartile range, stretching from the 25th to the 75th percentile, is from 0.46 to 0.73. The head-up rate for no gesture has a mean of 0.235, a standard deviation of 0.106, and a similar distribution pattern to involvement, with a minimum of 0 and a maximum of 0.57. For indicative gestures, this category has 61 observations and a mean involvement level of 0.547, slightly lower than that of no gesture. The standard deviation is higher at 0.231, denoting greater variability. The range of involvement is narrower, with a minimum of 0.05 and a maximum of 0.84, and a median of 0.62. The mean head-up rate for indicative gestures is 0.249, with a lower standard deviation of 0.092, indicating more consistent effects on head-up rates compared to the other categories. In descriptive gestures, with 54 observations, the mean involvement is 0.537, which is slightly lower than the indicative gestures but still within a close range. The standard deviation is 0.209, suggesting variability in the impact of descriptive gestures. The minimum engagement is higher at 0.07, and the maximum is 0.91, with a median of 0.61. The descriptive gestures show a mean head-up rate of 0.257, a standard deviation of 0.082, which is the lowest among the three categories, suggesting a more predictable effect on student head-up behavior.

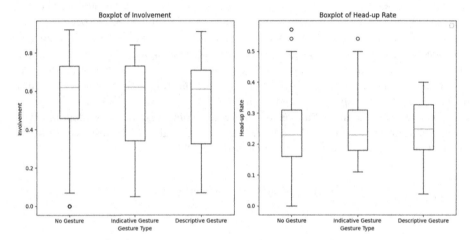

Fig. 3. The boxplot of different teaching gesture

A comprehensive overview of the distribution and central tendencies of student involvement and head-up rates across different teaching gesture types provides Fig. 3. To visually represent these statistics, boxplots were constructed for each variable, categorized by the three distinct gesture types: no gesture, indicative gestures, and descriptive gestures. The boxplots reveal no significant outliers or skewness in the data distribution for either variable, which is a prerequisite for conducting parametric tests such as ANOVA. The F-value and P-value obtained from the ANOVA tests provide statistical evidence to support or refute the visual observations made from the boxplots.

3.2 Inferential Statistics of Teaching Gesture

To further investigate the impact of different teaching gestures on student involvement and attention, an Analysis of Variance (ANOVA) was conducted (Table 3).

The ANOVA results for Involvement demonstrate a significant effect of teaching gestures ($F(2, n) = 374.20$, $p < .0001$). The mean levels of student involvement varied significantly across the three gesture types, with the no gesture condition showing the highest F-value and an extremely low P-value ($1.58e-58$), suggesting a substantial impact on student engagement. Similarly, the Head-up rate also revealed significant effects, with the highest F-value observed for the no gesture condition at 374.20 and a

Table 3. ANOVA results for teaching gestures

gesture	F-value	P-value
0	374.1971	1.58E−58
1	87.55254	5.85E−16
2	83.85045	4.43E−15

P-value of 1.58e−58. The indicative gesture and descriptive gesture conditions showed slightly lower but still highly significant F-values of 87.55 and 83.85, respectively, and P-values of 5.85e−16 and 4.43e−15, indicating a clear influence on students. Similarly, the Head-up rate also revealed significant effects, with the highest F-value observed for the no gesture condition at 374.20 and a P-value of 1.58e−58. The indicative gesture and descriptive gesture conditions showed slightly lower but still highly significant F-values of 87.55 and 83.85, respectively, and P-values of 5.85e−16 and 4.43e−15.

To understand the impact degree of different teaching gestures on student involvement and head-up rate, this study conducted Cohen's d analysis. The results of Cohen's d effect size for each comparison are summarized in Table 4.

Table 4. Cohen's d for different gesture

Gesture types	Involvement	Head-up rate
No gesture vs Gesture1	0.121369521	−0.1348181
No gesture vs Gesture2	0.168995846	−0.212767844
Gesture 1 vs Gesture2	0.04371	−0.087661005

When No gesture vs Gesture1, The Cohen's d value is 0.1214, indicating a small effect size. This suggests the effect is relatively minor. When No gesture vs Gesture2, The Cohen's d value is 0.1690, also indicating a small effect size. This result suggests that Gesture1 has a slightly greater impact on student involvement than Gesture2, but the overall effect remains small. When Gesture 1 vs Gesture2, The Cohen's d value is 0.0437, indicating a negligible effect size. This implies that there is very little difference in student involvement between Gesture1 and Gesture2. However, Head-up Rate is different, The Cohen's d value is −0.1348, indicating a small negative effect size. This suggests that the head-up rate is slightly higher when no gesture is used compared to Gesture1. The Cohen's d value is −0.2128, indicating a small to moderate negative effect size. This result suggests that the head-up rate is higher when no gesture is used compared to Gesture2. The Cohen's d value is −0.0877, indicating a negligible effect size. This implies that the difference in head-up rate between Gesture1 and Gesture2 is very small, with Gesture2 being slightly more effective in reducing the head-up rate.

4 Empirical Results

4.1 Distribution of Teaching Gestures

The distribution of teaching gestures is a critical aspect of understanding how these nonverbal cues are utilized in the classroom and their prevalence across different teaching scenarios. This section provides an empirical analysis of the frequency and distribution of the three gesture types observed in the study. To further understand the relative frequency, the proportion of each gesture type is calculated as a percentage of the total sample size. This allows for a normalized comparison of the frequency of each gesture type. Additionally, the temporal distribution of gestures is analyzed to determine if there are specific moments within a class where gestures are more likely to occur. This could be influenced by factors such as the complexity of the subject matter, teacher' habits, or the engagement level of individuals. The study also examines the variability in gesture usage across different instructors. This analysis is crucial for identifying individual teaching styles and preferences, which may have implications for the effectiveness of gestures in enhancing student involvement. Therefore, the same teacher and the same class were chosen for the follow-up analysis to try to avoid the influence of other factors. In summary, the distribution of teaching gestures is a multifaceted phenomenon that is influenced by various factors, including the instructional context, the subject matter, and the individual teaching style of the instructor. The results lay the groundwork for a deeper analysis of the relationship between gesture usage and student involvement.

4.2 Correlation Between Gestures and Student Involvement

The relationship between teaching gestures and student involvement is a nuanced one, with multiple factors contributing to the overall engagement of students in the classroom. Teaching gestures have been observed to have a direct impact on student involvement. The nonverbal cues provided by gestures can enhance understanding, emphasize key points, and maintain the flow of information, all of which contribute to increased engagement. However, the data analysis indicates that the influence of gestures on involvement is not isolated but is significantly mediated through the head-up rate. The head-up rate, which measures the frequency and duration for which students maintain an upright posture and make eye contact with the instructor, serves as a crucial intermediary in the relationship between gestures and involvement. When students are looking up and paying visual attention to the teacher, they are more likely to be receptive to the information being conveyed through gestures.

The empirical data presented in the previous sections provides evidence of the correlation between gestures and involvement. Specifically, the descriptive statistics and ANOVA results highlight significant differences in both involvement and head-up rate across the three gesture types. The Cohen's d analysis further quantifies the effect sizes, indicating that while the impact of gestures on involvement is small to moderate, the impact on head-up rate is more pronounced. The mediating role of head-up rate suggests that teaching gestures may not only capture students' attention directly but also indirectly by prompting them to look up and engage more actively in the learning process. This finding is consistent with theories of classroom communication and engagement, which emphasize the importance of visual attention in facilitating cognitive processing and emotional connection. For educators, understanding the correlation between gestures, head-up rate, and student involvement offers practical insights into how to optimize teaching strategies. By being mindful of the use of gestures and their potential to influence head-up rates, instructors can potentially enhance the overall involvement of their students.

5 Discussion and Conclusion

The study provides an evidence that teaching gestures play a significant role in enhancing student involvement in classroom. Specifically, the findings indicate that gestures, through their influence on the head-up rate, indirectly promote a higher level of student engagement. When students are more frequently looking up and making eye contact with the teacher, they are more likely to be cognitively and emotionally invested in the learning process. This relationship underscores the subtle but powerful way in which nonverbal communication can foster a more interactive educational environment. Teaching gestures serve multiple functions in the classroom. They can clarify complex concepts, emphasize key points, and regulate the flow of information. Moreover, gestures can act as a form of visual symbol, helping students to structure and organize the lecture content in their minds. The effectiveness of gestures in facilitating understanding and retention cannot be overstated, as they provide an additional layer of communication that complements verbal instruction. While the benefits of teaching gestures are clear, the manner and frequency of their use are equally important. Overuse or inappropriate gestures may distract students or dilute the intended message. Educators must be mindful of the type and timing of gestures to ensure they are used in a way that maximizes their pedagogical value. The study's findings suggest that a balanced and thoughtful approach to incorporating gestures into teaching can significantly contribute to a more engaging and effective learning experience.

Despite the findings of this study is valuable, there are limitations that must be acknowledged. The sample size is limited, may not fully represent the diversity of classroom environments and student populations. Additionally, the study' focus on specific types of gestures may not cover all aspects of nonverbal communication used by educators. Future research should aim to expand the scope of gesture types and explore their impact across different educational contexts and cultures. Furthermore, the study's subject limits the ability to draw comprehensive conclusions. In conclusion, this study reveals the pivotal role of teaching gestures in influencing student involvement through the mediating effect of the head-up rate. It highlights the importance of integrating gestures as a strategic component of instructional design. The intricate relationship between teaching gestures, head-up rates, and student involvement invites us to reconsider the foundational elements of pedagogical practice. Teaching gestures, once used only as an adjunct to verbal teaching, have become an important part of classroom interaction. The subtle changes of non-verbal communication provide educators with a medium for communicating with students that can engage, inspire and enhance the learning experience. This research presents practical insights, it also provides a little value for further exploration.

Acknowledgments. This study is derived from the Yunnan Normal University Graduate Student Research and Innovation Fund in 2023 (Project No. CIC2023006).

References

Matsumoto, Y., Dobs, A.M.: Pedagogical gestures as interactional resources for teaching and learning tense and aspect in the ESL grammar classroom. Lang. Learn. **67**, 7–42 (2017)

Alibali, M.W., et al.: Students learn more when their teacher has learned to gesture effectively. Gesture **13**, 210–233 (2013)

Goldin-Meadow, S.: Gesture's role in the learning process. Theory Pract. **43**, 314–321 (2004)

Roth, W.: Gestures: their role in teaching and learning. Rev. Educ. Res. **71**, 365–392 (2001)

Nafisi, J.: Gesture as a tool of communication in the teaching of singing. Aust. J. Music. Educ. **2**, 103–116 (2010)

Chue, S., Lee, Y., Tan, K.C.: Iconic gestures as undervalued representations during science teaching. Cogent Educ. **2** (2015)

Novack, M.A., Goldin-Meadow, S.: Learning from gesture: how our hands change our minds. Educ. Psychol. Rev. **27**, 405–412 (2015)

Liu, Q., Zhang, N., Chen, W., Wang, Q., Yuan, Y., Xie, K.: Categorizing teachers' gestures in classroom teaching: from the perspective of multiple representations. Soc. Semiot. **32**, 184–204 (2020)

Lazaraton, A.: Gesture and speech in the vocabulary explanations of one ESL teacher: a microanalytic inquiry. Lang. Learn. **54**, 79–117 (2004)

Zhang, J.R., Guo, K., Herwana, C., Kender, J.R.: Annotation and taxonomy of gestures in lecture videos. In: 2010 IEEE Computer Society Conference on Computer Vision and Pattern Recognition - Workshops, pp. 1–8 (2010)

Solomon, A., Guzdial, M., Disalvo, B., Shapiro, B.R.: Applying a gesture taxonomy to introductory computing concepts. In: Proceedings of the 2018 ACM Conference on International Computing Education Research (2018)

The Construction of ESP Digital Textbook Editorial Team Based on CLIL Concept

Haiyun Han[(⊠)], Dan Xian, and Yuanhui Li

Sanya Aviation and Tourism College, Sanya 572000, Hainan, China
`103238991@qq.com`

Abstract. Currently, numerous issues persist within the realm of ESP (English for Specific Purpose) digital textbooks, including a significant lack of deep integration between industry and education, emphasis on specialization knowledge rather than language skills, unsatisfied content, etc., which seriously hinders the enhancement of the teaching quality of ESP courses. The problems of textbooks are ultimately the problems of textbook editors, so building a diversified, professional and efficient editorial team is the guarantee of high-quality textbooks. This study takes the ESP teachers of three higher vocational colleges in SY city as the research object, guided by the concept of CLIL, investigates three aspects related to the core requirements of ESP digital textbooks' writing, and finds that the ESP teachers, as the main force of ESP digital textbooks' writing, have difficulties that cannot be overcome by themselves in short term, such as insufficient professional background knowledge and low level of information technology, so they cannot completely solve the problems of textbooks by themselves. Therefore, this paper put forward the construction of a TPT teachers' community, a tripartite synergy for the high-quality development of ESP digital textbooks.

Keywords: Digital textbooks · ESP Teachers · TPT Teachers' Community · CLIL

1 Introduction

1.1 Background

Textbook reform is a significant part of the "three-teaching" reform, and its position and role in the education system cannot be ignored. "Three-teaching" reform usually refers to the reform of the three major elements of teaching textbooks, teaching methods and teachers, which are interrelated and mutually influential and jointly play a role in the whole educational process. As a carrier of knowledge and information, textbooks are not only the basis of teaching but also an important medium for teachers to transfer knowledge and students to acquire knowledge. Therefore, the textbook reform is directly related to the whole education reform. Textbook reform mainly focuses on two aspects. One is the content of the textbook, i.e., presenting subject knowledge in a more accurate, cutting-edge, scientific and reasonable way. The second is the form of textbooks. The

K. Zhang et al. (Eds.): CSEI 2024, CCIS 2447, pp. 210–221, 2025.
https://doi.org/10.1007/978-981-96-3735-5_16

development of fusion media, the progress of digital communication technology and the popularization of internet have brought great changes to higher education. This change has not only changed the way in which college students read, learn, and are also presented with new challenges and opportunities for traditional paper textbooks. The digital transformation of paper textbooks has become a trend [1]. As a crucial tool to improve the effectiveness of education, digital textbooks can align with evolving digital transformation trends in the education sector. However, the digital transformation of paper textbooks is a complex systematic project that needs joint participation and efforts of many parties, and it is necessary to promote the orderly advancement of the digital transformation of textbooks under the premise of respecting the laws of education for the purpose of ensuring the quality of digital textbooks [2]. In the face of new challenges, traditional textbook editors, especially college teachers, must explore a new path of digital textbook construction that conforms to the trend and benefits students. This is not only an important step for education to realize digital transformation but also an important direction for their own cross-industry integration and development [3].

ESP textbooks are of great significance to English language teaching. ESP (English for Specific Purpose), also known as professional English or vocational English in the curriculum of colleges and universities, began to appear in the literature in the late 1960s. Halliday, as a pioneer, proposed the academic concept of English for specialized purpose (ESP), which advocates the development of specialized English for specific occupational groups, such as civil servants, police officers, magistrates, nurses, agricultural technicians and engineers [4]. ESP is also a very important part of the curriculum in higher vocational institutions. It highlights the integration of language learning and professional skills learning and highlights the professional and practical nature of English learning. ESP is designed to meet the English needs of students in specific fields or occupations and is indispensable in deepening the integration of industry and education and promoting school-enterprise cooperation in vocational education. Through the study of ESP, students can better adapt to the needs of their careers and improve their professional competitiveness.

ESP textbooks play a key role in supporting English language teaching. First, for those ESP teachers who have just transformed from EGP teachers, their reliance on ESP textbooks is even more obvious. This is because ESP materials can provide them with the necessary language teaching tools and references while teaching specialized knowledge, which undoubtedly enhances teaching effectiveness and students' learning experience. Second, for learners, ESP textbooks are the only formal way for them to combine professional learning with language learning. A high-quality ESP textbook not only stimulates students' interest in learning but also provides a standardized language model for learners [5], which is also confirmed by Hutchinson and Waters, who noted that good ESP textbooks have multiple positive effects, including facilitating teachers' organization of the teaching process in class and reflecting the authors' perceptions of the nature of language. Therefore, the level of authorship of ESP textbooks can seriously affect the quality of teaching and learning in ESP courses.

With the progress and innovation of modern education information technology, the pace of digital transformation of traditional paper-based textbooks is bound to accelerate. However, the number of digitized ESP textbooks is relatively small, and the quality varies. Therefore, the transformation of paper-based ESP textbooks into digital textbooks needs to follow the laws of the ESP discipline with the help of educational information technology and the concerted efforts of many parties to ensure the high-quality development of ESP digital textbooks.

The realization of the reform of ESP textbooks, whether in terms of inner content or outer form, ultimately depends on the editor. Therefore, the core of the construction of high-quality ESP textbooks is to build a high-quality editorial team.

1.2   Concept of Textbook Writing

To ensure the realization of educational goals, the author should follow a certain philosophy when writing textbooks. On the basis of the integration of English language and professional knowledge, this study chooses CLIL (Content and Language Integrated Learning) as the guiding concept for ESP textbook writing, which combines subject content and language teaching and emphasizes the development of language skills in the process of teaching subject knowledge so as to promote the mastery of subject knowledge through language learning. It integrates subject content and language through a model called "4C framework", i.e., content, communication, cognition and culture [6].

The combined characteristics of CILI discipline and foreign language learning are highly compatible with the interdisciplinary integration property. ESP textbooks writing guided by the CILI concept can strengthen the practicality, practicability and effectiveness of textbooks and ensure that the content of the textbooks meets academic standards and is close to actual needs, with the aim of better serving the all-round development of students.

1.3   Research Status at Home and Abroad

The digital construction of textbooks is inevitable for the digital transformation of education and has become a hot research topic in the field of education. In recent years, many scholars have studied the construction of digital textbooks. Qingchao, Lin Jian and other scholars discussed the construction directions and development paths of digital educational resources in the era of new education infrastructure [7]; Sun Yan, Li Xiaofeng studied digital textbooks in the background of digital transformation of education, the current situation and countermeasures [8]; Uluyol C and Agca R K proposed the way of integrating mobile multimedia into textbooks: 2D barcodes [9]. Research results concerning the development of traditional ESP textbooks for have also been reported. Deng Shiping explored the principles, status and path of the preparation of ESP textbooks for science and engineering from the perspective of new liberal arts and curriculum ideology [10]; Zhu Wenli studied the construction of ESP textbooks at music college [11]; and Deng Jing analyzed "learning-centered" ESP textbook preparation under a new situation with "Artificial Intelligence English Literacy Tutorial" as an example [12]. Du Wenxian took "Applied English for Pet Professionals" as an example to reflect on the writing of ESP textbooks for higher vocational English [13]. CLIL, a teaching method that combines content and language learning, there has been a hot spot of foreign language teaching research in recent years. In existing studies, CLIL is mostly used to guide classroom teaching or teacher development; for example, Zhou Hui studied the impact of the EU CLIL teacher training strategy on ESP teacher development [14], and Jiao Pei-hui, Wu Yang explored ESP teaching under the CLIL teaching concept [15, 16]. There are also many explorations of the guiding ideology, principles etc., for developing ESP textbooks, such as those based on the POA concept and multimodal theory. However, few studies have used the CLIL concept to guide the development of ESP textbooks, and few studies have used CLIL theory to guide ESP digital textbooks.

This study analyzes the challenges and countermeasures faced by textbook writers in the construction of ESP digital textbooks from the perspective of ESP textbook builders' editors, guided by CLIL theory, which is of great theoretical importance for the construction of ESP textbooks.

2 Problems With ESP Textbooks and the Reasons

2.1 Problems

Problem 1 Industry-teaching integration is not deep enough, and school-enterprise cooperation is a mere formality.

ESP emphasizes the integration of language learning and professional learning, highlights the professionalism and practicality of English learning, and aims to satisfy students' English requirements in specific fields or occupations, which is an aspect that cannot be ignored in deepening the integration of industry and education and promoting school-enterprise cooperation in vocational education. However, at present, many ESP textbooks are not characterized by strong integration of industry and education, and school-enterprise cooperation is just a formality or even the name of enterprise personnel.

Problem 2: Inaccurate positioning of content, emphasizing specialization over language.

ESP textbooks are the carriers and tools for teachers to implement teaching and learning, ESP textbooks are the learning resources for combining professional learning and language learning, and the goal of ESP teaching is to apply English language to professional knowledge to promote the acquisition of English. However, many existing ESP textbooks are not positioned correctly, and ESP textbooks are mistakenly regarded as English translations of corresponding professional textbooks. As a result, the textbooks emphasize the learning of professional skills and neglect the acquisition of English, and the content is too difficult and has too many vocabulary words, which seriously hinders the realization of their ESP teaching objectives.

Problem 3 The quantity of ESP digital textbooks is small, and their quality varies.

As a significant tool to enhance the quality of education, textbooks are capable of aligning with the evolving landscape of educational digital transformation and are a product of the times. At present, most ESP textbooks are in paper form, the number of digital ESP textbooks is small, there is a hard transition, the digital ESP textbooks are simply interpreted as electronic versions of paper textbooks, and the content quality also needs to be refined.

2.2 Reasons

The problem of ESP textbooks is ultimately the problem of textbook editors. Industry-teaching integration in the process of ESP textbooks' writing is not deep enough because ESP teachers, as the main force among ESP textbook editors, lack their own professional background knowledge and do not allow enterprise professionals to participate in the whole process of course teaching, learning, testing and evaluation. Owing to the authoritative requirements of ESP teaching industry-teaching integration and college-enterprise cooperation, enterprise professionals, who do not participate in actual teaching and textbook preparation, are forced to include enterprise professionals, and cooperation between colleges and enterprises has become a formality. In fact, the content of the textbooks is written according to the inherent language knowledge structure of ESP teachers, so the content of the textbooks cannot reflect the characteristics of the integration of industry and education.

ESP textbooks are not positioned correctly, and they are light on language and heavy on specialization. This is because many ESP textbook editors have insufficient knowledge of ESP course teaching and understand ESP textbooks as English translations of related professional textbooks. When ESP textbooks are compiled with English acquisition as the main goal and professional knowledge as the content carrier, they blindly apply the process-oriented or modularization compilation mode of engineering and compile professional English textbooks as English translations of related professional textbooks, which results in the content of the textbooks being overly difficult, with the frequent appearance of rare words and complicated knowledge structure, making it beyond understanding. Moreover, excessive specialization causes the language of ESP textbooks to lose its vividness, beauty and practicality. Consequently, students lose interest in language learning.

There are two principal causes for the small number and poor quality of ESP digital textbooks.

On the one hand, the editors do not have enough knowledge about digital textbooks and simply believe that digital textbooks are electronic versions of paper textbooks. In fact, in the era of information technology, digital textbooks have become a kind of three-dimensional textbook that combines the advantages of traditional paper-based textbooks and, at the same time, incorporates supporting study guides, diversified, information-based teaching resources and advanced digital platforms. It not only is an extension of the traditional paper textbook but also builds a new teaching platform with the help of modern information technology such as artificial intelligence. It not only provides an overall solution for curriculum implementation but also fully meets the requirements of new teaching modes in the digital era [17]. Moreover, the digital textbook also enhances the interactive experience; using the advantages of digital media, it can interactively present the work process and bring the students an immersive work scene or experience, especially in some work scenes with danger, which is especially important. At the same time, digital textbooks can also track technological development in a timely manner, and for fast-developing industries, new technologies, new techniques, and new standards can be quickly integrated into teaching resources, and the content of textbooks can be updated and revised in a timely manner according to teaching feedback.

On the other hand, the IT level of the editors is insufficient. Digital textbooks are an important symbol of the development of education digitization, which involves a variety of presentation methods, such as pictures, audio and video, animation, etc., and uses QR code technology, virtual simulation technology, cloud-based experimental platforms, and VR/AR/MR technology, which makes the content of the textbooks more vivid and graphic. This puts forward higher requirements for the editors' information technology level.

Therefore, the transformation of paper-based ESP textbooks to digital textbooks requires the editors to follow the rules of ESP subjects, use educational information technology, and make concerted efforts to ensure the high-quality development of ESP digital textbooks.

3 A Survey of ESP Teachers in Vocational Colleges

The problems of textbooks are ultimately the problems of editors, so are ESP teachers as editors capable of solving the above problems? To answer this question, this study investigated 41 ESP teachers in three existing higher education institutions in SY.

3.1 Questionnaire Design, Distribution and Collection

ESP digital textbooks are a new type of teaching tool that is based on ESP subject content (the integration of English language knowledge and industrial skills knowledge), builds a teaching platform assisted by contemporary information technology, such as artificial intelligence, integrates teaching resources, optimizes the learning environment, and promotes students' individual career development through the integration of theoretical and practical teaching design. ESP teachers are the key force in the construction of ESP digital textbooks; thus, the knowledge of ESP multidisciplinary integration, the ability to teach content design, and the level of educational formalization required for the construction of digital textbooks affect the quality of the construction of ESP digital textbooks.

In this study, we designed, distributed and collected questionnaires from ESP teachers at three vocational colleges in SY city. ESP teachers were requested to scan the QR code and answer questions online, and data were automatically collected via the backstage system. Finally, 41 effective questionnaires were obtained.

The basic information of the respondents in the recovered questionnaires revealed that the ESP teachers who took part in the survey ranged in terms of sex (female 73.17%, male 26.83%), age (25–35: 9.76%, 36–45: 73.17%, 46–55: 9.76%, ABOVE 55: 7.32%), teaching age (0–1: 14.63%, 2–3: 21.95%, 4–5: 9.76%, 6–10: 17.07%, ABOVE 10: 36.59%), title structure (assistant professor: 9.76%, lecturer: 51.22%, Associate Professor: 34.15%, Professor: 4.88%), and academic structure (Bachelor: 26.83%, Master: 70.73%, PhD: 2.44%), which are all in line with common sense, scientific and reasonable and can ensure the representativeness and coverage of the survey.

3.2 Reliability and Validity Test of the Questionnaire

First, to ensure the quality of the questionnaire on ESP teachers' proficiency related to textbook writing and to make the data collected more scientifically and accurately applicable for subsequent research and analysis, this questionnaire has undergone reliability and validity testing so that the real situation of the ESP teachers can be reflected in the survey.

3.2.1 Reliability Test

The reliability of a questionnaire refers to the consistency and stability of the measurements it provides across multiple measurements [18]. A reliable questionnaire will yield similar responses each time it is used, showing that the measurements are dependable and not greatly affected by random errors or variations. The first step is to administer the questionnaire on a case-by-case basis [20], with the findings presented in Table 1.

Table 1. Summary of case processing methods

Cases	Number	Percent (%)
Valid	41	38.0
Deletion	67	62.0
Total	108	100.0

Next, the reliability coefficients must be determined. There are different ways to assess the reliability of a questionnaire, such as Cronbach's alpha coefficient, test-retest reliability, and interrater reliability, which help determine the degree of consistency and dependability in the questionnaire's results. This study uses Cronbach's alpha coefficient as a reliability index for evaluating consistency because it is commonly considered by statisticians to be the most precise reliability index for assessing internal consistency [19]. The statistical software SPSS was then used to analyze the data, and the results of reliability test are presented in Table 2.

Table 2. Reliability statistics

Cronbach's Alpha	Standardized item-based Cronbach's Alpha	Number of items
.978	.978	18

As shown in Table 2, the calculation result of the overall Cronbach's alpha of the questionnaire is 0.978, which indicates excellent reliability and means that the data of ESP teachers' proficiency in editing ESP textbooks collected by the questionnaire are reliable.

3.2.2 Validity Test

The validity of a questionnaire is mainly about whether the questionnaire is actually capturing the construct or concept it is intended to assess, which ensures that the questionnaire is meaningful and relevant in measuring the specific construct. Hence, structural validity is used as the validity evaluation index in this research [20]. For the analysis methods, factor analysis is selected since it is commonly employed to test structural validity [20, 21]. SPSS was again used as the analysis tool, and the results are presented in Table 3. The significance was approximately 0 (less than 0.05), indicating that there were common factors among the questionnaire items and that factor analysis was suitable. The KMO value was 0.913 (greater than 0.8), indicating that the questionnaire had high validity, which provides confidence that the data collected truly represent the situations of the ESP teachers.

Table 3. KMO & Bartlett's Test

Sampling sufficient KMO measures	Bartlett's Test of Sphericity		
	Chi-square	df	Sig.
.913	969.449	153	0.000

Thus, the reliability and validity of this questionnaire are both excellent, which can provide reliable and valid data for next-step research. A valid questionnaire provides confidence that the data collected truly represent the phenomenon of interest.

3.3 Analysis of Results

The questionnaire was designed with 18 questions, of which 1–8 investigated the integration of ESP teachers' subject knowledge, which is the core of the content of digital textbook construction. Questions 9–18 investigated ESP teachers' information technology level, which is the technological basis of digital textbook construction. According to the results, ESP teachers performed poorly in both of the following aspects.

3.3.1 Poor Integration of Interdisciplinary Knowledge

ESP is a discipline that combines English language knowledge with industry skill knowledge, emphasizing school-enterprise cooperation and integration of industry and education, so the design of ESP textbooks should follow the characteristics of the ESP discipline, which requires ESP teachers not only to master the knowledge of English linguistics but also to understand the skill knowledge of the relevant industry; to take the work process of the post as the textbooks; to decompose the work tasks; to analyze the knowledge points related to the vocational ability, skills and vocational qualities; and to build learning units by organic integration with English to realize the docking of job competence and English learning; and to reflect the vocational nature of career competence development. Moreover, new technologies, new techniques or new specifications can be incorporated into textbooks in a timely manner, and the content of the textbooks can be optimized and iterated.

The survey results show that 60.98% of ESP teachers do not have practical experience in enterprises related to the courses they teach and do not understand real industry knowledge and actual workflows. Nearly 54% of ESP teachers are unable to conduct a needs analysis that includes various stakeholders (e.g., learners, professors, employers, schools). Approximately 34% of ESP teachers are unable to effectively negotiate and establish good interactions with different stakeholders, which means that they are unable to seek external help to learn about the industry and to compensate for their own shortcomings in knowledge. As ESP textbook writers, the lack of industry knowledge is a serious obstacle to the high-quality development of ESP textbook content.

3.3.2 Low Level of Information Technology

ESP digital textbooks reflect the level of development of educational digitization, and selecting the most appropriate digital presentation format tailored to the specific content of the textbooks, such as the use of pictures, audio/video, animation, QR code technology, virtual simulation technology, cloud-based experimental platforms, and VR/AR/MR technology, is essential. Digital textbooks can take advantage of digital media to interactively present the work process and bring immersive work scenes or work experiences, especially for dangerous work scenes. Therefore, the realization of digitized textbooks requires that editors can master a high level of information technology. The survey revealed that approximately 51% of ESP teachers are unable to use information technology well to meet the different needs of ESP learners or design ESP textbooks via information technology, and they are unable to improve their information technology level rapidly in a short period of time. Therefore, the IT level of editors cannot match the requirements of digital textbook construction, which severely restricts the development of digitized ESP textbooks.

In summary, we can conclude that the lack of ESP-related industry knowledge and the low level of information technology are the two major difficulties for ESP teachers in the construction of digital textbooks. ESP teachers cannot overcome this dilemma on their own in a short period of time.

4 Construction of the TPT Teachers' Communities

It is unrealistic to force ESP teachers to systematically compensate for relevant industry knowledge in the short run and rapidly improve their own information technology proficiency. For the high-quality construction of ESP digital textbooks, ESP teachers must seek help from outside to make up for their shortcomings and work together to build a community of teachers for the construction of textbooks.

First, according to the concept of CLIL and following the characteristics of industry-teaching integration, ESP teachers need to cooperate with industry experts (Professionals) in the collection of raw materials for textbooks, arrangement of content, design of teaching activities, realization of teaching evaluation, etc. ESP teachers contribute English linguistic knowledge for the construction of textbook content and provide learners with correct and standardized language models according to the scientific law of

English acquisition. Industry professionals take the job work process as the vein of textbooks; decompose work tasks; analyze knowledge points, skill points and vocational qualities related to vocational competence; and promptly integrate new technology, new techniques or new norms into textbooks. Teachers and experts complement each other's knowledge and cooperate sincerely to guarantee the content construction of ESP textbooks and enhance the practicality, practicability and timeliness of the textbooks.

Second, teachers and professionals guarantee the content of digital textbooks, and the presentation of the content requires the help of IT technologists to build a platform and create an environment for the operation of digital textbooks. Compared with traditional paper textbooks, digital textbooks have the following characteristics:

Strong interactivity: Digital textbooks can be presented through multimedia, animations and other ways of presenting content but also with a variety of interactive teaching tools and interactive learning software so that the students can engage it actively and the learning experience should be enhanced to make it more enjoyable and interactive. High degree of visualization: Digital textbooks can use pictures, videos, animations and other multimedia elements to make the learning content more vivid and intuitive and easy to understand and remember.

Diversity: Digital textbooks are rich in content, diverse and easy to update. Teachers can independently develop, select, modify and update the content of textbooks according to the different needs of students and the characteristics of the subject to meet the needs of teaching.

Personalization: Digital textbooks can provide personalized educational resources and learning environments for different students according to their different learning levels and interest characteristics so that students can learn at their own pace and in their own way and better develop their potential.

Strong real-time: Digital textbooks are characterized by online interaction and real-time updating; thus, students can obtain the latest content and information of textbooks at any time.

The specialties of digital textbooks require the construction of a digital platform, and the construction of the platform requires the professional assistance of IT technologists.

Therefore, a high-quality ESP textbook development team should includes ESP teachers, professionals (industry experts), and IT technologists, which compose the TPT teachers' community. The three parties work together to take the content of digital textbooks as the core, with tools and software, terminal facilities and network platforms as the supportive environment, on the basis of which the integration of the construction of the curriculum, textbooks, teaching, and evaluation is realized to develop a trinity of teachers, professionals, and technologists who can provide all-around services in the construction of ESP digital textbooks.

5   Conclusions

Through a survey of ESP teachers, we found that, as the main force in writing ESP digital textbooks, ESP teachers face two major dilemmas, i.e., poor interdisciplinary integration of industry and education and a low level of information technology. In addition, they cannot overcome the dilemma by their own strengths in short term. Therefore, the construction of a TPT teachers' community, which includes ESP Teachers, industry Professionals, and IT Technologists, has become a path to guarantee the high-quality development of ESP digital textbooks in an all-round and all-process way.

Acknowledgments. This research was supported by the Education Department of Hainan Province, project number: Hnjg2024-245.

First, I would like to thank my friends and colleagues for their firm support and generous help, especially Li Yuanhui, who helped me with the data processing.

Second, my sincere gratitude goes to my friends, Xian Dan, who helped me with data collection and the format revision work.

In general, this paper would not be completed so successfully without their help.

References

1. Shaoyang, D.: Research on the Construction of Digital Platform for Publication and Supply of Textbooks in Colleges and Universities. Zhengzhou University (2024)
2. Wenying, W.: The problems and countermeasures of the digital transformation of textbooks. J. Publ. Copyr. **9**(1) (2014)
3. Xiaoqing, G., Lele, Z.: The construction direction and development path of digital textbooks in the era of educational digital transformation. Univ. Discip. **3**(4), 82–89 (2022)
4. Halliday, M.A.K., McIntosh, A., Strevens, P.: The Linguistic Sciences and Language Teaching. Longmans, London (1964)
5. Tom, H., Alan, W.: English for Special Purposes. Shanghai Foreign Language Education Press, Shanghai (2002)
6. Bing, G.: ESP autonomous learning model based on CLIL theory. Foreign Lang. Lit. Stud. **34**(01), 21–28 (2017)
7. Qingchao, K., Jian, L., Xiu, M., et al.: The construction direction and development path of digital education resources in the era of new educational infrastructure. E-educ. Res. **42**(11), 7 (2021)
8. Yan, S., Xiaofeng, L.: The development demand, present situation and countermeasures of digital textbooks against the background of educational digital transformation. Chian Univ. Teach. **12**, 85–91 (2023)
9. Uluyol, C., Agca, R.K.: Integrating mobile multimedia into textbooks: 2D barcodes. Comput. Educ. **59**(4), 1192–1198 (2012)
10. Shiping, D.: ESP textbook compilation of science and engineering from the perspective of new liberal arts and curriculum thought and politics: principle. Present Situat. Path Foreign Lang. Study **00**, 24–43 (2023)
11. Wenli, Z.: Research on ESP textbook construction and teaching practice in music colleges–taking Sichuan conservatory of music as an example. J. Xichang Univ. Soc. Sci. Ed. **34**(03), 124–128 (2022)
12. Jing, D.: The compilation and development of "learning-centered" ESP textbook under the new situation– taking the artificial intelligence English reading and writing course as an example. Chin. J. ESP **02**(63–69), 114–115 (2022)
13. Wenxian, D.: Practice and reflection on the compilation of English ESP textbooks in higher vocational colleges–taking applied English for pet majors as an example. J. Liaoning Agric. Tech. Coll. **24**(01), 12–15 (2022)
14. Hui, Z.: The enlightenment of EU CLIL teacher training strategy to ESP teacher development. J. Changchun Norm. Univ. **36**(11), 173–175 (2017)

15. Peihu, L., Jiangxia, L.: ESP teaching of medical English based on CLIL theory. Constr. Old Base Areas **14**, 56–58 (2016)
16. Yang, W.: The enlightenment of CLIL model to the teaching of engineering ESP course. J. Guangxi Radio TV Univ. **32**(05), 88–91 (2021)
17. Pan, H., Dongqing, W., Jun, X., et al.: Morphological characteristics and functional models of digital textbooks. Mod. Distance Educ. Res. **2**(7), 93–98 (2014)
18. Zeng, W.Y.: Analysis of the reliability and validity of questionnaires. Stat. Inf. Forum **6**(20), 11–15 (2005)
19. Halkidi, M.: Hierarchical clustering. In: Liu, L., Özsu, M.T. (eds.) Encyclopedia of Database Systems, pp. 1684–1689. Springer, New York (2018). https://doi.org/10.1007/978-1-4614-8265-9_604
20. Xia, Y.F.: SPSS Statistical Analysis Essentials and Example Detailed Explanation, 1st edn. Electronic Industry Press (2010)
21. Han, H., Li, Y.: Building of the 6C English education system for Sanya citizens under the background of Hainan free trade port construction. In: Fourth International Conference on Computer Science and Educational Informatization (CSEI 2022) (2022)

Automatic Knowledge Graph Construction and Dynamic Fusion Method Using LLMs and Graph Embedding for Medical Informatics Education

YongTing Zhang[1,2,3], HuanHuan Wang[2,3], Pauline Shan Qing Yeoh[1], ZeHua Yu[2,3], BaoWen Zou[2,3], Khairunnisa Hasikin[1], Khin Wee Lai[1(✉)], and Xiang Wu[1,2,3(✉)]

[1] The Faculty of Engineering, Universiti Malaya, 50603 Kuala Lumpur, Malaysia
`wuxiang@um.edu.my`
[2] Yunlong Lake Laboratory of Deep Underground Science and Engineering, Xuzhou 221000, China
[3] The Institute of Medical Information Security, Xuzhou Medical University, Xuzhou 221004, China

Abstract. Knowledge graphs (KGs) have great potential in various practical applications, especially in education. Educational KGs are of major importance in course design and personal learning. They collected and integrated data from multiple sources, such as textbooks and education guidelines, to provide systematic knowledge architecture for learners, gradually improving education quality. Previous work focused on massive manual operations and professional knowledge to build KGs and presented many limitations, such as increased time consumption. To address the above issues, this study proposes a pipeline that combines large language models (LLMs) and a graph embedding method to support KG construction for medical informatics, LLM-MIKG. Specifically, the entire construction process can be divided into three critical phases. First, we adopt a top-down approach to create an ontology, dividing medical informatics into clinical informatics, bioinformatics, pharmaceutical informatics, medical intelligence, medical information security, and intelligent medicine. Second, the prompting engineering should be optimized. This study designs a recursive prompting strategy to extract the entities and relationships of each knowledge node from top to bottom, forming many local KGs. Then, a graph embedding method is used to fuse local KGs to merge duplicate entities, establishing a complete medical informatics KG. Finally, the experimental results demonstrated the superiority of the proposed pipeline. We visualized 30,000 nodes on neo4j and deployed it on a self-developed medical informatics lifelong education platform to support further educational applications, which is an innovative attempt at medical informatics.

Keywords: Automatic knowledge graph construction · large language model · knowledge fusion · graph embedding method · neo4j

K. Zhang et al. (Eds.): CSEI 2024, CCIS 2447, pp. 222–240, 2025.
https://doi.org/10.1007/978-981-96-3735-5_17

1   Introduction

Knowledge graphs (KGs) generally represent the structure of knowledge by creating relationships for any entity. They are structured as a graph with nodes (entities) and edges (relationships) that organize and integrate large-scale information from different data sources [1, 2]. KGs can enhance the semantic understanding of knowledge with diverse sources. The application of KGs covers various domains, including medical research [3], education [4], finance [5], etc. In education, KGs display education content in an intuitive, interconnected manner, which helps learners understand complex knowledge by visualizing relationships between different concepts. KGs facilitate the development of personalized learning, intelligent tutoring systems, etc. [6, 7]. Especially for medical informatics, which encompasses vast and intricate subjects, KGs enable the visualization of these diverse topics. By simplifying complex subjects, medical informatics KGs help learners quickly grasp knowledge.

Currently, many KGs have been created for education to improve learning efficiency, as shown in Table 1. Educational KGs offer several advantages. One of the primaries is their ability to help learners understand complex relationships between concepts. Additionally, they support personalized learning and can provide more targeted educational experiences. However, there are also several limitations. For example, creating and maintaining a high-quality knowledge graph can be time-consuming. Moreover, the scope of courses covered in educational KGs is limited. Some interdisciplinary courses do not have dedicated knowledge graphs.

The construction process of KGs involves multiple steps, such as ontology design and entity-relationship extraction. In ontology design, the current mainstream ontology construction methods are still primarily based on manual processes. The most notable strategies for ontology construction include IDEF [17], skeletal methodology [18], TOVE [19], the general ontology construction method [20], the cyclic acquisition method [21], and the seven-step method [20]. In entity-relationship extraction, as surveyed by Chen et al. [22], the main processes include named entity recognition (NER) and relationship extraction. On the one hand, traditional NER methods can be categorized into three main approaches: rule-based, unsupervised learning, and feature-based supervised learning. Rule-based methods rely heavily on hand-crafted rules, whose typical methods include LaSIE-II [23], SAR [24], FASTUS [25], and LTG [26]. Feature-based supervised learning methods, including hidden Markov models [27], decision trees [28], and conditional random fields [29], define NER as a multiclass classification or sequence labeling task. On the other hand, most existing research on relationship extraction exploits neural network-based approaches. The traditional methods of CNN, RNN, and transfer learning-based models were dominant, as shown in Table 2. However, these methods suffer from expensive labeled data and still require an external dependency parser. With the development of artificial intelligence, NER and relationship extraction technology based on large language models (LLMs) have become popular research topics. Representative methods include LLaMA (Large Language Model Meta AI) [30] and T5 (Text-to-Text Transfer Transformer) [31], which are open-source large models released by Meta AI and Google teams, respectively. In general, these LLMs can better understand and analyze text semantics and contextual information, showing the powerful representation

Table 1. The state of the art of educational knowledge graphs

References	KGs	Description
[8]	The electronic information major KG	Li et al. proposed the visual KG for the electronic information major, which analyzed course relationships and ranked key knowledge concepts
[9]	The ideological and political KG	Chen et al. created the KG to describe the relationship between educational psychology and ideological and political courses
[10]	The electric circuits course KG	Wang et al. constructed the electric circuits course KG based on unstructured data by storing in MongoDB and Neo4j
[11]	The "Introduction to the Internet of Things" course KG	Hu et al. designed the KG for "Introduction to the Internet of Things" course to enhance the relevance of course content
[12]	The general CourseKG	Li proposed the general CourseKG for education, contributing the quality of teaching
[13]	JobEdKG used for career selection	Yoursa et al. introduced the JobEdKG, which was used to recommend the suitable job for students. JobEdKG also covered the online courses and skills required for career roles
[14]	The overview of KGs in cybersecurity	Zhao et al. surveyed the KGs constructed in cybersecurity
[15]	The KG for "Information Technology in Secondary Schools"	Liu et al. designed the KG for "Information Technology in Secondary Schools," which described the relationship between the knowledge points in subject courses
[16]	The KG created for "undergraduate computer science course"	Lee et al. constructed the novel KG for undergraduate computer science course

ability and good generalizability of large language models. However, these methods are still limited to open-source general fields and have poor interpretability.

Therefore, this study intends to use LLMs to construct interdisciplinary medical informatics KGs to further enrich educational KGs. The procedure integrated LLMs and the graph embedding method (LLM-MIKG) are introduced. First, this study employs a top-down ontology construction strategy, dividing medical informatics into clinical informatics, bioinformatics, pharmaceutical informatics, medical intelligence, medical information security, and intelligent medicine. Second, we tune the prompt of the LLMs and design the recursive prompt to extract the entities and relationships of each knowledge node from top to bottom, obtaining the local knowledge graph. This study adopts a graph embedding-based method to fuse local knowledge graphs, merge duplicate entities and create a complete medical informatics knowledge graph. The innovations of this study are as follows:

- A novel pipeline is proposed for extracting entity relationships via LLMs to automatically construct KGs.
- The specific ontology is designed for an interdisciplinary medical informatics knowledge base.
- The graph embedding method is introduced to fuse knowledge to facilitate the quality of medical informatics KGs.

The remainder of this paper is organized as follows. Section 2 presents the methodology of this study in detail. The experimental results are listed in Sect. 3. Section 4 summarizes and describes the future work of this study.

2 Methods

As medical informatics involves massive amounts of interdisciplinary knowledge, the relationships among types of knowledge are more complex. To improve the combination and presentation of this knowledge, this study uses a knowledge graph. We design a dynamic knowledge graph construction method using LLMs on the basis of the top-bottom ontology modeling method (LLM-MIKG). Compared with the general knowledge graph construction pipeline, the proposed LLM-MIKG can automatically construct and dynamically fuse knowledge. The main process of the LLM-MIKG is shown in Fig. 1, including the data layer, knowledge layer, and application layer. The data layer includes the introduction of data sources and data processing. The knowledge layer mainly shows the process and visualization of automatically generated medical informatics knowledge graphs via LLM in this study. The application layer is responsible for describing the potential future applications of the medical informatics knowledge graph constructed in this study.

2.1 Information Extraction via the LLM and Recursive Strategy

A. Data Source: Based on medical informatics education characteristics, the data are divided into textbooks, ppt, and other tutorial materials.

B. Data Processing: Read and segment the text via Jieba. Then, the stop words are filtered out via the stop word list. Jieba segments the given Chinese text into words and converts it into a sequence of words. The aim of filtering out stop words is to eliminate some high-frequency words that lack significant meaning, such as words with connective relationships [41]. These words contribute little semantic content and are not particularly beneficial for information extraction. Additionally, the removal can decrease the time and computational load required for text processing. Each word must be compared against the stop word list. If it is identified as a stop word, it will be discarded. If not, it will be saved. We select the most commonly used Baidu stop word list. Moreover, to meet

Table 2. The state-of-the-art traditional relationship extraction methods are CNN-based and RNN-based.

References	Methods	Description
[32]	Integrate the CNN and attention	This study combined the attention model in CNN to capture both entity-specific attention and relation-specific attention
[33]	End-to-end RNN model	Miwa et al. used the RNN to extract the relationship facilitating the construction of the KG
[34]	Combine LSTM and attention	Lee et al. Used integrated bidirectional LSTM and attention to efficiently extraction entity
[35]	The transfer learning-based model	Liu et al. adopted the supervised model with prior knowledge learned from relevant task of entity classification by transfer learning
[36]	The end-to end reinforcement learning-based model	Takanobu et al. presented the end-to-end reinforcement learning model to extract the entity relationship
[37]	Pretrained model	The pretrained model was employed to extract relationship
[38]	The pretrained model	This study introduced the pretraining and fine-tuning strategy to automatically extract related information using pretrained biomedical large language models (LLM)
[39]	The pretrained model based on self-designed prompt	He et al. proposed a prompt-based pretrained model to guide the process of the information extraction
[40]	The pretrained large language model fine-tuned	Gill et al. designed the automated extraction framework

the input restriction requirements of LLMs, this study divides the content according to chapter knowledge points for the textbook text.

C. Ontology Design: The critical task of knowledge graph construction is ontology design. An ontology primarily serves to define the types of entities within a target domain and to describe their attributes. A good ontology is the basis for subsequent reasoning over the knowledge graph. There are two ways to construct an ontology model [42]: top-down and bottom-up. The top-down method begins with broad concepts and relationships and then refines and expands upon them to develop more detailed entities and relationships. Conversely, the bottom-up approach begins with specific entities and relationships and gradually synthesizes and infers higher-level concepts and relationships. Textbooks have relatively consistent structures. Thus, this study employs a top-down

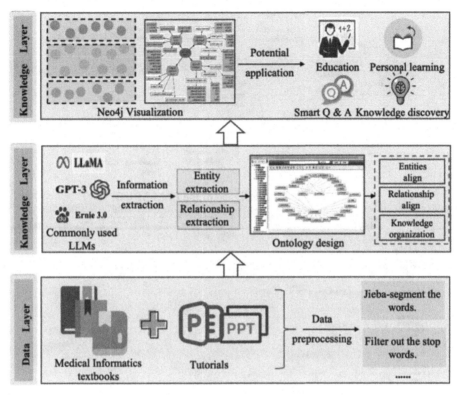

Fig. 1. The main modules of the proposed LLM-MIKG.

approach to build a medical informatics ontology. Since interdisciplinary knowledge in medical informatics is vast, this study focuses on medical informatics knowledge, common issues, case studies, and examination tests, which are all key points in medical informatics. The medical informatics knowledge nodes are defined as follows: clinical informatics, bioinformatics, pharmaceutical informatics, medical informatics, medical information security, and intelligent medicine. In addition, the common issue nodes can be identified as knowledge acquisition and operational challenges. The case analysis nodes may encompass application scenarios and technical cases. Examination test nodes can range from section tests to chapter tests, standardized tests, and adaptive tests. "Medical information knowledge"-"common issues" is a "still exists" relationship; "Medical information knowledge"-"examination tests" is a "test" relationship; "Medical information knowledge"-"case studies" is a "refer" relationship. The relationship between the subordinate nodes is "including." The resulting ontology model is depicted in Fig. 2.

D. Automatic Entity-Relationship Extraction via LLMs via a Recursive Strategy: Medical informatics textbooks are lengthy documents that require preprocessing. They are divided into text chunks based on sections according to knowledge points to accommodate the maximum input length requirements of LLMs. These chunks are successively uploaded into the LLMs as inputs via a recursive strategy and undergo

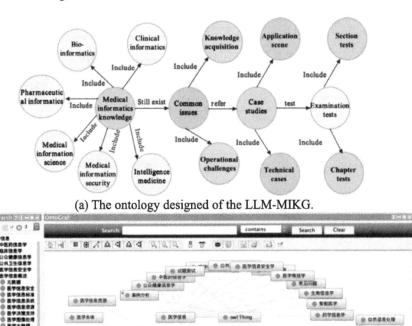

(a) The ontology designed of the LLM-MIKG.

(b) The construct protégé

Fig. 2. The ontology created in this study is displayed.

information extraction processes, such as entity and relation recognition. The necessary triples for knowledge graph construction are subsequently obtained. We selected three LLMs as the in-formation extraction models, including ChatGPT, kimi, and ERNIE Bot.

(1) Promotion design

It is a two-stage conversation process. A prompt is given to conduct the knowledge extraction task and employ self-verification for LLMs, as shown in Fig. 3.

Referring to Zhang and Shao et al. [43, 44], we design the LLMs task description to extract knowledge. First, to obtain full medical informatics knowledge captured by LLMs, this study instructs LLMs to assume the role of medical informatics education experts and informs them of the tasks they need to complete. "【 】" represents the identified entities. The identified entities of this study are the chapter names. Second, we provide a set of entity relationships as prompts for the relationship extraction process to improve accuracy. Finally, we explicitly specify the output format as CSV to standardize the data storage. The proposed recursive strategy operates as follows: The text chunks are segmented on the basis of specific knowledge points within each section

<Task Descriptions>

As an expert in medical informatics, you specialize in extracting knowledge from PDFs, such as "clinical information systems." Your task involves extracting knowledge from the uploaded documents and fulfill the following criteria: 1) Return the relationship between the 【 】 and other entities in a rigorous triple. 2) The set of entity relationships is {definition, classification, characteristics, properties, functions, features, related technologies and methods, implementation methods, cases, and associated issues}. 3) Output the information in a CSV table format: {Entity 1, Relationship, Entity 2}.

<Self-Verification>

You are very skilled in named entity recognition and relation extraction. Can you confirm that the entities and relations in the above output correspond to the correct content? Can you confirm that they belong to the field of medical informatics? Please answer "yes" or "no".

Fig. 3. The prompt designed for information extraction.

under study. Entity and relationship extraction occurs in two rounds. First, LLMs were extracted from individual sections, followed by extraction at the chapter level. This same process applies across different medical informatics textbooks; thus, it is referred to as the recursive extraction strategy.

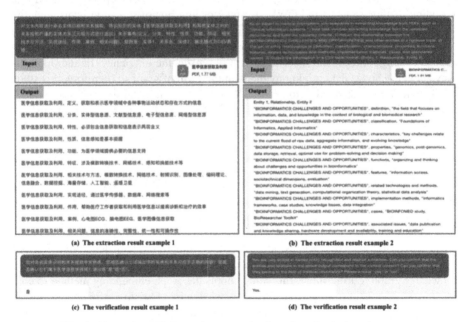

(a) The extraction result example 1

(b) The extraction result example 2

(c) The verification result example 1

(d) The verification result example 2

Fig. 4. Examples of information extraction based on the designed prompt.

To address the challenges posed by hallucination issues in LLMs, we designed self-validation to verify that the entity extracted from documents belongs to a specific entity type. Assuming that the knowledge extracted in the previous stage may be incomplete and inaccurate, this study employs a self-verification prompt to address the errors and omissions from the earlier extraction process, thereby validating the output results and allowing for the reextraction of knowledge. Consequently, self-verification is utilized primarily to confirm whether the entity–relationship pairs extracted from specific documents are categorized correctly.

To demonstrate the accuracy of the extracted knowledge, validation encompasses the entire process of information extraction: if the entities match the relationships, the output is "Yes"; otherwise, if they do not match, the output is "No". According to the above process, LLMs are recursively called according to the chapter chunks to extract entity–relationship triples in sequence, thus realizing automatic calling and extraction. Examples of information extraction according to the designed prompt are shown in Fig. 4.

2.2 Data Normalization and Storage

This study stores the processed data in the form of triplets. The most commonly used ontology representation languages are the resource description framework (RDF) and Web Ontology Language (OWL). RDF and OWL can formulate the semantic foundation, whose aim is to share and reuse the knowledge. RDF is more flexible and offers scalable knowledge. The form of RDF is triplets that represent the properties. OWL is more expressive and has more robust logical constructs. Its ability is to provide knowledge reasoning. Although RDF and OWL are superior in terms of semantic interpretability for machines, they have insufficient capacity to handle massive amounts of knowledge data. In contrast, the advantage of the graph database is obvious, especially for large-scale knowledge indices and queries, which optimizes the efficiency. In addition, it is convenient to choose data mining methods in the form of graphs. Therefore, this study uses the graph database as the storage tool. Neo4j is chosen as the structured knowledge storage tool. The nodes and edges express medical informatics entities and relationships, respectively.

2.3 Knowledge Fusion

The extracted knowledge is represented in the form of a triple, such as <head entity, relationship, tail entity>, which is displayed visually by Neo4j. The created ontology is used to construct a medical informatics knowledge graph and achieve conversion from the original data to structured data. Knowledge fusion is a pivotal process in the construction of knowledge graphs [45]. It involves integrating knowledge from various sources and resolving duplicates, enhancing the consistency and completeness of the knowledge graph. Furthermore, this study adopts the graph embedding method to conduct knowledge fusion, which transforms knowledge into low-dimensional knowledge. In the low-dimensional domain, the semantic associations are calculated, and the invalid knowledge is removed.

First, the definition of the knowledge base $K(E, F, G)$ is given. E is the head entity. F denotes the tail entity, and G represents the relationship between E and F. The process of graph embedding is as follows:

$$f : g_i \rightarrow v_i \in R^d \tag{1}$$

g_i represents the i-th node, and v_i is the embedding value. d denotes the number of dimensions of the matrix. The number of d nodes is less than the number of graph nodes.

The head and tail entities are embedded into a low-dimensional domain. Then, the reasonableness of the embedding process is evaluated.

$$\frac{e}{i} = M_{re}\,\overrightarrow{e} \tag{2}$$

$$\frac{f}{i} = M_{rf}\,\overrightarrow{f} \tag{3}$$

where $\overrightarrow{e}$ and $\overrightarrow{f}$ represent the embedding vectors of the head entity and the tail entity, respectively. M_{re} and M_{rf} are the embedding matrices. Specifically,

$$M_{re} = s_m e_m + u^{m \times n} \tag{4}$$

$$M_{rf} = \overrightarrow{s_m}\,\overrightarrow{f} + u^{m \times n} \tag{5}$$

s denotes the relationship between the head entity and the tail entity. $u^{m \times n}$ represents the unit matrix. The evaluation process is shown in Eq. (6) by calculating the difference between the head and tail entities.

$$dif\left(\overrightarrow{e}, \overrightarrow{f}\right) = \|\frac{e}{i} + \overrightarrow{s} - \overrightarrow{f_i}\|_2^2 \tag{6}$$

After completing the graph node embedding, the importance and relevance A of nodes η_i are calculated to filter duplicate nodes.

$$\eta_i = \frac{\sum_{i=1}^{n} v_i + \frac{n}{2} - 1}{n(n-1)} \tag{7}$$

$$A = \sum_{ij} \omega_{ij} \|v_i - v_j\|_2^2 \tag{8}$$

n denotes the number of graph nodes. ω_{ij} represents the nodes' weights. v_i and v_j are the vector values in low-dimensional space.

Finally, to facilitate knowledge fusion, we need to further calculate the similarity L of the nodes.

$$L = \frac{\overline{v_i} \cdot \overline{v_j}}{\|\overline{v_i}\| \cdot \|\overline{v_j}\|} \tag{9}$$

$\overline{v_i}$ and $\overline{v_j}$ are the vector features of entities i and j, respectively.

The content of a medical informatics knowledge graph encompasses interdisciplinary knowledge, with varying degrees of consistency in the extracted information across different disciplines. To address this issue, this study introduces a slicing method to organize the knowledge graph, as depicted in Fig. 5. Each discipline is represented by a distinct knowledge graph. These diverse knowledge graphs encompass subject-related information, which is systematically organized within the graphs on the basis

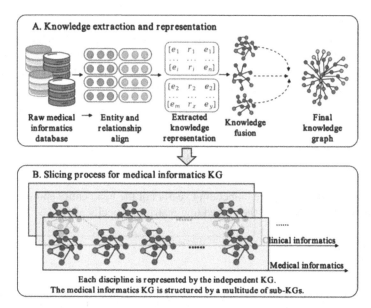

Fig. 5. The graph embedding method for fusing knowledge.

of the predefined ontology. The medical informatics knowledge graph is structured by a multitude of subknowledge graphs. Furthermore, comprehensive medical informatics knowledge graphs can also be divided into various subknowledge graphs.

In general, we utilize LLMs and refine their prompt engineering to automatically extract key information. The extracted content is stored in the form of structured triples. Considering the interdisciplinary nature of the data, a segmented knowledge graph is subsequently formed, and ultimately, a comprehensive medical informatics knowledge graph is constructed. This knowledge graph can offer support for interdisciplinary educational initiatives.

3   Experiments

This section first introduces the experimental data and metrics and then describes the experimental settings. Finally, we present the experimental results.

3.1   Data Collection

To verify the ability of LLMs to perform automatic KG construction tasks within interdisciplinary medical informatics, this study established a dataset based on the following criteria. Our focus was on selecting medical informatics knowledge entities. This study ensured that the topics of the datasets were as broad as possible, covering clinical informatics, as well as artificial intelligence technology. This breadth is crucial for fully reflecting the interdisciplinarity and complexity of medical informatics research. In addition, the selected textbooks need to be logically structured and content rich, which

Table 3. Introduction of the collected data

Topic	Total Books	Explanation
Medical informatics	15	It holds the importance of healthcare, medical data management, etc.
Clinical informatics	12	It is the clinical application of medical informatics using modern technology to improve the efficiency of solving clinical issues
Bioinformatics	16	It utilizes the computer science to analyze and explain the biological data to push the development of life sciences
Pharmaceutical informatics	3	It is the critical branch in medical informatics, which uses the information technology to drug discovery
Medical intelligence	2	It represents the guideline of how to search and obtain the high-quality medicine-related electronic materials
Medical information security	7	The sensitivity of medical data is obvious. The existing research conduct the series of privacy preserving
Intelligent medicine	14	There are so many auxiliary equipment, like Internet of Things to support the health monitoring

is essential for models to comprehend the context and extract knowledge entities effectively. By complying with these criteria, our goal was to construct a dataset that truly displays the potential of LLMs in constructing medical informatics KGs.

Therefore, we carefully selected 69 medical informatics-related textbooks, as shown in Table 3. In addition, considering the token limit of LLMs, we segment all the textbooks according to the chapters to preserve the contextual semantic integrity to the greatest extent. Moreover, this study prelabeled part of the samples to contribute to the comparative experiments and ablation study, which made it easy to obtain the precision, recall and F1 score performance.

3.2 Experimental Setup

The experiments used ChatGPT, kimi, and ERNIE Bot as the LLM components. These models were employed to extract entities and relationships, represent them in triplicate, and save them in csv format. The context length was set to a default of 4096, and the maximum number of tokens generated per output sequence was limited to 1024. Neo4j is used to batch import and visualize the CSFV data. The Neo4j operation was deployed locally. In addition, traditional knowledge extraction methods were compared to demonstrate the effectiveness of LLMs in capturing complex relationships and enhancing the knowledge graph construction process.

3.3 Evaluation Metrics

In the KG construction task, precision, recall, and the F1 score are the most commonly used evaluation metrics to determine the effectiveness of accurately extracting entities and relationships from large-scale data [46]. Specifically, the definitions of these metrics are as follows.

Precision represents the proportion of accurately extracted entities in all extracted entities. The higher the precision value *is*, the more entities that are correctly extracted.

$$Precision = \frac{TP}{TP + FP} \tag{10}$$

where *TP* and *FP* are the numbers of true positives and false positives, respectively.

Recall that the proportion of accurately extracted entities should be correctly extracted entities. The high recall showed that the LLMs could proficiently extract all relevant entities and minimize omission.

$$Recall = \frac{TP}{TP + FN} \tag{11}$$

where *FN* represents the omission number of the identified positive entities.

The *F1 score* is the harmonic mean of precision and recall, which is a comprehensive metric, as shown in Eq. (12).

$$F1 - score = 2 \cdot \frac{Precision \cdot Recall}{Precision + Recall} \tag{12}$$

3.4 Ontology Modeling

The KG ontology was vital because it could provide a formalized structure that defined the rules of entities and relationships within the graph. The ontology serves as the backbone of the KG, ensuring its scalability, maintainability, and robustness. This study formulated the rules of medical informatics KGs, first constructing the ontology according to the educational objective, as shown in Fig. 6. Educational KGs focus on knowledge introduction, common issue lists, case studies and examination test provisions. Figure 6 shows the ontology model of medical informatics. After completing the ontology modeling, it was necessary to refine the involved individuals to display the completeness of the knowledge.

3.5 Knowledge Fusion Performance

To resolve the issue of duplicated entities and relationships, this study adopted a graph embedding method to fuse knowledge. It first involves the conversion of semantic knowledge (transfer into low-dimensional knowledge). Referring to [47], owing to entities and relationships all in Chinese, we coded them using one-hot. The KG is transformed into one matrix. Then, we calculate the semantic association to remove invalid and repeat knowledge. To demonstrate the effectiveness of the proposed knowledge fusion method,

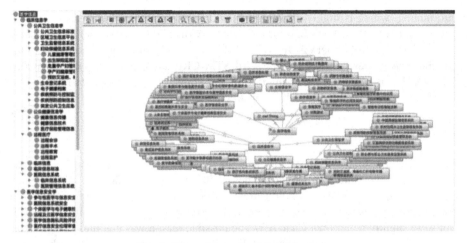

Fig. 6. The ontology model of this study.

this section presents comparative experiments. We selected some fusion methods as the baselines. Word2vec-BILSTM [48] was proposed to serve as the word vector model to extract key features from semantic information. It can capture more complex semantic features, improving the understanding capability for long texts. Liu et al. [49] proposed the Word2Vec-BiLSTM-CRF method to improve the efficiency of NER. BERT-BiLSTM-CRF was used by Qi et al. [50] to fuse graph structure features and mine more valuable information. The former V2-BiLSTM-CRF [51] was designed to fuse medical entities. The comparative results are shown in Table 4.

Table 4. Comparative results.

Methods	Precision/%	Recall/%	F1-score/%
Word2vec-BILSTM	75.2	72.6	73.9
Word2Vec-BiLSTM-CRF	77.9	77.7	77.8
BERT-BiLSTM-CRF	82.1	87.1	84.5
RoFormerV2-BiLSTM-CRF	83.8	88.1	85.9
Our	90.1	88.2	89.1

The proposed knowledge fusion method obtained the best results and obtained the best precision, recall, and F1 values, all of which exceeded 88%. This finding showed that the proposed method had a more comprehensive range of applicability in information extraction and fusion. In contrast, the ability of the Word2vec-BILSTM method to fuse knowledge was inferior to that of the other three comparative methods. The possible reason is that these three methods integrate a conditional random field (CRF) model. The advantage of integration is that the CRF can capture dependencies between sequential information, which is highly effective for entity recognition and relationship extraction tasks. BERT-BiLSTM-CRF and RoFormerV2-BiLSTM-CRF had almost the same effect. However, RoFormerV2-BiLSTM-CRF was slightly superior to the former. One possible reason was that RoFormerV2-BiLSTM-CRF adopted processed and labeled data, which was beneficial for fusing information. In general, the proposed method was superior in fusing knowledge of KG construction.

3.6 Ablation Study

This study aims to show the performance of three used LLMs with and without the prompt word and validation strategy. The results are shown in Table 5. We conclude that the prompt word and verification strategies designed in this study are effective and greatly improve the accuracy of entity and relationship extraction. Kimi and ERNIE Bot were slightly better than ChatGPT. The possible reason was that these two models were easier to understand in Chinese. The difference did not exceed 1%, which was within an acceptable range. Overall, the ablation study simply showed the effectiveness of the proposed method. In the future, we will design more appropriate prompt words to improve the accuracy of extracting triple data.

Table 5. Ablation study results.

LLMs	Task	Precision/%	Recall/%	F1-score/%
ChatGPT	Few prompt	60.3	68.7	64.2
	Rish prompt	77.9	74.1	76.1
	Rish prompt+validation strategy	79.4	77.5	78.4
Kimi	Few prompt	56.2	58.9	59.1
	Rish prompt	79.6	74.8	77.1
	Rish prompt+validation strategy	80.1	78.8	79.4
ERNIE Bot	Few prompt	58.9	62.3	60.6
	Rish prompt	76.6	72.5	74.5
	Rish prompt+validation strategy	81.2	77.7	79.4

3.7 Data Visualization and Storage via Neo4j

Using the above data collection, processing and extraction methods, medical informatics KGs that contained different fields of knowledge were obtained with 30,000 nodes. This study used Neo4j to visualize this KG. The local KG is displayed in Fig. 7.

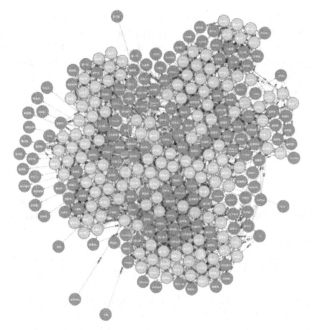

Fig. 7. The presentation of partially medical informatics-related entities.

4   Conclusion

This study presents a pipeline for constructing medical informatics knowledge graphs via large language models and a graph embedding method, LLM-MIKG. First, we design an ontology suitable for medical informatics within the LLM-MIKG framework, initially formulating the construction rules for the educational knowledge graph. Additionally, we optimize the prompt wording for large language models to extract entity–relationship information, incorporating a validation strategy. The models extract entities and relationships for each knowledge node hierarchically, building local knowledge graphs on the basis of individual knowledge points. Furthermore, LLM-MIKG integrates multiple local graphs via the graph embedding method. This step aims to eliminate duplicate and invalid entities, resulting in a complete knowledge graph. Comparative experiments demonstrate the effectiveness of the proposed pipeline, and visualization confirms the completeness of the constructed medical informatics knowledge graph. Notably, by changing the input data, the framework can be adapted for different fields. For example, using clinical medicine textbooks as inputs allows the construction of a clinical medicine knowledge graph. We acknowledge certain limitations in this study. For example, the knowledge incorporated into the graph requires continuous updates. Thus, the practical application of the proposed LLM-MIKG needs further exploration. Future research will focus on two areas: (1) developing automatic methods for knowledge graph completion and (2) implementing an end-to-end system for real-world applications.

238   Y. Zhang et al.

Acknowledgments. This work was supported by the Cooperation project between Yunlong Lake Laboratory and the Affiliated Hospital of Xuzhou Medical University under Grant no. 104024005, the Xuzhou Science and Technology Plan Project under Grant no. KC22298, the National Key Project on Online Course Construction and Teaching Research for Postgraduates in Medicine under Grant no. YXC2022-02-01 10, the Xuzhou Medical University Postgraduate Education and Teaching Reform Key Project under Grant no. XYJGKT202402, the Xuzhou Science and Technology Project under Grant no. KC23310, and the Jiangsu Province Industry-Education Integration First-Class Course Project.

References

1. Yuan, C., Yu, T., Pan, J., Lin, W.: KGScope: interactive visual exploration of knowledge graphs with embedding-based guidance. IEEE Trans. Vis. Comput. Graph., 1–14 (2024)
2. Liu, X., Mao, T., Shi, Y., Ren, Y.: Overview of knowledge reasoning for knowledge graph. Neurocomputing **585** (2024)
3. Wang, X., Zhang, R., Zhao, B., Yao, Y., Zhao, H., Zhu, X.: Medical knowledge graph completion via fusion of entity description and type information. Artif. Intell. Med. **151** (2024)
4. Wu, X., Wang, H., Zhang, Y., et al.: A tutorial-generating method for autonomous online learning. IEEE Trans. Learn. Technol. **17** (2024)
5. Zhang, H., Dang, Y., Zhang, Y., Liang, S., Liu, J.: Chinese nested entity recognition method for the finance domain based on heterogeneous graph network. Inf. Process. Manag. **61**(5) (2024)
6. Sun, J., Du, S., Liu, Z., Yu, F., Liu, S., Shen, X.: Weighted heterogeneous graph-based three-view contrastive learning for knowledge tracing in personalized e-learning systems. IEEE Trans. Consum. Electron. **70**(1), 2838–2847 (2024)
7. Zhu, M., Qiu, L., Zhou, J.: Meta-path structured graph pretraining for improving knowledge tracing in intelligent tutoring. Expert Syst. Appl. **254** (2024)
8. Li, Z., Cheng, C., Zhang, C., Zhu, X., Zhao, H.: Multi-source education knowledge graph construction and fusion for college curricula. In: 2023 IEEE International Conference on Advanced Learning Technologies (ICALT), pp. 359–363 (2023)
9. Chen, S., Ma, Y., Lian, W.: Fostering ideological and polical education via knowledge graph and KNN model: an emphasis on positive psychology. BMC Psychol. **12**(170) (2024)
10. Wang, N., Liang, D., Dou, R.: Construction of electric circuits course knowledge graph. In: 2023 IEEE International Conference on Advanced Learning Technologies (ICALT), pp. 161–165 (2023)
11. Hu, X., Zhou, Y., Qi, J.: Research on the teaching model of knowledge graph for professional introduction course based on OBE. In: 35th Chinese Control and Decision Conference (CCDC), pp. 1928–1933 (2023)
12. Li, Y., Liang, Y., Yang, R., Qiu, J., Course, K,G.: An educational knowledge graph based on course information for precision teaching. Appl. Sci. **14**(2710), (2024)
13. Yousra, F., Adil, B., Mounir, G.: JobEdKG: an uncertain knowledge graph-based approach for recommending online courses and predicting in-demand skills based on career choices. Eng. Appl. Artif. Intell. **131** (2024)
14. Zhao, X., Jiang, R., Han, Y., Li, A., Peng, Z.: A survey on cybersecurity knowledge graph construction. Comput. Secur. **136** (2024)
15. Liu, C., Zhang, J., Zhang, H., Li, X.: Group cooperative teaching design with knowledge graphs in project-driven learning. Int. J. Inf. Commun. Technol. Educ. (IJICTE) **19**(1), 1–11 (2019)

16. Lee, C., Wang, M., Chen, C., Reformat, M., Nojima, Y., Kubota, N.: Knowledge graph-based genetic fuzzy agent for human intelligence and machine co-learning. In: 2023 IEEE International Conference on Fuzzy Systems (FUZZ) (2023)
17. Shang, Z., Zhu, S., Han, D., Yin, Y.: Knowledge representation and data management of ontology-based vessel man-machine-environment system. Int. J. Mater. Prod. Technol. (IJMPT) 53(2), 116–136 (2016)
18. Morbach, J., Yang, A., Marquardt, W.: OntoCAPE-A large-scale ontology for chemical process engineering. Eng. Appl. Artif. Intell. 20(2), 147–161 (2007)
19. Chen, Z., Qian, H., Gao, Y., Lyu, G., Wang, Q.: Ontology construction of city hotline service for urban grassroots governance. In: 2022 IEEE International IOT, Electronics and Mechatronics Conference (IEMTRONICS), pp. 1–10 (2022)
20. Luo, L., Deng, M.: An ontology construction method for educational domain. In: 2013 Fourth International Conference on Intelligent Systems Design and Engineering Applications, pp. 99–102 (2013)
21. Gao, Z., Liang, Y.: The ontology construction approach for the Chinese tax knowledge domain. In: 12th International Conference on Fuzzy Systems and Knowledge Discovery (FSKD), pp. 1693–1697 (2020)
22. Chen, Y., Ge, X., Yang, S., Hu, X.: A survey on multimodal knowledge graphs: construction, completion and applications. Mathematics 11(8) (2023)
23. Humphreys, K., Gaizauskas, R., Azzam, S., Huyck, C., Mitchell, B.: University of Sheffield: description of the LaSIE-II system as used for MUC-7. In: MUC-7 (1998)
24. Aone, C., Halverson, L., Hampton, T., Ramos-Santacruz, M.: SRA: description of the IE2 system used for MUC-7. In: MUC-7 (1998)
25. Appelt, D., Hobbs, J., Bear, J., Israel, D., Kameyama, M.: SRI international FASTUS system: MUC-6 test results and analysis. In: MUC-6, pp. 237–248 (1995)
26. Mikheev, A., Moens, M., Grover, C.: Named entity recognition without gazetteers. In: EACL, pp. 1–8 (1999)
27. Eddy, S.: Hidden Markov models. Curr. Opin. Struct. Biol. 6(3), 361–365 (1996)
28. Quinlan, J.: Induction of decision trees. Mach. Learn. 1(1), 81–106 (1986)
29. Lafferty, J., McCallum, A., Pereira, F.: Conditional random fields: probabilistic models for segmenting and labeling sequence data. In: International Conference on Machine Learning, pp. 282–289 (2001)
30. Touvron, H., Lavril, T., Izacard, G., Martinet, X.: LLaMA: open and efficient foundation language models. arXiv (2023)
31. Raffel, C., Shazeer, N., Roberts, A., Lee, K., Narang, S.: Exploring the limits of transfer learning with a unified text-to-text transformer. arXiv (2023)
32. Shen, Y., Huang, X.: Attention-based convolutional neural network for semantic relation extraction. In: 26th International Conference on Computational Linguistics, pp. 2526–2536 (2016)
33. Miwa, M., Bansal, M.: End-to-end relation extraction using LSTMs on sequences and tree structures. In: 54th Annual Meeting of the Association for Computational Linguistics (2016)
34. Lee, J., Seo, S., Choi, Y.: Semantic relation classification via bidirectional LSTM networks with entity-aware attention using latent entity typing. Symmetry 11(785) (2019)
35. Liu, T., Zhang, X., Zhou, W., Jia, W.: Neural relation extraction via inner-sentence noise reduction and transfer learning. In: 2018 Conference on Empirical Methods in Natural Language Processing, pp. 2195–2204 (2018)
36. Takanobu, R., Zhang, Z., Liu, J., Huang, M.: A hierarchical framework for relation extraction with reinforcement learning. In: 33th AAAI Conference on Artificial Intelligence, pp. 7072–7079 (2019)

37. Yamada, I., Asai, A., Shindo, H., Takeda, H., Matsumoto, Y.: LUKE: deep contextualized entity representations with entity-aware self-attention. In: 2020 Conference on Empirical Methods in Natural Language Processing, pp. 6442–6454 (2020)
38. Zhang, Y., et al.: RDscan: extracting RNA-disease relationship from the literature based on pretraining model. Methods **228**, 48–54 (2024)
39. He, Q., Chen, G., Song, W., Zhang, P.: Prompt-based word-level information injection BERT for Chinese named entity recognition. Appl. Sci. **13**(5) (2023)
40. Gill, J., Chetty, M., Lim, S., Hallinan, J.: Large language model-based framework for automated extraction of genetic interactions from unstructured data. PLoS ONE **19**(5) (2024)
41. Zhang, M., Li, X., Yue, S., Yang, L.: An empirical study of TextRank for keyword extraction. IEEE Access **8**, 178849–178858 (2020)
42. Xi, J., Wu, X., Wu, M.: Design and construction of lightweight domain ontology of tectonic geomorphology. J. Earth Sci. **34**, 1350–1357 (2023)
43. Zhang, Y., Hao, Y.: Traditional Chinese medicine knowledge graph construction based on large language models. Electronics **13**(7) (2024)
44. Shao, W., Zhang, R., Ji, P., Fan, D.: Astronomical knowledge entity extraction in astrophysics journal articles via large language models. Res. Astron. Astrophys. **24** (2024)
45. Yang, X., Yu, X., Gao, X., Wang, H., Zhang, J., Li, T.: Federated continual learning via knowledge fusion: a survey. IEEE Trans. Knowl. Data Eng. **36**(8), 3832–3850 (2024)
46. Wen, Y., Wang, Z., Sun, J.: MindMap: knowledge graph prompting sparks graph of thoughts in large language models. arXiv (2024)
47. Shen, X., Li, X., Zhou, B., Jiang, Y., Bao, J.: Dynamic knowledge modeling and fusion method for custom apparel production process based on knowledge graph. Adv. Eng. Inform. **55** (2023)
48. Zhang, W., Wang, M., Han, G., Feng, Y.: A knowledge graph completion algorithm based on the fusion of neighborhood features and vBiLSTM encoding for network security. Electronics **13**(9) (2024)
49. Liu, M., Tu, Z., Zhang, T.: LTP: a new active learning strategy for CRF-based named entity recognition. Neural. Process. Lett. **54**, 2433–2454 (2022)
50. Qi, D., Wang, B., Zhao, Q., Jin, P.: Research on the spatial network structure of tourist flows in Hangzhou based on BERT-BiLSTM-CRF. ISPRS Int. Jo. Geo-Inf. **13**(4) (2024)
51. Ke, J., Wang, W., Chen, X., Gou, J., Gao, Y., Jin, S.: Medical entity recognition and knowledge map relationship analysis of Chinese EMRs based on improved BiLSTM-CRF. Comput. Electr. Eng. **108** (2023)

Kendall's Rank Correlation Coefficient-Based Monotonic Decision Tree for the Analysis of Students' Stress Factors

Yashuang Mu[1], Yan Sun[2(✉)], Lidong Wang[3], Yueyang Zheng[2], and Jingjing Wang[1]

[1] School of Artificial Intelligence and Big Data, Henan University of Technology, Zhengzhou 450001, People's Republic of China
[2] College of Information Science and Engineering, Henan University of Technology, Zhengzhou 450001, People's Republic of China
16627050393@163.com
[3] School of Science, Dalian Maritime University, Dalian 116026, People's Republic of China

Abstract. Data mining technology can extract important information from numerical data to help students develop better, and a good mental state can help improve students' academic performance. A decision tree is a machine learning technique that can be utilized to complete data mining tasks and predict students' mental health. Traditional decision trees can complete this task, but they pay less attention to the monotonic constraint relationship between students' personal reasons and external environment and the degree of psychological stress. To address this problem, this paper proposes a Kendall's rank correlation coefficient-based monotonic decision tree model (KCC-tree). This algorithm can consider monotonic constraints in the data mining process, which accurately predicts the stress level of students. With the use of Kendall's rank correlation coefficient, the proposed KCC-tree method can be used to evaluate the monotonic consistency of features and labels. This approach allows for the selection of qualified candidate features, which are then used to determine the split point. Moreover, the analysis of classification accuracy, mean absolute error and precision reveals that the monotonic classification decision tree method discussed here is feasible for predicting the stress level of students. In addition, this paper illustrates the effectiveness and feasibility of the algorithm by comparing the KCC-tree with classic decision trees such as BFT, C4.5, LAD, and SC.

Keywords: Education Data Mining · Prediction Model · Monotonic Classification · Decision Tree

1 Introduction

Recently, the educational landscape has increasingly transitioned from traditional teacher-led models to student-centered learning paradigms [6]. This shift

K. Zhang et al. (Eds.): CSEI 2024, CCIS 2447, pp. 241–257, 2025.
https://doi.org/10.1007/978-981-96-3735-5_18

reflects a growing emphasis on fostering students' autonomous learning processes and abilities, alongside heightened awareness of mental health and stress levels among students. The high-pressure environment characteristic of traditional teaching models can exacerbate stress, whereas contemporary student-centered approaches prioritize the creation of adaptable and inclusive learning environments. Despite these advancements, challenges remain, particularly concerning mental health issues arising from autonomous learning. Factors such as academic pressure continue to significantly influence students' learning outcomes and overall development [23]. To conduct accurate and personalized psychology assessments of students, multiple factors must be considered comprehensively [7]. Educational data mining can not only be applied to students' academic data, but also combine students' behavioral data, learning environment data with their psychological state and stress levels to provide more comprehensive assessments and intervention measures [14]. As information technology continues to advance, a substantial volume of data pertaining to students' academic performance and stress has accumulated in the education management system. By analyzing these data, it is possible not only to predict students' academic performance [12], but also to identify students who are at risk of mental health problems due to excessive stress. Teachers can use these data to better understand students' psychological states, intervene in a timely manner and adjust teaching strategies to help students relieve learning pressure and promote their overall development, thereby ensuring that students make academic progress in a healthy psychological environment.

In this context, machine learning technologies have emerged as valuable tools for educators seeking to monitor students' learning statuses, stress levels, and mental well-being. By analyzing learning performance and stress-related data, machine learning algorithms can effectively identify students at risk of experiencing high stress. This proactive identification enables educators to implement timely interventions, offer psychological support, and modify teaching strategies accordingly, thereby fostering a more balanced and supportive educational environment [24].

Monotonic classification tasks are commonly encountered in everyday life and professional settings. For example, consumers select products in the market by considering quality and price, employers assess candidates on the basis of their academic credentials and proficiency, and stockholders make decisions about stocks by evaluating potential appreciation and associated risks [4]. Similarly, predicting students' academic performance is also a typical monotonic classification problem. Students who study longer and have more solid knowledge should perform better. Although many algorithms have been used to predict students' stress levels, they often ignore the inherent monotonic constraints between daily performance, external factors, and stress levels. Therefore, the concept of monotonicity is also applicable in this field. To develop an effective prediction model for assessing students' stress levels, it is necessary to combine the monotonicity constraint with the correlation between features and labels to ensure that students' psychological state and stress level are considered during the evaluation process. This approach enhances both the accuracy and fairness of predictions while also fostering the overall development and mental well-being of students.

To address monotonic classification tasks, a new metric named rank mutual information [10], derived from the dominance rough set [5] served as a new metric to assess the quality of feature in 2010. This measure combines the robustness of Shannon's entropy with the ability of dominant rough set to obtain rank information originating from monotonic datasets. Owing to its effectiveness and resilience, particularly in noisy datasets, the metric is also utilized to construct decision tree-based classifiers. Hu et al. [9] proposed a robust and interpretable algorithm, REMT (rank entropy method tree), specifically for monotonic classification challenges. Analyses, both theoretical and experimental, reveal that the metric is highly effective in addressing monotonic classification tasks [3,21].

However, despite being a valuable assessment tool for assessing the quality of features, traditional monotonic decision trees that use this metric often face time-consuming processes for determining splitting attributes and points [17]. To address this issue, this article proposes an enhanced decision tree algorithm tailored for monotonic classification tasks. The algorithm optimizes the classic decision tree framework by integrating rank mutual information and further refines the feature selection process via Kendall's rank correlation coefficient [1, 18]. This approach aims to increase the computational efficiency and robustness of feature selection, making it more suitable for complex datasets.

The proposed Kendall's rank correlation coefficient-based monotonic decision tree (KCC-tree) addresses this gap by ensuring a monotonic relationship between students' internal factors and the external environment and stress levels. In addition, it provides both prediction accuracy and a transparent and interpretable framework to identify key factors affecting students' stress.

The structure of this paper is as follows. Section 2 offers an overview of preliminary knowledge. In Sect. 3, a Kendall's rank correlation coefficient-based monotonic decision tree for classification tasks is proposed. The outcomes from the research experiments are detailed in Sect. 4. Finally, Sect. 5 wraps up this paper.

2 Preliminary

2.1 Monotonic Classification

Let $DT = \langle U, A, D \rangle$ be a decision table, where $U = \{x_i\}_{i=1}^{N}$ is a set representing samples, $A = \{a_k\}_{k=1}^{n}$ is a set of features, and D is a set representing the labels of the instances. The value of sample x_i with respect to feature $a_k \in A$ or D is expressed as $v(x_i, a_k)$ and $v(x_i, D)$, respectively.

The sequential relationship among instances with respect to a or D is indicated by '$\geq$' or '$\leq$'. We say that x_j is not worse than x_i concerning a or D if $v(x_i, a) \leq v(x_j, a)$ or $v(x_i, D) \leq v(x_j, D)$, denoted by $x_i \leq_a x_j$ and $x_i \leq_D x_j$, respectively. Conversely, $x_i \geq_a x_j$ and $x_i \geq_D x_j$ can be defined to indicate the opposite relationship.

If $A \supseteq B$ and $v(x_i, B) = v(x_j, B)$ for all $a \in B$, then $v(x_i, a) = v(x_j, a)$ can be inferred.

Definition 1. Given a feature a, let $B = A - \{a\}$. For $x_i, x_j \in U$, under the restriction $v(x_i, B) = v(x_j, B)$, if $v(x_i, a) \geq v(x_j, a)$, then $v(x_i, D) \geq v(x_j, D)$, or if $v(x_i, a) \leq v(x_j, a)$, then $v(x_i, D) \leq v(x_j, D)$, we say that the decision attribute D is monotonically increasing with respect to the feature a. Otherwise, if $v(x_i, a) \geq v(x_j, a)$, then $v(x_i, D) \leq v(x_j, D)$, or if $v(x_i, a) \leq v(x_j, a)$, then $v(x_i, D) \geq v(x_j, D)$, we say that the decision attribute D is monotonically decreasing with respect to the feature a.

In problems involving monotonic constraints, irregular monotonic relationships are characterized by increasing trends, whereas others exhibit decreasing trends. This phenomenon is commonly observed in reality. For example, with respect to vocabulary mastery, a student's proficiency may improve when they regularly practice and review new words, and it may decline if they fail to engage in consistent study and review.

2.2 Dominance Rough Set and Rank Mutual Information

1) Dominance rough set

Definition 2. If $DT = \langle U, A, D \rangle$ is a decision table and $A \supseteq B$, we define the following sets:

$$[x_i]_B^{\leq} = \{x_j \in U \mid x_i \leq_B x_j\} \tag{1}$$

$$[x_i]_D^{\leq} = \{x_j \in U \mid x_i \leq_D x_j\} \tag{2}$$

By us, the following attributes can be ascertained:

(a) If $C \subseteq B \subseteq A$, we have $[x_i]_C^{\leq} \supseteq [x_i]_B^{\leq}$;
(b) If $x_i \leq_B x_j$, we have $x_j \in [x_i]_B^{\leq}$ and $[x_j]_B^{\leq} \supseteq [x_i]_B^{\leq}$;
(c) $[x_i]_B^{\leq} = \bigcup \left\{ [x_i]_B^{\leq} \mid x_j \in [x_i]_B^{\leq} \right\}$;
(d) $\bigcup \left\{ [x_i]_B^{\leq} \mid x_j \in U \right\} = U$.

The sets mentioned above are referred to as dominance rough sets, a concept established by Greco et al. [5]. Similarly, we can define a disadvantaged rough set and derive its properties.

2) Rank mutual information

Definition 3. Let $DT = \langle U, A, D \rangle$, $A \supseteq B$. The forward rank mutual information between B and D in the set U is defined as follows:

$$RMI^{\leq}(B, D) = -\frac{1}{|U|} \sum_{i=1}^{|U|} \log \left(\frac{|[x_i]_B^{\leq}| \times |[x_i]_D^{\leq}|}{|U| \times |[x_i]_B^{\leq} \cap [x_i]_D^{\leq}|} \right) \tag{3}$$

where $[x_i]_{\overline{B}}^{\leq}$ and $[x_i]_{\overline{D}}^{\leq}$ are defined by **Definition 2**.

Correspondingly, the backward rank mutual information between B and D in the set U is defined as follows:

$$RMI^{\geq}(B, D) = -\frac{1}{|U|} \sum_{i=1}^{|U|} \log \left(\frac{|[x_i]_{\overline{B}}^{\geq}| \times |[x_i]_{\overline{D}}^{\geq}|}{|U| \times |[x_i]_{\overline{B}}^{\geq} \cap [x_i]_{\overline{D}}^{\geq}|} \right) \tag{4}$$

Owing to the lack of robustness of the dominance rough set in dealing with practical tasks, Hu Qinghua proposed a new metric derived from the dominance rough set to evaluate the ordered consistency between two attributes under the framework of information theory, which is called ordered mutual information. Rank mutual information possesses both stability in information entropy and the capacity to assess the monotonicity between features [9].

2.3 Kendall's Rank Correlation Coefficient

In statistics, Kendall's rank correlation coefficient is a nonparametric coefficient that assesses the level of monotonic agreement between variables [13]. The calculation of the coefficient is based on the number of consistent and inconsistent pairs between two vectors.

Typically, Kendall's rank correlation coefficient between two vectors α_i and α_j is defined as the correlation coefficient of the two vectors:

$$\text{Tau}(\alpha_i, \alpha_j) = \frac{\text{Con} - \text{Inc}}{\sqrt{\text{Con} + \text{Inc} + T_{\alpha_i}} \times \sqrt{\text{Con} + \text{Inc} + T_{\alpha_j}}} \tag{5}$$

where Con is the number of consistent pairs between α_i and α_j, Inc is the number of inconsistent pairs between α_i and α_j, and T_{α_i} and T_{α_j} are the numbers of ties for α_i and α_j, respectively.

Given two vectors a and b, $a = (a_i)_{i=1}^n$ and $b = (b_i)_{i=1}^n$, $\text{Con}, \text{Inc}, T_a$, and T_b are defined as:

$$\text{Con} = |\{(i, j) \mid 1 \leq i < j \leq n, \ (a_j - a_i)(b_j - b_i) > 0\}| \tag{6}$$

$$\text{Inc} = |\{(i, j) \mid 1 \leq i < j \leq n, \ (a_j - a_i)(b_j - b_i) < 0\}| \tag{7}$$

$$T_a = |\{(i, j) \mid 1 \leq i < j \leq n, \ (a_j - a_i)(b_j - b_i) = 0, \ (b_j - b_i) \neq 0\}| \tag{8}$$

$$T_b = |\{(i, j) \mid 1 \leq i < j \leq n, \ (a_j - a_i)(b_j - b_i) = 0, \ (a_j - a_i) \neq 0\}| \tag{9}$$

where $a_i, a_j \in a$, $a_j > a_i$; $b_i, b_j \in b$, $b_j > b_i$.

Kendall's rank correlation coefficient can be used for both samples and populations. The range of values for the correlation coefficient of samples and populations is from -1 to 1. When the value is 1, the significance indicates that the two variables have a strong correlation, and their changing trends are completely consistent; when it is -1, the significance indicates that the two variables have a strong correlation, and their changing trends are completely opposite. When the value is 0, there is no significant monotonicity in the relationship between the two variables. Feature selection is a crucial technique for reducing dimensionality and is widely applied across various fields [15]. The method aims to find the most significant subset of features according to specific standards. Kendall's correlation coefficient has been proven effective for feature selection [13].

3 A Kendall's Rank Correlation Coefficient-Based Monotonic Decision Tree

3.1 Feature Selection and Splitting Point Selection

A key challenge in the creation of algorithms for training decision tree models is feature evaluation [25]. It determines the splitting rules as the decision tree develops [16]. A Kendall's rank correlation coefficient-based monotonic decision tree is shown here, which uses Kendall's rank correlation coefficient as a metric to measure features, removes redundant features, and obtains candidate features that meet the criteria. The rank mutual information is subsequently calculated via the criterion for selecting the split point to obtain the optimal split point.

Kendall's rank correlation coefficient is a nonparametric coefficient that measures the extent of the monotonic relationship between two variables. This paper applies it as a measure of impurity to assess the quality of features and initially filters out features that satisfy the monotonic constraint condition, preparing them as candidates for optimal split points.

In essence, the relationships between features and labels can be quantified via rank mutual information. Typically, it functions as a metric to evaluate feature effectiveness and identify the best splitting points. However, applying this measure throughout the entire process of monotonic classification tasks can be time intensive [17]. Consequently, we need to focus only on features that satisfy the monotonic constraint, select them as candidate features, and calculate the rank mutual information solely for these candidates to identify the split point.

3.2 Construct Kendall's Rank Correlation Coefficient-Based Monotonic Decision Tree

In light of the decision tree construction process, three key aspects should be taken into account beforehand [19].

First, in KCC-tree, Kendall's rank correlation coefficient is employed to reduce the feature dimensions by filtering out irrelevant features. Then, the split point can be identified through rank mutual information.

The stopping criterion represents the second key aspect. The first condition states that if all instances within a node originate from the same category, the expansion of the tree halts at that node. The second condition involves the threshold ε. If the proportion of samples in the subset is less than this value, we also cease the expansion of the tree, which is crucial for preventing overpartitioning issues [9]. The last stopping criterion is that the features that meet the conditions cannot be screened out, that is the Kendall correlation coefficient is less than or equal to 0.

For a batch of instances X with n candidate features $\{a_j\}_{j=1}^m$ and a label attribute D, assume that c is a value used to divide the value range of a_k. The rank mutual information $RMI^\leq(a_j, c, D)$ is as follows:

$$RMI^\leq(a_j, c, D) = -\frac{1}{|X|}\sum_{x\in X}\log\left(\frac{|[x]_{a_j}^\leq| \times |[x]_D^\leq|}{|X| \times |[x]_{a_j}^\leq \cap [x]_D^\leq|}\right) \tag{10}$$

Algorithm 1: The proposed KCC-tree splitting rule.

Input: A root node $X = \{x_i\}_{i=1}^N$, where x_i is the i−th instance with n condition attributes $\{A_k\}_{k=1}^n$ and one decision attribute D.

Output: The best splitting feature A_k, the splitting point cp_{k^*}, and the rank mutual information $RMI_{cp_{k^*}}(A_{k^*})$.

1 Initialize one set C;
2 **for** *each attribute* A_k, $k = 1, 2, \ldots, n$ **do**
3 | Compute $Tau(A_k, D)$;
4 | **if** $Tau(A_k, D) > 0$ **then**
5 | | add A_k to C.
6 | **end**
7 **end**
8 **for** *each attribute* a_j, $j = 1, 2, \ldots, m$ **do**
9 | **for** *each value* cp_l *in* a_j **do**
10 | | Initialize two subsets X_1 and X_2;
11 | | **for** *each* x *in* X **do**
12 | | | **if** $v(x, a_j) \leq cp_l$ **then**
13 | | | | $v(x, a_j) = 1$ and add x to X_1.
14 | | | **else**
15 | | | | $v(x, a_j) = 2$ and add x to X_2.
16 | | | **end**
17 | | **end**
18 | | Compute $RMI_{cp_l}(a_j) = RMI^\leq(a_j, cp_l, D)$;
19 | **end**
20 | $cp_l^*(a_j) = \arg\max_{cp_l} RMI_{cp_l}(a_j)$.
21 **end**
22 $A_{k^*} = \arg\max_{a_j} RMI_{cp_l^*}(a_j)$, $cp_{k^*} = cp_l^*(a_j)$.
23 **return** A_{k^*}, cp_{k^*}, $RMI_{cp_{k^*}}(A_{k^*})$.

Finally, with respect to the labeling rules, three scenarios need to be considered. First, if all instances within a node originate from the same category, the class label is given to the leaf node. Second, if the instances in a leaf node originate from various classes, the class of the node is the median of the samples. Finally, if two classes have an equal number of instances in a node, and the present node is the right descendant of its predecessor, the more favorable class is designated to the node; if not, the less favorable class is designated.

By utilizing the rules described earlier, KCC-tree can be developed via a top-down recursive approach, which is in line with the usual decision tree construction method. The specific procedure for the splitting rule can be observed in Algorithm 1.

4   Experiment

This section highlights several experimental investigations. An overview of the datasets and assessment metrics is presented in Sect. 4.1. Section 4.2 inspects the impact of the stopping criteria on the algorithm. Furthermore, Sect. 4.3 offers an in-depth comparative evaluation of several "classical" decision tree classifiers.

4.1   Datasets and Assessment Metrics

Throughout the trials, all methods are executed in Java, utilizing the data structures offered by WEKA. All the trials are carried out on hardware with an Intel(R) Core(TM) i5-12490F 3.00 GHz processor, 16 GB of RAM, and a 64-bit Windows 10 operating system.

We selected two datasets from Kaggle (https://www.kaggle.com/). One that focuses on students' stress levels to predict their pressure. Furthermore, to study the applicability of the proposed KCC-tree in the education field, we selected a dataset on students' academic performance. The datasets related to the students can be found in Table 1. To investigate the feasibility of the suggested algorithm, evaluating its performance alongside several traditional decision tree classifiers is crucial. For this purpose, 6 datasets were selected for a comparative analysis. The other 6 datasets are obtained from UCI (https://archive.ics.uci.edu/). Table 2 displays the pertinent information for these real datasets. In the course of the experiments, any instances with missing values are discarded.

The student stress factor dataset comprises 1,100 records and 20 features, which are categorized into five groups:

(1) Psychological factors such as the level of anxiety and self esteem.
(2) Environmental factors such as breathing problems, blood pressure and sleep quality.
(3) Physiological factors such as the level of noise and living conditions.
(4) Academic factors such as grade, and the relationships between teachers and students.
(5) Social factors such as pressure stemming from peers and bullying.

This dataset categorizes samples into three groups on the basis of stress level: low, medium, and high stress. Specifically, there are 373 samples with low stress levels, 358 samples with medium stress levels, and 369 samples with high stress levels.

The dataset related to student academic performance includes 480 records and 16 features, which are categorized into three main groups:

(1) Demographic features such as sex and nationality.
(2) Academic background features such as educational stage, grade level and section.
(3) Behavioral features such as raised hands on class, opening resources, answering surveys by parents, and school satisfaction.

Students' academic performance is classified into three levels on the basis of their grades. If the score falls between 0 and 69, it is considered low-level; between 70 and 89, it is considered middle-level; and between 90 and 100, it is considered high-level. There are 211 samples in the low-level category, 127 samples in the middle-level category, and 142 samples in the high-level category.

Table 1. Details of Student stress factors and Student academic performance.

Datasets	Features	Class	Data size (KB)	Instances
Student Stress Factors	20	3	49	1100
Student Academic Performance	16	3	6	480

Table 2. Detailed information on the datasets in the real world.

Datasets	Features	Class	Data size (KB)	Instances
Australian	9	3	5	150
Breast-cancer-w-o	9	2	16	699
Credit approval	15	2	30	690
Parkinsons	22	2	34.3	195
Iris	4	3	4.4	150
Vechicle	18	4	53.8	846

To assess the classifier performance, we use accuracy, mean absolute error (MAE), and precision.

The MAE is a metric that indicates the proximity of predictions to the actual outcomes, and is defined as:

$$MAE = \frac{1}{n}\sum_{i=1}^{n}|y_i' - y_i| \tag{11}$$

where n represents the count of instances in the test set, y_i' represents the output generated by the algorithm, and y_i represents the true output of the i-th sample.

4.2   Influence of the Stopping Criteria on the KCC-Tree

We investigate the influence of the stopping criterion ε on the suggested algorithm's performance, concentrating on testing accuracy, the MAE, and precision within the datasets presented in Table 1. The parameter ε ranges from 0.01 to 0.1, increasing by 0.01. For every value, the estimated outcomes are the average outcomes derived from ten iterations of 10-fold cross-validation. Figures 1, 2, and 3 illustrate how ε influences the performance of the proposed algorithm across the various datasets.

As shown in Figs. 1, 2 and 3, the proposed KCC-tree performs better on the student stress factor dataset and slightly worse on the student academic performance dataset from the perspective of accuracy, MAE, and precision. The proposed approach is less sensitive to parameters related performance, that is, the model is more robust to the feature selection and decision rules of the input data.

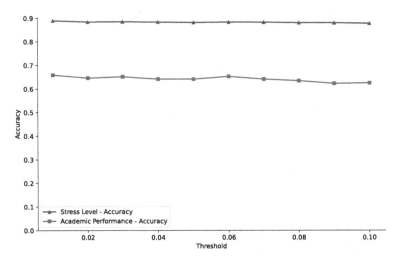

Fig. 1. The accuracy of student stress factors and student academic performance as the threshold changes.

To test the efficacy of the proposed KCC-tree, we compare it with the widely used decision tree classifier C4.5 [20]. We use the C4.5 model to predict students' stress level and academic performance, and select the results of the three stopping criteria of the KCC-tree for comparison.

From the perspective of accuracy, precision, and MAE, Tables 3, 4 and 5 show the proposed KCC-tree outperforms C4.5 on the student stress factor dataset, while there is still room for improvement on the student academic performance dataset.

Figure 4 shows the comparison of the three stopping criteria, and the sizes of the generated trees (the overall count of tree nodes) are also compared. The results

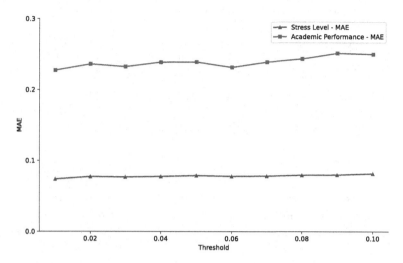

Fig. 2. The MAEs of the student stress factors and student academic performance as the threshold changes.

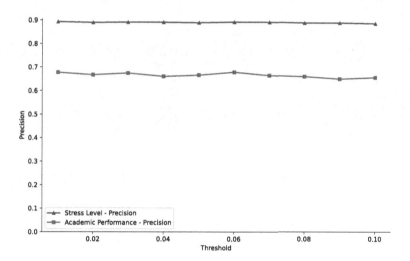

Fig. 3. The precision of student stress factors and student academic performance as the threshold changes.

Table 3. Accuracy of the KCC-tree and C4.5 algorithms.

Datasets	KCC-tree			C4.5
	$\varepsilon = 0.03$	$\varepsilon = 0.06$	$\varepsilon = 0.09$	
Stress Level Factors	0.8847	0.8832	0.8800	0.8758
Student Academic Performance	0.6513	0.6525	0.6227	0.7264

Table 4. MAEs of the KCC-tree and C4.5 algorithms.

Datasets	KCC-tree			C4.5
	$\varepsilon = 0.03$	$\varepsilon = 0.06$	$\varepsilon = 0.09$	
Stress Level Factors	0.0768	0.0779	0.0800	0.2157
Student Academic Performance	0.2325	0.2316	0.2515	0.0910

Table 5. Precision of the KCC-tree and C4.5 algorithms.

Datasets	KCC-tree			C4.5
	$\varepsilon = 0.03$	$\varepsilon = 0.06$	$\varepsilon = 0.09$	
Stress Level Factors	0.8910	0.8918	0.8881	0.8818
Student Academic Performance	0.6743	0.6782	0.6497	0.7393

indicate that the proposed algorithm produces a smaller tree size, which further proves the good generalization ability of the model and makes the decision-making process more transparent.

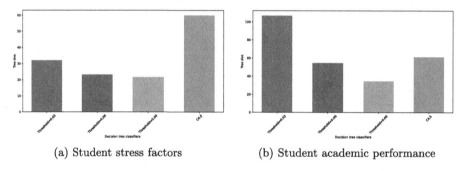

(a) Student stress factors   (b) Student academic performance

Fig. 4. Comparison of the effects of tree size between the C4.5 and KCC-tree models on student stress factors and student academic performance.

From these results, it is evident from these results that the proposed KCC-tree is a model with good performance and suitable for predicting students' stress levels.

According to the above analysis, the Kendall's rank correlation coefficient-based monotonic decision tree effectively identifies students' stress levels, providing valuable insights into their psychological states and enabling teachers to identify potential issues in a timely manner. This method allows teachers to monitor each student's stress in real time. Additionally, it can serve to anticipate students' academic performance in a timely manner, offering valuable predictions for their academic outcomes and helping students understand their shortcomings in a timely manner.

4.3 Comparative Analysis of Typical Decision Tree Models and the KCC-Tree

To analyze the efficacy of the KCC-tree, we conduct a comparison with several classic tree classifiers based on decision rules: BFT [22], C4.5, LAD [8], NBTree [11], and SC [2]. Each classifier is realized via the Weka machine learning toolkit (version 3.6.9), with parameters configured to their default settings. In this standard configuration, BFT, C4.5, and SC engage in pruning during tree induction, whereas LAD and NBTree lack this parameter. Therefore, the outcomes for BFT, C4.5, and SC are based on trimmed decision trees. Furthermore, three values of the stopping criterion ε (0.03, 0.06, 0.09) are appraised in the proposed algorithm.

The comparative analysis focuses on accuracy and tree size, using precision and MAE calculated via Weka classifiers. Evaluation to assess model performance. The results are detailed in Tables 6, 7, and 8, which present averages from tenfold cross-validation. The classic model, indicated in brackets, outperforms the proposed KCC-tree, particularly for parameters 0.03, 0.06, and 0.09.

Table 6 reveals that, compared with the proposed KCC-tree, the traditional classifiers—BFT, C4.5, LAD, NBT, and SC–achieve superior performance on only 1, 1, 1, 2, and 1 datasets out of a total of 6, respectively. On the basis of the average testing accuracies across all datasets, KCC-tree demonstrates strong predictive accuracy.

Table 6. 'Accuracy comparison of the tree models across the 6 datasets.'

Datasets	KCC-tree			BFT	C4.5	LAD	NBTree	SC
	$\varepsilon = 0.03$	$\varepsilon = 0.06$	$\varepsilon = 0.09$					
Australian	0.8399	0.8458	0.8451	0.8440	0.8240	0.7977	0.8451	0.8359
Breast-cancer-w-o	0.9465	0.9455	0.9473	0.9323	0.9321	0.9450	0.9705	0.9320
Credit approval	0.8577	0.8556	0.8484	0.8439	0.8197	0.7963	0.8468	0.8278
Parkinsons	0.8792	0.8929	0.8693	0.8734	0.8662	0.8693	0.8664	0.8644
Iris	0.9460	0.9513	0.9407	0.9380	0.9403	0.9333	0.9343	0.9423
Vehicle	0.6919	0.6874	0.6434	0.6992	0.7034	0.7034	0.7006	0.7058
Avg.	0.8602	0.8631	0.8490	0.8551	0.8476	0.8408	0.8606	0.8514
Better than KCC-tree				(1/6)	(1/6)	(1/6)	(2/6)	(1/6)

Table 7 shows that compared with the KCC-tree, the conventional classifiers BFT, C4.5, LAD, NBT, and SC only demonstrate superior performance on 2, 1, 1, 2, and 1 datasets, respectively, out of a total of 6. On the basis of the average precision across all test datasets, the proposed algorithm performs well in terms of the precision of prediction.

If we look at the problem from the perspective of monotonic tasks, it is more appropriate to use the MAE as an evaluation indicator. From Table 8, it is

Table 7. Precision comparison of the three models across the 6 datasets.

Datasets	KCC-tree			BFT	C4.5	LAD	NBTree	SC
	$\varepsilon = 0.03$	$\varepsilon = 0.06$	$\varepsilon = 0.09$					
Australian	0.8456	0.8504	0.8494	0.8509	0.8269	0.8199	0.8474	0.8383
Breast-cancer-w-o	0.9472	0.9455	0.9499	0.9330	0.9462	0.9450	0.9717	0.9330
Credit approval	0.8599	0.8556	0.8558	0.8220	0.8203	0.7963	0.8496	0.8306
Parkinsons	0.8915	0.9064	0.8889	0.8850	0.8809	0.8693	0.8796	0.8797
Iris	0.9557	0.9594	0.9560	0.9461	0.9469	0.9411	0.9431	0.9500
Vechicle	0.7009	0.6950	0.6497	0.7013	0.7075	0.7049	0.7071	0.7113
Avg.	0.8668	0.8687	0.8583	0.8564	0.8334	0.8548	0.8460	0.8572
Better than KCC-tree				(2/6)	(1/6)	(1/6)	(2/6)	(1/6)

Table 8. MAE comparison of the three models across the 6 datasets.

Datasets	KCC-tree			BFT	C4.5	LAD	NBTree	SC
	$\varepsilon = 0.03$	$\varepsilon = 0.06$	$\varepsilon = 0.09$					
Australian	0.1601	0.1542	0.1550	0.1998	0.2057	0.2028	0.2008	0.2096
Breast-cancer-w-o	0.0535	0.0548	0.0527	0.0800	0.0791	0.0801	0.0794	0.0794
Credit approval	0.1423	0.1444	0.1516	0.2053	0.2122	0.2068	0.2111	0.2052
Parkinsons	0.1207	0.1071	0.1307	0.1501	0.1581	0.1554	0.1621	0.1612
Iris	0.0378	0.0324	0.0396	0.0436	0.0434	0.0448	0.0451	0.0434
Vehicle	0.1541	0.1563	0.1783	0.1559	0.1543	0.1532	0.1553	0.1523
Avg.	0.1114	0.1097	0.1180	0.1391	0.1421	0.1405	0.1423	0.1419
Better than KCC-tree				(1/6)	(1/6)	(1/6)	(1/6)	(1/6)

evident that compared with the KCC-tree model, the general BFT, C4.5, LAD, NBT and SC tree models outperform only the KCC-tree model on 1, 1, 1, 1 and 1 datasets out of the 6 datasets. This means that the proposed KCC-tree model has a better fit to the data and can more accurately capture the patterns and trends in the data. Ultimately, the classification performance of the proposed model is comparable to or even surpasses that of existing traditional tree models.

Figure 5 shows the sizes of the trees generated by these decision tree algorithms on different datasets. Two pieces of information can be obtained from the figure. First, the size of the decision tree decreases as the threshold increases. Second, under the condition that the performance does not change much, the number of tree nodes is also less than that of the traditional decision tree, which means that the amount of calculation during prediction is reduced, thereby improving the calculation efficiency.

The above analysis effectively improves the process of feature selection for the classic monotonic decision tree; that is, the proposed Kendall's rank correlation coefficient-based monotonic decision tree algorithm is feasible.

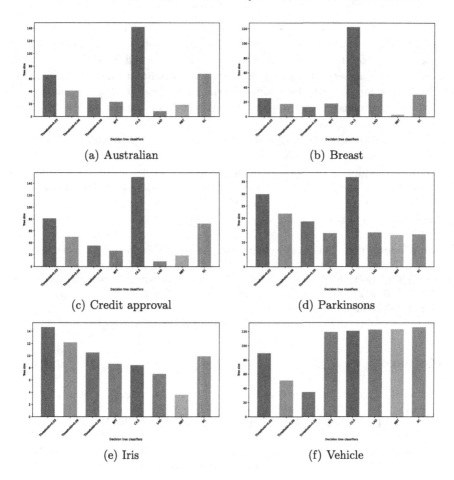

Fig. 5. Tree size comparison of the tree models across the 6 datasets.

5 Conclusion

This study presents a novel decision tree algorithm during the induction process of the decision tree, which uses Kendall's rank correlation coefficient to eliminate redundant attributes before node splitting and selects the best splitting attributes to optimize the feature selection process. This study applies an algorithm to predict students' mental health and stress levels. Using this model, educators can understand students' mental health in real time, identify and respond to students' mental health problems on the basis of various factors, conduct targeted interventions and guidance, promote students' overall development, and improve their mental health. In addition, the model is also applicable to scenarios involving monotonic feature constraints, such as studying the connection between students' daily activities and academic performance, which has great practical value and significance. By evaluating the performance of the KCC-tree on two datasets, student stress factors and student academic performance, the feasibility of the proposed algorithm in educational problems is demonstrated. To assess the effectiveness and feasibility of the proposed KCC-tree algorithm across various datasets, this study uses the UCI benchmark dataset to compare the KCC-tree model with traditional decision tree models. The results indicate that the performance of the proposed algorithm is comparable to that of established decision tree models.

There are two aspects of this study that are worth pointing out: First, the stopping criterion ε effectively addresses the oversegmentation problem during tree growth. Exploring methods to optimize the parameter ε provides an effective avenue for future research. Second, this paper considers only the impact of a single feature on the results, ignoring the correlation between features. We will address this issue in the future.

Acknowledgments. This work is supported by the National Natural Science Foundation of China under Grants (Nos. 62173053, 62006071, 62006033), the Science and Technology Project of Science and Technology Department of Henan Province (Nos. 242102210016, 212102210149), and the Backbone Teacher Training Program of Henan University of Technology.

References

1. Abdi, H.: The Kendall rank correlation coefficient. Encycl. Meas. Stat. **2**, 508–510 (2007)
2. Breiman, L.: Classification and Regression Trees. The Wadsworth & Brooks/Cole (1984)
3. Chen, J., Li, Z., Su, H., Zhai, J.: Self-adaptive interval dominance-based feature selection for monotonic classification of interval-valued attributes. Int. J. Mach. Learn. Cybern. **15**(6), 2209–2228 (2024)
4. Chen, J., Li, Z., Wang, X., Su, H., Zhai, J.: Fusing multiple interval-valued fuzzy monotonic decision trees. Inf. Sci. **676**, 120810 (2024)
5. Greco, S., Matarazzo, B., Slowinski, R.: Rough approximation of a preference relation by dominance relations. Eur. J. Oper. Res. **117**(1), 63–83 (1999)
6. Gull, H., Saqib, M., Iqbal, S.Z., Saeed, S.: Improving learning experience of students by early prediction of student performance using machine learning. In: 2020 IEEE International Conference for Innovation in Technology (INOCON), pp. 1–4. IEEE (2020)
7. Gupta, S., Agarwal, J.: Machine learning approaches for student performance prediction. In: 2022 10th International Conference on Reliability, Infocom Technologies and Optimization (Trends and Future Directions) (ICRITO), pp. 1–6. IEEE (2022)
8. Holmes, G., Pfahringer, B., Kirkby, R., Frank, E., Hall, M.: Multiclass alternating decision trees. In: Elomaa, T., Mannila, H., Toivonen, H. (eds.) ECML 2002. LNCS (LNAI), vol. 2430, pp. 161–172. Springer, Heidelberg (2002). https://doi.org/10.1007/3-540-36755-1_14
9. Hu, Q., Che, X., Zhang, L., Zhang, D., Guo, M., Yu, D.: Rank entropy-based decision trees for monotonic classification. IEEE Trans. Knowl. Data Eng. **24**(11), 2052–2064 (2011)

10. Hu, Q., Guo, M., Yu, D., Liu, J.: Information entropy for ordinal classification. SCIENCE CHINA Inf. Sci. **53**, 1188–1200 (2010)
11. Kohavi, R., et al.: Scaling up the accuracy of Naive-Bayes classifiers: a decision-tree hybrid. In: KDD, vol. 96, pp. 202–207 (1996)
12. Kong, C., Zhang, X., Li, X., Wang, M., Feng, Y.: Analysis of influencing factors of middle school students' learning based on c5.0 decision tree. In: Fourth International Conference on Computer Science and Educational Informatization, CSEI 2022, vol. 2022, pp. 94–100. IET (2022)
13. Kursa, M.B.: Kendall transformation brings a robust categorical representation of ordinal data. Sci. Rep. **12**(1), 8341 (2022)
14. Li, X., Li, C.: Research on construction of student academic early warning model based on ensemble learning. In: Gan, J., Pan, Y., Zhou, J., Liu, D., Song, X., Lu, Z. (eds.) International Conference on Computer Science and Educational Informatization, pp. 217–228. Springer, Heidelberg (2023). https://doi.org/10.1007/978-981-99-9499-1_18
15. Luo, C., Pi, H., Li, T., Chen, H., Huang, Y.: Novel fuzzy rank discrimination measures for monotonic ordinal feature selection. Knowl. Based Syst. **240**, 108178 (2022)
16. Mu, Y., Liu, X., Wang, L.: A Pearson's correlation coefficient based decision tree and its parallel implementation. Inf. Sci. **435**, 40–58 (2018)
17. Mu, Y., Wang, L., Liu, X.: A fast rank mutual information based decision tree and its implementation via map-reduce. Concurrency Comput. Pract. Exp. **30**(10), e4387 (2018)
18. Okoye, K., Hosseini, S.: Correlation tests in R: Pearson Cor, Kendall's Tau, and Spearman's Rho. In: R Programming: Statistical Data Analysis in Research, pp. 247–277. Springer, Heidelberg (2024). https://doi.org/10.1007/978-981-97-3385-9_12
19. Potharst, R., Bioch, J.C.: Decision trees for ordinal classification. Intell. Data Anal. **4**(2), 97–111 (2000)
20. Quinlan, J.R.: C4.5: Programs for Machine Learning. Elsevier (2014)
21. Şenozan, H., Soylu, B.: A flexible non-monotonic discretization method for preprocessing in supervised learning. Pattern Recogn. Lett. **181**, 77–85 (2024)
22. Shi, H.: Best-first decision tree learning [thesis]. University of Waikato, Hamilton (2007)
23. Shvetcov, A., et al.: Passive sensing data predicts stress in university students: a supervised machine learning method for digital phenotyping. Front. Psych. **15**, 1422027 (2024)
24. Tyulepberdinova, G., Mansurova, M., Sarsembayeva, T., Issabayeva, S., Issabayeva, D.: The physical, social, and mental conditions of machine learning in student health evaluation. J. Comput. Assist. Learn. **40**(5), 2020–2030 (2024)
25. Yang, Y., Chen, D., Ji, Z., Zhang, X., Dong, L.: A two-way accelerator for feature selection using a monotonic fuzzy conditional entropy. Fuzzy Sets Syst. **483**, 108916 (2024)

Cultivating Computational Thinking in High School Information Technology Classrooms: A Practical Study of Tiered Teaching in a Smart Education Environment

Chaojun Yang⑩, Lingyan Liu⑩, Bo Zhao$^{(\boxtimes)}$, and Yiqiang Rao⑩

Yunnan Normal University, Kunming 650500, China
ykzb63@126.com

Abstract. The rapid development of information technology affects social life, education, etc. At the same time, new requirements for the future development of human beings to adapt to and promote the development of society faster and better, i.e., computational thinking to solve real-world problems, innovate and create, and the actual differences between people cannot be ignored, so combination with the current status quo of education, under the guidance of wisdom education, we explore the impact of computational thinking-oriented hierarchical teaching on the development of the computational thinking of students. Therefore, in light of the current education situation and under the guidance of smart education, we explore the impact of computational thinking-oriented teaching on students' computational thinking and provide students with appropriate learning resources and content to promote the development of computational thinking.

Keywords: Computational Thinking · Tiered Instruction · Lag Sequence Analysis

1 Overview of the Study

1.1 Background of the Study

The traditional technological division of labor and the supply chain cannot meet the rapid development of current social science and technology, which has led to the innovation of talent and education. As a product of the education revolution triggered by computers, the internet and other information technologies, smart education has been highly emphasized in various fields. Smart education focuses on the development of students' intelligence in a smart environment and requires students to have comprehensive digital literacy while cultivating the masters of the information society. Computational thinking is one of the indispensable thinking skills of human beings in the information society, i.e., human beings face complex real-world problems, determine problems, decompose problems, construct models and solve problems through teamwork and computers or systems. Computational thinking has been listed as a core literacy in China's general high school information technology (IT) curriculum, triggering a wave of teaching reforms. The IT curriculum itself is characterized by both practical and theoretical features, taking into account both instrumental and ideological qualities, and is therefore very important to the future development of learners. In reality, there are differences in the development of each person's thinking ability and level of knowledge, and it is difficult to promote high-quality and balanced development of education through "one-size-fits-all" education and the use of layered teaching to promote effective teaching in the classroom.

1.2 Computational Thinking and Tiered Teaching

Since WING J M (2006) first defined computational thinking as "a series of thinking activities that use the basic concepts of computer science to solve problems, design systems, and understand human behavior," various scholars have actively explored the meaning of computational thinking. Since then, different scholars have actively explored the meaning of computational thinking, which is defined by the International Society for Technology in Education & Computer Science Teachers Association (ISTE & CSTA) as "the use of computers and other tools to solve problems in a problem-solving manner. The International Society for Technology in Education & Computer Science Teachers Association (ISTE & CSTA) defines it as "Representing problems in a problem-solving manner using computers and other tools; Logically organizing and analyzing data; Representing data abstractly using models or simulations; Using algorithmic thinking to build automated solutions; Identifying, analyzing, and implementing possible solutions with the goal of integrating the most efficient steps and resources; Generalizing and migrating the problem-solving process." Computing at School (CAS) considers computational thinking to be the process of cognition or thinking through logical reasoning, which primarily encompasses the ability to think algorithmically, to think analytically, and to think about generalization and the ability to identify and utilize patterns, to think abstractly, and to think with respect to assessment. At present, there is no definite concept of computational thinking, but after synthesizing the above definitions, there is a consensus that computational thinking is a collection of abilities to use new and old knowledge to clarify the problem, decompose the problem, and sort out the structure to solve the problem in the problem-solving process, and it is an ability that urgently needs to be cultivated and upgraded to adapt to the current society.

The educational idea of hierarchical teaching on the basis of student differences can be traced back to the "teaching according to ability" proposed by Confucius during the Spring and Autumn and Warring States periods in China. There are real differences in human talent and intelligence, and different contents and forms of teaching can be chosen according to different levels. The definition of hierarchical teaching in this study is "an educational and teaching method based on the classroom system, which stratifies students according to their learning status, cognitive level and other differences, and guides them to effectively master knowledge and develop their thinking skills". On the basis of collective education, individual differences are emphasized, and the learning content and objectives of each level are designed and taught according to students' differences to improve their level of computational thinking.

1.3 Computational Thinking Assessment Method

To better cultivate computational thinking, researchers have proposed various theories and methods. Owing to the diversity of interpretations of the concept of computational thinking in the academic community, the current assessment of computational thinking includes scale assessment, work analysis assessment, interview assessment, and question test assessment. To better cultivate computational thinking, researchers have proposed various theories and methods. At present, the assessment of computational thinking includes scale assessment, work analysis assessment, interview assessment, and question test assessment, such as scale-based assessment based on the CTS (2017), CTSS (2018), and CPSES (2017), and trial-based assessment based on Bebras Tasks (2008), CTt (2017), etc. Some researchers have chosen to use a combination of approaches depending on the needs of the study, such as Eric Wiebe et al., who combined Roman-Gonzalez's CTt scale with Bebras to develop a "lean" computational thinking assessment tool with high facial validity for grades 6—8 (2019). The above assessment methods focus on outcome performance, whereas computational thinking involves process performance, which makes it more difficult to accurately reflect the development of students' computational thinking. Therefore, this study used lagged sequence analysis to assist in studying the process of students' computational thinking development.

2 Teaching Practice Research Design

2.1 Subjects of the Study

A total of 103 students in the first year of high school in School S were used as the research subjects, including 51 students in Class S in the experimental group and 52 students in Class D in the control group. Selecting a Python Programming Fundamentals course in the discipline of Information Technology for an experiment in layered instruction geared toward computational thinking in a smart environment. The research subjects are in the primary stage of learning Python programming, there are deficiencies in basic knowledge and skills in Python programming, and their programming knowledge, methods and skills need reasonable guidance from teachers.

2.2 Research Tools

Basic Learning Survey Questionnaire. To understand the students' learning foundation, attitudes and interest, combined with the existing learning interest questionnaire, according to the actual situation of the research object and the environment, the questionnaire was modified and distributed before the experiment, and 103 valid questionnaires, were recovered. The questionnaire reliability was 0.892, and the validity was 0.774, which shows that the questionnaire has good validity and credibility.

Computational Thinking Questionnaire. According to the common skills of computational thinking, such as decomposition, abstraction, debugging, iteration, generalization, algorithms and their design, we combine the elements of computational thinking involved in students' programming process, and understand the current development status of computational thinking in terms of decomposition, abstraction, generalization, modeling, algorithmic design, and evaluation dimensions. The post-experimental test distributed and recovered 103 valid questionnaires; the reliability of the computational thinking questionnaire was 0.957, and the validity was 0.926, indicating that the questionnaire had good reliability and validity.

Pretest and Posttest Papers. The pretest paper had an internal consistency reliability of 0.95, a difficulty coefficient of 0.62, and a differentiation coefficient of 0.20, whereas the posttest paper had an internal consistency coefficient of 0.94, a difficulty coefficient of 0.65, and a differentiation coefficient of 0.24, which suggests that the test paper has a good level of reliability, an appropriate level of difficulty, and an average level of differentiation.

Computational Thinking Test. Considering the actual learning situation and basic content of the students, 12 questions from the International Computational Thinking Challenge (Bebras Tasks) were selected; each question was worth 5 points, and the total score was 60 points. The internal consistency reliability of the computational thinking test questions is 0.88, the difficulty is 0.67, and the degree of differentiation is 0.31, which indicates that the computational thinking test questions have good reliability, appropriate difficulty, and good differentiation.

Lag Sequence Analysis of Computational Thinking Mapping Programming Behavior. Compared computational thinking and programming behavior, lag sequence analysis was used to analyze the programming behavior of students at different levels in the practice and extension sessions of the classroom teaching process and infer the development process of students' computational thinking through their outward behavior. There is more behavioral coding of learners' classroom behavior, online learning behavior, and mature theoretical research, such as the coding table of learners' coding behaviors and the coding table of the types of errors in the programming process (2006). Among them, the study of Blikstein (2011, 2014) et al. serves as a reference for many people to conduct behavioral coding research. Blikstein classified learners' behaviors in the programming process into coding behaviors and noncoding behaviors. In view of the content of the behavioral coding table above, this study combines the key elements of computational thinking with the acquired data to form a computational thinking mapping programming behavioral coding table, as shown in Table 1 (Tables 2 and 3).

2.3 Research Process and Cases

Research Process. In the prestudy period, through listening and observing classes, experiencing lectures, and consulting full-time teachers to understand and familiarize themselves with the research subjects, the students in class S were divided into A, B, and C according to the pretest results at a ratio of 1:2:1 for the hierarchical exploration of the teaching of downward computational thinking in the field of wisdom education, and class D was taught in accordance with the general teaching method. After three rounds of action research to implement the practice of teaching computational thinking from the perspective of wisdom education, students' knowledge and skills were posttested via test papers, students' computational thinking was posttested via international computational thinking test questions (Bebras Tasks), and students' development of computational thinking was analyzed in detail via data comparison combined with lagged sequence analysis at the later stage of the study.

Table 1. Computational Thinking Mapping Programming Behavior Coding Table

Organizing Plan	Norm	Description of Indicators	Programming Behavior	Encodings
Computational Thinking	Decomposition Problem	Break down problems into smaller, more manageable or solvable parts	Ability to write code in clear and structured steps, with clear and explainable logic between steps	CT-FW
	Pattern Recognition	Identify features or rules to recognize and classify data	Choose the appropriate algorithmic structure to write code to solve a problem, e.g., choose an if, for, or while algorithmic structure	CT-RS
	Abstraction	Categorize and summarize the decomposed problem information to eliminate useless information and identify useful information	Rationalize the code to represent critical information for problem solving, such as variables	CT-A
	Arithmetic	Use executable instructions to describe the problem solution	Write code	CT-DZ
			Leveraging platform resources to write code	CT-DJ
			Modify the code according to the error message after running	CT-DX
	transfer and apply	The processes and methods of problem solving using computers transfer to other problem solving related to them	Facing a new problem, modify the previous code to solve the task	CT-M

(continued)

Table 1. (*continued*)

Organizing Plan	Norm	Description of Indicators	Programming Behavior	Encodings
	Valuation	Evaluation of the problem solutions developed	Question the code and make changes to it before the program is run	CT-EQ
			Run the program after it is written	CT-EZ
Irrelevant Behavior	Nonbehavioral	No manipulative behavior to the point of being unable to observe learner behavior	No operational behavior	OB-W
	Supportive Behavior	Learner operational behavior does not map to computational thinking	Learning-related behaviors such as opening IDLE programming software occur	OB-O
	Negative Behavior		Presence of nonlearning related behaviors such as logging into social software	OB-N

Teaching Research Case. Taking the while cycle teaching content in Chapter 4, Sect. 4 of the high school information technology textbook is used as an example.

Teaching Environment Analysis. The intelligent teaching environment is the basis for the implementation of computational thinking-oriented layered teaching in the intelligent education environment, which in this study includes the intelligent environment of one person, one computer with a high-speed network, the UMU interactive learning platform, the Ruijie cloud classroom and so on.

Hierarchical Design of Teaching Objectives. This lesson describes the learning objectives for Level A students as follows: students will be able to describe the basics and use of the while loop structure, design a well-developed algorithm based on a real-world problem, and be able to use the while loop to solve a problem. The learning objectives for Level B students are described as follows: students can describe the basics and use of the while loop structure and can recognize and use the while loop structure in more complex problems. The learning objectives for Level C students are described as follows: students will be able to describe the basic syntax and use the while loop structure and will be able to use the while loop to solve simple problems.

Layered Design and Implementation of Teaching Activities. The layered teaching process of computational thinking in the field of intelligent education is shown in Fig. 1.

Table 2. Pre- and posttest performance of Class S and Class D

Testing Time	Class Number	Average Score	variance (statistics)	Upper Quartile	Maximum Value	Minimum Score
Prestudy Testing	Class S	63.25	67.60	63.50	80.75	42.00
	S Class Level A	72.55	17.43	72.30	80.75	68.10
	S Class Level B	64.00	10.32	65.25	68.05	58.95
	S Class Level C	53.10	37.31	55.50	58.70	42.00
	Class D	64.10	62.74	64.60	85.25	48.30
Posttesting	Class S	67.40	78.32	67.15	93.15	53.10
	S Class Level A	80.14	63.63	74.60	93.15	70.40
	S Class Level B	67.19	14.39	67.15	77.65	61.55
	S Class Level C	57.28	9.51	56.40	64.80	53.10
	Class D	67.21	82.92	65.20	92.70	54.10

Table 3. Performance of Class S and Class D in Computational Thinking Test Scores

Class Number	Average Score	variance (statistics)	Upper Quartile
Class S	40.49	59.25	40.00
S Class Level A	48.85	46.47	50.00
S Class Level B	39.40	31.92	40.00
S Class Level C	34.23	19.03	35.00
Class D	37.79	46.48	40.00

Before class, students complete self-study of the key knowledge of the classroom through the use of the UMU interactive learning platform, combined with the relevant information released by the teacher in advance to complete the precourse learning diagnosis, and the teacher combines the diagnostic situation of the feedback from the UMU platform and the use of the Ruijie cloud classroom to show the PPT and other relevant information to sort out and explain the while structure, its differences and similarities with the loop structure and other knowledge. The teacher combed and explained the while structure, its similarities and differences with respect to the loop structure, combined it with examples to illustrate the breakthrough point of using the while loop structure to clarify the three elements of the loop, guided the students to sort out and summarize the methods of solving the examples and the points of error, and then gave the students time to perform practical exercises. In the classroom activities, different levels of students are issued exercises of different difficulties and extension exercises to give students enough time to think and operate. After the extension exercises, students can show their own code through the RAGE Cloud Classroom sharing screen, exchange their thoughts on the problems and then complete the classroom summary.

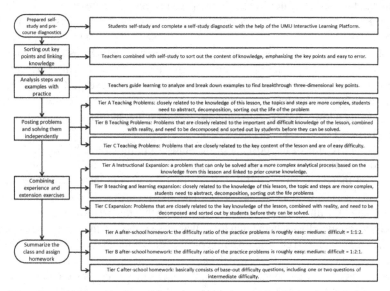

Fig. 1. Flowchart of hierarchical teaching of computational thinking under the vision of smart education

Teaching Evaluation Layered Design. Combined with the feedback of the UMU platform data, the overall situation of the students can be quickly understood, according to the different learning objectives of the A, B, and C level students and the degree of difficulty of the content of the assignment, to develop different evaluation standards and methods. The evaluation criteria for Level A students in this lesson are as follows: students recognize when to use the while loop structure on the basis of recognizing the while loop structure and method, and design a perfect algorithm according to the actual problem and write a program to run to solve the problem. Students at Level B are evaluated on their ability to recognize when to use the while loop structure on the basis of their knowledge of the structure and methodology of the while loop and their ability to organize and write simple correct code to solve general problems. Students at Level C are evaluated for their ability to correctly state the basic concepts and syntactic structure of the while loop structure, identify when to use the while loop structure, and independently write code to solve basic problems with the while loop structure.

3 Analysis of Findings

3.1 Overall Achievements

The overall results of the prestudy test were integrated from the pretest paper and the Attitude and Interest in Learning Questionnaire at a ratio of 9:1. Analysis of the test results revealed that the students' performance on the pretest paper and the performance of learning attitudes and interests were compatible overall. There was an overall difference of 0.85 points between Class S and Class D in terms of mean scores, with a variance of 4.86, and the mean scores of the classes were close to the median scores, which indicated that the distribution of the performance of Classes S and D was symmetrical, with Class S being lower than Class D in terms of the mean value and with a greater degree of internal variability. In terms of the performance of each level in Class S, there is a significant difference in student performance between the three levels, with students in Level C having a lower mean score than the median score, indicating that there are more students in Level C with scores below 55.5.

The overall results of the posttest of the study were integrated by the posttest paper and the computational thinking questionnaire at a ratio of 9:1. Analysis of the test results revealed that there was an overall difference of 2.2 points in the mean scores between Class S and Class D, with a variance of 4.6. The mean scores of Class S were higher than those of Class D, with a smaller variance, indicating that the performance of the students in Class S was generally high and that there was less variability in the performance of the students among themselves. The difference between the mean scores of Class S and the median score of Class S was 0.25, which can be regarded as a symmetrical distribution of the performance of the students in Class S. Class D's mean scores were greater than the median score, indicating that the performance of the students in Class D was greater. The mean score of class D is greater than the median score, indicating that the performance of students in class D has a large skewed value, and overall there is a large difference in performance between students in class D. There is a significant difference in the performance of the three levels in class S. The variance of the performance of students in Level A is the largest, and the mean score is greater than the median score, indicating that the performance of students in Level A has a large difference in performance and a skewed value.

A comparison of the results of the pretest and pretest revealed that the overall performance of Class S is slightly lower than that of Class D. The highest and lowest scores of Class S are lower than those of Class D, and there is a greater difference in the performance of Class S students. After the tiered teaching experiment, the highest score in class S is larger than the highest score in class D. Even though the lowest score in class S is still smaller than that in class D, the gap between the two is significantly narrowed, the mean score in class S exceeds that in class D, and the variance is smaller than that in class D, which indicates that the overall performance of the stu-dents in class S grows, and the differences in the performance of the students are reduced. Second, the overall achievement of all tiers in Class S has increased substan-tially. Among them, the average score of the students in level A increased by 7.59 points, which is the greatest increase; the average score of the students in level B increased by 3.19 points, and the average score was higher than the overall average score of class S. The average score of the students in level C increased by 4.18 points, which is the most centralized in terms of the overall score. The results of the above analyses show, to some extent, that tiered instruction for computational thinking in the smart education environment is effective.

3.2 Computational Thinking Test Questions

After completing the computational thinking test after layered instruction in computational thinking from a smart education perspective, the overall performance on the computational thinking test revealed that the median score in Class D was higher than the mean score, indicating that more students in Class D scored less than 40 points. In addition, Class S was 2.7 points higher than Class D. The overall mean score of Level A students in Class S was lower than the median score and had the highest variance, indicating that more students in Level A scored less than 50 points and that fewer students scored higher. The mean scores for Level B students and the overall mean score for Class D students were close to the median, and the scores for Level B students tended to be closer to 40. The average score for students in Level C, although not reaching 60% of the total score, was closer to 36 points. 60% of the total score, but it is closer to 36 points, and the variance is smaller, indicating that the performance of students in Level C tends to be 34.23. To a certain extent, this finding shows that tiered instruction oriented toward computational thinking in the smart education environment can promote the development of students' computational thinking.

3.3 Lagged Series Analysis

The overall performance of each level of Class S and Class D, the computational thinking test and other related test performance analyzed from the data belongs to the exogenous results, whereas the students' thinking process in the programming process is an implicit response. To better understand the students' thinking process in the process of layered teaching of computational thinking in the field of smart education, by recording the students' programming process in the classroom, one student was randomly selected from each level of Class S and Class D. The specific results of the lag sequence analysis of the students' three programming behaviors in the classroom according to Table 1 are as follows.

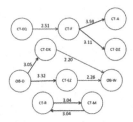

Fig. 2. Programming behavior transformation diagram for Level A students in Class S

First, as shown in Fig. 2, Level A students in class S (CT-R → CT-M, Z score = 3.04) tend to migrate to apply previously learned knowledge to solve new problems

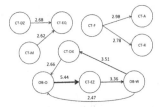

Fig. 3. Programming behavior transformation diagram for Level B students in Class S

before and after writing a program for pattern recognition. The level A students (CT-EQ → CT-F, Z score = 2.51) evaluate and modify the written program before proceeding to the next step of program writing and later decompose the problem for abstraction or write the program directly (CT-F → CT-A, Z score = 3.59; CT-F → CT-DZ, Z score = 3.11). The students demonstrated strong computational thinking skills in transferring and applying, pattern recognition and evaluation in the programming process. Second, as shown in Fig. 3, students in Level B of Class S (CT-M → CT-EQ, Z score = 2.62) tended to copy and paste the original code and then modify it to solve new problems, indicating that students in Level B were able to utilize their original knowledge to solve problems to a certain extent. Figure 4 shows that when new problems are solved (OB-O → CT-M, Z score = 2.96), students in Level C in class S tend to copy the original code after referring to the relevant knowledge content in the platform materials, and then think about how these codes should be used (CT-M → CT-F, Z score = 1.97), and the tendency of toward negative behavior is more obvious for students in Level C after running the program (CT-EZ → OB-N, Z score = 3.65), indicating that students are not yet able to flexibly apply what they have learned. Figure 5 shows that students in class D tend to modify the original code after copying it when solving a new problem (CT-M → CT-EQ, Z score = 4.47), and they know when and how to use the while structure to a certain extent, but they are not yet flexible enough and skillful enough.

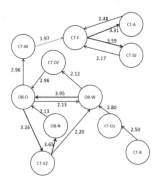

Fig. 4. Programming behavior transformation diagram for Level C students in Class S

Second, in the debugging process, A-level students of class S (OB-O → CT-DX, Z score = 3.05) tend to refer to relevant information or browse the original program and

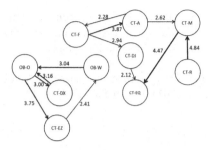

Fig. 5. Programming behavior transformation diagram for Class D students

then modify the program according to the error prompts; B-level students of class S (CT-DX → OB-O, Z score = 2.66) tend to locate the error prompts in the running results during the debugging process, and try to modify the program. After that, they carry out auxiliary behaviors such as checking related materials. The debugging behaviors of Level C students in class S were less common because they relied more on external auxiliary materials for writing programs. When debugging, students in class D (OB-O → CT-DX, Z score = 3.00; CT-DX → OB-O, Z score = 3.16) refer to the platform re-sources or browse the program code and then, after modifying the code according to the prompts and referring to the related resources or message program code again, become more rigorous and meticulous in the debugging process.

4   Research Summary and Outlook

From the broad perspective of intelligent education, the exploration of layered teaching for computational thinking is beneficial to the individual development of students on the basis of the reality of classroom teaching. Summarizing the research on teaching practice, the teaching strategy helps students learn effectively according to their own abilities, and the smart education environment provides strong technical support for the stratified cultivation of computational thinking, which promotes the teaching process to be intelligent and interactive. Teachers use the data feedback for the design of teaching and the allocation of learning resources, leave the classroom for students to do more hands-on work, solve problems by searching for information, browsing through the code, etc., so that the students can internalize their knowledge into experience. After encountering problems, students can solve them by searching for information, browsing written code, etc., so that they can internalize their knowledge into the experience. Overall, this teaching strategy can effectively improve students' basic knowledge memorization, comprehension and application ability as well as their computational thinking ability.

In the future, we will further deepen the theoretical research on tiered teaching, lengthen the time for practising the teaching model, and explore the teaching model in classroom teaching that is geared toward the development of students' computational thinking in a precise manner. While technological development brings infinite possibilities to education, it also poses new challenges. For students to better adapt to and promote the future development of society, subsequent research also needs to pay attention to technology and humanistic care so that students can comply with the compliance behavior of qualified citizens in the information society.

Acknowledgments. This study is derived from the Yunnan Normal University Graduate Student Research and Innovation Fund in 2023 (Project No. YJSJJ23-B162).

References

Wing, J.M.: Computational thinking. Commun. ACM **49**(3), 33–35 (2006)

ISTE: Operational definition of computational thinking for K-12 education. https://cdn.iste.org/www-root/ct-documents/computational-thinking-operational-definition-flyer.pdf. Accessed 28 Jun 2024

Korkmaz, Ö., Çakir, R., Özden, M.Y.: A validity and reliability study of the computational thinking scales (CTS). Comput. Hum. Behav. **72**, 558–569 (2017)

Kong, S.-C., Chiu, M.M., Lai, M.: A study of primary school students' interest, collaboration attitude, and programming empowerment in computational thinking education. Comput. Educ. **127**, 178–189 (2018)

Gökçearslan, Ş, Günbatar, M.S., Kukul, V.: Computer programming self-efficacy scale (CPSES) for secondary school students: development, validation and reliability. Eğitim Teknolojisi Kuram ve Uygulama **7**(1), 158 (2017)

Dagienė, V., Futschek, G.: Bebras international contest on informatics and computer literacy: criteria for good tasks. In: Mittermeir, R.T., Sysło, M.M. (eds.) Informatics Education - Supporting Computational Thinking. ISSEP 2008. Lecture Notes in Computer Science, vol. 5090, pp. 19–30. Springer, Heidelberg (2008). https://doi.org/10.1007/978-3-540-69924-8_2

Román-González, M., Pérez-González, J.-C., Jiménez-Fernández, C.: Which cognitive abilities underlie computational thinking? Criterion validity of the computational thinking test. Comput. Hum. Behav. **72**, 678–691 (2017)

Wiebe, E., London, J., Aksit, O., Mott, B.W., Boyer, K.E., Lester, J.C.: Development of a lean computational thinking abilities assessment for middle grades students. In: Proceedings of the 50th ACM Technical Symposium on Computer Science Education, 22 February 2019

Shute, V.J., Sun, C., Asbell-Clarke, J.: Demystifying computational thinking. Educ. Res. Rev. **22**, 142–158 (2017)

Blikstein, P.: Using learning analytics to assess students' behavior in open-ended programming tasks. In: Proceedings of the 1st International Conference on Learning Analytics and Knowledge, 27 February 2011

Blikstein, P., Worsley, M., Piech, C., Sahami, M., Cooper, S., Koller, D.: Programming pluralism: using learning analytics to detect patterns in the learning of computer programming. J. Learn. Sci. **23**(4), 561–599 (2014)

Jadud, M.C.: Methods and tools for exploring novice compilation behavior. In: Proceedings of the Second International Workshop on Computing Education Research, 9 September 2006

A Predictive Model for Self-Directed Learning Ability that is Based on Learning Behaviors

Huining Wang, Zhengzhou Zhu$^{(\boxtimes)}$, and Jian Chen

Peking University, No.5 Yiheyuan Road Haidian District, Beijing, People's Republic of China
zhuzz@pku.edu.cn

Abstract. Currently, there is a shift from one-time academic education to lifelong learning, highlighting the necessity of self-directed learning ability. To cultivate learners with a high level of autonomy, it is essential to predict and diagnose their self-directed learning abilities. Given the limitations of existing diagnostic methods for self-directed learning ability, this paper focuses on students in the software engineering course at Peking University. It constructs a hybrid learning behavior feature on the basis of Zimmerman's self-regulated learning model and characteristic instructional design. A predictive model for self-directed learning ability based on learning behaviors is designed to enhance teaching quality and improve self-directed learning ability.

Keywords: Learning behavior · self-directed learning ability · ability prediction · machine learning · self-regulated learning theory

1 Introduction

Social change and technological advancement are progressing at an increasingly accelerated pace, with transformation cycles continuously shortening. Moreover, the average lifespan is increasing, meaning that individuals face more changes throughout their lives. To thrive in the "university of society", one must possess strong self-directed learning abilities. Notably, the newly released engineering education accreditation standards highlight the need for students to be aware of self-directed and lifelong learning, along with the to continuously learn and adapt to societal developments [1]. How teachers can cultivate self-directed learning abilities is a significant educational reform challenge facing education today and in the future.

In many applied studies on educational intervention implementation, measuring, diagnosing, or predicting self-directed learning ability is a critical step in assessing intervention effectiveness. Research in the field of self-directed learning continues to focus on and address the challenges of diagnosing self-directed learning. However, most current studies on diagnosing self-directed learning ability rely on subjective statements or objective observations, with limitations related to learners' subjectivity and the resource-intensive nature of research methods [2]. Thus, existing research still faces challenges in achieving objective, large-scale, and timely diagnoses of self-directed learning ability.

© The Author(s), under exclusive license to Springer Nature Singapore Pte Ltd. 2025
K. Zhang et al. (Eds.): CSEI 2024, CCIS 2447, pp. 271–285, 2025.
https://doi.org/10.1007/978-981-96-3735-5_20

In many applied studies on educational intervention implementation, measuring, diagnosing, or predicting self-directed learning ability is a critical step in assessing intervention effectiveness. Research in the field of self-directed learning continues to focus on and address the challenges of diagnosing self-directed learning. However, most current studies on diagnosing self-directed learning ability rely on subjective statements or objective observations, with limitations related to learners' subjectivity and the resource-intensive nature of research methods [2]. Thus, existing research still faces challenges in achieving objective, large-scale, and timely diagnoses of self-directed learning ability.

In recent years, as educational information has progressed, blended teaching models that combine online and offline methods have gradually emerged. The extensive learning behavior data provided by these models offer new perspectives for research on the timely diagnosis of self-directed learning ability. Learning behaviors, especially those that are unconscious and scattered, often better reflect learners' true thoughts and states during the learning process [2]. This paper constructs a predictive model for self-directed learning ability on the basis of learners' learning behaviors in a blended teaching environment, characterized by objectivity, real-time feedback, and user imperceptibility.

2   The Experimental Dataset

2.1   Research Subjects

A certain college at Peking University offers a software engineering course that uses a blended teaching model, combining "classroom instruction+online learning" with project practice. Students are required to form their own teams and apply software engineering knowledge in a development project, completing various reports and engaging in software implementation, testing, and maintenance.

The course employs a teaching strategy aimed at enhancing students' self-directed learning abilities by boosting their engagement, reflection, and autonomy. It combines theoretical explanations with case analyses, using outcome-based education (OBE) and real project cases to promote interaction and extracurricular exploration. Online learning is supported by platforms such as Moodle and Touge for video lessons, exercises, and collaborative work. The study involves 95 Peking University undergraduates over 18 weeks, with assessments based on project grades, exams, online practice, attendance, class performance, and extracurricular exploration, each with a different weight in the final grade.

2.2   Self-Directed Learning Ability Scale

This study used Li Xikun's self-directed learning ability scale, adjusting item 12 to "I frequently watch professional conferences and instructional videos to better master professional knowledge and skills." This section covers the data collection and analysis of the questionnaire's reliability and validity.

Questionnaire Data Collection
In the spring semester of 2023, a questionnaire survey on self-directed learning ability

was conducted with 95 students from a college at Peking University after the completion of the software engineering course (on July 1). A total of 65 questionnaires were collected, resulting in a response rate of 68.4%.

The scale includes 22 items and employs a five-point Likert scale for scoring. The total score of the scale is obtained by summing the scores of each item. To provide a more intuitive assessment of students' self-directed learning abilities, the original total score of the scale is converted into a five-point scale via the following formula. The resulting scores $X_{standardscore}$ range from a minimum of 1 to a maximum of 5.

$$X_{standardscore} = \frac{X_{originscore}}{QuestionNumbers}$$

Reliability and Validity Analysis

SPSS 26 was used to analyze the reliability and validity of the adapted self-directed learning ability scale to ensure its suitability for measurement. Reliability was assessed via Cronbach's alpha coefficient, with all values above 0.7 meeting accepted standards for both total and subscale reliability. This indicates that the questionnaire is highly reliable, as detailed in Table 1.

Table 1. Results of Questionnaire Reliability Analysis

Scale Dimensions	Number of Items	Cronbach's Alpha	Cronbach's Alpha
Overall Scale	22	.928	.932
Learning Motivation	5	.634	.730
Planning	5	.877	.879
Learning Environment	5	.753	.758
Self-Management	7	.881	.886

The structural validity of the questionnaire was tested via the KMO test and Bartlett's test of sphericity, and the results are presented in Table 2. The KMO value is not less than 0.8, and Bartlett's test of sphericity has a significance level of 0.000, indicating a high level of structural validity for the questionnaire.

Table 2. Results of the Questionnaire Validity Analysis

KMO		.800
Bartlett's Test of Sphericity	Approximate Chi-Square	932.845
	Degrees of Freedom	231
	Significance	.000

3 Multidimensional Learning Behavior Characteristics

This section separately analyzes online and offline blended learning behaviors to construct multidimensional learning behavior characteristics. The aim is to capture learners' behavior patterns in different learning environments more comprehensively, enhancing the understanding of the learning process and evaluating learning abilities.

3.1 Online Learning Behavior Analysis

The self-regulated learning theory model provides a comprehensive perspective on the various factors influencing self-directed learning. It reveals mechanisms and strategies that stimulate self-directed learning and offers educational guidance for clarifying the impact mechanisms of behaviors on self-directed learning [6]. While researchers have proposed different models from their own perspectives, planning, performance, and reflection are stages that self-regulated learners typically experience throughout their activity cycles. Therefore, to more accurately describe and explain the online learning process and systematically analyze online learning behaviors, this paper uses Zimmerman's self-regulated learning model as the theoretical basis. Zimmerman [7] provided a detailed explanation of the three stages of the self-regulated learning model: planning, performance, and reflection. These stages occur before learning begins, during learning, and after learning ends, respectively, and each stage has its subprocesses.

Planning Stage (Pre-Learning)
As the initial stage, the planning phase involves task analysis, which includes setting expected goals and planning learning strategies. In an online learning environment, learners need to interpret learning tasks independently, define process goals, and develop personalized learning plans using available resources. Variations in this process can lead to differences in learning outcomes. Self-motivation beliefs, as implicit factors in the planning stage, include self-efficacy and outcome expectations. These beliefs influence behavior in subtle ways. Students who believe that they have strong capabilities are more likely to set high goals and engage more actively in learning tasks and activities. During the planning stage, students organize learning plans and resources to complete tasks, demonstrating autonomous learning behaviors such as setting learning goals, formulating plans, and acquiring resources [8].

Performance Stage (During Learning)
In the performance stage, self-control involves learners actively employing learning strategies to enhance focus and efficiency. Viewing and participating in discussion posts is crucial for significantly impacting learning outcomes [9]. Williamson's research indicates that learners seek help from others or offer help through interpersonal communication during learning activities [10]. Self-observation includes metacognitive monitoring and self-recording, tracking one's performance and environmental influences. Self-recording behaviors, a form of implicit cognitive and psychological activity, are typically not easily recorded by online learning platforms. Metacognitive monitoring involves comparing current learning states with goal states and making judgments and adjustments. During this stage, students monitor and adjust their learning processes to

better complete tasks, including executing learning activities, monitoring, and regulating learning processes [11].

Reflection Stage

The reflection stage, the final stage of the self-regulated learning model, includes self-judgment and self-response, which significantly impact the learning process in the next cycle. For self-judgment, teachers typically set chapter tests and learning summaries in online teaching environments to assist students in self-assessment and causal attribution. Wang's research revealed that self-assessment and self-reflection improve final achievements and involve regulating problem-solving activities [12]. Self-response has a significant effect on learning orientation, such as self-satisfaction, which can stimulate interest in learning, enhance self-efficacy, and guide students toward final learning goals, resulting in periodic self-regulation. Common tools reflecting self-response include self-evaluations, which reflect learners' levels of self-satisfaction. In the course plan of the study's subjects, weekly chapter quizzes are set, but self-evaluations and learning summaries are not yet included.

3.2 Classroom Learning Behavior Analysis

Effective teacher–student interactions and appropriate course planning also have a significant effect on promoting students' self-directed learning [3]. The software engineering course attended by the study subjects was specifically designed to promote self-management and develop students' self-directed learning abilities. Kim's research revealed that when learners feel closely related to or actively engaged in learning content, they are more likely to use self-directed learning strategies [13]. In other words, learners' self-directed learning is related to their perceptions of the course's value [14]. Reeve argued that self-directed learning includes activities that are fully or partially controlled by students and is strongly related to the level of participation in the learning process [15]. Student engagement can be defined as the degree of attention, enthusiasm, and interest exhibited by students during learning [16, 17]. It is reflected in three dimensions, namely, behavioral, emotional, and cognitive engagement [3], with specific manifestations under different dimensions, as shown in Table 3.

Among these, emotional engagement and cognitive engagement reflect the students' internal interest in and passion for the learning content, which are difficult to measure through quantifiable indicators. However, these internalized, implicit thought processes can be expressed through external behaviors. Therefore, this paper uses student behavioral engagement related to classroom learning activities as one of the feature dimensions for measuring self-directed learning ability.

3.3 Data Construction

On the basis of the above analysis, this study combines Zimmerman's self-regulated learning theory model and a specialized teaching design aimed at developing self-directed learning abilities in a software engineering course. It constructs multidimensional hybrid learning behavior features from the learning process, as illustrated in Fig. 1.

Table 3. Specific Manifestations of Student Engagement

Dimensions of Student Engagement	Specific Manifestations
Behavioral Engagement	Attendance, active participation, engaging in discussions, taking on leadership roles, etc
Emotional Engagement	Feelings of enjoyment or interest generated by the learning content
Cognitive Engagement	Deep understanding of learning materials, striving for higher standards, and approaching challenges with enthusiasm

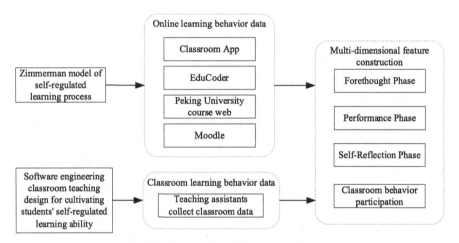

Fig. 1. Construction of the feature diagram

To ensure that the selected learning behavior features accurately represent students' self-directed learning abilities—beyond their performance against assessment criteria—this section focuses on features that highlight genuine student autonomy. This involves excluding metrics such as the "Touge Challenge Completion Rate," "Touge Challenge Scores," "Attendance Scores," and "Classroom Performance Scores," which may be more indicative of adherence to assessment requirements than true self-directed learning. The final set of 30 behavior features collected, reflecting self-directed learning, are detailed in Table 4.

The course included 9 tests conducted through the Classroom app. These consisted of 2 pretests aimed at assessing students' preparation before key classes and 7 posttests designed to evaluate their participation and understanding during the course. The tests targeted crucial chapters, such as Detailed Design and Object-Oriented Analysis and Design, to measure comprehension of the core content. Additionally, because assignments on the Classroom app are completed in groups, they were not included in the analysis, as they do not adequately capture individual levels of autonomy. Similarly, group-based project features were excluded to maintain the focus on individual self-directed behaviors, ensuring that the analysis remains relevant to personal learning initiatives rather than collaborative outcomes.

Table 4. Characteristics of Autonomous Learning Behavior

Characteristic Dimension	Code	Characteristics of Autonomous Learning Behavior
Planning Stage (Before Learning)	p1	Number of Classroom Platform Material Clicks
	p2	Number of Teaching Network Course Visits
	p3	Number of Teaching Network Learning Video Clicks
Performance Stage (During Learning)	m1	Number of Attempts in "Software Engineering Practice Teaching Case Based on Trustie" on Topway
	m2	Number of Attempts in "Software Engineering Theory and Practice" on Topway
	m3	Online Duration on Teaching Network Platform
	m4	Duration of Teaching Network Learning Video Viewing
	m5	Number of Teaching Network Discussion Board Visits
	m6	Number of Posts on Teaching Network Discussion Board
	m7	Number of Moodle Video Viewing Actions
Reflection Stage (After Learning)	r1–r9	Classroom Platform Test Scores for Each Chapter
	r10–r18	Time Spent on Classroom Platform Tests for Each Chapter
Classroom Behavior Participation	t1	Extracurricular Exploration Score
	t2	Role in Project

On the Touge platform, there are two practical courses available for students to assess their learning outcomes: "Software Engineering Practice Cases Based on Trustie" and "Software Engineering Theory and Practice." During the challenge process, students who complete the same level and achieve the same score may have experienced different numbers of attempts—some pass on the first try, whereas others may pass after several failures. Owing to course assessment requirements, students' Touge challenge completion rates are generally 100%. Therefore, the number of attempts in practical courses can be used to compare different learning behaviors exhibited by students who use various learning strategies.

On the Moodle learning platform, the system records 17 types of behaviors during video viewing. These behaviors can be categorized into video viewing interactions and user interface operations. We use the cumulative number of video viewing behaviors on the Moodle platform as a data feature to reflect the self-directed learning process.

In the context of the software engineering classroom-related activities of the research subjects, extracurricular exploration includes the total number of activities, such as participation in "One" series events (e.g., One Story Software Engineering, One Paper Software Engineering), awards from competitions, publication of reflections, and articles posted on the class public account. Although extracurricular exploration is one of the course assessment standards, the sample data indicate that students significantly participate in these activities, with real scores generally far exceeding the maximum threshold set by the assessment standard. Thus, the true scores for students' extracurricular exploration are also used as one of the features for constructing classroom behavior participation. Additionally, the role in the project indicates whether the student serves as a team leader or a member in group projects, reflecting the student's initiative and enthusiasm in task-taking.

4 A Self-Directed Learning Ability Prediction Model

Accurate assessment of self-directed learning ability is crucial for both educators and students. The self-directed learning ability prediction model in this paper aims to predict the quantitative indicators of students' self-directed learning ability on the basis of multidimensional learning behavior features. This section first details the design of the sample weighting algorithm on the basis of questionnaire response times and then introduces the experimental process of the self-directed learning ability prediction model, including feature selection, model training and parameter tuning, and model results, as shown in Fig. 2. Finally, the predictive effects between learning behavior features and self-directed learning ability are analyzed.

4.1 Sample Weighting Algorithm

The analysis of the self-directed learning questionnaire shows good reliability and validity, indicating that it provides stable measurements. However, this does not guarantee that all the responses are careful and accurate. Some students who complete the questionnaire unusually quickly tend to give uniform or extreme answers, such as always choosing "Strongly Agree" or "Strongly Disagree." Such inattentive responses can obscure meaningful results and introduce noise into the data, impacting analysis.

To address this, the study employs sample weighting. A relationship between the response time and sample weight is established, and each sample's weight is calculated. During regression model training, the loss function is adjusted by multiplying each sample's loss by its weight. This approach prioritizes higher-quality samples and reduces the influence of inattentive answers. The model is trained iteratively to minimize the weighted loss, optimizing parameters while considering sample quality. The weighted

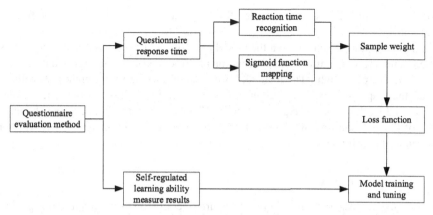

Fig. 2. A Self-Directed Learning Ability Prediction Model.

model's performance is then compared to that of a baseline model to assess the impact of weighting adjustments. The weighting algorithm based on the response time is shown in Fig. 3.

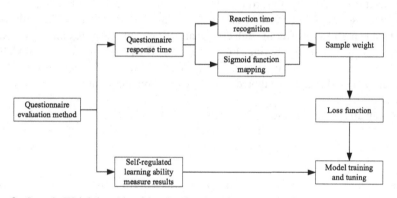

Fig. 3. Sample Weighting Algorithm Design Based on the Questionnaire Response Time.

Reaction time identification is a postprocessing method for handling careless responses in surveys [18]. It is generally believed that if the duration of questionnaire completion is too short, the provided answers may not accurately represent the respondent's true thoughts. Online survey tools (such as the Questionnaire Star) can automatically record the response time of participants. For sample i, let the response time of the questionnaire be, the sample weight be, and the number of items in the scale be n. To facilitate subsequent calculations of sample weights, the response time is first processed on the basis of a reaction time threshold. An empirical method for setting the reaction time threshold is commonly used [18]. Huang et al. [19] reported that participants are unlikely to respond faster than 2 s per item. This threshold is widely adopted [18]. On the basis of factors such as item type, difficulty, respondent age, and education level, this study sets the upper limit of the reaction time threshold to 4 s. Thus, spending 4 s or more on an item is considered a thoughtful and valid response. Therefore, the formula is as follows.

After obtaining, to ensure that the model's sensitivity to response time varies across different intervals, a nonlinear transformation is introduced using the sigmoid function to derive the sample weight. The formula for calculating the sample weight is as follows. When the response time is less than or equal to the lower limit of the reaction time threshold 2*n, the sample weight is set to 0. When the response time exceeds the upper limit of a reaction time threshold of 4*n, the sample weight approaches 1, which is essentially the original weight.

4.2   Feature Selection

This section uses the RFE algorithm for feature selection on the data features organized in Table 4. The features are ranked according to their importance, and the top 10 features with a rank of 1 are selected for subsequent model training and prediction. The results of the learning behavior feature selection are shown in Table 5.

4.3   Self-Directed Learning Ability Prediction Results

The dataset was randomly divided into 70% for training and 30% for testing. The training set was used to train both the baseline model and the weighted model with sample weights, and a grid search along with cross-validation methods were employed to determine the optimal parameter settings for each model. The performance of the models was compared via an independent test set. Tables 6 and 7 present the prediction results for the baseline model and the weighted model, respectively, in terms of the MSE, RMSE, MAE, and MAPE.

Among all the model results, 7 models have a MAPE value of less than 10%. Compared with the other models, the Lasso model with sample weights performs better across all four evaluation metrics and can be used for predicting self-directed learning ability.

4.4   Predictive Effect of Learning Behavior on Self-Directed Learning Ability

Using the top 10 most important features selected for model training, the prediction model achieved an MSE of 0.18 and a MAPE of 8.9% on an independent test set, indicating that these 10 learning behavior features have a significant predictive effect on self-directed learning ability. This finding quantitatively confirms the relationship between internal personal self-directed learning ability and external learning behaviors. Such confirmation can provide reference recommendations for educational practice, suggesting that educators should consider both students' self-directed learning abilities and their exhibited learning behaviors when designing courses and guidance strategies. This section analyzes the features in conjunction with feature dimensions and Pearson correlations to help educators more precisely support students in achieving learning goals through effective learning strategies and behaviors, thereby enhancing their self-directed learning ability.

In the planning phase of the online self-directed learning cycle, the "number of clicks on class materials" feature has the highest importance for predicting self-directed learning ability among all learning behavior features and has a positive predictive effect on the model. This finding indicates that, in the early stages of the self-directed learning

Table 5. Learning Behavior Feature Selection Results

Number	Learning Behavior Feature	Rank	Selected
p1	Classroom App Material Clicks	1	√
t1	Extracurricular Exploration Score	1	√
r3	Classroom App Test 3 Score	1	√
r2	Classroom App Test 2 Score	1	√
m6	Teaching Network Forum Posts Count	1	√
r9	Classroom App Test 9 Score	1	√
r5	Classroom App Test 5 Score	1	√
r8	Classroom App Test 8 Score	1	√
r1	Classroom App Test 1 Score	1	√
r7	Classroom App Test 7 Score	1	√
m1	Touge "Software Engineering Practice Teaching Case Based on Trustie" Challenge Attempts	2	×
r17	Classroom App Test 8 Response Time	3	×
r18	Classroom App Test 9 Response Time	4	×
r12	Classroom App Test 3 Response Time	5	×
m2	Touge "Software Engineering Theory and Practice" Challenge Attempts	6	×
r16	Classroom App Test 7 Response Time	7	×
t2	Project Role	8	×
r10	Classroom App Test 1 Response Time	9	×
m5	Teaching Network Forum Visits Count	10	×
r14	Classroom App Test 5 Response Time	11	×
m7	Moodle Video Viewing Behavior Count	12	×
r11	Classroom App Test 2 Response Time	13	×
r4	Classroom App Test 4 Score	14	×
p2	Teaching Network Course Visits Count	15	×
m3	Teaching Network Platform Online Duration	16	×
r6	Classroom App Test 6 Score	17	×
m4	Teaching Network Learning Video Viewing Duration	18	×
p3	Teaching Network Learning Video Clicks Count	19	×
r15	Classroom App Test 6 Response Time	20	×
r13	Classroom App Test 4 Response Time	21	×

Table 6. Performance of the Base Model

Model	MSE	RMSE	MAE	MAPE
Lasso	0.19	0.44	0.37	9.5%
Decision Trees	0.27	0.52	0.43	11.1%
Random Forests	0.22	0.48	0.39	10.2%
GBDT	0.23	0.48	0.40	10.3%
XGBoost	0.22	0.47	0.39	10.1%

Table 7. Performance of the weighted model

Model	MSE	RMSE	MAE	MAPE
Lasso	0.18	0.43	0.35	8.9%
Decision Trees	0.23	0.47	0.39	10.1%
Random Forests	0.22	0.47	0.39	9.9%
GBDT	0.19	0.44	0.37	9.2%
XGBoost	0.21	0.46	0.38	9.7%

process, learning behaviors related to selecting and acquiring learning resources are crucial for developing self-directed learning ability. Educators can meet learners' needs by providing diverse learning resources and stimulating their interest, thereby facilitating more effective self-directed learning.

In the performance phase, the "number of posts on the discussion board" on the educational network has a strong positive predictive effect on self-directed learning ability. Self-directed learning does not mean that students learn in isolation; students can achieve their learning goals by participating in discussions to gain or provide help. Educators can act as guides and facilitators, encouraging students' active participation in communication and discussion. In contrast, browsing behaviors such as the "number of visits to the educational network discussion board" have a significant degree of randomness and a smaller predictive effect on self-directed learning ability.

In the reflection phase, multiple features related to "class test scores" have a high predictive effect on self-directed learning ability. This suggests that students with stronger self-directed learning abilities effectively evaluate and reflect on their learning process and outcomes on the basis of test scores, adjusting their learning strategies when necessary. Out of the 9-chapter tests, 7 test score features are of greater importance, whereas the remaining are lower. To explore the reasons, this study analyzed the test papers of each chapter, as shown in Table 8.

The difficulty index of the test paper is given by the following formula, where P represents the difficulty index, and X represents the average score of the sample and represents the total score of the test paper. The closer P *is* to 1, the lower the difficulty

Table 8. Analysis of Chapter Test Papers.

Number	Total Score	Average Score	Standard Deviation	Difficulty	Discrimination	Selected
1	100	59.4	26.2	0.59	1.3	✓
2	100	78.7	13.8	0.79	0.62	✓
3	100	80.2	11.5	0.80	0.55	✓
4	100	93.7	9.9	**0.94**	**0.4**	✗
5	100	60.0	20.3	0.60	1	✓
6	100	96.4	6.7	**0.96**	**0.25**	✗
7	48	33.1	9.61	0.69	1	✓
8	10	8.8	1.36	0.88	0.62	✓
9	100	82.3	13.9	0.82	0.65	✓

of the test paper.

$$P = \frac{X}{W}$$

The formula for calculating the test paper's discrimination index is as follows, where D represents the discrimination index, X_H represents the average score of the top 27% of D students, and X_L represents the average score of the bottom 27% of D students. The larger D is, the better the ability of the test paper to differentiate between students. A discrimination index above 0.4 indicates that the test paper has excellent discrimination ability.

$$D = \frac{2 * (X_H - X_L)}{W}$$

Table 8 shows that the "Classroom Test 4 Scores" and "Classroom Test 6 Scores", which have a smaller impact on self-directed learning ability, have relatively lower test difficulty and poorer discrimination than the other tests do. These findings indicate that tests with better discrimination and moderate difficulty can assist students in making more accurate self-assessments and adjustments. Educators can increase students' self-directed learning ability by designing high-quality tests and encouraging them to engage in thorough self-evaluations and reflection.

With respect to classroom-related learning behavior, "extracurricular exploration scores" demonstrated a significant predictive effect on self-directed learning ability, with a positive correlation. Educators should encourage and support students' extracurricular exploration activities and provide necessary guidance and resources to help them develop and enhance their self-directed learning skills.

5 Conclusion

This paper presents a predictive model for self-directed learning ability on the basis of learners' behaviors. By utilizing data from blended teaching environments, the model enhances the understanding of students' learning processes, enabling educators to develop more effective teaching strategies and personalized interventions. However, the study has several limitations. While it employs extensive behavioral data, the model may overlook contextual factors such as individual motivation, prior knowledge, and external support. Future research should address these limitations by examining a wider range of factors influencing self-directed learning, including qualitative studies to capture individual learner experiences and cross-institutional validations. The incorporation of advanced techniques such as machine learning could further increase the model's accuracy and adaptability. Overall, further investigations should aim to establish a comprehensive framework for diagnosing and promoting self-directed learning abilities, contributing to effective educational practices in a rapidly changing societal landscape.

Acknowledgments. This paper is supported by the Humanities and Social Sciences Research Planning Fund Project of the Ministry of Education: "Research on Metacognitive Diagnosis Theory and Technology Driven by Multimodal Learning Data" (23YJA880091) and the Fundamental Research Funds for the Central Universities. Additionally, we would like to acknowledge the Undergraduate Teaching Reform Project of Peking University in 2024: "Gamified Interactive Experimental Teaching in Software Engineering" (Project No. 7100903145).

References

1. China Engineering Education Accreditation Association: Engineering Education Accreditation Standards [S/OL]. China Standards Press, Beijing (2022). https://www.ceeaa.org.cn/gcj yzyrzxh/rzcxjbz/gcjyrzbz/index.html. Accessed 28 Mar 2024
2. Hu, Y., Gu, X., Zhao, C.: Online learning behavior analysis modeling and mining. Open Educ. Res. **20**(2), 102–110 (2014)
3. Zhu, Z., Zhang, Q., Song, X.: A classroom teaching design for software engineering aimed at cultivating students' autonomous learning ability. Comp. Educ. **05**, 155–159 (2023)
4. Li, X.: Research on the Compilation and Evaluation of the Autonomous Learning Ability Scale for Physical Education Students at Beijing Sport University. Master's Thesis, Beijing Sport University (2017)
5. Wu, M.: Practical Statistical Analysis of Questionnaires. Chongqing University Press, Chongqing (2010)
6. Li, Y., Jiang, Q., Zhao, W.: Research on the structure and mechanism of online learning behavior in the digital age—a self-regulation theory perspective. Mod. Distance Educ. **01**, 61–70 (2023)
7. Zimmerman, B.J.: Becoming a self-regulated learner: an overview. Theory Pract. **41**(2), 64–70 (2002)
8. Knowles, M.S.: Self-directed learning: a guide for learners and teachers. J. Contin. Educ. Nurs. **7**(3), 60 (1975)
9. Soffer, T., Cohen, A.: Students' engagement characteristics predict success and completion of online courses. J. Comput. Assist. Learn. **35**(3), 378–389 (2019)

10. Williamson, S.N.: Development of a self-rating scale of self-directed learning. Nurse Researcher **14**(2) (2007)
11. Kim, R., Olfman, L., Ryan, T., et al.: Leveraging a personalized system to improve self-directed learning in online educational environments. Comput. Educ. **70**, 150–160 (2014)
12. Wang, F.H.: An exploration of online behavior engagement and achievement in flipped classroom supported by learning management system. Comput. Educ. **114**, 79–91 (2017)
13. Kim, D., Jung, E., Yoon, M., et al.: Exploring the structural relationships between course design factors, learner commitment, self-directed learning, and intentions for further learning in a self-paced MOOC. Comput. Educ. **166**(6), 104171 (2021)
14. Fischer, G.: Beyond hype and underestimation: identifying research challenges for the future of MOOCs. Distance Educ. **35**(2), 149–158 (2014)
15. Reeve, J.: A self-determination theory perspective on student engagement. In: Christenson, S., Reschly, A., Wylie, C. (eds.) Handbook of Research on Student Engagement, pp. 149–172. Springer, Boston (2012). https://doi.org/10.1007/978-1-4614-2018-7_7
16. Trowler, V.: Student engagement literature review. High. Educ. Acad. **11**(1), 1–15 (2010)
17. Carini, R.M., Kuh, G.D., Klein, S.P.: Student engagement and student learning: testing the linkages. Res. High. Educ. **47**, 1–32 (2006)
18. Zhong, X., Li, M., Li, L.: Control and identification of nonserious responses in questionnaire surveys. Adv. Psychol. Sci. **29**(2), 13 (2021)
19. Huang, J.L., Curran, P.G., Keeney, J., et al.: Detecting and deterring insufficient effort responding to surveys. J. Bus. Psychol. **27**, 99–114 (2012)
20. Liu, B., Wu, Y., Shu, H., et al.: Uncovering the predictive effect of behaviors on self-directed learning ability. Brit. J. Educ. Technol. (2024)

The Indoor Fusion Algorithm Based on INS and UWB

Yu Meng[1,2], Kangni Huang[1,2], Jin Hui[1,2,3(✉)], and Keliu Long[1,2(✉)]

[1] Jiangxi Province Key Laboratory of Multidimensional Intelligent Perception and Control, Jiangxi University of Science and Technology, Ganzhou 341000, China
huijin@hdu.edu.cn, keliulong@jxust.edu.cn
[2] School of Information Engineering, Jiangxi University of Science and Technology, Ganzhou 341000, China
[3] School of Information Engineering, Hangzhou Dianzi University, Hangzhou 310018, China

Abstract. Ultra-wideband (UWB) positioning is highly susceptible to environmental factors, whereas inertial navigation system (INS) positioning suffers from cumulative errors over time. To address these limitations, this paper investigates the fusion of UWB and INS positioning techniques to increase the positioning accuracy. This study provides a comprehensive analysis of UWB and INS positioning principles and presents a novel approach for their integration. In the experimental setup, the time of arrival (TOA) method was employed for UWB positioning evaluation, and separate experiments were conducted to assess the performance of the INS system. The experimental results confirm that UWB positioning is prone to environmental disturbances, causing interruptions in continuous signal transmission. In contrast, the INS system experiences progressive error accumulation, which significantly degrades the positioning accuracy over time. To overcome these challenges, this paper proposes a fusion approach based on a Kalman filter algorithm aimed at combining the strengths of both positioning technologies. Comparative analysis with standalone positioning methods demonstrates that the proposed fusion algorithm significantly enhances accuracy and mitigates error accumulation, thereby validating its effectiveness.

Keywords: UWB · INS · Indoor Fusion Positioning · TOA · Kalman Filter

1 Introduction

In recent years, with the rapid development of society and the progress of science and technology, people have become increasingly intense in their quest for smart and convenient lifestyles. The demand for various location-based services has increased sharply, including autonomous driving, warehouse logistics, emergency rescue, unmanned supermarkets, travel navigation, and personnel tracking [1]. When positioning is applied to indoor environments, GNSS signals are severely attenuated because of the occlusion of buildings, and the signals may become weak or even difficult to detect, making it difficult to provide stable and reliable data [2]. Therefore, many scholars have studied indoor positioning. After years of development, the current main indoor positioning technologies include infrared positioning technology [3], Wi-Fi positioning technology [4], Bluetooth positioning technology [5], ultrasonic positioning technology [6], radio frequency identification positioning technology (RFID) [7], ZigBee positioning technology [8], UWB positioning technology [9] and INS positioning technology [10]. Among them, UWB technology has become a major technology in the field of indoor localization because of its advantages of high temporal resolution, strong penetration, good anti-interference performance and low energy consumption. However, indoor environments are complex and variable. UWB signals are susceptible to non-line-of-sight (NLOS) propagation [11] because of the obstruction of people, objects, or walls, leading to problems such as low accuracy and poor stability of UWB positioning techniques. Therefore, it is difficult to achieve high-precision positioning in complex environments with only a single type of sensor. INS is an independent navigation technology that has the advantage of not being affected by changes in the external environment, so there is no need to consider channel attenuation or NLOS errors. It is capable of outputting high-frequency signals in excess of 200 Hz, so it has excellent measurement accuracy over a short period of time. In addition to precise position and velocity information, the INS can also provide the output of the attitude data. However, since the algorithm involves integration, the error of inertial sensors accumulates with time, leading to long-term navigation error increasing constantly and making it difficult to maintain the accuracy of high-precision positioning services for a long time [12]. Considering the shortcomings of using UWB and INS positioning singly, this paper adopts the fusion of INS and UWB, resulting in good complementarity. On the one hand, the long-term positioning accuracy of UWB technology can be used to reduce the accumulation of INS errors and solve the problem of INS localization results drifting with time in the LOS environment. On the other hand, in a non-line-of-sight environment, UWB technology is affected by NLOS errors; at this time, the short-term positioning accuracy of the INS can be utilized to mitigate the impact of NLOS errors on the positioning accuracy to ensure the continuity of the positioning and form a fusion positioning technology with high positioning accuracy and stable performance.

2 Overview of UWB and INS and Fusion Positioning Technology

2.1 UWB Positioning Technology

UWB technology is a wireless communication technology. Unlike the traditional sinusoidal carrier method, UWB uses nanosecond nonsinusoidal narrow pulses to transmit data.

The TOA method mainly measures the time of unidirectional transmission of the electrical signal from the base station to the measured object and uses the distance value obtained by multiplying the measured time by the speed of light to estimate the straight-line distance from the base station to the object. Assuming that the coordinates of the three base stations are known, they are (X_1, Y_1), (X_2, Y_2) and (X_3, Y_3), and the coordinates (X_0, Y_0) of the measured object are unknown. The base station transmits an electric wave signal at the moment of T1 and reaches the object at the moment of T2. T represents the time of electric wave transmission, and the distance between the base station and the object can be estimated according to Eq. (1).

$$d = c \times T \tag{1}$$

where d is the distance between the base station and the object and where c is the speed of light. The position of the object is solved via triangulation, and the equation is as follows:

$$\begin{cases} d_1{}^2 = (X_0 - X_1)^2 + (Y_0 - Y_1)^2 \\ d_2{}^2 = (X_0 - X_2)^2 + (Y_0 - Y_2)^2 \\ d_3{}^2 = (X_0 - X_3)^2 + (Y_0 - Y_3)^2 \end{cases} \tag{2}$$

By solving Eq. (2), the object coordinate equation can be obtained as:

$$\begin{bmatrix} X_0 \\ Y_0 \end{bmatrix} = \frac{1}{2} \begin{bmatrix} X_1 - X_3 & Y_1 - Y_3 \\ X_2 - X_3 & Y_2 - Y_3 \end{bmatrix}^{-1} \# \\ \begin{bmatrix} X_1^2 - X_3^2 + Y_1^2 - Y_3^2 + d_3^2 - d_1^2 \\ X_2^2 - X_3^2 + Y_2^2 - Y_3^2 + d_3^2 - d_2^2 \end{bmatrix} \tag{3}$$

2.2 INS Positioning Technology

INS is an independent navigation technology that neither relies on external signals nor radiates any form of energy outward. On the basis of Newton's laws of motion, this system obtains the velocity and displacement by recording the acceleration of the object in the inertial reference frame, integrating these measured accelerations over time, and then converts them to a navigational coordinate system. Accordingly, the velocity, heading angle and specific position of the object can be determined.

(1) Attitude solution.
    The definition of a quaternion is similar to that of a complex number, except that the imaginary part of a quaternion has three parts, which are based on a linear combination of pairs $\{1, i, j, k\}$, and the quaternion can be transformed into vectors as follows:

$$q = \begin{bmatrix} 1 & i & j & k \end{bmatrix} \begin{bmatrix} q_0 \\ q_1 \\ q_2 \\ q_3 \end{bmatrix} \# \\ = q_0 + q_1 i + q_2 j + q_3 k \tag{4}$$

where q_0 is the real part, q_1, q_2, and q_3 are the imaginary parts, and i, j, k are the units of the imaginary parts.
(2) Velocity solution.
    The velocity solution can be obtained by integrating the acceleration information. Its differential equation is as follows:

$$\dot{v} = C_b^n a - g \tag{5}$$

where $a = \begin{bmatrix} a_x & a_y & a_z \end{bmatrix}$ represents the measured acceleration and where $g = \begin{bmatrix} 0 & 0 & g_0 \end{bmatrix}$ represents the gravitational acceleration.

The general solution of this differential equation is as follows:

$$\Delta v = (C_b^n a - g) \Delta t \tag{6}$$

(3) Position solution.

The differential form of the position is as follows:

$$\dot{p} = v \tag{7}$$

When the general solution of the velocity is substituted, the general solution form of the position is as follows:

$$\Delta p = v \Delta t + \tfrac{1}{2} a \Delta t^2 \tag{8}$$

2.3 Kalman Filter

The Kalman filter is an algorithm that uses linear system state equations to estimate the state of the system optimally by outputting observation data from system inputs. The optimal estimation is for more accurate measurements, and the predicted value is calculated from a linear mathematical model and then combined with the measured value of the sensor.

Assume that there is a linear dynamic system; in that case, its state can be described via state transfer Eq. (9) and observation Eq. (10):

$$x_k = A x_{k-1} + B u_k + w_{k-1} \tag{9}$$

$$z_k = H x_k + v_k \tag{10}$$

where x_k represents the state of the current moment, A represents the state transition matrix, B represents the control input matrix, u_k represents the control input, and w_{k-1} represents the process noise. z_k is the observed quantity, H is the observation matrix, and v_k is the observation noise.

The key process of the Kalman filter includes prediction and updating. In the prediction stage, the current state is estimated and predicted via the state transfer equation.

(1) Prediction stage.

predict the current state:

$$\hat{x}_{k|k-1} = A\hat{x}_{k-1|k-1} + B u_k \tag{11}$$

where $\hat{x}_{k|k-1}$ represents the state estimation at time point (k) under the condition that all the information until time point (k-1) has been given.

Covariance of the prediction error:

$$P_{k|k-1} = A P_{k-1|k-1} A' + Q \tag{12}$$

where $P_{k|k-1}$ is the covariance of the prediction error, indicating the uncertainty of the prediction state. Q represents the covariance matrix of the process noise.

(2) Update stage.
  Kalman gain:

$$K_k = P_{k|k-1}H^T \left(HP_{k|k-1}H^T + R\right)^{-1} \tag{13}$$

where K_k represents the Kalman gain, which determines the weights between the observation and predicted values, and R represents the covariance matrix of the observation noise.

3 Experiments and Analysis of Results

3.1 Setup of Experiments

The position area is set within a square area with a side length of 10 m. The TOA position method needs at least 3 base stations, but in this paper, four base stations are used for TOA localization with coordinates (0, 0), (10, 0), (10, 10), and (0, 10). Moreover, a rectangular trajectory with a length of 7 m and a width of 4 m is set to represent the pedestrian walk path. The velocity of the pedestrian walk is set to 1.5 m per second, and the measurement frequency is set to 50 Hz. The pedestrian walks at a uniform velocity following the trajectory, and the sampling points are uniformly distributed on the trajectory according to the speed and frequency. The pedestrian starts walking from (2, 2) and walks along the trajectory in a circular pattern.

3.2 The Experimental Results and Analysis of UWB Localization

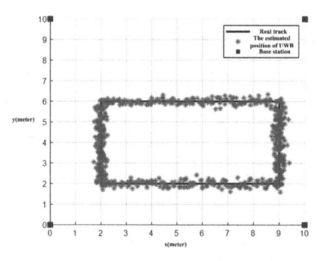

Fig. 1. TOA localization position estimation chart

As shown in Fig. 1, the estimation positions of TOA localization are distributed mainly in the adjacent area around the real track, and few points have large errors combined with the real position. Therefore, the accuracy of TOA localization is initially considered high. Figure 2 shows that the error is concentrated in a narrow range between 0.05 m and 0.35 m. This finding indicates that TOA localization technology is able to provide highly accurate localization results. Only a small portion is within the range of 0.3--0.35 m, and a very small portion is distributed above 0.35 m.

As shown in Table 1, the maximum error of TOA localization is 0.475 m, and the average error is 0.19 m. Therefore, TOA localization technology demonstrates a localization ability with small errors, good stability and high accuracy.

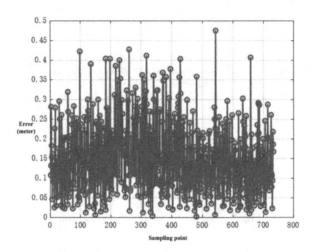

Fig. 2. Error of TOA localization

Table 1. The error of TOA localization

Error	Maximum error	Minimum error	Average error
Error value (meter)	0.475	0.03	0.190

3.3 The Experimental Results and Analysis of INS Localization

Figure 3 shows that the results of INS localization are terrible, and the difference between the estimated position on the track and the real position is large. Moreover, ideally, the final localization point should be within a small range near the starting position, but the position of INS localization is very far from the starting point. Figure 4 shows that the error increases gradually as the positioning continues, which confirms that INS localization leads to the accumulation of error with increasing time. Together with the results in Table 2, the maximum error is as high as 6.266 m, and the average error is 2.844 m, which is a very large error in a square area with a side length of 10 m. Therefore, the results of INS localization are not good because of large deviations and accumulate over time.

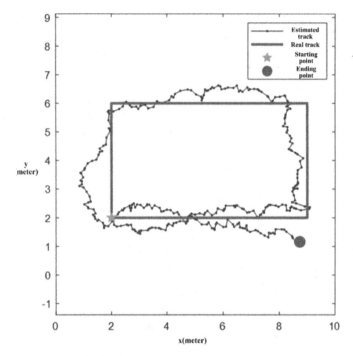

Fig. 3. Estimated track of INS localization

Table 2. Errors in INS localization

error	Maximum error	Average error
Error value (meter)	6.266	2.844

3.4 Subsection Sample

Figure 5 shows the resulting graph of the INS and UWB localization algorithms after fusion via weights. The black rectangle represents the real track, the blue squares at the four corner positions are the four base stations of UWB localization, the blue dotted line represents the track of INS localization, the magenta star-shaped point represents the estimated position point of UWB localization, and the red solid line represents the trajectory after fusion . Figure 5 and Fig. 4 show that as the track estimation proceeds,

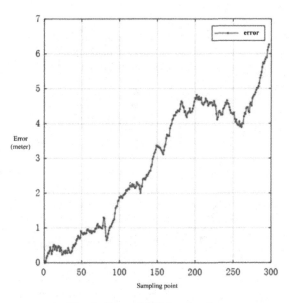

Fig. 4. Error of INS localization

Table 3. Comparison of the localization errors before and after fusion

Localization method	Max error	Min error	Average error
UWB	0.629	0.024	0.203
INS	7.243	0.021	1.436
The fusion	0.511	0.010	0.171

the INS localization error gradually tends to accumulate, and the localization accuracy is low. Figure 2 shows that the error of the UWB localization position estimation point is small. The fused track is essentially consistent with the real trajectory, except that the fused track still has a slightly larger error due to the excessive error of the INS during the final localization. Table 3 shows that the maximum error, minimum error and average error of the fused localization are all lower than those of the single localization, and the analysis of Fig. 6 reveals that the deviation of the fused localization is concentrated between 0.05 and 0.2 m, which indicates that the localization is more stable after fusion. Through the overall analysis, it is concluded that the fusion localization algorithm can make very good use of the high accuracy of UWB localization, and the fusion localization has a better localization performance than the two localization algorithms do.

294   Y. Meng et al.

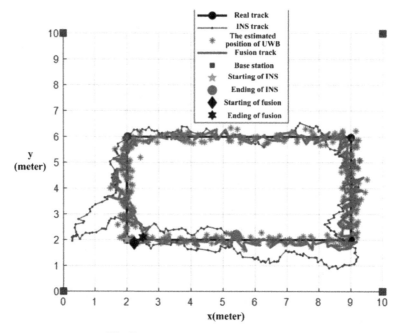

Fig. 5. Fusion results of INS and UWB

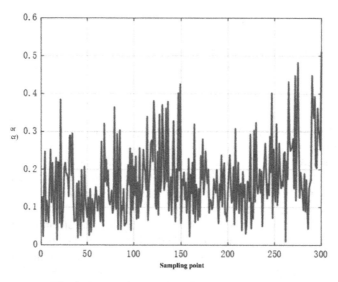

Fig. 6. Errors of INS and UWB fusion localization

4   Conclusions

This paper presents experimental evaluations of UWB and INS localization algorithms. The results confirm that when used individually, UWB localization is highly susceptible to environmental disturbances, whereas INS localization suffers from cumulative errors over time, both of which negatively impact positioning accuracy. To address these limitations, this study proposes a fusion algorithm that integrates UWB and INS localization to achieve more accurate and stable positioning. The fusion algorithm was developed and evaluated through a series of experiments, with comparative analysis of the results from the UWB, INS, and fused localization approaches. The findings demonstrate that the fusion algorithm effectively mitigates the environmental sensitivity of UWB positioning and prevents the error accumulation inherent in INS technology. The results validate that the fused localization approach significantly outperforms the standalone methods.

Acknowledgments. This work is supported by the College Student Innovation and Entrepreneurship Training Program of Jiangxi University of Science and Technology under Grant No. 202410407040.

References

1. Song, Z.: Automatic positioning technology of warehouse logistics robot based on visual servo. Tech. Autom. Appl. **40**(8), 70–74 (2021)
2. Zhu, X., Li, Z., Li, S., et al.: Indoor localization method based on adaptive wavelet threshold analysis. Autom. Control. Comput. Sci. **57**(5), 523–533 (2023)
3. Damir, A., Sandi, L.: Indoor localization based on infrared angle of arrival sensor network. Sens. (Basel, Switz.) **20**(21), 6278 (2020)
4. Qiaolin, P., Youkun, C., Zhou, M., Zhengwei, Y., Yukun, Z.: Indoor Wi-Fi localization algorithm based on the improved contrastive learning and parallel fusion neural network. Chin. J. Sci. Instrum. **45**(1), 101–110 (2024)
5. Limin, C., Yuning, C.: Research on indoor positioning method based on bluetooth wireless technology. Wirel. Internet Technol. **20**(13), 21–23 (2023)
6. Ijaz, F., Yang, H.K., Ahmad, A.W., et al.: Indoor positioning: a review of indoor ultrasonic positioning systems. In: Proceedings of the 2013 15th International Conference on Advanced Communications Technology (ICACT), pp. 1146–1150. IEEE (2013)
7. Paolo, T., Salvatore, D., Matteo, U.: Efficient localization in warehouse logistics: a comparison of LMS approaches for 3D multilateration of passive UHF RFID tags. Int. J. Adv. Manufact. Technol. **120**(7), 4977–4988 (2022)
8. Uradzinski, M., Guo, H., Liu, X., et al.: Advanced indoor positioning using zigbee wireless technology. Wireless Pers. Commun. **97**, 6509–6518 (2017)
9. Zhang, Y., Tan, X., Zhao, C.: UWB/INS integrated pedestrian positioning for robust indoor environments. IEEE Sens. J. **20**(23), 14401–14409 (2020)
10. Meng, S., Yunjia, W., David, P., et al.: Indoor localization using mind evolutionary algorithm-based geomagnetic positioning and smartphone IMU sensors. IEEE Sens. J. **22**(7), 7130–7141 (2022)
11. Venkatesh, S., Buehrer, R.M.: Non-line-of-sight identification in ultrawideband systems based on received signal statistics. IET Microwaves Antennas Propag. **1**(6), 1120–1130 (2007)
12. Kaijun, X., Yun, D., Yong, Y.: Analysis of IMU error characteristics in strapdown inertial navigation system. J. XIAN Aeronaut. Univ. **42**(1), 1–6 (2024)

Research on the Current Status and Implications of Mobile Learning in International Higher Education

Xiuming Li[✉] and Nana Zhang

Qinghai Minzu University, Xining, Qinghai, China
lixiumingwhs@163.com

Abstract. Mobile learning (M-Learning) has been widely used in education. With the rapid development of mobile internet and communication technology, mobile terminal equipment is increasingly widely used. Mobile learning has been the focus of the educational department, and it has become the main position of mobile learning. For the purpose of developing mobile learning, this research investigated mobile learning in the WEB of SCIENCE and identified 326 samples. On the basis of the analysis of the concept, the research method, the influential factors, and the application of mobile learning, the status quo in the world can be summarized.

Keywords: Mobile learning · higher education · mobile technology · international

1 Introduction

Starting in the United States, mobile learning has been widely studied worldwide. With the development and renewal of technology, mobile learning has become a major trend in the educational field. In international higher education, mobile learning has become an important mode of study. Many colleges have started to integrate mobile learning into their education system. Mobile learning has been widely applied in many areas of higher education, such as social science, natural science and engineering technology. Through the development of mobile learning applications and the establishment of mobile learning platforms, universities provide students with learning resources and communication opportunities at any time. Additionally, some international colleges support distance learning and online learning through mobile learning, which offers more flexibility and diversity to students. Many governments and enterprises pay much attention to mobile learning and have introduced related policies and investments to support mobile learning. A number of international organizations have also actively promoted and cooperated with each other to promote mobile learning in international higher education.

The WEB of SCIENCE was searched for via key words such as mobile learning, M-learning, mobile education, M-education, and higher education. The search period was limited to January 1, 2001, to January 1, 2024. For the first time, 421 articles were retrieved, and duplicates and irrelevant articles were removed. Finally, 326 samples

K. Zhang et al. (Eds.): CSEI 2024, CCIS 2447, pp. 296–306, 2025.
https://doi.org/10.1007/978-981-96-3735-5_22

were collected and analyzed. In this paper, the author analyses the status quo of mobile learning in international higher education from four aspects: the evolution of the concept of mobile learning, the methods used, the influential factors, and the application of mobile learning. Finally, suggestions are made for the development of mobile learning in China [1].

2 The Evolution of the Concept of Mobile Learning

With the rapid development of IT and the increasing popularity of mobile terminals, mobile learning has become a new and important method of digital learning. The definition of mobile learning varies, and its definition has evolved with the development of mobile learning. There are two ways to classify the definition: one is to emphasize the use of mobile equipment, and the other is to emphasize the learning process.

2.1 Emphasize the Application of Hardware Mobile Devices

Traxler (2005) proposed from the perspective of users that mobile learning is the primary assistance provided by handheld devices for education, and this definition focuses more on the role of technology [2]. Yousuf (2007) suggested that mobile learning refers to education and training conducted through mobile devices, including digital assistants and smartphones [3]. Mobile learning can be used in noneducational activities. One of the characteristics of mobile learning is that it is easy to use and inexpensive. Sad and Goktas see mobile learning as an extension of digital learning, primarily through smartphones, tablets, and laptops [4] (see Fig. 1).

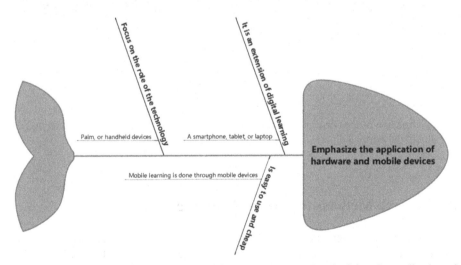

Fig. 1. Evolution of the Concept of Mobile Learning based on Emphasizing the application of hardware and mobile devices

2.2   Emphasizing the Mobility of Learners and Learning Processes

The mobility of mobile learning not only manifests in the movement of hardware devices but also includes the movement of learners and the movement of the learning process [5]. O'Malley et al. (2005) proposed that mobile learning refers to learning anytime or anywhere [6]. Learners use mobile devices to learn from any nonfixed location [7]. Alexander (2006) proposed that mobile learning learners have a wandering nature similar to herdsmen, and they use mobile devices to complete their learning. Learners can upload, download, browse, and publish information through mobile devices anywhere on campus. Both definitions emphasize the mobility of learners in the process of mobile learning. Wang et al. (2009) proposed that mobile learning refers to learning at any time and place through wireless networks and mobile terminal devices [8]. Kukulska Hulme and Traxler (2005) proposed that mobile learning refers to the teaching process that is no longer constrained by time and space. El Hussein and Cronje (2010) further deepened the concept of mobile learning, stating that it includes the movement of learners, devices, information flows, and learning processes, and emphasized that learning in education is the generation of any type of learner, technology (device), and process in the learning environment [9] (see Fig. 2).

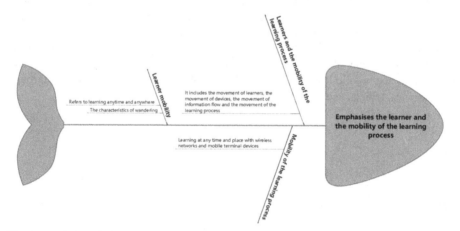

Fig. 2. Evolution of the Concept of Mobile Learning based on Emphasizing the learner and the mobility of the learning process

3   Research Methods for Mobile Learning

In this study, 326 sample papers were categorized and summarized. Among the 326 papers, a total of 201 papers explicitly used the research methodology, whereas 125 papers did not. Among the 201 articles that clearly use research methods, quantitative research is the most common (93 articles), qualitative research ranks second (62 articles), and mixed research ranks third (38 articles). Action research and comparative research are scarce. Quantitative research mainly adopts experimental research methods and survey research methods, whereas qualitative research mainly adopts observation methods, case study methods, and interview methods. Foreign scholars often conduct short-term surveys and experimental studies on mobile learning in the field of higher education, but relatively few long-term follow-up studies exist. Only two papers adopt action research. In the process of education, research on mobile technology and devices requires long-term collaboration between researchers and teaching practitioners. For example, Davison and Lazaros (2015) conducted a survey on the application of mobile technology in university classroom teaching in multiple countries in 2010 and compared and analyzed the survey results between 2010 and 2006. Through changes in time, they analyzed the changes in the research object [10].

3.1 Quantitative Research Methods

Sevillano Garcia (2015) conducted a quantitative study on the acceptability of tablets and mobile phones in European higher education [11]. This study used a questionnaire survey method to establish five main influencing factors related to acceptance, namely, self-efficacy, effort expectations, performance expectations, learning activities, and general abilities. On the basis of the Pearson test, a structural equation model was applied to analyze the influence of mobile terminal devices on learners' learning ability.

Zha Xiaoyu (2024) demonstrated the feasibility of the combination of mobile learning and traditional classrooms. Mobile learning extends the availability of knowledge and information resources and allows students to learn actively from passive study to active learning. It improves the sharing of knowledge, communication and cooperation and solves problems that cannot satisfy the practical needs of teachers and students [12].

3.2 Qualitative Research Methods

Gikas and Grant (2013) carried out an in-depth study on the use of mobile devices for university students and the role of social media in learning [13]. Led by researchers, teachers from three United States colleges used mobile devices to teach. Through the implementation of the project, 2–4 students who participated in mobile learning from the three colleges were selected for the interviews and recording. Then, with the help of Glaser's grounded theory, an iterative study was carried out to gather data. This paper analyses and sums up the advantages of mobile devices for students' learning and the problems they encounter in using mobile devices.

3.3 Mixed Research Method

In this research, a combination of quantitative and qualitative methods is used. Ke and HSU (2015) conducted research on improving teachers' TPACK knowledge of subject teaching through the use of mobile smartphones, augmented reality (AR) product creation, and related mobile learning activities. Researchers selected 40 fourth-year teacher trainees from the United States as participants and randomly divided them into two groups. Among them, 34 participants successfully completed the research task. The study adopted a method of having participants watch short videos on YouTube, with the goals of creating videos and understanding the design methods of educational animations. The first group of teacher trainees used animated videos from smartphones to assist in animation production. The theme of the animation was the concept of buoyancy, and the students published the animation on the website for evaluation. The second group of teacher trainees watched videos on educational resource websites related to buoyancy themes and then communicated on mobile websites. Researchers conducted interviews with participants before, during, and after the intervention in the experiment and conducted qualitative analysis on the interview data. After the experiment, the subjects were tested for their ability to perform TPACK. The results showed that both groups of mobile learning methods improved the TPACK ability of normal students and that the production of mobile products (AR) had a significant effect on the integration of content knowledge and technical ability. Watching mobile video clips has an advantage in terms of the ability of normal students to acquire knowledge.

4   Analysis of the Influencing Factors of Mobile Learning

The results revealed three aspects in this study: first, the self-perception of university students' mobile learning; second, the impact of mobile terminal usage habits and the validity of mobile learning. This paper analyzes the influential factors from the perspective of teachers, students and learning activities.

4.1   The Perspective of Teachers

Teachers are also an important factor affecting mobile learning [14]. Sad and Goktas (2014) conducted survey research on 1087 prospective teachers to investigate the cognitive status of mobile learning devices (including smartphones and laptops) [4]. The study revealed that prospective teachers had a greater advantage in laptops than in smartphones and chose to use different mobile learning tools according to the environment they were in; there were no significant differences in sex, age, or mobile phone use, and prospective teachers did not have a strong sense of mobile learning. Alrcsheedi and Caprctz (2015) investigated the factors affecting the effectiveness of mobile learning from the perspective of teachers [15]. He reported that the factors with the most significant influence on the validity of mobile learning are learner autonomy and network connectivity.

4.2   The Perspective of Students

To analyze the behavior of mobile learning, the researcher sets up a model on the basis of different application contexts and explores the influential factors of mobile learning behavior. The research results show that the major influencing factors are self-efficacy, attitudes and achievement expectations.

Cheon (2012) analyzed the factors influencing mobile learning among college students [16]. The study was divided into four phases. In the first phase, 17 students' basic personal data were acquired. In phase two, they were asked to watch a video on mobile learning. In phase three, students listen to a mobile learning report, and in phase four, they conduct a survey and analysis of mobile learning outcomes. The results indicate that mobile learning attitudes and behavioral difficulty positively influence mobile learning intentions. Pak (2012) creatively constructed a general model on the basis of the technology acceptance mode [17]. The general model builds a relationship from perceived utility, usability, behavior intention, attitude, self-efficacy, accessibility, and professional relevance [18]. In this study, 288 college students in South Korea were selected as the study objects, and a structural equation model was applied to demonstrate that the model could be used to explain students' behavioral intentions. On the basis of rational behavior theory and the technology acceptance model, Althunibat (2015) established a research model and reported that the main factors affecting mobile learning were usability and service quality [19].

4.3   The Perspective of the Learning Activity

The success or failure of learning determines the validity of mobile learning. The design and organization of learning activities have a positive effect on mobile technology, which can reduce the interference caused by the technique. Tindell and Bohlander (2012) conducted a survey and research on the use of text information in classrooms among 269 undergraduates [20]. The results revealed that 95 percent of the students brought their mobile phones to class, 92 percent used SMS, and 10 percent received at least one SMS during a test. Most students say that they use cell phones in class, but most of them do not know about it. Gikas and Grant (2013) conducted a survey and research on college students' mobile learning experience [21]. After the teacher used the mobile terminal equipment during the course, the researcher interviewed the students who took part in the program. The results indicate that the greatest benefit of using mobile terminal equipment is that the learners can obtain more information quickly, cooperate with each other and communicate more easily. However, mobile terminal equipment has several shortcomings, such as a small operation disc, difficulty inputting large volume information, and other information that can easily interfere with mobile learning.

5   Application Forms of Mobile Learning in Higher Education

With the integration of mobile networks and multimedia technology, mobile learning can be realized in time, which results in different learning experiences for learners. Mobile learning can adjust the learning process flexibly and simultaneously enhance the learning experience.

5.1   Applied to Self-Regulated Learning

Sha and Looi et al. (2012) combined mobile learning with social cognitive theory to explore the use of mobile learning in self-regulated learning [22]. In this research, the self-adjustment of the mobile learning process is considered an agent, which has the characteristics of being forward-looking, goal-oriented and self-reactive. The true learning behavior, the mobile learning process and the triangle structure of the metacognition process constitute the self-adjusting three-dimensional model. On the basis of the 3D model, a software package was developed to customize the installation of the software on the mobile phone. Detailed learning consists of clarifying tasks, setting goals, and concluding remarks. Learners control the learning process and provide feedback on the situation. Research has shown that mobile technology can significantly increase learners' ability to interpret knowledge and improve their own judgment (for example, familiarity with the study content) [23]. Through the questionnaire survey, the following conclusions are drawn: the stronger the motivation of mobile learning is, the greater the degree of self-regulation.

Tabuenca and Kalz (2015) selected university students in New Zealand as research objects. In the process of geographical knowledge learning, mobile technology helps college students self-regulate their learning time [24]. When learners browse each knowledge node on the web page, the monitor will have prompts to record the learning time and urge learners to self-regulate the learning process, prompting them to "how much time is needed for the next task to complete and ready to start". Through such a set of monitoring training, learners' time control ability is obviously improved, and their academic performance is also improved to a certain extent.

In self-regulated learning, the emphasis on the use of mobile technology to improve learners' metacognitive process helps learners avoid losing direction in the learning process and enhances their self-feedback awareness.

5.2 Application to Cooperative Learning

Mobile learning can make use of the contextualized learning experience in the process of cooperation to improve the learning effect [25]. Ting (2013) studied the form of cooperative learning in the process of mobile learning [26]. The communication among learners, between learners and teachers, and between learners and content is integrated into mobile technology, and knowledge is internalized through the communication between various elements. When faced with a new situation, learners will show excitement and integrate information from multiple sensory channels through communication to complete knowledge learning. Knowledge can be expressed through body language, and knowledge rules can be transmitted by mobile technology to enhance learners' understanding of knowledge and deepen their mastery of knowledge rules.

Ryu (2012) selected college students aged between 20 and 28 years as subjects and designed an online training system, which was installed on the smartphone devices of the subjects [27]. Two people work in teams to complete security questions for virtual locations through an online training system. In the designed online system, there are questions, regional overview guidance, electronic maps and other menus. Once one party in the group touches the location or menu, the other party will receive information, give the other party feedback information, and complete the cooperation task. Through cooperative learning and questionnaire surveys, the research results show that two members of the same group are full of curiosity and strong motivation to learn and have a good grasp of safety knowledge.

6 Implications of Mobile Learning for China in the Field of International Higher Education

To analyze the current situation of mobile learning in international higher education, the author adopts the methods of theory and practice. Therefore, research on mobile learning in international higher education is highly important for Chinese mobile learning.

6.1 Mobile Learning Platform Construction

Platform building is not only the fundamental link of mobile learning but also the essential guarantee for mobile learning to develop smoothly. Yang Xianmin (2022) and others noted that mobile education platforms pay increasing attention to the exploration of data resources and the in-depth application of intelligent technology, transforming it from a large knowledge dissemination platform into a new platform[28]. Platform construction based on mobile learning in universities is a systematic project involving multiple functional departments, such as the Academic Affairs Office, library, network information center, Student Affairs Office and various departments. On the basis of many studies and requirements analyses of mobile learning, a specialized group is in charge of the top-level design of the mobile learning platform. The group consists of department leaders, teachers, students, network information centers and academic affairs offices.

Gao Wei (2021) and others believe that if massive structured, semistructured and unstructured data cannot be effectively processed, their in-depth development and utilization of big data will be severely restricted. Therefore, mobile learners need not only scattered or fragmented data but also a platform to integrate and mine all kinds of relevant data to meet their overall knowledge and information requirements. When building a mobile learning platform, we should conduct extensive consultation with students and listen to the real needs of the audience so that they can conduct more convenient and personalized learning in the mobile network environment[29]. Mobile learning platform construction can be carried out from four aspects. First, the mobile learning module includes teaching videos, teaching courseware, mobile libraries, and related learning software. The second module is the learning support service module, which includes curriculum queries, grade queries, study room queries, educational administration information, and teaching evaluations. The third is the social activity module, which includes mutual assistance between teachers and students, resource sharing, and online Q&A. The fourth is the life support module. These data include college students' water, electricity, campus card payments, employment information, etc.

6.2 Content Construction of Mobile Learning

Content construction is the core element of attracting learners to complete mobile learning [30]. Two points should be taken into account when constructing the content of mobile learning: first, the systematic presentation of subject professional content; second, cultivating learners' ability to process and integrate fragmented information. The view of neo-constructivism is that in the internet era, the method used to process knowledge fragments and complete meaning construction is the learning strategy of "fractional storage and total collection" [31].

There is a difference between mobile learning and traditional studies and digitized studies. The mobility of mobile learning reflects the fragmentation of content, and learners tend to be shallow. How to deepen shallow-level learning and integrate fragmented knowledge to form systematic knowledge is the focus of mobile learning in content construction.

Given the rapid development of mobile technologies and pedagogies that prioritize learner-centered, participatory activities, it is critical to define mobile learning in a holistic way. This definition should be used as a foundation for research and practice on mobility. This ensures that the unique features and potential of mobile learning as a means of education are clearly understood.

Emphasis is placed on the importance of the use of mobile technology for the purpose and selection of mobile learning. Studies have shown that mobile learning is most effective when it is combined with the classroom, has a clear learning objective, and has the guidance of a knowledgeable teacher. With the increasing independence of students, teachers gradually cut back on their support. Studies such as that of Kondo et al. support the idea that teacher guidance and scaffolding play crucial roles in maximizing the benefits of mobile learning [32].

6.3 System Design of Mobile Learning

In the process of education and teaching and the application of mobile technology to promote education reform, concept change, including the concepts of administrators and teachers, is key. The acceptance of the application of mobile terminal equipment in teaching, the conscious use of equipment, and the design and improvement of the system are the upper guarantees for carrying out mobile learning. This approach can be promoted in the following ways: First, the teaching form can be improved, the form of the flipped classroom can be adopted, students can use mobile terminals to learn independently after class, and teachers can carry out group discussions in class to internalize knowledge. The second is the adjustment of the evaluation system, which previously paid too much attention to the result evaluation, mainly through examination methods. The learning assessment of mobile learning should focus not only on results-based course examination but also on process evaluation. Students are evaluated on the basis of the network platform, learning track, logins, duration, and topics discussed. Policymakers and education developers should explore the potential of mobile testing platforms as new assessment tools, especially for distance learning. A hybrid approach is needed to assess the effectiveness and applicability of these platforms, especially at the graduate level. The study conducted by Alshah et al. offers insight into the feasibility and benefits of using mobile testing platforms in education assessment [33].

7 Conclusion

Mobile learning is an excellent example of how to transform the teaching process by adopting the latest IT tools and technologies. In this study, 276 studies on mobile learning between 2001 and 2024 were reviewed to identify possible areas for further research. Although previous studies have explored the benefits and trends of mobile learning, this study offers a new perspective and direction for future research. Research on mobile learning has been conducted abroad, and many achievements have been achieved in foreign higher education. Although mobile learning in China developed relatively late, it has developed very quickly. Currently, China's mobile learning is still far from the world. Over the last several decades, China has made great strides in the development of mobile learning and economic and educational development. Mobile teaching is a new method of distance education that combines computer networks, hand-held devices and communication techniques. Instead of the traditional desktop model, it uses smartphones, tablets, laptops, and even e-books to teach on the internet. On this basis, it is very important to establish a uniform standard for mobile education. However, the shortage of teachers and teachers has also become a bottleneck to the development of mobile education. Therefore, we should strengthen the study of mobile teaching, such as teacher training, development, design and support, to develop a path for the continuous development of mobile teaching in China.

Acknowledgments. 1.This research is supported or partially supported by School-level projects of Qinghai Minzu University. (Nos.:23GCC06). 2. This research is supported or partially supported by the Education Science Planning Project of Qinghai Province during the 14th Five Year Plan period (Nos.:24QJG77).

References

1. Statista: Petroc Taylor Mobile Network Subscriptions Worldwide 2028.https://www.statista.com/statistics/330695/number-of-smartphone-users-worldwide/. Accessed 2 Sep 2023
2. Traxler, J.: Defining mobile learning [OB/OL]. https://www.researchagte.net/publication/228637407. Accessed 25 Nov 2017
3. Yousuf, M.I.: Effectiveness of mobile learning in distance education. Turk. Online J. Distance Educ. **8**(4), 114–124 (2007)
4. Sad, S.N., Gokas, O.: Preservice teacher perceptions about using mobile phones and laptops in education as mobile learning tools. Br. J. Educ. Technol. **45**(4), 606–618 (2014)
5. Liu, M., Zhang, Q.: Research on mobile learning in international higher education: review and prospect. Open Educ. Res. **22**(06), 81–92 (2016)
6. O'Malley, C., et al.: Guidelines for learning/teaching/tutoring in a mobile environment [EB/OL]. https://hal.archives-ouvertes.fr/hal-00696244/document. Accessed 26 Nov 2017
7. Du, Q.: Reflections on mobile language learning. J. Yunnan Open Univ. **19**(02), 18–22 (2017)
8. Wang, J., Zhao, C., Zhang, Z.: Study of several questions on mobile learning and its implementation. J. High. Correspondence (Nat. Sci. Ed.) **04**, 6–8 (2006)
9. El-Hussein, M.O.M., Cronje, C.J.: Defining mobile learning in the higher education landscape. Educ. Technol. Soc. **13**(3), 12–21 (2010)
10. Davison, C.B., Lazaros, E.J.: Adopting mobile technology in the higher education classroom. J. Technol. Stud. **41**(1), 30–39 (2015)
11. Sevillano-Garcia, M.L., Vazquez-Cano, E.: The impact of digital mobile devices in higher education. Educ. Technol. Soc. **18**(1), 106–119 (2015)
12. Cha, X.: Empirical study on the introduction of mobile learning in information literacy cultivation among normal university students. Coll. Educ. (03), 132–135+148 (2024)
13. Gikas, J., Grant, M.M.: Mobile computing devices in higher education: student perpectives on learning with cellphones, smartphones & social media. Internet High. Educ. **28**(19), 18–26 (2013)

14. Ke, F., Hsu, Y.-C.: Mobile augmented-reality artifact creation as a component of mobile computer-supported collaborative learning. Internet High. Educ. **44**(26), 33–41 (2015)
15. Alrasheedi, M., Capretz, L.F.: An empirical study of critical success factors of mobile learning platform from the perspective of instructors. Procedia Soc. Behav. Sci. **200**(176), 211–219 (2015)
16. Cheon, J., Lee, S., Crooks, S.M., Song, J.: An investigation of mobile learning readiness in higher education based on the theory of planned behavior. Comput. Educ. **59**(3), 1054–1064 (2012)
17. Park, S.Y., Nam, M.-W., Cha, S.-B.: University students' behavioral intention to use mobile learning: evaluating the technology acceptance model. Br. J. Edu. Technol. **43**(4), 592–605 (2012)
18. Zhou, C.: Study on the influencing factors of mobile learning based on the TPB and DTPB theories. J. Hexi Univ. **32**(05), 39–45 (2016)
19. Althunibat, A.: Determining the factors influencing students' intention to use m-learning in Jordan higher education. Comput. Hum. Behav. **66**(52), 65–71 (2015)
20. Tindell, D.R., Bohlander, R.W.: The use and abuse of cell phones and text messaging in the classroom: a survey of college students. Coll. Teach. **60**(1), 1–9 (2012)
21. Gikas, J., Grant, M.: Mobile computing devices in higher education: student perspectives on learning with cellphones, smartphones & social media. Internet High. Educ. **28**(19), 18–26 (2013)
22. Sha, L., Looi, C.K., Chen, W.: Recognizing and measuring self-regulated learning in a mobile learning environment. Comput. Hum. Behav. **28**(2), 88–95 (2012)
23. Kiat, L.B., Ali, M.B., Halim, N.D.A., Ibrahim, H.B.: Augmented reality, virtual learning environment and mobile learning in education: a comparison. In: Proceedings of the 2016 IEEE Conference on e-Learning, e-Management and e-Services (IC3e), Langkawi, Malaysia, pp. 23–28, 10–12 October 2016
24. Tabuenca, B., Kalz, M., Drachsler, H., et al.: Time will tell: The role of mobile learning analytics in self-regulated learning. Comput. Educ. **89**, 53–74 (2015)
25. Chang, Y., Lee, S., Wong, S.F., Jeong, S.-P.: AI-Powered learning application use and gratification: an integrative model. Inf. Technol. People **35**, 2115–2139 (2022)
26. Ting, Y.L.: Using mobile technologies to create interwoven learning interactions: an intuitive design and its evaluation. Comput. Educ. **60**(1), 1–13 (2013)
27. Ryu, H., Parsons, D.: Risky business or sharing the load?--Social flow in collaborative mobile learning. Comput. Educ. **58**(2), 707–720 (2012)
28. Yang, X., Zhang, Y.: How to solve the contradiction between education scale and individuation?—Logical framework and practical path of data-driven scale aptitude. Distance Educ. China (8), 42–52+79 (2022)
29. Wei, G., Zhang, Y.: The generation, characteristics and application of "Big Data+Ideological and political Education." Theor. Guide **9**, 123128 (2021)
30. Zheng, W., Song, J., He, G.: Research on the development status of mobile learning in universities -- a case study of universities in Fujian Province. Heilongjiang High. Educ. Res. (02), 21–24 (2017). Tong, Y., Zhang, L., Zhang, Y.: Research progress and evaluation of mobile learning at home and abroad. Educ. Career (02), 101–106 (2017). (in Chinese)
31. Feng, C.: Research on Web-based mobile Learning Course Design for college students. Harbin Normal University (2012)
32. Kondo, M., Ishikawa, Y., Smith, C., Sakamoto, K., Shimomura, H., Wada, N.: Mobile assisted language learning in university EFL courses in japan: developing attitudes and skills for self-regulated learning. ReCALL **24**, 169–187 (2012)
33. Alshurideh, M.T., et al.: Factors affecting the use of smart mobile examination platforms by universities' postgraduate students during the COVID-19 pandemic: an empirical study. Informatics **8**, 32 (2021)

Design of Blockchain-Based Intelligent Storage Cabinets

Xiaodong Zhang[1], Shuxin Chen[1,2], Yongchao Li[1], Zhong Zhang[3],
and Renzheng Xue[1(✉)]

[1] Qiqihar University, Qiqihar, Heilongjiang Province, China
[2] School of Intelligent Computing Engineering, Tianjin Ren'ai College, Tianjin City, China
[3] Tianjin University, Tianjin City, China

Abstract. With the recovery of the economy and the resurgence of the tourism industry, the need for secure storage of personal belongings in public spaces has become increasingly prominent. Traditional storage methods require substantial human resources. This paper explores the design and implementation of a blockchain-based intelligent cabinet system that enhances the efficiency of item storage and retrieval, optimizing the user experience. The front end uses Vue.js and React Native, whereas the back end employs PHP for API development, which is supported by the FISCO BCOS consortium blockchain for data management. The system ensures efficient front-and-back-end interaction through Ajax technology, allowing users to conveniently deposit, retrieve, and borrow items, as well as make order inquiries. Administrators can monitor order status and locker usage via a management interface, enhancing management efficiency. The test results indicate that the system operates stably and meets user needs.

Keywords: Intelligent storage cabinet · Blockchain technology · Item security · Smart campus

1 Introduction

The advent of blockchain-based smart locker systems represents a major technological breakthrough. Leveraging Internet of Things (IoT) technology, these systems allow users to easily access, borrow, and return items via smart devices [1]. Smart storage solutions are increasingly utilized in various environments, including residential communities, libraries, train stations, and airports [2, 3]. Blockchain integration is particularly critical for these systems, as it enhances operational efficiency and security while offering flexible services tailored to users' needs. The development of secure, efficient, and user-friendly smart lockers holds substantial practical value.

Blockchain smart locker systems significantly improve item management in public spaces, optimize the user experience, and lower operational costs. By incorporating blockchain technology, these systems ensure data transparency and security throughout the item storage and transaction process, thereby strengthening user trust (Fig. 1).

X. Zhang—(1996–), male, from HeiHe, HeiLongJiang, with primary research interests in PLC and electrical control.

© The Author(s), under exclusive license to Springer Nature Singapore Pte Ltd. 2025
K. Zhang et al. (Eds.): CSEI 2024, CCIS 2447, pp. 307–313, 2025.
https://doi.org/10.1007/978-981-96-3735-5_23

Fig. 1. Blockchain-Based Intelligent Service Cabinet

2 Challenges Faced by Traditional Storage Cabinets

In today's fast-paced society, the demand for efficiency has risen sharply. Secure and convenient item storage solutions are particularly essential in scenarios such as shopping, travel, and commuting [5, 6]. Traditional lockers, especially those relying on keys, pose challenges, including inconvenient access, complex mechanisms, and high manufacturing costs [7]. These issues are even more pronounced in crowded public spaces such as airports and shopping malls, diminishing the overall user experience and satisfaction.

Although intelligent locker systems are still in the early stages of development in the domestic market, there is significant potential for growth [8]. Compared with established international systems, domestic solutions are often limited in technological capabilities and application breadth. However, with ongoing technological advancements and growing market demand, domestic intelligent locker systems are poised to expand their use, leading to more intense market competition. Research and development of blockchain-based smart lockers could greatly increase public service efficiency while simultaneously reducing operational and management costs [9].

3 System Design

3.1 Data Design

In an intelligent locker system, it is essential to clearly define the primary entities and their interrelationships. These entities include users, lockers, and transaction records. The user entity holds personal and authorization information, the locker entity represents the physical lockers, and the transaction record entity logs the details of all the transactions. Each entity's attributes must be defined carefully, with a strong emphasis on data access and security.

To facilitate data management, suitable data access layer interfaces (APIs) and data access objects (DAOs) should be implemented to encapsulate database operations. These interfaces enable the creation, deletion, updating, and retrieval of data [10]. Furthermore, sensitive data, including user information and transaction details, must be encrypted to ensure the privacy and integrity of the data.

The user table contains essential information for all system users, as shown in Table 1. This includes usernames, phone numbers, and passwords. Such data are crucial for verifying user identity during login. To safeguard user privacy and prevent unauthorized access, passwords are encrypted before being stored, ensuring protection even if the database is compromised (Table 2).

Table 1. User Table

Field Name	Length	Not Null	Constraints	Remarks
id	50	no	Primary Key	Identifier
name	100	no		User's nickname
phone	50	no		User's phone number
password	100	no		User's password
created	50	yes		Creation timestamp
updated	50	yes		Update timestamp
deleted	50	yes		Deletion timestamp

Table 2. Cabinet Table

Field Name	Data Type	Length	Allow Null	Constraints
id	int	50	no	Primary Key
name	vartchar	255	no	
camput	Int	100	no	
address	vartchar	255	no	
code	vartchar	255	no	
content	vartchar	255	yes	
created	datetime	255	yes	
updated	datetime	100	yes	
deleted	datetime	100	yes	

3.2 Deposits and Retrieval Process Design

The borrowing and returning functions are central to the intelligent locker system and involve two key steps: item deposit and retrieval. The system supports various transaction modes, including one-to-one, many-to-one, and one-to-many transactions. When an order is placed, the system identifies the order type and ensures that only users with the appropriate roles are authorized to create orders. Moreover, the system checks the availability of the locker to prevent double booking. All records of deposit and retrieval operations are permanently stored on the blockchain, ensuring data integrity and transparency. This approach strengthens the system's security and enhances operational efficiency by providing a clear, immutable transaction history. These mechanisms enable the intelligent locker system to effectively manage the borrowing and returning process, contributing to a more secure, streamlined, and efficient user experience.

Design of the Item-Deposit Process

The storage process is illustrated in Fig. 2. First, users access the service interface and select an available intelligent locker. The system generates form data and provides the user with a deposit code. Upon reaching the locker, the user selects the deposit option and enters the provided code. After verification, the locker door opens automatically, allowing the user to place the items inside. The recipient is notified of the deposit. The system then generates a storage record that includes item details, the locker number, and the storage time, all of which are securely recorded on the blockchain.

Fig. 2. Design of the item-deposit process

Design of the Item Retrieval Process

The retrieval process is illustrated in Fig. 3. First, users select the "retrieval item" function on the intelligent locker and retrieve the retrieval code from their mobile device. Before submitting the retrieval request, the system verifies the user's permissions. If the user's credentials are valid, the system generates a new order, updates its status to "retrieval," and provides the corresponding retrieval code. Users then enter the code, and upon successful verification, the locker door opens automatically, allowing them to retrieve the item. After the item is retrieved, the system updates the storage record on the blockchain, marking the item as "retrieved."

3.3 Overall System Architecture Design

The interface system adopts the MVVM (Model-View-ViewModel) design pattern for developing user interface (UI) applications. It follows a three-tier architecture, as depicted in Fig. 4, which consists of a system layer, a server layer, and a presentation layer. This architecture divides the application's functions and responsibilities into

Fig. 3. Design of the item retrieval process

three distinct tiers, each serving a specific role. This layered structure improves code maintainability, scalability, and reusability.

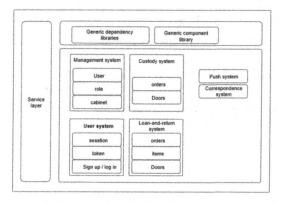

Fig. 4. Overall System Architecture Design

4   System Implementation

4.1   System Environment

The environment configuration during the development phase is summarized in Table 3. We installed phpstudy_pro on Windows 11, which includes Nginx 1.12.11, MySQL 5.7.26, and PHP 7.3.5. After launching the application, we downloaded Composer 2.5.8 from the software management interface. To establish the front-end environment, we visited the official website of Node.js to install the long-term support version of Node.js v18.

In the deployment phase, we deploy the application on CentOS 7.6. First, we install Nginx and PHP, ensuring that port 80 is open, followed by deploying the FISCO alliance chain on Ubuntu.

Table 3. Environment Configuration Details

Application Environment	Version	Application Environment	Version
Windows	11	Centos	7.6
Node.js	18.18.2	NPM	9.8.1
PHP	8.3	Composer	2.5.8
Nginx	2.4	MySQL	8.0
JAVA SDK	11	Android SDK	10
FISCO BCOS	2.11.0	Ubuntu	20.4

Table 4. Order creation test data

Test ID	Test Conditions	Expected Result	Actual Result	Pass/Fail
1	No parameters provided	Error message prompt	Error message prompt	Pass
2	Other parameter types	Error message prompt	Error message prompt	Pass
3	Only one parameter input	Error message prompt	Error message prompt	Pass
4	All parameters correct	Error message prompt	Success message prompt	Pass

4.2 Functional Testing

Verifying the functionality of the interface against specifications and expectations is crucial. This process involves validating both requests and responses to ensure that the system processes the user input correctly and returns the appropriate results. Additionally, it is important to conduct parameter validity checks to ensure that the interface can handle various input scenarios, including both valid and invalid parameters. The testing should also assess the effectiveness of the error-handling mechanism, ensuring that the system provides clear error messages in exceptional situations without compromising stability or security. The experimental results show that the system tests performed as expected, with all the interfaces functioning correctly. The test data, presented in Table 4, cover a variety of scenarios, including valid parameter requests, invalid parameter requests, and boundary condition testing.

5 Conclusion

This paper provides a comprehensive study and design of a blockchain-based intelligent locker system, exploring its potential applications in item management within public spaces. By integrating the Internet of Things (IoT) and blockchain technologies, the system significantly enhances the efficiency of item storage and retrieval, improves the user experience, and ensures data transparency and security. The results from testing indicate that the system operates reliably and effectively meets user needs. As technology evolves and the market continues to mature, blockchain-based intelligent locker systems are expected to be adopted in an increasing number of public spaces and applications, further enhancing the intelligence and convenience of item management.

Fund Project. Tianjin Special Fund Project for High-Quality Development of the Manufacturing Industry (20232184): Application of Innovative Mechanisms for Blockchain + Smart Form Management in Education

References

1. Lan, G., Huang, M., Li, F., et al.: Design of an intelligent express storage cabinet based on STM32. Electron. Prod. **31**(04), 35–37+27 (2023)
2. Wei, F., Li, P.: Design and implementation of an intelligent storage cabinet system for hazardous chemical reagents in laboratories. Lab. Res. Explor. **40**(06), 158–163 (2021)
3. He, M., Qi, X., Wang, W., et al.: Hardware design of an intelligent cabinet based on STM32F103RBT6. IoT Technol. **13**(07), 108–111 (2023)
4. Luo, L., Zhu, Y., Huanan: Research on distributed storage technology for college platforms. Henan Sci. Technol. **42**(01), 28–33 (2023)
5. Chenyue, W.: Design of a new type of intelligent express cabinet based on the internet of things. Digit. Commun. World **05**, 77–79 (2024)
6. Liang, J., Chen, W.: Design of an intelligent express cabinet based on GSM. Shanxi Electron. Technol. **5**, 56–57+64 (2023)
7. Ye, Q., Lu, R., Liang, H., et al.: Research on improvement of express center management: a case study of the express center in Jiangning University Town. China Collective Econ. **24**, 87–88 (2021)
8. Xue, J., Yao, Y., Wu, X.: Analysis and prediction of factors influencing shared accommodation in Hangzhou: based on data from the Airbnb platform. Stat. Sci. Pract. **12**, 44–48 (2018)
9. Qin, L.: Integrated optimization of agricultural product supply chains based on "internet plus". Bus. Econ. **6**, 116–118+129 (2022)
10. Wang, C.: Design and implementation of a Chairman's mailbox based on J2EE. Comput. Program. Skills Maintenance **20**, 11–13 (2016)
11. Li, X., Jin, X., Bai, W.: An express cabinet with drone and unmanned vehicle for pickup and delivery, Shaanxi Province: CN201810551804.9, 19 January 2021

A MarkBERT Semantics with Global Contextual Mechanism for Chinese Named Entity Recognition

He Ning[1,2], Haifeng Wang[1,2(✉)], Wenbin Wang[1,2], and Kezhen He[1,2]

[1] Yazhou Bay Innovation Institute, Hainan Tropical Ocean University, Sanya, China
[2] Hainan Tropical Ocean University, Sanya, China
hfwang@hntou.edu.cn

Abstract. This paper presents an innovative approach that combines MarkBERT-BiLSTM with contextual CRF modeling and is designed to address key challenges in Chinese named entity recognition (NER). These challenges include the difficulty in recognizing subtle features, the complexity involved in feature extraction, ambiguous lexical boundaries and the intricate nature of contextual semantics. The method commences with the utilization of the MarkBERT model for preprocessing, which generates vectors that convey information regarding lexical boundaries. These pretrained vectors are subsequently fed into a BiLSTM framework, wherein the global context mechanism facilitates the integration of both forward and backward sentence information into the BiLSTM structure in an effective manner. Ultimately, a CRF layer is employed. At the entity labeling and classification stage, the generation of the optimal predicted sequence is ensured. The experimental results indicate that the model performs exceptionally well on the MSRA dataset, achieving a high F1 score of 95.75%. This outcome highlights the significant advantages of the proposed model in addressing the complexities of Chinese NER.

Keywords: named entity recognition · deep learning · pre-training language model

1 Introduction

Named entity recognition (NER) is a sequence labeling task that is primarily focused on information extraction. It is beneficial for handling a wide range of downstream tasks in NLP. NER plays a critical role in fields such as intelligent question-answering systems, sentiment analysis and knowledge graphs. However, Chinese NER is frequently more challenging, because the intricate structure of entities, nuanced characteristics, absence of rigid naming conventions, vast array of entity types, strong contextual dependencies, intricate linguistic traits, ambiguous entity boundaries, and other factors, collectively increasing the complexity and difficulty of Chinese NER.

© The Author(s), under exclusive license to Springer Nature Singapore Pte Ltd. 2025
K. Zhang et al. (Eds.): CSEI 2024, CCIS 2447, pp. 314–327, 2025.
https://doi.org/10.1007/978-981-96-3735-5_24

In traditional NER tasks, the identification of named entities relies mainly on rules and templates designed by domain experts. In [1], Akkasi A et al. proposed an enhanced rule-based tagger called CHemTok, which primarily utilizes rules extracted from training data. These rules are employed to merge tokens segmented in earlier steps, thereby generating longer and more distinctive tokens. This method effectively improves the performance of NER in the chemical domain. In [2], Eftimov T et al. proposed an innovative method called drNER, which is specifically designed for gathering dietary information. This method emphasizes accurately identifying and organizing dietary-related entities. However, such rule-based and dictionary-based methods are overly reliant on expert design, which leads to a lack of interconnectivity between different domains and results in low cross-domain recognition accuracy. Furthermore, domain-specific dictionaries require regular maintenance by professionals.

Subsequently, statistical machine learning (ML) approaches, such as the construction of probabilistic models to predict entity tokens for each word or phrase, are employed to input the annotated corpus set and feature templates into HMM [3], MEMM [4], CRF [5], SVM [6], and other models. To predict entities and their entity classes. In [7], CS Malarkodi et al. proposed a method uses CRF to extract named entities from agricultural data across different agricultural domains, significantly improving the accuracy of agricultural systems. In [8], K Liu et al. improved the CRF model, enabling the enhanced model to extract higher-level clinically named entities from Chinese EMRs. However, these traditional statistical machine learning (ML) approaches rely heavily on extensive data annotation by researchers, and the feature engineering process is complex, requiring the manual design of numerous features. This not only consumes a significant amount of time and effort but also depends heavily on the expertise of domain specialists. Additionally, it is difficult for these methods to capture complex contextual information. With the ongoing progress of technology and advent of DL, traditional machine learning methods have been gradually supplanted. Deep learning effectively addresses issues such as capturing long-distance dependencies and automating feature extraction, demonstrating strong generalizability capabilities and robust model adaptability. Common models include RNN [9], LSTM [10], and CNN [11], among others.

In [12], G. Lample and colleagues proposed the BiLSTM-CRF model. This model captures contextual information through LSTM networks and uses CRF to capture the dependencies between labels. The model is capable of handling strong label dependencies. Furthermore, it employs dropout techniques to prevent overfitting, thereby enhancing its generalizability. For the CoNLL-2003 dataset, the model achieves a relatively high F1 score of 90.94%. In [13], Bu Zhou Tang and others applied the CNN-LSTM-CRF model, when combined with attention mechanism, has been shown to be effective for Chinese clinical text NER. This model is capable of automatically selecting important contextual information relevant to the current character, thereby enhancing its ability to recognize entity boundaries. Furthermore, the model has been demonstrated to be applicable to a range of entity types, including both continuous and discontinuous entities, which illustrates its adaptability across different entity types. However, these deep learning-based methods, which depend on conventional word embedding models to generate static representations, focus solely on the extraction of features between characters, words, or word-to-word relationships. They are unable to distinguish the semantics and nuances of the same word in context. However, many models based on the transformer architecture have effectively solved this issue. In their seminal work, in [14], Devlin and colleagues proposed the BERT pre-training model employs large-scale bidirectional pre-training to facilitate the acquisition of rich language representations. In contrast to traditional unidirectional language models, BERT is capable of making predictions by integrating both left and right context information. This results in the generation of more comprehensive bidirectional representations, which in turn facilitates superior semantic comprehension of the same word in disparate contexts. The BERT-base and BERT-large models demonstrated considerable performance enhancements across all tasks within the GLUE benchmark, with average accuracy improvements of 4.5% and 7.0%, respectively.

In [15], YiHan Liu and colleagues proposed an enhanced BERT pre-training model. This model retained the same architectural design and training objectives as the original, but underwent several modifications to extend the training duration, increase batch sizes, and incorporate additional training data. Furthermore, they employed a dynamic masking strategy, which markedly enhanced the model's performance. This approach yielded significant outcomes across nine development tasks within the GLUE benchmark. In [16], Linyang Li and colleagues proposed a BERT model with inserted word boundary markers to address the traditional out-of-vocabulary (OOV) problem. This model can add word-level learning objectives to the markers, thereby enriching semantic information. However, the addition of boundary markers can cause the sequence length to exceed the model's maximum limit, resulting in the loss of some contextual information, which negatively impacts the model's performance. To overcome the previously mentioned problems, we propose a MarkBERT-BiLSTM-Context-CRF model. This model employs a MarkBERT module to pre-train vectors with word boundary information, thereby addressing the out-of-vocabulary (OOV) problem. It then fully learns text features and inputs the vectors to a BiLSTM module, which addresses the gradient vanishing problem and captures the sequence. The information is combined with the global context mechanism [17] to obtain the whole sentence information, which is then incorporated into the representation of each word. This approach addresses the insufficiency of BiLSTM in generating sentence representations. The global context mechanism retrieves the past (forward) sentence representation from the last BiLSTM unit and the future (backward) sentence representation from the initial unit and comprises a gating mechanism, which is used to fuse the representations of the sentences with the representations of the hidden states at every time point. Subsequently, the CRF module is subsequently utilized to globally optimize the label sequence, thereby avoiding unreasonable label combinations and ultimately decoding the best-predicted sequence. The findings from the experiments demonstrate that the proposed model results in an F1 score of 95.75% on the MSRA dataset, thereby illustrating its superior performance. The principal contributions of the current research are as follows:

This study investigates the complex process of using pre-training models for NER and proposes an enhanced named entity recognition model based on Mark-BERT. This model innovatively integrates MarkBERT's ability to handle word boundaries with a global context mechanism, thereby alleviating the challenges of processing entities with ambiguous word boundaries and overcoming the limitations of context representation. As a result, it improves the model's accuracy in recognizing Chinese entities and its semantic representation capability.

2   System Model and Problem Description

2.1   Overview of the System Model

The significant influence of BERT on named entity recognition has resulted in this field becoming a prominent area of research. The MarkBERT-BiLSTM-Context-CRF model, which is outlined in Fig. 1, comprises four main modules: The initial module is the Embedding layer, wherein the pre-trained MarkBERT model is employed to pre-process the tokenized text sequence, thereby obtaining a vector that incorporates word boundary information. The subsequent module is the BiLSTM layer, which processes the vectors generated by MarkBERT with the objective of capturing the contextual information and long-range dependencies inherent to the input sequence. The third module is the Context layer, which integrates global contextual information to compensate for the limitations of the BiLSTM layer, which uses only local contextual information at each time step. The fourth module is the CRF layer, which decodes the label sequence output from the BiLSTM layer integrated with the global context mechanism to improve prediction accuracy, thereby generating the optimal observation sequence.

2.2   MarkBERT Module

The pre-training model has been demonstrated to markedly increase the precision of Chinese NER recognition in a multitude of research studies. The Chinese NER process is conducted primarily by extracting global features via the BERT pre-training model, which is built upon the encoder part of the transformer architecture [18]. This is specifically the multilayered bi-directional transformer, which enables it to consider contextual information at all levels simultaneously. The pre-training process of BERT comprises two tasks: Masked Language Modeling (MLM) and Next Sentence Prediction (NSP). During the pre-training phase, BERT is trained using a substantial corpus of unlabeled text. Upon completion of the pre-training phase, it can be fine-tuned to adapt to a range of downstream tasks. BERT significantly enhances its performance in named entity recognition tasks through its robust bidirectional encoding and pre-training mechanisms.

The MarkBERT [16] model is a Chinese pre-training model that improves upon the BERT model to enhance performance in tasks such as Chinese named

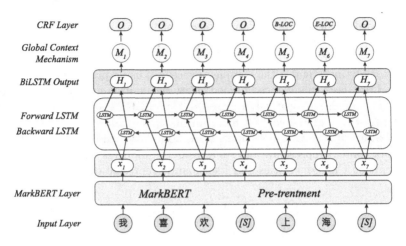

Fig. 1. MarkBERT-BiLSTM-Context-CRF Model Architecture Diagram.

entity recognition by introducing word boundary markers. MarkBERT inserts special markers (e.g., [S]), which facilitate the processing of arbitrary words regardless of whether they have appeared in the pre-training data. This enables the model to process arbitrary words, irrespective of whether they have been included in the pre-training data. Traditional Chinese BERT models typically encode characters as the fundamental unit, which fails to consider the nuances of the Chinese vocabulary and consequently performs poorly, particularly when confronted with out-of-vocabulary (OOV) issues.

In the MLM task, the MarkBERT model uses both the MLM and whole-word masking strategies. In addition, it incorporates the Replacement Word Detection (RWD) task, which is designed to improve the model's comprehension of word boundaries by substituting specific words and requiring the model to identify these substitutions. Specifically, synonyms or phonetically similar words are employed to replace the original words. The model is subsequently required to ascertain whether the replacements have occurred on the basis of the marked words. Therefore, in addition to predicting the masked characters, the model must also identify word boundaries and the replaced words. These improvements explicitly incorporate word-level information into a character-level pre-trained model, which results in a notable enhancement of the model's performance.

In the pre-training phase, the masking rate is maintained at 15% of the total characters, in accordance with the BERT model. However, in 30% of instances, no markers are inserted, indicating that it is capable of operating without markers. In 50% of cases, the whole word masking strategy is applied. In this strategy, MarkBERT selects whole words for masking, rather than masking only part of the characters within a word. To illustrate, if the word "Beijing" is selected for whole-word masking, the entire word is concealed, and the model must be capable of predicting the complete word on the basis of the surrounding context rather than focusing on individual characters. In other cases, the model performs the standard masked language model prediction. In the case of inserting markers, 30% of the time, words are replaced by homophones or synonyms, and the model must predict these replacements. In the remaining time, the words remain normal. The model calculates the loss for only 15% of the regular markers to prevent label imbalance during the process of learning markers.

In conclusion, the MLM and RWD tasks increase the model's capacity to comprehend contextual and word-level information in greater depth. The incorporation of homophones and synonym confusion words augments the model's ability to process intricate linguistic phenomena. Additionally, MarkBERT can be downgraded to the original BERT model, thus enhancing its adaptability to diverse task requirements.

2.3   BiLSTM Module

LSTM [10] is designed to address the vanishing and exploding gradient issues that arise when RNNs process extensive data sequences. We can refer to Fig. 2. The LSTM structure mainly regulates the flow of information through the incorporation of memory cells and gate controls. The gating mechanism comprises three gates: the input gate, the forget gate and the output gate. The memory cell is the core component responsible for storing and transmitting long-term dependency information. The input gate controls which data from the present input and the preceding hidden state should be stored in the memory cell. The forget gate determines what data in the memory cell should be kept or removed. The output gate determines which portions of the information stored in the memory cell will be released, thereby influencing the hidden state in the subsequent time step. The corresponding formulas are as follows:

$$i_t = \sigma(W_i \otimes [H_{t-1}, x_t] + b_i) \tag{1}$$

$$f_t = \sigma(W_f \otimes [H_{t-1}, x_t] + b_f) \tag{2}$$

$$o_t = \sigma(W_o \otimes [H_{t-1}, x_t] + b_o) \tag{3}$$

$$C_t = f_t \otimes C_{t-1} + i_t \otimes \tilde{C}_t \tag{4}$$

$$\tilde{C}_t = \tanh(W_C \otimes [H_{t-1}, x_t] + b_c) \tag{5}$$

$$H_t = o_t \otimes \tanh(C_t) \tag{6}$$

Here, σ is the activation function, W is the weight matrix, b is the bias vector, x_t is the input at the current time step, i_t is the output value of the input gate, f_t is the output value of the forget gate, o_t is the output value of the output gate, C_t is the cell state at the current time step, $\tilde{C}_t$ is the candidate cell state, and H_t is the hidden state of the memory cell.

The BiLSTM model represents an advancement over the traditional LSTM. It comprises two LSTM layers: one processes input in a forward manner (from left to right), and the remaining one processes input in a reverse direction (from right to left). In contrast to the LSTM, which can only learn from past information, the BiLSTM is capable of learning from both past and future information

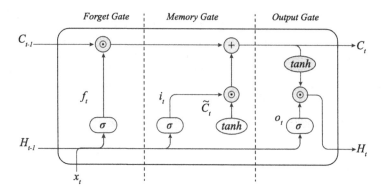

Fig. 2. LSTM Model Architecture Diagram.

simultaneously, thereby generating more comprehensive representations for each element in the sequence.

The forward LSTM is:

$$\overrightarrow{H_t} = \overrightarrow{LSTM}(x_t, H_{t-1}) \tag{7}$$

The backward LSTM is:

$$\overleftarrow{H_t} = \overleftarrow{LSTM}(x_t, H_{t+1}) \tag{8}$$

The ultimate hidden state after connecting the forward and backward LSTM is:

$$H_t = [\overrightarrow{H_t}; \overleftarrow{H_t}] \tag{9}$$

2.4   Global Context Mechanism

The BiLSTM in Chinese NER tasks has led experts to gradually discover its shortcomings when dealing with long texts. Specifically, BiLSTM can only use partial contextual information at each time step. In other words, BiLSTM can integrate only partial fragments of preceding and succeeding context into the representation of the current word, but it cannot form a complete sentence representation.

Given the limitations of BiLSTM in handling NER tasks and the need for global information, a global context mechanism [17] has been introduced. This mechanism extracts global information from the last forward output and the first backward output of BiLSTM, which represent the forward and backward representations of the whole sentence, respectively. The equation is given by:

$$\overrightarrow{G} = \overrightarrow{H}_n \quad | \quad \overleftarrow{G} = \overleftarrow{H}_1 \tag{10}$$

$\overrightarrow{G}$ represents the forward global data, and $\overleftarrow{G}$ represents the backward global data.

The gating mechanism enables the selective fusion of global information, as well as the representation at the present time step. In particular, the local representation, denoted by H_t, at each time step and the global information, represented by G, are linearly mapped to obtain a representation that is employed in the computation of the weights. Subsequently, an activation function is applied to compute the fusion weights for the local representation and the global information. The local representation and the global context are then fused via weighted averaging on the basis of the computed weights. Finally, the fused representation is passed to the classification layer to produce the ultimate prediction outcome. The equation is given by:

$$O_t = H_t \parallel G \tag{11}$$
$$R_H = W_H O_t + b_H \tag{12}$$
$$R_G = W_G O_t + b_G \tag{13}$$
$$i_H = \text{sigmoid}(R_H) \tag{14}$$
$$i_G = \text{sigmoid}(R_G) \tag{15}$$
$$M_t = i_H^t \otimes H_t \parallel i_G^t \otimes G \tag{16}$$

where O_t is the representation obtained by concatenating H_t and G,W is the trainable weight matrix,b is the bias vector,R is the intermediate representation after linear mapping,i is the fusion weight calculated through the activation function, M_t is the fused representation that combines local and global information.

2.5 CRF Module

CRF [5] is a widely used statistical model for sequence labeling tasks. It is a discriminative probabilistic model. While the BiLSTM layer excels at handling long-range contextual relationships, and the Global Context mechanism serves as a complement to the BiLSTM layer, neither can accurately predict the dependencies between successive labels in text.

Therefore, in this paper, the output sequence of the global context mechanism module is used as the input sequence for the CRF module to perform label sequence prediction. By modeling the transition properties between labels, CRF can effectively handle these label dependencies and ensure the coherence of the label sequence. Through the decoding process, CRF finds the label sequence with the highest probability among all possible label sequences. Specifically, CRF calculates the score for the predicted sequence M by using the output from the global context mechanism module as input. The scoring function is as follows:

$$\text{Score}(M, Y) = \sum_{i=0}^{n} A_{y_i, y_{i+1}} + \sum_{i=0}^{n} P_{i, y_i} \tag{17}$$

where M is the output sequence of the given text, Y represents the corresponding predicted label sequence, A represents the transition score matrix within the

CRF, and P is the score matrix from the upper layer. The parametric form of the conditional probability and model parameters is as follows:

$$P(Y \mid M) = \frac{e^{S(M,Y)}}{\sum\limits_{\tilde{Y} \in Y_m} e^{S(M,\tilde{Y})}} \tag{18}$$

$\tilde{Y}$ represents all possible prediction sequences corresponding to the text sequence M. To address the issue of label imbalance, the CRF layer introduces a loss function for optimization. The final loss function is obtained through log-likelihood, as follows:

$$L_{\text{loss}} = -\sum_{t \in T} \log_e \left(P(Y_t \mid M_t) \right) \tag{19}$$

Where T represents the collection of all sentences in the training data, M_t represents the input sequence associated with sentence t, and Y_t represents the predicted sequence associated with sentence t.

The CRF can effectively learn the constraints between labels, generate logically consistent label sequences, and optimize through global probability distribution, thus better addressing the Chinese NER task and improving the model's effectiveness.

3   Experimental Results And Analysis

3.1   Evaluation Dataset

The model will undergo comparative experiments on the Chinese dataset MSRA. The MSRA Chinese dataset, released by Microsoft Research Asia, is a commonly used annotated dataset for Chinese NLP and is one of the datasets for the entity recognition task in SIGNAN backoff 2006. It is also an important benchmark for evaluating performance in Chinese NER tasks. The dataset is annotated with part-of-speech tags and entity types according to the standard format for NER, as presented in Table 1.

3.2   Experimental Environment And Parameter Configuration

The experiment was conducted via PyTorch 2.1.2, Python 3.10, and CUDA 11.8. The GPU used was an RTX 3090 (24 GB), and the CPU was an Intel(R) Xeon(R) Platinum 8362 CPU @ 2.80 GHz. As presented in Table 2.

Table 1. Introduction to the Dataset Size (Unit: Sentences)

Dataset	Training Set	Development Set	Test Set
MSRA	43634	——	4365

Table 2. Experimental Environment

Experiment Environment	Parameter
Version	2.1.2
Python Version	3.10
CUDA Version	11.8
GPU	RTX 3090 (24 GB)
CPU	Intel(R) Xeon(R) Platinum 8362 CPU @ 2.80 GHz

We used the MarkBERT-BiLSTM-Context-CRF model to pre-train the dataset, obtaining a 768-dimensional representation. The Adam optimizer was utilized, with a learning rate set to 1e−5, a batch size of 10, cls_hidden set to 128 layers, Dropout set to 0.3, cls_head set to 2, word_embed_dim set to 100, and the number of epochs was set to 20. As presented in Table 3.

Table 3. Parameter setting

Parameter	Set Value
Representation Dimension	768
Optimizer	Adam
Learning Rate	1e−5
Batch Size	10
Cls_hidden	128
Dropout	0.3
Cls_head	2
Word_embed_dim	100
Epochs	20

3.3 Data Preprocessing

This paper adopts the BMES annotation scheme, where the initial character of an entity is labeled as "B" (beginning), the central characters of an entity are labeled as "M" (middle), the last character of an entity is labeled as "E" (end), and a single character entity is labeled as "S" (single). All non-entity characters and placeholders are labeled as "O" (outside). The entity types in this paper include the following: person names ("NR"), place names ("NS"), and organization names ("NT") from the MSRA dataset.

3.4   Evaluation Index

To evaluate the model's performance, the study employs, three distinct metrics are employed: Precision (P), Recall (R), and the F1 score (F1). The calculation formulas are listed below:

$$P = \frac{TP}{TP + FP} \tag{20}$$

$$R = \frac{TP}{TP + FN} \tag{21}$$

$$F_1 = \frac{2 \times P \times R}{P + R} \tag{22}$$

TP represents the number of samples correctly classified as belonging to the positive class, whereas FP denotes the number of samples that have been misclassified as positive.

3.5   Comparison Experiment

To assess the performance of the proposed MarkBERT-BILSTM-Context-CRF model, a comparative analysis was carried out using different models.

As shown in Fig. 3, we use the MSRA public dataset to evaluate the performance of the NER model. The CNN-BiLSTM-CRF model [19] extracts character-level features for each Chinese character via CNN, combines character feature vectors with local context features, and finally outputs via CRF, thereby improving the model's NER performance. The BERT-BiLSTM-CRF model [20] uses pre-trained dynamic word vectors as inputs combined with downstream tasks, which allows it to learn rich semantic features and demonstrates extremely high performance in entity recognition. Compared with the CNN-BiLSTM-CRF model, the F1 increased by 3.56%. The BERT-BiLSTM-ATT-CRF model [21], which is based on the previous model, incorporates an attention mechanism and further trains through this mechanism to extract important semantic features, resulting in significant performance improvements on both datasets. The ALBERT-BiLSTM-CRF model [22] primarily utilizes the embedding capabilities of the pre-trained ALBERT model and fine-tunes the subsequent connection parameters to achieve further performance improvements.

The aforementioned entity recognition models demonstrate significant improvements in performance; however, the enhanced models do not effectively address the OOV (Out-Of-Vocabulary) issue and the constraints of context information. In contrast, the MarkBERT-BiLSTM-Context-CRF model proposed in this study integrates the strengths of the MarkBERT model and the context mechanism effectively addresses the shortcomings discussed above, achieving an F1 of 95.75%. A comparative analysis of the models presented in this study and the aforementioned models reveals that the model yields excellent results on the MSRA dataset, indicating superior precision in recognizing entities within the MSRA dataset compared with the other models.

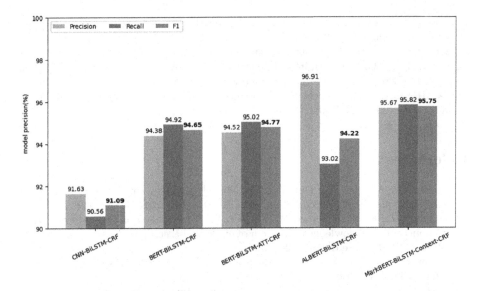

Fig. 3. Comparison of Models on the MSRA Dataset.

4 Conclusion

This study focuses on Chinese named entity recognition and proposes a model
that significantly improves the accuracy of recognizing entities in the MSRA
dataset. This is achieved by effectively combining MarkBERT, BiLSTM, and
CRF, and by integrating a global context mechanism to increase recognition precision. The MarkBERT The pre-processing model generates the requisite word
vectors, which are then fed into the BiLSTM layer for additional processing.
The incorporation of the global context mechanism facilitates the handling of
information from the entire sentence. Finally, the CRF layer applies constraints
to improve the effectiveness of NER.

Moreover, our findings indicate that the MarkBERT-BiLSTM-Context-CRF
model displays robust performance on the identified datasets, establishing a
robust foundation for knowledge graphs. This also offers a broader range of
options for further research in this field.

In the future, we intend to introduce more detailed information regarding
the features in question, as well as datasets encompassing multiple domains and
types, on the basis of the MarkBERT-BiLSTM-Context-CRF framework. This
will serve to increase the accuracy and breadth of NER.

Acknowledgments. This study was funded by the Major Science and Technology Program of Yazhou Bay Innovation Institute of Hainan Tropical Ocean University (2023CXYZD001), the Key Research and Development Project of Hainan Province (ZDYF2024SHFZ051), the Hainan Tropical Ocean University School-Level Research and Practice Projects in Emerging Engineering, Agriculture, and Liberal Arts Disciplines (RHYxgnw2024), and the Special Project of Science and Technology Innovation of Sanya City (2022KJCX30).

References

1. Akkasi, A., Varoğlu, E., Dimililer, N.: ChemTok: a new rule based tokenizer for chemical named entity recognition. Biomed. Res. Int. **2016**(1), 4248026 (2016)
2. Eftimov, T., Koroušić Seljak, B., Korošec, P.: A rule-based named-entity recognition method for knowledge extraction of evidence-based dietary recommendations. PLoS ONE **12**(6), e0179488 (2017)
3. Rabiner, L., Juang, B.: An introduction to hidden Markov models. IEEE ASSP Mag. **3**(1), 4–16 (1986)
4. McCallum, A., Freitag, D., Pereira, F.C., et al.: Maximum entropy Markov models for information extraction and segmentation. In: ICML, vol. 17, pp. 591–598 (2000)
5. Lafferty, J., McCallum, A., Pereira, F., et al.: Conditional random fields: probabilistic models for segmenting and labeling sequence data. In: ICML, vol. 1, no. 2, p. 3, Williamstown, MA (2001)
6. Yanan, Z., Dagang, T.: Research on text classification based on GloVe and SVM. Softw. Guide **17**(6), 45–48 (2018)
7. Malarkodi, C., Lex, E., Devi, S.L.: Named entity recognition for the agricultural domain. Res. Comput. Sci. **117**(1), 121–132 (2016)
8. Liu, K., Hu, Q., Liu, J., Xing, C.: Named entity recognition in Chinese electronic medical records based on CRF. In: 2017 14th Web Information Systems and Applications Conference (WISA), pp. 105–110. IEEE (2017)
9. Elman, J.L.: Finding structure in time. Cogn. Sci. **14**(2), 179–211 (1990)
10. Hochreiter, S.: Long short-term memory. Neural Comput. **9**(8), 1735–1780 (1997)
11. LeCun, Y., et al.: Backpropagation applied to handwritten zip code recognition. Neural Comput. **1**(4), 541–551 (1989)
12. Lample, G.: Neural architectures for named entity recognition. arXiv preprint arXiv:1603.01360 (2016)
13. Tang, B., Wang, X., Yan, J., Chen, Q.: Entity recognition in Chinese clinical text using attention-based CNN-LSTM-CRF. BMC Med. Inform. Decis. Mak. **19**, 89–97 (2019)
14. Devlin, J.: BERT: pre-training of deep bidirectional transformers for language understanding. arXiv preprint arXiv:1810.04805 (2018)
15. Liu, Y.; RoBERTa: a robustly optimized BERT pretraining approach. arXiv preprint arXiv:1907.11692 (2019)
16. Li, L., Dai, Y., Tang, D., Qiu, X., Xu, Z., Shi, S.: MarkBERT: marking word boundaries improves Chinese BERT. In: Liu, F., Duan, N., Xu, Q., Hong, Y. (eds.) Natural Language Processing and Chinese Computing, NLPCC 2023. LNCS, vol. 14302, pp. 325–336. Springer, Cham (2023). https://doi.org/10.1007/978-3-031-44693-1_26
17. Xu, C., Shen, K., Sun, H.: Supplementary features of BiLSTM for enhanced sequence labeling. arXiv preprint arXiv:2305.19928 (2023)

18. Vaswani, A.: Attention is all you need. In: Advances in Neural Information Processing Systems (2017)
19. Jia, Y., Xu, X.: Chinese named entity recognition based on CNN-BiLSTM-CRF. In: 2018 IEEE 9th International Conference on Software Engineering and Service Science (ICSESS), pp. 1-4. IEEE (2018)
20. X. T, Y. J. N, L. H: Chinese entity recognition based on BERT-BILSTM-CRF model. Comput. Syst. Appl. **29**(7), 48–55 (2020)
21. Li, D., Tu, Y., Zhou, X., Zhang, Y., Ma, Z.: End-to-end Chinese entity recognition based on BERT-BiLSTM-ATT-CRF. ZTE Commun. **20**(S1), 27 (2022)
22. D. B. Y, C. L. L: Chinese named entity recognition method based on Albert. Comput. Sci. Appl. **10**, 883 (2020)

Home-Hosted Learning Management System for Online and Blended Learning: A Case Study

Riyad Dhuny[1]([✉]), Arshad Ahmud Iqbal Peer[1], Aslam Aly El-Faïdal Saib[1],
Nassirah Laloo[1], Leila Hafeeza Mohammad Denmamode[1],
Nawaz Ali Mohamudally[1], and Fangli Ying[2]

[1] School of Innovative Technologies and Engineering, University of Technology, Mauritius, La
Tour Koenig, Pointe-aux-Sables, Port Louis 11134, Mauritius
{dhuny,apeer,asaib,nlaloo,ldenmamode,alimohamudally}@utm.ac.mu
[2] Department of Computer Science, East China University of Science and Technology, Xuhui,
Shanghai, China
yfangli@ecust.edu.cn

Abstract. Learning management systems (LMSs) play a crucial role in facilitating the tasks of educators in the management and administration of classes. Nevertheless, many teaching staff still do not have access to an LMS for various reasons, including several linked to hosting purposes. Cloud hosting an LMS presents challenges, including latency, high costs, data privacy concerns, and limited functionality. Educators often struggle to evaluate LMS benefits due to a lack of access and may be deterred by technical setup complexities. These issues highlight the need for alternative LMS deployment strategies that address cloud computing drawbacks while maintaining educational effectiveness. To address these challenges, recent studies have shown that running an LMS from a microserver such as the Raspberry Pi hardware is now possible, supporting multiple students simultaneously. Consequently, this work investigates the feasibility of home-hosting an LMS as a viable alternative in two distinct ways. In one method, the microserver's performance for hosting an LMS at home was evaluated under laboratory conditions by simulating an Internet Service Provider's bandwidth values. In the second approach, a home-hosted LMS was operated in a production environment for four years, servicing more than 420 students. In this paper, we dive into the system as a case study, collecting statistics to justify evidence that the system has operated purposefully. In conclusion, this paper demonstrates the viability of a home-hosted LMS solution as an alternative to traditional centralized systems. It offers insights into this approach's practical implementation, performance, and potential benefits for more accessible and customisable e-learning solutions in various educational contexts.

Keywords: eLearning · home-hosted · Learning Management System ·
technology-enhanced · e-learning · H5P · portable · Raspberry Pi and IoT

K. Zhang et al. (Eds.): CSEI 2024, CCIS 2447, pp. 328–340, 2025.
https://doi.org/10.1007/978-981-96-3735-5_25

1 Introduction

While hosting a Learning Management System (LMS) in the cloud might appear to be the ideal solution in most situations, cloud computing also introduces several issues such as latency [1], where data have to travel longer distances to centralized servers; cost, as high data transfer, storage volumes, and use of more CPU cores can lead to significant expenses over time [2]; potential vendor lock-in [3], where educators face challenges migrating their content if they wish to switch providers; data privacy concerns, with fears that content may be compromised; and limited functionality, as providers may restrict specific settings or prevent the installation of essential plugins [4]. Another challenge is that educators often lack access to an LMS to evaluate its potential benefits [5], and the technical hurdles involved in setting up such a system may discourage them from initiating this process.

This paper proposes a decentralized model of an LMS that gives educators full access to a personal cloud at home to host their own LMS. Such a model is made possible, as previous investigations demonstrated that mobile computing devices could be used as servers to host LMSs [6]. This work aims to share our acquired experience to help other educators globally decide if this model would suit their needs. While this model was tested at the tertiary level, there are indications that it can also be used in primary and secondary education. Under different circumstances, it can also be used as a portable LMS.

E-Learning requires many aspects at different levels, namely, the technological, pedagogical, e-Learning, organisational and psychological levels [7, 8]. It is more than initiatives ensuring that students have access to IT equipment, such as learning tablets [9–11] or laptops, similar to the 'One Laptop per Child' project [12, 13]. Similarly, this is more than the sole initiative of making computing devices more accessible to a broader audience for mobile learning [14] or making e-textbooks available as pre-installed devices [15–17]. These previously mentioned initiatives made available, IT infrastructure, to enable e-learning. The major setback is that technology does not stand by itself and is accompanied by a vision that directs its use—one where educators can monitor each student's progress. Without teaching and learning strategies, teachers distance themselves from devices and rarely use them for class educational purposes, as observed by Kraemer et al. [13] and Ugwuede [17]. One crucial tool is the LMS, which assists the educator in administering, documenting, tracking, reporting, and delivering training programmes and educational courses [18]. LMS requires a computer server and networking to operate, which often hinders LMS adoption for various reasons, including cost and difficulty in setting up.

The emergence of a low-cost, Single-Board Computer (SBC) hardware named Raspberry Pi (RPI) has led to changes in many fields, including education. The RPI can be used as a power-efficient portable web server [19, 20] capable of supporting the operations of an LMS. The previously mentioned setup was even tested in a war conflict zone in the Central African Republic and areas with limited internet connectivity [4, 21]. An LMS provides educators with insight into the class's day-to-day progress and is necessary to support education from primary to tertiary levels. Moodle is the most popular open-sourced LMS, with more than 179,000 active deployments in 242 countries [22]. From a popularity point of view, for 38 features compared, Moodle topped the list of

LMSs [23]. Other comparative studies to find viable LMSs for distance education and online learning ranked Moodle among the top, given that it is open source and free [24, 25]. Moodle LMS is also used in special needs education for people who are deaf or hard of hearing in Jordan [26] and was even found to be the most predominant LMS used in e-learning for medical education in low- and middle-income countries [27]. This influenced our decision to opt for Moodle as an LMS.

While Moodle provides a robust foundation for e-learning, as evidenced in the previous paragraph, its capabilities can be further enhanced through the integration of interactive content creation tools. One relatively new tool in e-learning is H5P interactive content [28]. H5P is a game changer for active learning and provides a wide range of interactive tools for LMSs. Among the capabilities of H5P is adding YouTube videos as an LMS activity and placing specific interactive questions on top of the videos to enable active learning. H5P pauses the video to allow learners to answer the questions. Unfortunately, H5P is not available for Google Classroom. Moodle is currently the only LMS with free self-host H5P plugin integration [23], allowing educators to host multimedia content directly on Moodle, eliminating the need for external links or internet connectivity when operating on a local network. Some examples of H5P usage worth visiting are laboratory safety training and active learning in engineering and bioscience education [29–31]. H5P triggered our interest in exploring an alternative to Google Classroom and using Moodle as the central LMS on an RPI.

Historically, RPI appeared on the market in 2012 to become the world's third-best-selling computer platform [32] after five years because of its relatively low cost and usage in many areas [33]. The latest version of RPI, version 4 (RPI4) [34], as shown in Fig. 1, is available with a quad-core ARM 64-bit processor of 1.5 GHz and 2 gigabytes (GB), 4 GB or 8 GB of Random Access memory (RAM) with prices ranging from US$39–85 [35]. The basic RPI configuration meets and exceeds the minimum hardware

Fig. 1. Image of a Raspberry Pi 4 with a ruler demonstrating the small form factor of the hardware, which is close to the size of a credit card.

requirements to install the latest Moodle version. In their work, Dhuny *et al.* [6] measured the performance of a 1.5 GHz CPU-powered RPI4 against Moodle. They reported that hardware could support 30 users from a Secure Digital (SD) card and up to 40 users if a Solid State Disk (SSD) was employed, and the scarce resource preventing more users from being supported was the CPU. Their tests, however, exclude any 'think time', which represents the time users take between operations with the system. The experiments were carried out on a course size categorized as medium per Moodle test plans [36].

This study pushes the previous experiments [6] into production mode by home-hosting an LMS using one of Mauritius's lowest and most affordably-priced bandwidth packages available. A laboratory test is also carried out to measure the LMS output quality for prospective users. As described by previous experiments [6], a small-sized course was used for the laboratory tests, as it closely resembles the course size running in production. Additionally, we share our experience regrouping the RPI, Moodle, and H5P components for a home-hosted solution. A ready-for-use software disk image has also been made available.

The remainder of this paper is structured as follows: Sect. 2 presents the decentralized model and the economics of having a home-hosted solution. Section 3 covers the system's statistics and meaningful numbers collected during the operation of the LMS. Section 4 shares the load tests and results carried out on the home-hosted solution. The conclusion is presented in Sect. 5.

2 Decentralized Model and the Economics of Having a Home-Hosted Solution

Educational institutions offering access to web-based LMSs use a centralized server approach, as shown on the left in Fig. 2. With this model, all educators and students can access the same server hosting the LMS. This model requires a powerful server, different user roles and many administrative tasks to grant and restrict authorization to users accordingly. Such control and flexibility make the management of an LMS complex and challenging at times, and it is catered by the institution for staff and students. Another alternative available is the Software as a Service offered by some providers. In this model, the LMS provider has some LMS already hosted on the internet and provides account access to educators against a fee. This model is for stand-alone educators willing to add an LMS to their toolbox. Apart from its costs, the disadvantage of this model is that the host or LMS provider often has several server restrictions to protect its infrastructure. These restrictions translate to the service provider limiting the choice of extra features, such as installing extra Moodle plugins, leading to a poor user experience. The monthly cost to the educator also depends on the number of learner users associated with an educator account on the LMS and the space available for the LMS operation. For example, Moodle Cloud [37] offers packages to support 50 users with 250 MB storage for US$ 140 yearly, where a user means anyone with an account. Using such a model, educators are locked in a situation where they must constantly renew their subscriptions to ensure that their students' assignments are not lost. Any payment delay is stressful because of the fear of losing content. Another approach reserved for technical savvy is to take a hosting account and host an LMS in the cloud. This approach has a running cost ranging on average from

US$8.49 to 23.95/month [38, 39], mainly for renting disk, CPU and memory usage from a provider to keep the LMS accessible over the internet.

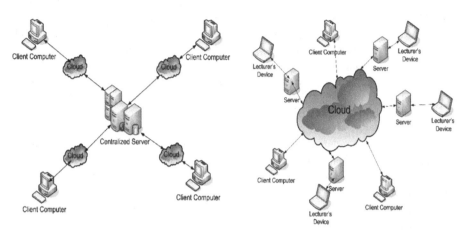

Fig. 2. The figure represents two different models for hosting consideration purposes. On the left is a centralized model, and on the right is a decentralized model.

This work proposes and implements a decentralized server approach, as shown on the right in Fig. 2, where academicians can have their own server host an LMS on-premises/at home to service the students. As an advantage, the educator connects directly to the LMS from a local area network with zero lag, and all submitted assignments are stored on the educator's premises. The educator has full access and control of the LMS, including the possibility of installing extra features and plugins. The yearly operational cost is drastically reduced for those who already have good internet connectivity, which is the case for most educators. Home-hosted LMS represents a one-off investment for acquiring RPI4 hardware and, optionally, a domain with a starting yearly price of US$

Table 1. A comparison between the Moodle Cloud and a Moodle hosted on an RPI4 for specific features.

Support Feature	Moodle Cloud	RPI4*
Number of users	50	30 - (SD Card)/40 - (SSD) [6]
Disk Space	250 MB	240 GB*(depends on disk size)
Can install additional plugins	No	Yes
Scalable	Yes	No
Cost	USD 140/year	USD 107*/one-off

* The RPI4 hardware used for comparison purposes is an RPI4 with 4GB of RAM, a 240 GB SSD, an SSD to USB Cable Connector, a Casing and a 3.1A Adaptor, with a total cost of $107 as of October 2024, with the price originating from the Raspberry Pi Approved reseller store, The Pi Hut.

12–30 [40], depending on the chosen domain name. A comparison table between an entry-level package for a Moodle Cloud and a home-hosting solution using an RPI4 is displayed in Table 1.

3 Statistics Collected from the System

A home-hosted LMS was tested over eight semesters spanning four years to support one lecturer and 19 cohorts. More than 420 user accounts were recorded, during which no significant issues, difficulties, incidents or complaints were received regarding the system's operation. Given the RPI's small form factor and relatively low cost, the system's usage statistics are impressive and are used as evidence to demonstrate the home-hosted model's capabilities and success. First, from April 2020 to April 2024, the system remained live, representing more than 35,000 h of operation for the pi. The underlying database houses more than 450 tables with over 750,000 records. It serviced cohorts containing, on average, 15 students and a maximum of 28 concurrently accessing the system. During that period, the users performed 3,821,096 operations, from signing into the system to submitting an assignment, as reported by the Moodle logs. More than 2,200 assignments were graded. For video-related assignments, students uploaded their work on YouTube as unlisted videos or kept them on their Google Drive and shared the links for grading via LMS. This approach helps reduce bandwidth usage, making it feasible to home-host the LMS. Video contents created for the lessons were also uploaded on YouTube and called via the H5P plugin inside the LMS. H5P loads the video directly from the provider, which offloads the server. The course sizes, excluding the assignments, remained low and were backed up with a file size of less than 10 MB.

3.1 Working with LMS Plugins

With no limitations on installing plugins inside the home-hosted LMS, selected plugins were installed and used for specific purposes to ensure the smooth running of classes. The OAuth2 [41] plugin module of Moodle was activated for GMAIL accounts inside Moodle, allowing students to sign in using Google Single Sign-On, as shown in Fig. 3.

Learners do not need to create an account and additional credentials for Moodle. For online sessions, Google Meet and Zoom are the most widely used tools at the University of Technology, Mauritius (UTM), and Moodle has Google Meet for Moodle [42] and Zoom Meeting [43] plugins.

By default, the Moodle student activity log already helps educators by providing an overview of the time spent on the module. The attendance plugin helps by adding the functionality to allow students to mark their attendance only during the session slot [44]. The H5P plugin [28] helps include external resources such as YouTube videos and allows interactive elements on top of the videos. Finally, after the semester, assignments are graded, exported in spreadsheet format and submitted to the School Examination Unit, which Moodle appropriately handles. The Turnitin module [45] was installed for cases requiring antiplagiarism checks, allowing seamless integration with the Moodle assignment submission system.

Fig. 3. The login form of Moodle as depicted here contains a Google Sign in. The Use of OAuth2 plugin inside Moodle to enables this Single Sign-On.

4   Load Tests and Results on the Home-Hosted LMS

With a home-hosted LMS in place, it is essential to know how many concurrent users the system can support and the quality of the user experience as measured by the application performance index (Apdex) [46, 47]. The Apdex results depend on the server resources and the bandwidth the Internet Service Provider (ISP) provides. Load tests were carried out on the home-hosted LMS via a previously published method [6] to measure these values. Maro *et al.* also employed a similar method [48, 49]; however, they measured the quality of response in milliseconds rather than Apdex.

By default, Moodle allows the generation of sample test courses, different cohorts as test sizes, and the necessary scripts to conduct server load tests. Using a test course size categorized as small (S) [36], representing a file size of 10 MB, load tests were carried out for cohort sizes ranging from 10–60 users, as noted by the Apdex. Under Apdex, an application is expected to load within a certain amount of time, after which the user becomes frustrated. During the tests, two load time scenarios were considered: (1) a load time of 0.5–1.5 s, for which the user is expected to react to a frustration threshold after 1.5 s, and (2) a load time of 1–3 s, for which the user reaches the frustration threshold after 3 s. The server was connected to a 20 Mbps internet connection with an 8 Mbps upload rate. The tests were carried out from another Home ADSL-connected computer using an internet connection speed of a 10 Mbps download rate and a 2 Mbps upload rate, representing the smallest home internet speed offered by the primary telecom provider in Mauritius. Both internet connections used My.T as the service provider. The tests represent several users trying to use their internet connection at home to connect to the server simultaneously to access the resources. The users were simulated via Apache JMeter [50]. The network was restricted by the bandwidth offered by the ISP provider. The connection speeds were checked with the 'iperf' [51] command on the Linux terminal to ensure that they were within the expected range before the experiments.

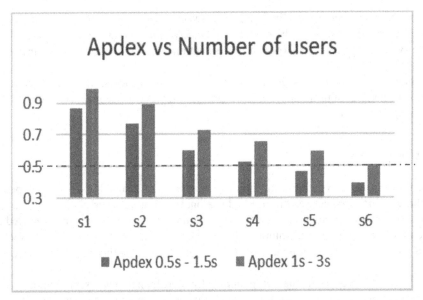

Fig. 4. This graph shows the impact of an increasing number of users on Apdex when operating with bandwidth restrictions.

The Apdex values are measured from 0 to 1, with values lower than 0.5 considered unacceptable. Fig. 4 shows the Apdex values for tests from s1–s6, which represent 10–60 simultaneous users. The home-hosted solution could withstand up to 40 concurrent

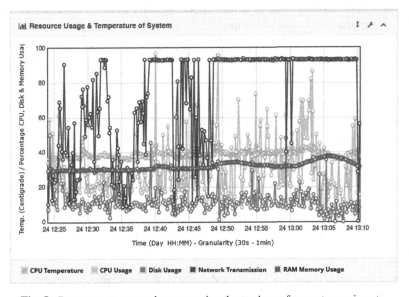

Fig. 5. Resource usage graph representing the tendency for most experiments.

users with an acceptable load time ranging between 0.5 s and 1.5 s, for which Apdex is above 0.5, as represented by the red line in Fig. 4. When up to 20 more users are added to the system, the pages are expected to load within 3 s, as represented by s5 and s6 of Fig. 4,

The server's resource usage was plotted for the experiments, and it was observed that as the number of users increased, the network resource usage reached its ceiling, as shown in Fig. 5.

5   Conclusion

Not all LMSs are built equal; some are more advantageous than others, but this depends on the viewing perspective. From an educational institution's perspective, a solution such as Google Classroom is free of charge, requires no maintenance and is hosted in the cloud, making it an ideal solution. Some educators who require more features in an LMS prefer other LMSs for better classroom management, but this comes with an extra cost.

With our LMS experimental setup running for more than four years, we demonstrated that it was possible to operate a Moodle LMS using a home-hosted solution with additional features and advantages than a commercial provider would offer. These include the ability to install LMS plugins without restrictions, assignments are delivered next to the home router, and zero monthly subscription costs are required to a hosting provider. In an experimental setup, the home-hosted LMS was hosted on a 20 Mbps download and 8 Mbps upload internet connectivity from My.T, which is reasonably priced in Mauritius. The decentralized model distributes the number of students on many small home-hosted servers. Educational institutions that use a dedicated server receive higher loads during peak hours, and server failures or delays affect operations institution-wide. This case would not happen in a decentralized model.

For educators, particularly those who have yet to adopt an LMS for various reasons, a recommendation would be to start with an LMS using RPI. First, the LMS can be operated locally or on an intranet for testing purposes, allowing for increased confidence in using the system. Given that the need to support a group of users arises, the first area to consider for an upgrade is the bandwidth, such as the graphs of **Fig. 5**. Demonstrated that it is the limiting factor. The bandwidth value of 8 Mbps uploads used in production for the past four years represents one of the lowest bandwidths in Mauritius. Applying such a low value made it more probable that similar or better conditions would be met by prospective users worldwide.

Furthermore, the performance evaluation was carried out without a 'think time' to maintain the same experimental conditions as Dhuny *et al.* [6]. However, users do require a think time while processing the information they are reading. This approach reduces the traffic on the network resources (Fig. 5), which is expected to improve the server's overall response, making it further usable in production mode with an upload bandwidth of 8 Mbps.

When simulating users via Apache JMeter [49], the performance evaluation results revealed that up to 40 users could be supported for a small-sized course, as represented by the blue bar of s4 in Fig. 4 crossing the 0.5 mark on Apdex 0.5 s–1.5 s. This result indicates that, on average, users would be able to receive a response from the server within one and a half seconds of initiating a request. The results are also an indication for educators who have class sizes with up to 40 students, as is the case for most of them in Mauritius, that such small hardware will be able to handle the job as expected. Additionally, even if the number of users is further increased to up to 60 users, the server's response quality is expected to be, on average, three seconds, as represented by the orange bar in Fig. 4. This work supplements previous work in the field [6], which demonstrated that the full potential of RPI4 in an unconstrained network is capable of supporting up to 40 concurrent users for a medium-sized course running from an SSD.

Better performing computer hardware and higher bandwidth internet connectivity will be required to support more users. Connectivity is where ISP providers can help the education sector by providing reasonably priced, tailored internet packages with higher upload bandwidths for educators. With respect to future work, the authors believe that commercial potential is associated with this work. For example, router manufacturers might consider integrating RPI modules or similar SBCs to allow users to host 3-tiered applications such as Moodle. This work and previous works in the field contributed to the production of RPI64box [52], which is available for download and is ready for use to produce a portable LMS.

References

1. Srivastava, S., Singh, S.P.: A survey on latency reduction approaches for performance optimization in cloud computing. In: Proceedings of the 2016 Second International Conference on Computational Intelligence & Communication Technology (CICT), pp. 111–115 (2016). https://doi.org/10.1109/CICT.2016.30
2. Dikaiakos, M.D., Katsaros, D., Mehra, P., Pallis, G., Vakali, A.: Cloud computing: distributed internet internet computing for IT and scientific research. IEEE Internet Comput. **13**(5), 10–13 (2009). https://doi.org/10.1109/MIC.2009.103
3. Opara-Martins, J., Sahandi, R., Tian, F.: Critical analysis of vendor lock-in and its impact on cloud computing migration: a business perspective. J. Cloud Comput. **5**(1), 4 (2016). https://doi.org/10.1186/s13677-016-0054-z
4. Ndassimba, N.G., Ndassimba, E., Kossingou, G.M., Ouya, S.: Digital elementary school solution with moodlebox in a conflict zone: the case of the Central African Republic. In: Proceedings of the 2021 23rd International Conference on Advanced Communication Technology (ICACT), pp. 382–386, February 2021. https://doi.org/10.23919/ICACT51234.2021.9370681
5. Linhalis, F., Silva, A.: Solutions to enable the use of TIC in education in regions with low internet connectivity: a literature review. Cad. Educ. Tecnol. e Soc. (2023). https://api.semanticscholar.org/CorpusID:269047337
6. Dhuny, R., Peer, A.A.I., Mohamudally, N.A., Nissanke, N.: Performance evaluation of a portable single-board computer as a 3-tiered LAMP stack under 32-bit and 64-bit operating systems. Array **15**, 100196 (2022). https://doi.org/10.1016/j.array.2022.100196
7. Tankeleviciene, L., Damasevicius, R.: Towards a conceptual model of learning context in e-learning. In: Proceedings of the 2009 Ninth IEEE International Conference on Advanced Learning Technologies, pp. 645–646, July 2009. https://doi.org/10.1109/ICALT.2009.184
8. McLain, T.R.: Learning management systems adoption conundrums; technological and pedagogical dilemmas that arise for higher education. J. Educ. Train. **4**, 124–130 (2017)

9. Fernández, L., Correa, J.M., Losada, D.: OLPC project in the Basque Country: Eskola 2.0. Procedia Soc. Behav. Sci.a Soc. Behav. Sci. **15**, 2207–2213 (2011). https://doi.org/10.1016/j.sbspro.2011.04.081

10. Mora, T., Escardíbul, J.O., Di Pietro, G.: Computers and students' achievement: an analysis of the one laptop per child program in Catalonia. Int. J. Educ. Res. **92**, 145–157 (2018). https://doi.org/10.1016/j.ijer.2018.09.013

11. Tarek, S.A.: Impact of tablet based training in empowering remote rural community of South West Bangladesh to acquire disaster preparedness skills. Procedia Econ. Financ. **18**, 287–295 (2014). https://doi.org/10.1016/S2212-5671(14)00942-3

12. Freudenberg, B., Ohshima, Y., Wallace, S.: Etoys for one laptop per child. In: Proceedings of the 2009 Seventh International Conference on Creating, Connecting and Collaborating through Computing, pp. 57–64, January 2009. https://doi.org/10.1109/C5.2009.9

13. Kraemer, K.L., Dedrick, J., Sharma, P.: One laptop per child (OLPC): a novel computerization movement?. In: Proceedings of the 2011 44th Hawaii International Conference on System Sciences, pp. 1–10, January 2011. https://doi.org/10.1109/HICSS.2011.327

14. Oyelere, S.S., Suhonen, J., Sutinen, E.: M-Learning: a new paradigm of learning ICT in Nigeria. Int. J. Interact. Mob. Technol. **10**(1), 35 (2016). https://doi.org/10.3991/ijim.v10i1.4872

15. Clarke, B., Svanaes, S., Zimmermann, S.: One-to-one tablets in education: tablets for schools 1 (2013). http://tabtimes.com/news/education/2011/10/31/schools-will-have-more-tablets-they-do-computers-2016. Accessed 5 Apr 2021

16. Sanusi, I.T., Oyelere, S.S., Suhonen, J., Olaleye, S.A., Otunla, A.O.: Exploring students and teachers activities, experiences and impact of Opón Ìmò mobile learning device on teaching and learning. In: Proceedings of the 2017 IEEE AFRICON Science, Technology and Innovation of Africa, AFRICON 2017, pp. 788–793 (2017). https://doi.org/10.1109/AFRCON.2017.8095583

17. Ugwuede, K.: Rethinking learning tablet initiatives and their impact on education in Africa—TechCabal (2020). https://techcabal.com/2020/03/09/digital-learning-tablets-for-africa/. Accessed 5 Apr 2021

18. Tjong, Y., Sugandi, L., Nurshafita, A., Magdalena, Y., Evelyn, C., Yosieto, N.S.: User satisfaction factors on learning management systems usage. In: Proceedings of the 2018 International Conference on Information Management and Technology (ICIMTech), pp. 11–14, September 2018. https://doi.org/10.1109/ICIMTech.2018.8528171

19. Runia, M., Kanwalinderjit, G.: Raspberry Pi webserver. In: The Steering Committee of The World Congress in Computer Science, Computer Engineering and Applied Computing (WorldComp), pp. 62–67 (2015)

20. Ginting, B., Sawaluddin, S., Zarlis, M., Sihombing, P.: Raspberry-Pi as portable web server e-learning moodle for student learning and assignment. In: Proceedings of the Proceedings of the 2nd International Conference of Science Education in Industrial Revolution 4.0, ICONSEIR, 17th December 2019, Medan, North Sumatra, Indonesia, pp. 3–8 (2020). https://doi.org/10.4108/eai.17-12-2019.2296003

21. CIA: Internet users - The World Factbook (2019). https://www.cia.gov/the-world-factbook/field/internet-users/. Accessed 6 Apr 2021

22. Moodle statistics (2021). https://stats.moodle.org/. Accessed 6 Apr 2021

23. Karadimas, N.V.: Comparing learning management systems from popularity point of view. In: Proceedings of the 2018 5th International Conference on Mathematics and Computers in Sciences and Industry (MCSI), pp. 141–146, August 2018. https://doi.org/10.1109/MCSI.2018.00040

24. Dobre, I.: Learning management systems for higher education - an overview of available options for higher education organizations. Procedia Soc. Behav. Sci.a Soc. Behav. Sci. **180**, 313–320 (2015). https://doi.org/10.1016/j.sbspro.2015.02.122

25. Poulova, P., Simonova, I., Manenova, M.: Which one, or another? Comparative analysis of selected LMS. Procedia Soc. Behav. Sci.a Soc. Behav. Sci. **186**, 1302–1308 (2015). https://doi.org/10.1016/j.sbspro.2015.04.052
26. Khwaldeh, S.M.I.A.: Implementation, use and analysis of open source learning management system 'Moodle' and e-learning for the deaf in Jordan. PhD thesis, University of Central Lancashire (2011)
27. Barteit, S., Guzek, D., Jahn, A., Bärnighausen, T., Jorge, M.M., Neuhann, F.: Evaluation of e-learning for medical education in low- and middle-income countries: a systematic review. Comput. Educ. **145**, 103726 (2019). https://doi.org/10.1016/j.compedu.2019.103726
28. H5P: Set up H5P for Moodle—H5P (2016). https://h5p.org/moodle. Accessed 20 May 2021
29. Chilukuri, K.C.: A novel framework for active learning in engineering education mapped to course outcomes. Procedia Comput. Sci. **172**, 28–33 (2020). https://doi.org/10.1016/j.procs.2020.05.004
30. Sinnayah, P., Salcedo, A., Rekhari, S.: Reimagining physiology education with interactive content developed in H5P. Adv. Physiol. Educ. **45**(1), 71–76 (2021). https://doi.org/10.1152/advan.00021.2020
31. Viitaharju, P., Yliniemi, K., Nieminen, M., Karttunen, A.J.: Learning experiences from digital laboratory safety training. Educ. Chem. Eng. **34**, 87–93 (2021). https://doi.org/10.1016/j.ece.2020.11.009
32. The MagPi: Sales soar above Commodore 64. The MagPi **56**, 8 (2017)
33. Johnston, S.J., et al.: Commodity single board computer clusters and their applications. Futur. Gener. Comput. Syst. **89**, 201–212 (2018). https://doi.org/10.1016/j.future.2018.06.048
34. Halfacree, G.: Introducing Raspberry Pi4. The MagPi **83**, 26–29 (2019)
35. Pimoroni: Raspberry Pi 4 Model B (2021). https://shop.pimoroni.com/products/raspberry-pi-4?variant=29157087445075. Accessed 6 Apr 2021
36. Moodle Docs: JMeter test plan generator - MoodleDocs. https://docs.moodle.org/405/en/JMeter_test_plan_generator. Accessed 30 Oct 2024
37. Dougiamas, M.: Moodle (2002). https://moodle.org/. Accessed 19 Jul 2022
38. Contabo: Contabo VPS Hosting (2022). https://contabo.com/en/vps/. Accessed 29 Dec 2021
39. Hostgator: Hostgator VPS Hosting (2022). https://www.hostgator.com/vps-hosting. Accessed 31 Dec 2021
40. Google domains, p. 2017 (2015). https://domains.google/. Accessed 25 Dec 2022
41. Moodle Documentation: OAuth 2 services - MoodleDocs. https://docs.moodle.org/405/en/OAuth_2_services. Accessed 28 Oct 2024
42. Santos, R.: Google Meet^{TM} for Moodle. https://moodle.org/plugins/mod_googlemeet. Accessed 3 Nov 2021
43. Champ, J., Bader, S.: Zoom meeting Moodle Plugin. https://moodle.org/plugins/mod_zoom. Accessed 3 Nov 2021
44. Marsden, D.: Moodle plugins directory: attendance. https://moodle.org/plugins/mod_attendance. Accessed 27 Oct 2021
45. McGettrick, J., Dawson, P., Winn, D.: Moodle plugins directory: turnitin plagiarism plugin. https://moodle.org/plugins/plagiarism_turnitin. Accessed 27 Oct 2021
46. Relic, N.: Apdex: measure user satisfaction—New relic documentation (2013). https://docs.newrelic.com/docs/apm/new-relic-apm/apdex/apdex-measure-user-satisfaction/. Accessed 6 Apr 2021
47. Sevcik, P.J.: Defining the application performance index. Bus. Commun. Rev. **20**, 8–10 (2005). http://apdex.org/docs/Defining_The_Application_Performance_Index.pdf
48. Maro, S.H., Kondoro, A.W., Mtebe, J.S., Proctor, J., Komba, A., Haßler, B.: Exploring the feasibility of deploying technology enhanced school-based teacher continuous professional development in internet-limited environments in Tanzania. Int. Rev. Res. Open Distrib. Learn. **25**(2), 60–76 (2024). https://doi.org/10.19173/irrodl.v25i2.7428

49. Maro, S., Kondoro, A., Haßler, B., Mtebe, J., Proctor, J.: Deployment of offline learning management systems: comparing the performance of selected micro-servers in Tanzania. J. Learn. Dev. **10**(2), 280–296 (2023). https://doi.org/10.56059/jl4d.v10i2.835
50. Apache JMeter: Apache JMeter (1998). https://jmeter.apache.org/. Accessed 30 May 2021
51. Dugan, J., Elliott, S., Mah, B.A., Poskanzer, J., Prabhu, K.: iPerf - The TCP, UDP and SCTP network bandwidth measurement tool (2014). https://iperf.fr/. Accessed 6 Apr 2021
52. Dhuny, R., Mohamudally, N.A.: RPI64Box: a portable 3-tiered LAMP stack in a 64-bit operating system environment. Softw. Impacts **14**, 100390 (2022). https://doi.org/10.1016/j.simpa.2022.100390

Author Index

Printed in the United States
by Baker & Taylor Publisher Services